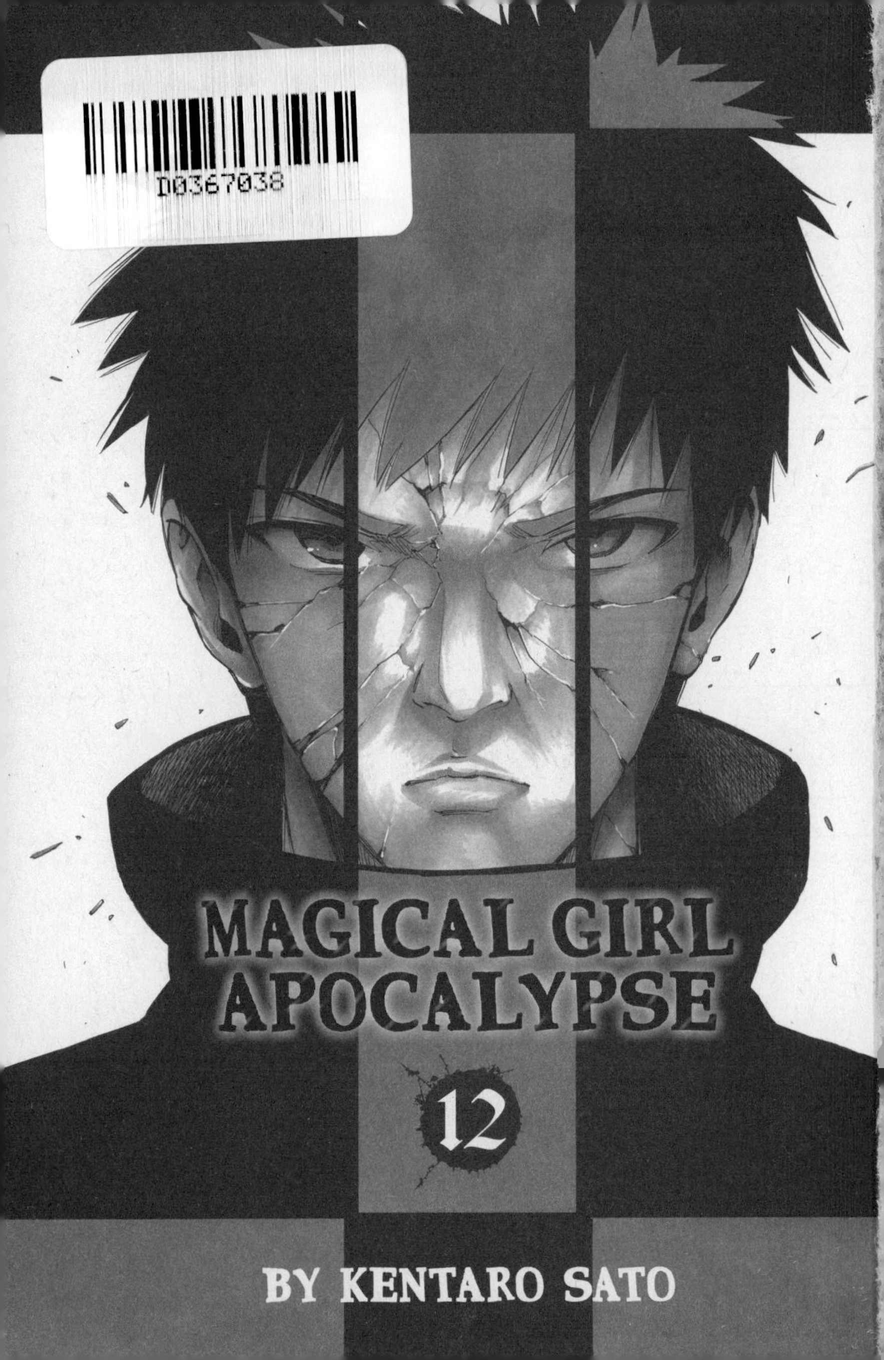

# MAGICAL GIRL APOCALYPSE

12

BY KENTARO SATO

# Previously, in *Magical Girl Apocalypse...*

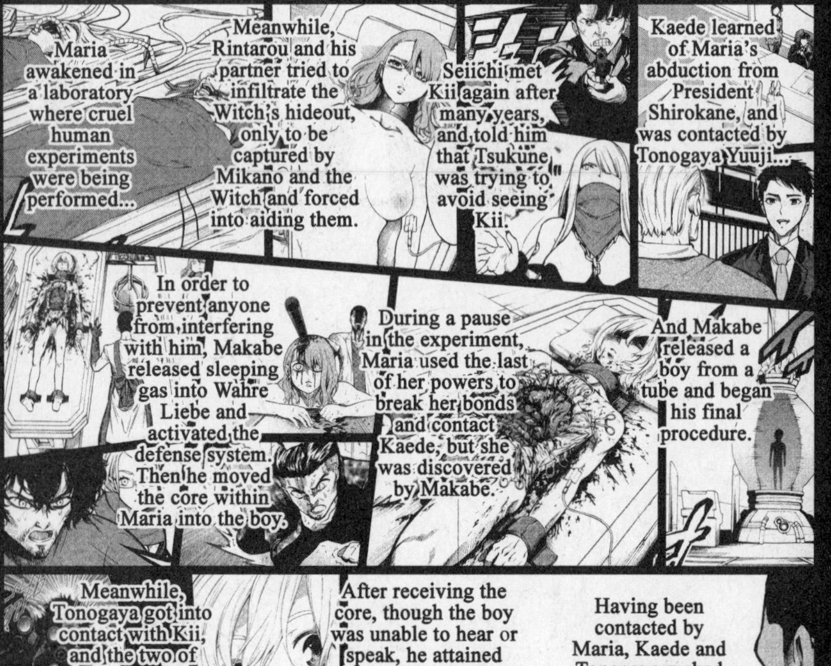
Kaede learned of Maria's abduction from President Shirokane, and was contacted by Tonogaya Yuuji...
Seiichi met Kii again after many years, and told him that Tsukune was trying to avoid seeing Kii.
Meanwhile, Rintarou and his partner tried to infiltrate the Witch's hideout, only to be captured by Mikano and the Witch and forced into aiding them.
Maria awakened in a laboratory where cruel human experiments were being performed...
And Makabe released a boy from a tube and began his final procedure.
During a pause in the experiment, Maria used the last of her powers to break her bonds and contact Kaede, but she was discovered by Makabe.
In order to prevent anyone from interfering with him, Makabe released sleeping gas into Wahre Liebe and activated the defense system. Then he moved the core within Maria into the boy.
Having been contacted by Maria, Kaede and Tonogaya rushed to Wahre Liebe. But while she was looking for a way to enter, Kaede was captured by Makabe.
After receiving the core, though the boy was unable to hear or speak, he attained incredible magical power. Makabe named the boy "Wataru," and then set off to find Tsukune and collect the last piece of the "Revelations of the Apocalypse."
Meanwhile, Tonogaya got into contact with Kii, and the two of them went into Wahre Liebe. They made it to the underground laboratory, but as soon as they entered, they were caught in an explosion...

## CAST

**KOGAMI KII**

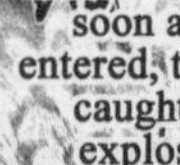

He is in a relationship with Kaede, and they live together. He is the one in charge of doing the household chores.

**ABENO MARIA**

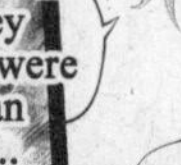

A researcher at Wahre Liebe. She is the Lab Director. She has gigantic breasts. She is engaged to marry Tonogaya Yuuji.

**SAYANO KAEDE**

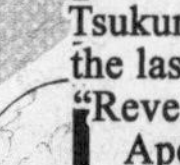

A researcher at Wahre Liebe. She is the Assistant Lab Director. She is in a relationship with Kii and lives with him.

**HANAKAI MIKANO**

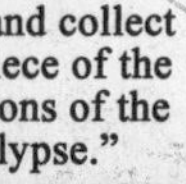

A very strong-spirited high school girl. She lives next door to Shinobu, and they are childhood friends.

**SHIROKANE SOU**

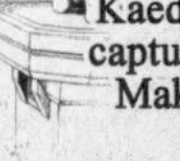

Shinobu's father. He is the CEO of the world-renowned pharmaceutical company Wahre Liebe.

**SHIROKANE SHINOBU**

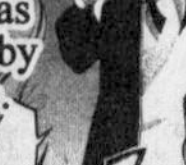

A genius instrumental in developing several new drugs for his father's pharmaceutical company. He lives next door to his childhood friend, Mikano.

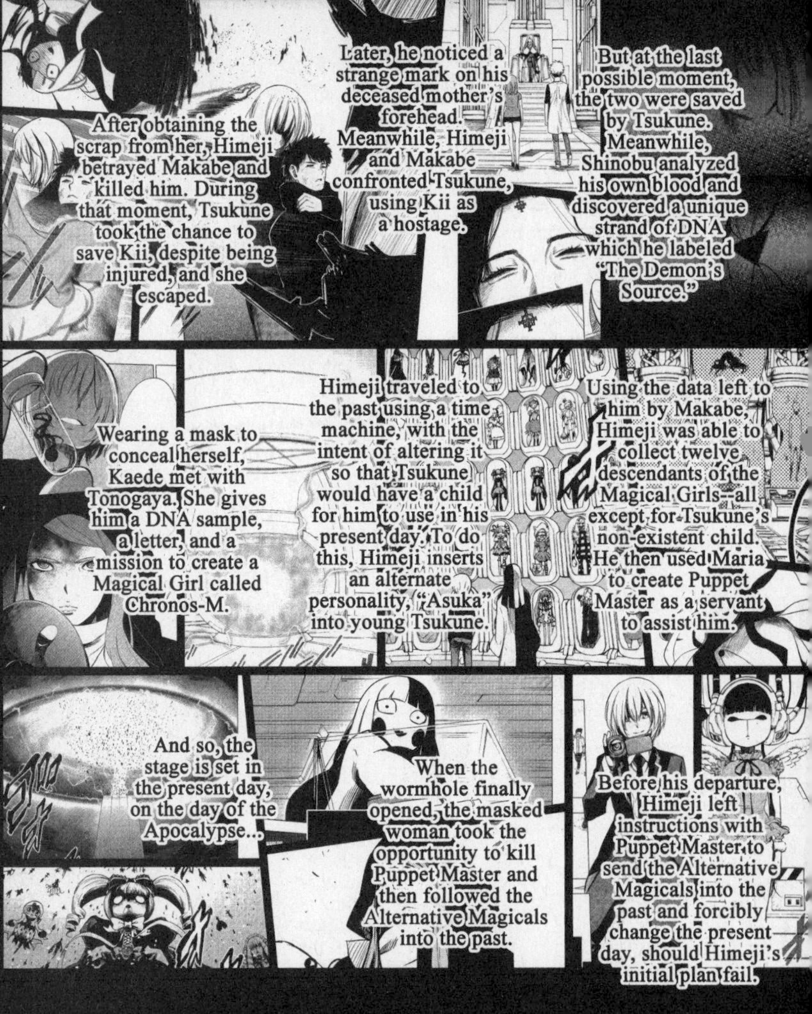
But at the last possible moment, the two were saved by Tsukune. Meanwhile, Shinobu analyzed his own blood and discovered a unique strand of DNA which he labeled "The Demon's Source."
Later, he noticed a strange mark on his deceased mother's forehead. Meanwhile, Himeji and Makabe confronted Tsukune, using Kii as a hostage.
After obtaining the scrap from her, Himeji betrayed Makabe and killed him. During that moment, Tsukune took the chance to save Kii, despite being injured, and she escaped.
Using the data left to him by Makabe, Himeji was able to collect twelve descendants of the Magical Girls--all except for Tsukune's non-existent child. He then used Maria to create Puppet Master as a servant to assist him.
Himeji traveled to the past using a time machine, with the intent of altering it so that Tsukune would have a child for him to use in his present day. To do this, Himeji inserts an alternate personality, "Asuka" into young Tsukune.
Wearing a mask to conceal herself, Kaede met with Tonogaya. She gives him a DNA sample, a letter, and a mission to create a Magical Girl called Chronos-M.
Before his departure, Himeji left instructions with Puppet Master to send the Alternative Magicals into the past and forcibly change the present day, should Himeji's initial plan fail.
When the wormhole finally opened, the masked woman took the opportunity to kill Puppet Master and then followed the Alternative Magicals into the past.
And so, the stage is set in the present day, on the day of the Apocalypse...

**MAKABE KEITO**

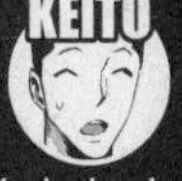

A mad scientist who has performed countless human experiments. The creator of Himeji Wataru. He was planning to perform a ritual described in the "Revelations of the Apocalypse," but he was killed by Himeji first.

**TONOGAYA YUUJI**

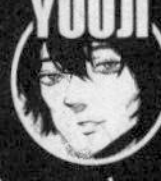

A researcher of nanotechnology who has many achievements to his name. Engaged to marry Maria.

**HIMEJI WATARU**

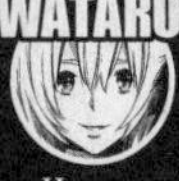

He was created to replace the original female Wataru. Maria's core was transferred into him.

**FUKUMOTO SEIICHI**

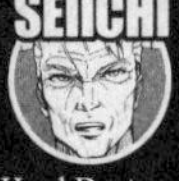

Head Doctor at Kairin University Hospital. He gave Sou a vial of magical girl blood and suggested that he should look for the Witch.

**AKUTA RINTAROU**

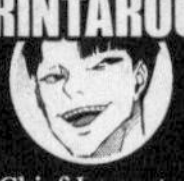

Chief Inspector of 1st Division Criminal Investigations at Tokyo Police HQ. Still just as infatuated with high school girls.

# SEVEN SEAS ENTERTAINMENT PRESENTS

# MAGICAL GIRL APOCALYPSE

## story and art by KENTARO SATO    VOLUME 12

TRANSLATION
**Wesley Bridges**

ADAPTATION
**Janet Houck**

LETTERING AND LAYOUT
**Meaghan Tucker**

LOGO DESIGN
**Phil Balsman**

COVER DESIGN
**Nicky Lim**

PROOFREADER
**Shanti Whitesides**

ASSISTANT EDITOR
**Jenn Grunigen**

PRODUCTION ASSISTANT
**CK Russell**

PRODUCTION MANAGER
**Lissa Pattillo**

EDITOR-IN-CHIEF
**Adam Arnold**

PUBLISHER
**Jason DeAngelis**

MAHO SYOJYO OF THE END Volume 12
© Kentaro Sato 2016
Originally published in Japan in 2016 by Akita Publishing Co., Ltd..
English translation rights arranged with Akita Publishing Co., Ltd. through
TOHAN CORPORATION, Tokyo.

Seven Seas books may be purchased in bulk for promotional, educational, or
business use. Please contact your local bookseller or the Macmillan Corporate
and Premium Sales Department at 1-800-221-7945, extension 5442, or by
e-mail at MacmillanSpecialMarkets@macmillan.com.

Seven Seas and the Seven Seas logo are trademarks of
Seven Seas Entertainment, LLC. All rights reserved.

ISBN: 978-1-626925-07-6

Printed in Canada

First Printing: July 2017

10 9 8 7 6 5 4 3 2 1

## FOLLOW US ONLINE: *www.gomanga.com*

# READING DIRECTIONS

This book reads from *right to left*, Japanese style.
If this is your first time reading manga, you start
reading from the top right panel on each page and
take it from there. If you get lost, just follow the
numbered diagram here. It may seem backwards at
first, but you'll get the hang of it! Have fun!!

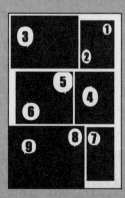

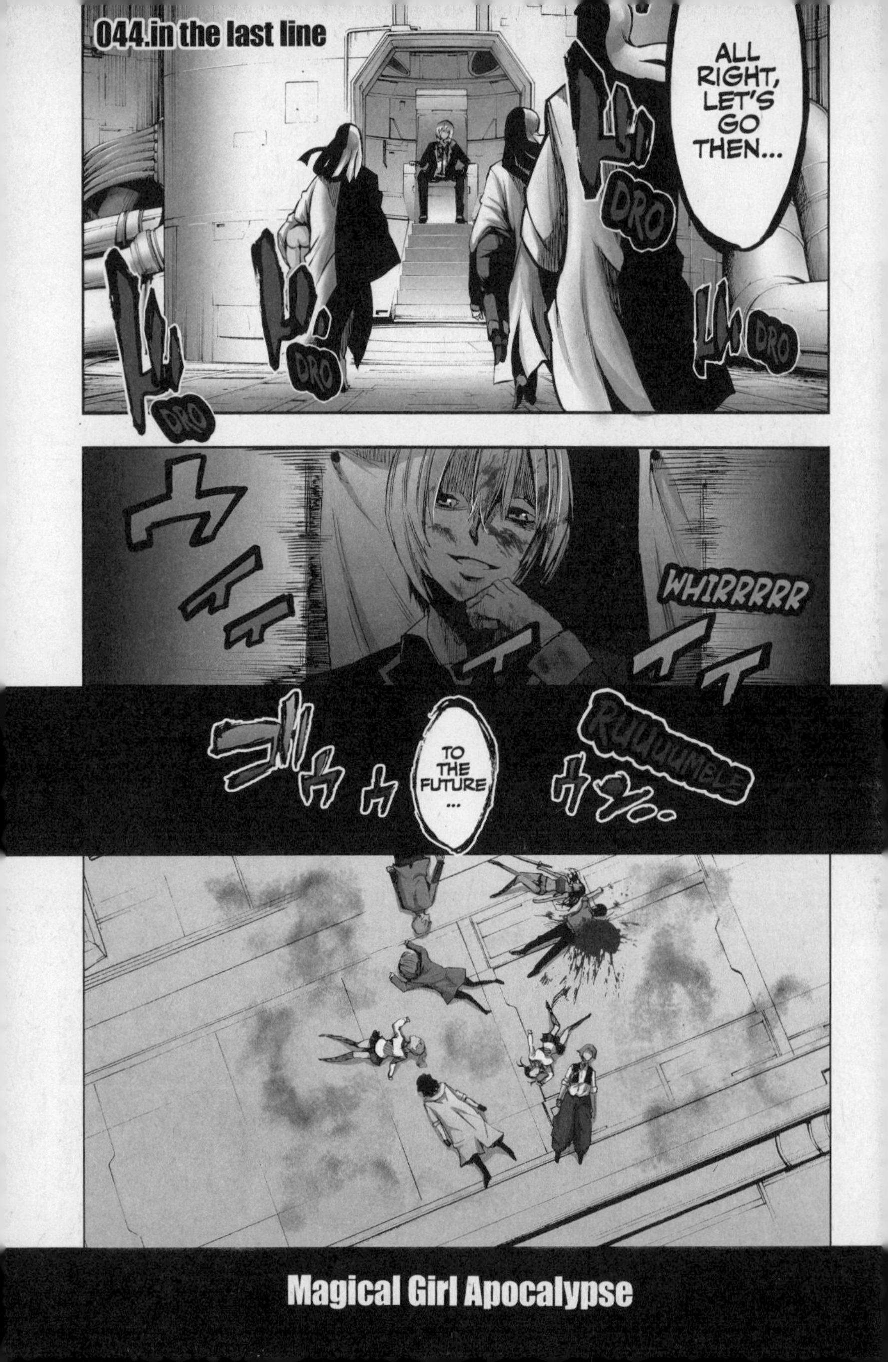
044.in the last line
ALL RIGHT, LET'S GO THEN...
DRO
DRO
DRO
DRO
WHIRRRRR
RUUUUMBLE
TO THE FUTURE ...

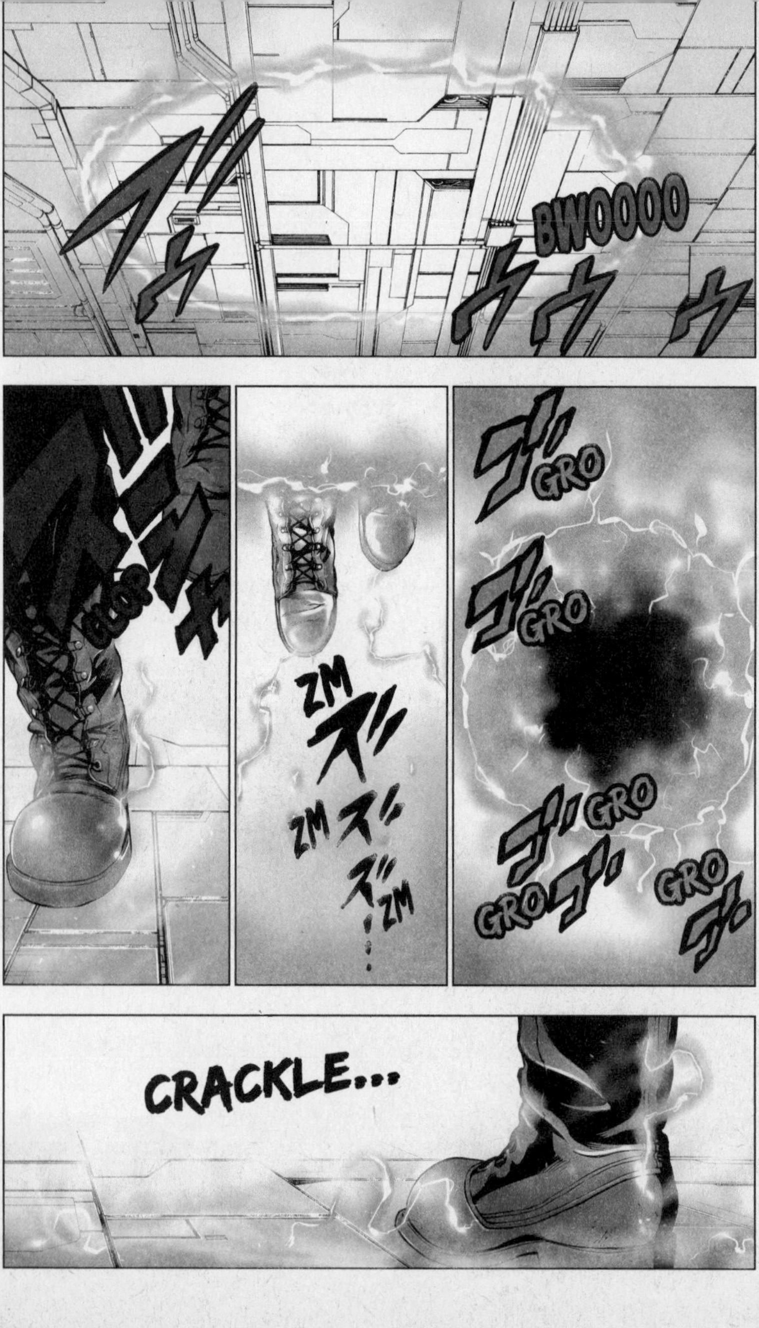
BWOOOO
GRO
GRO
GRO
GRO
GRO
ZM
ZM
ZM
CLOP
CRACKLE...

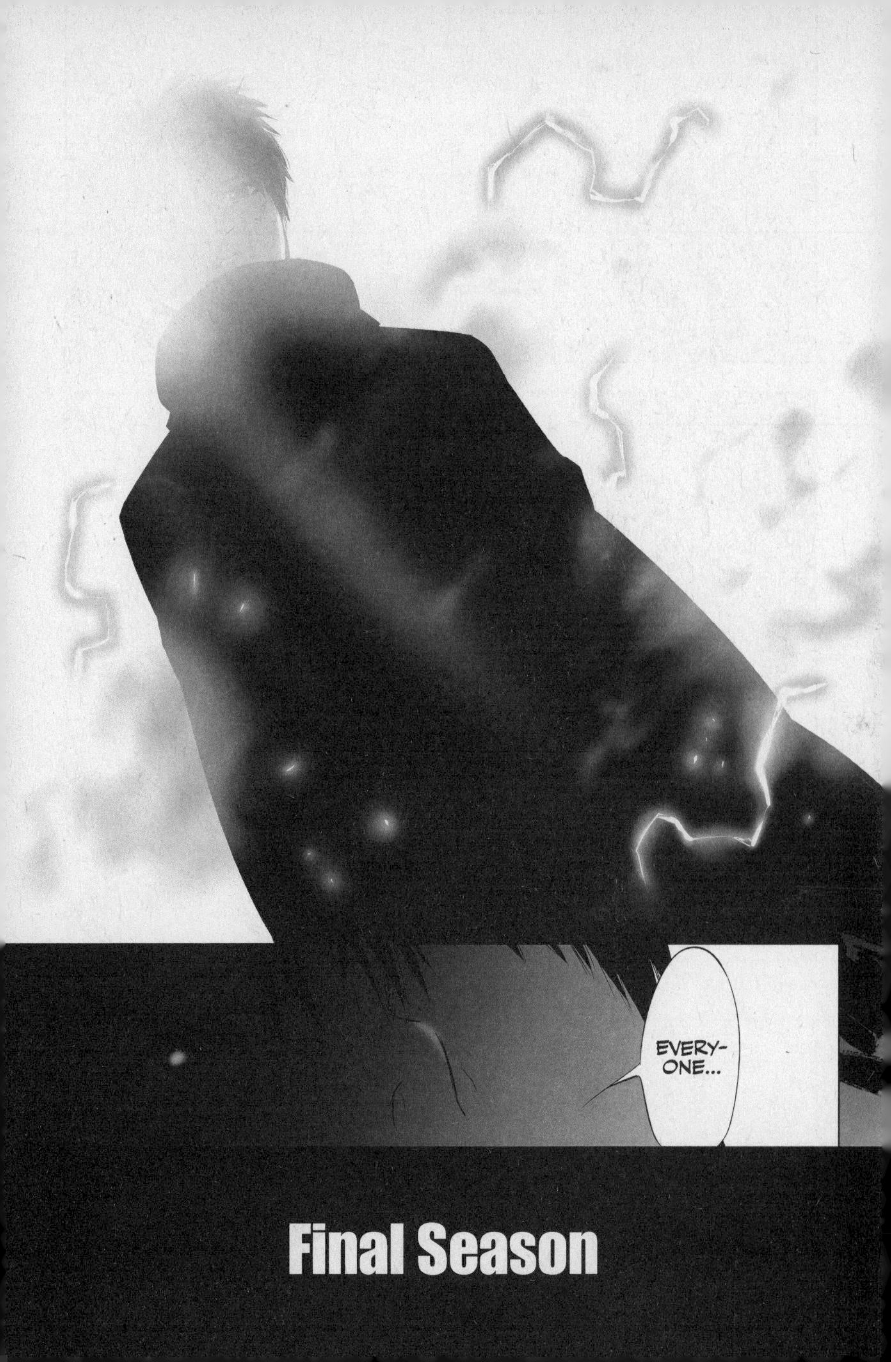
EVERY-
ONE...

# Final Season

# 044.in the last line

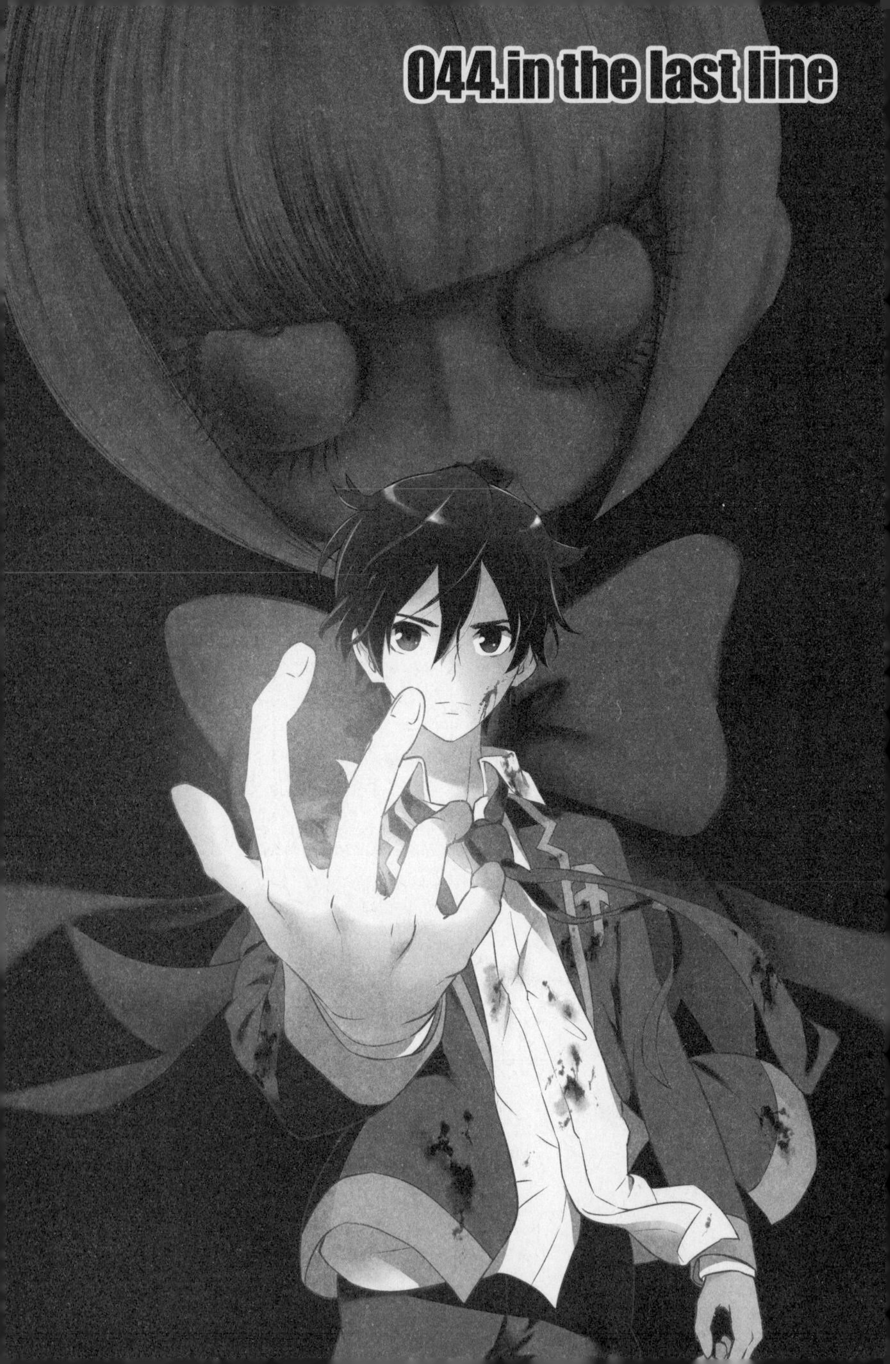

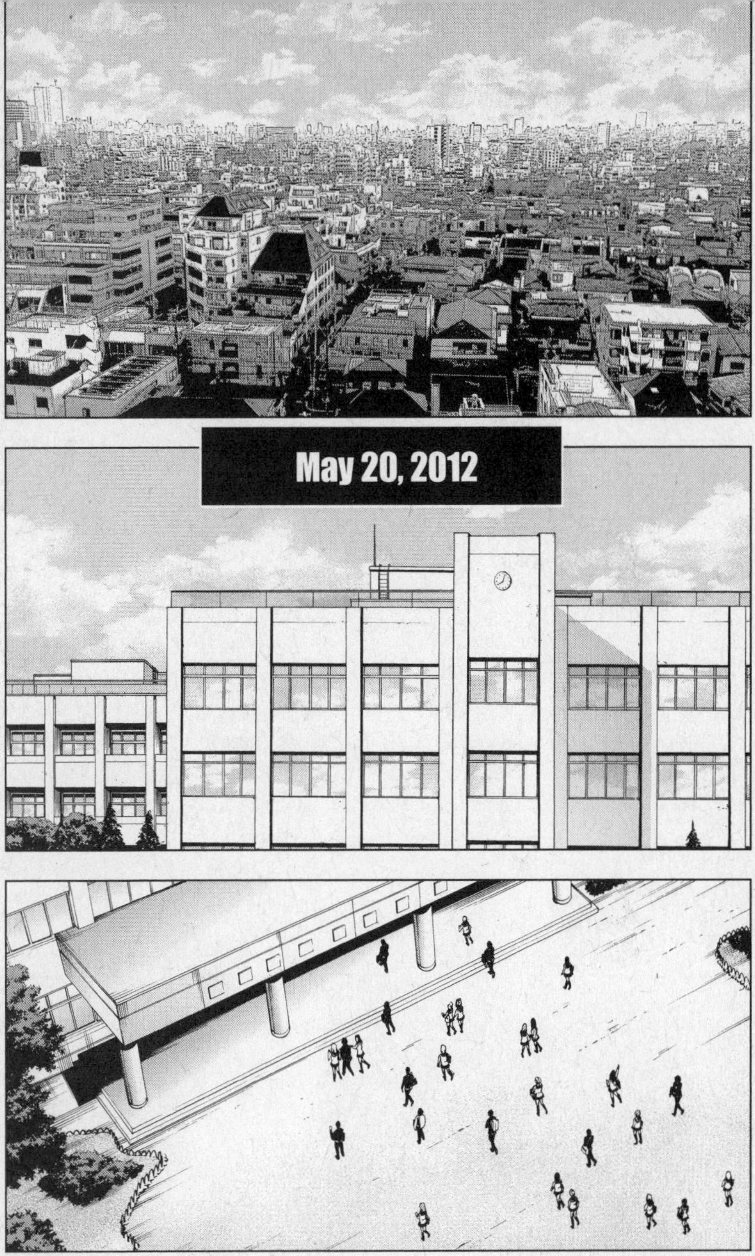
May 20, 2012

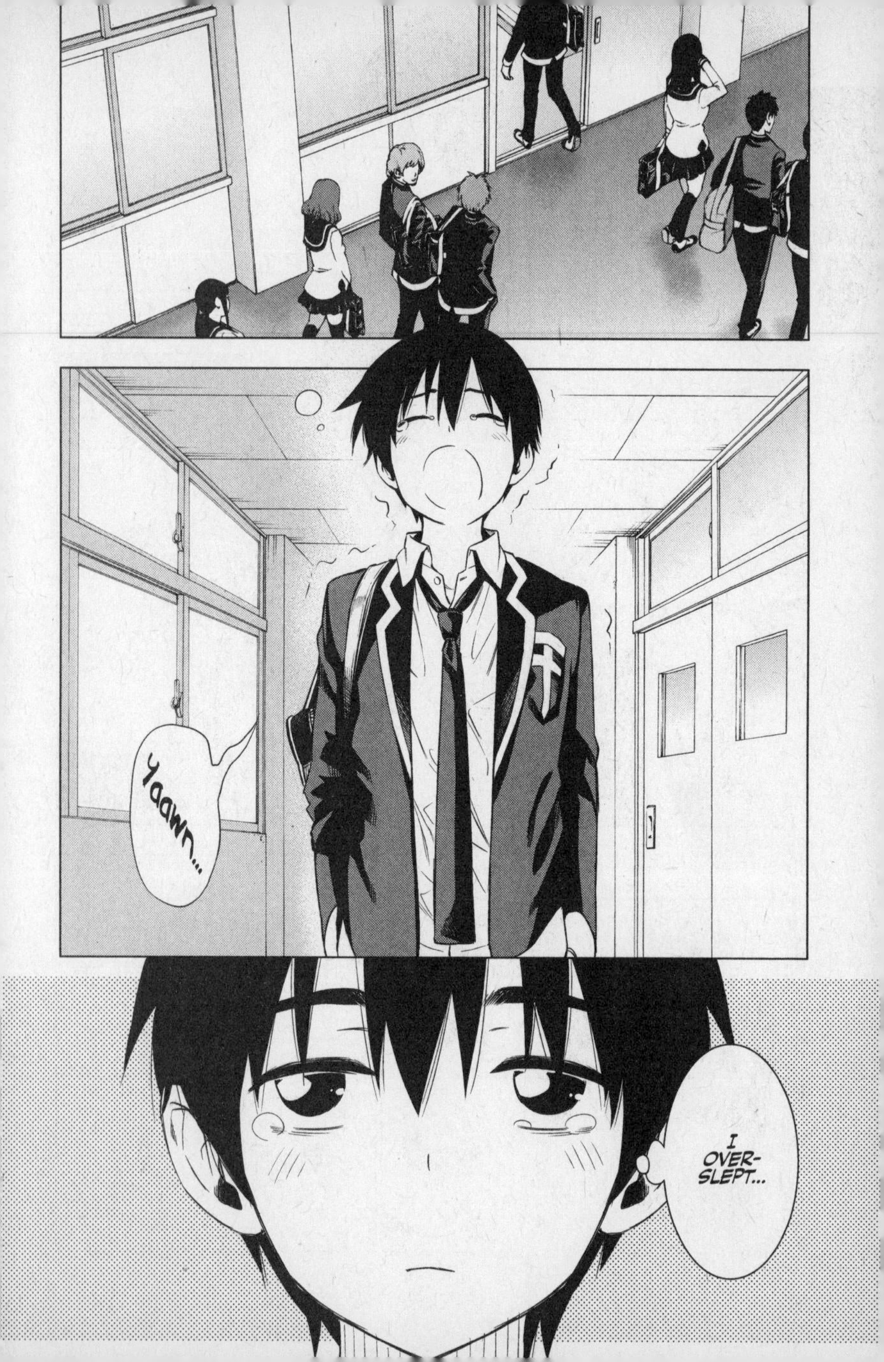
Yaawn...
I OVER-SLEPT...

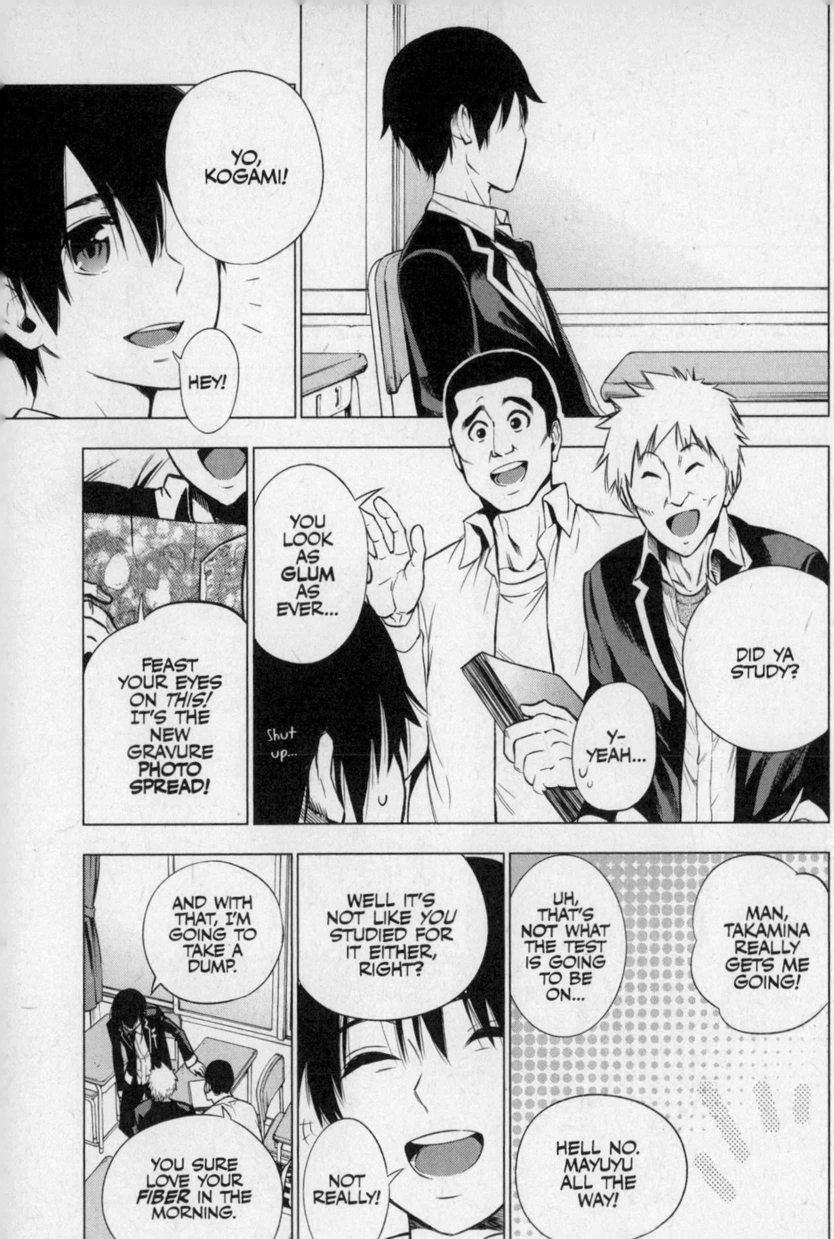
YO, KOGAMI!
HEY!
YOU LOOK AS GLUM AS EVER...
DID YA STUDY?
Y-YEAH...
Shut up...
FEAST YOUR EYES ON *THIS!* IT'S THE NEW GRAVURE PHOTO SPREAD!
MAN, TAKAMINA REALLY GETS ME GOING!
UH, THAT'S NOT WHAT THE TEST IS GOING TO BE ON...
HELL NO. MAYUYU ALL THE WAY!
WELL IT'S NOT LIKE *YOU* STUDIED FOR IT EITHER, RIGHT?
NOT REALLY!
AND WITH THAT, I'M GOING TO TAKE A DUMP.
YOU SURE LOVE YOUR *FIBER* IN THE MORNING.

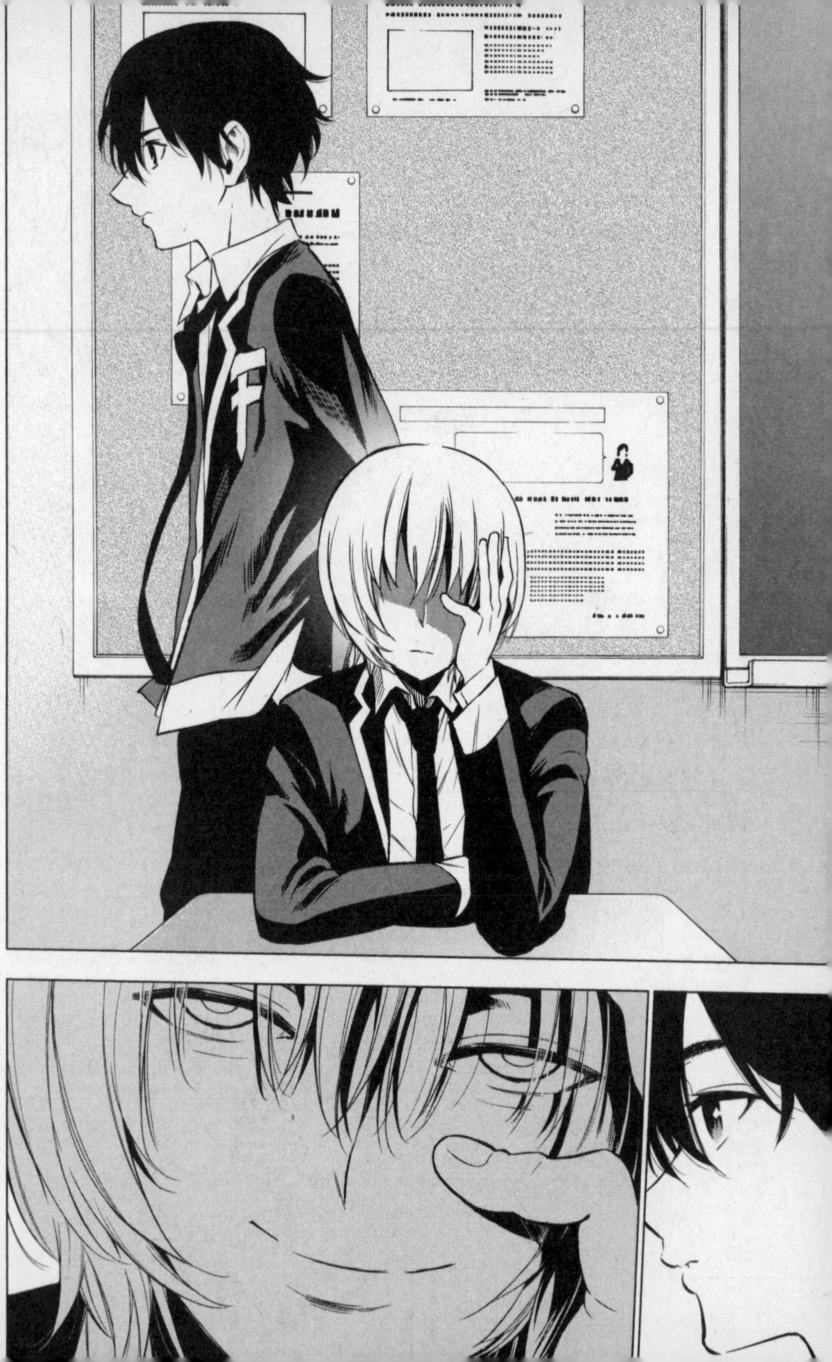

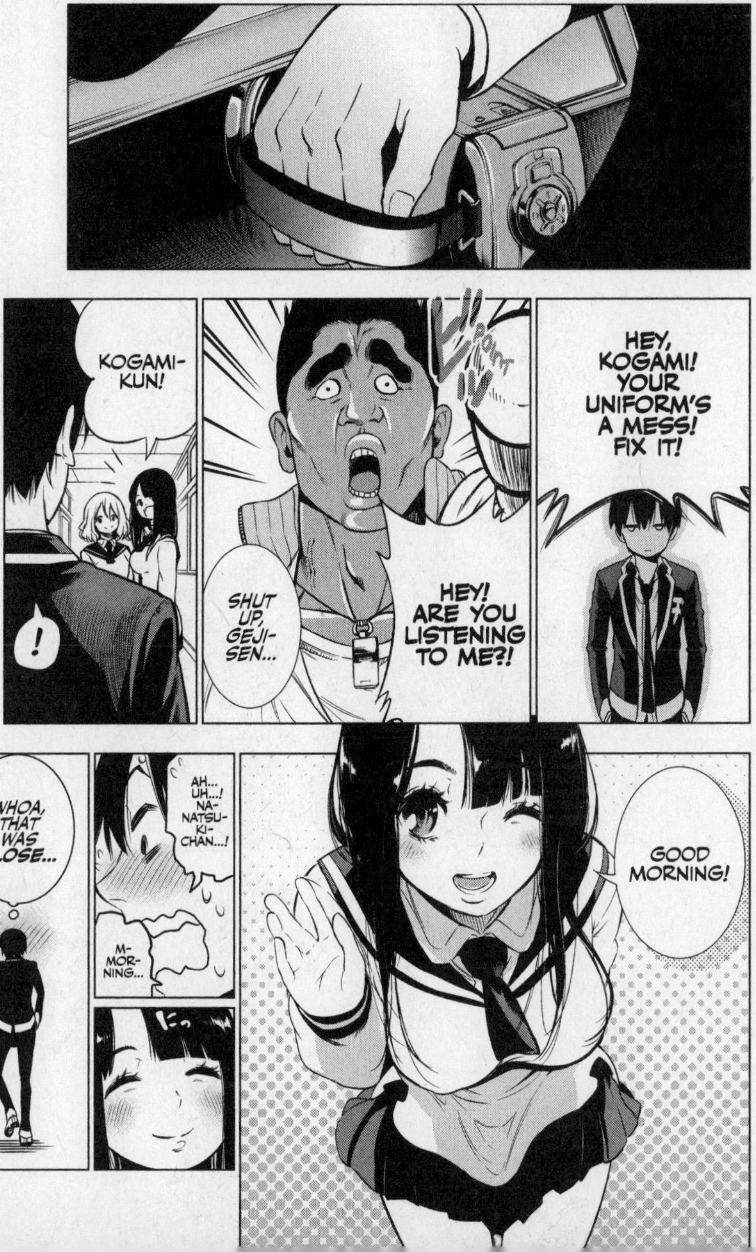
HEY, KOGAMI! YOUR UNIFORM'S A MESS! FIX IT!
HEY! ARE YOU LISTENING TO ME?!
SHUT UP, GEJI-SEN...
KOGAMI-KUN!
!
GOOD MORNING!
AH... UH...! NA-NATSUKI-CHAN...!
M-MORNING...
WHOA, THAT WAS CLOSE...

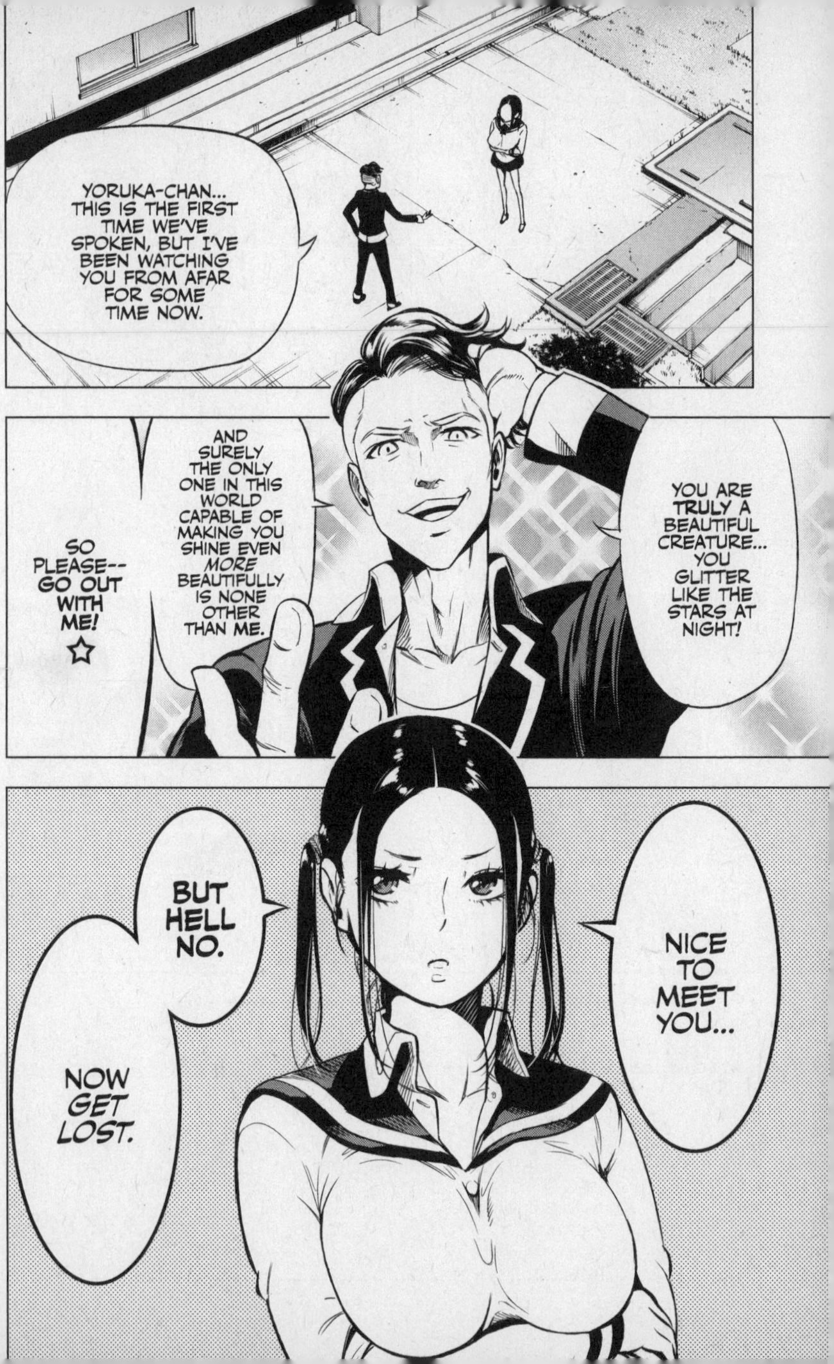
YORUKA-CHAN... THIS IS THE FIRST TIME WE'VE SPOKEN, BUT I'VE BEEN WATCHING YOU FROM AFAR FOR SOME TIME NOW.
YOU ARE TRULY A BEAUTIFUL CREATURE... YOU GLITTER LIKE THE STARS AT NIGHT!
AND SURELY THE ONLY ONE IN THIS WORLD CAPABLE OF MAKING YOU SHINE EVEN MORE BEAUTIFULLY IS NONE OTHER THAN ME.
SO PLEASE-- GO OUT WITH ME! ☆
NICE TO MEET YOU...
BUT HELL NO.
NOW GET LOST.

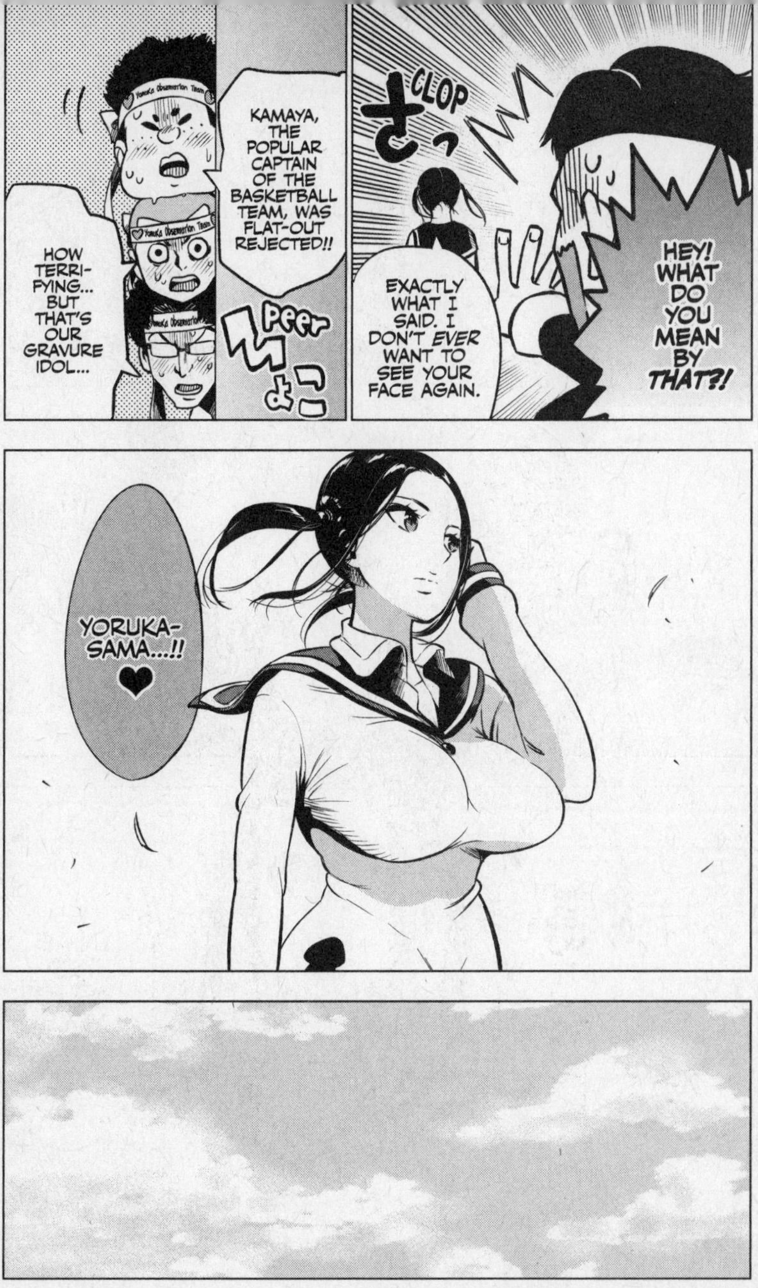
CLOP
さっ
HEY! WHAT DO YOU MEAN BY *THAT?!*
EXACTLY WHAT I SAID. I DON'T *EVER* WANT TO SEE YOUR FACE AGAIN.
KAMAYA, THE POPULAR CAPTAIN OF THE BASKETBALL TEAM, WAS FLAT-OUT REJECTED!!
Yoruka Observation Team
Yoruka Observation Team
Yoruka Observation Team
peer
ひょこ
HOW TERRI-FYING... BUT THAT'S OUR GRAVURE IDOL...
YORUKA-SAMA...!! ♥

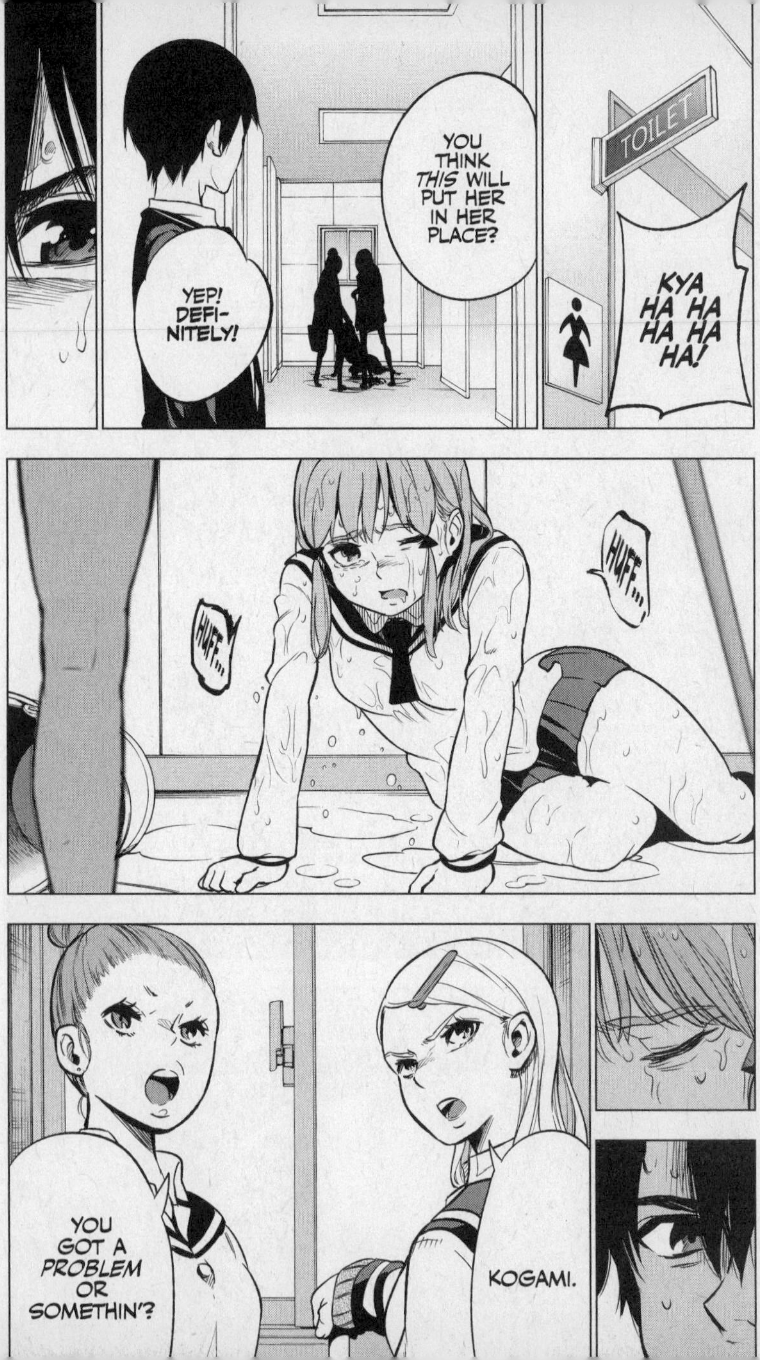
TOILET
KYA HA HA HA HA HA!
YOU THINK THIS WILL PUT HER IN HER PLACE?
YEP! DEFINITELY!
HUFF...
HUFF...
YOU GOT A PROBLEM OR SOMETHIN'?
KOGAMI.

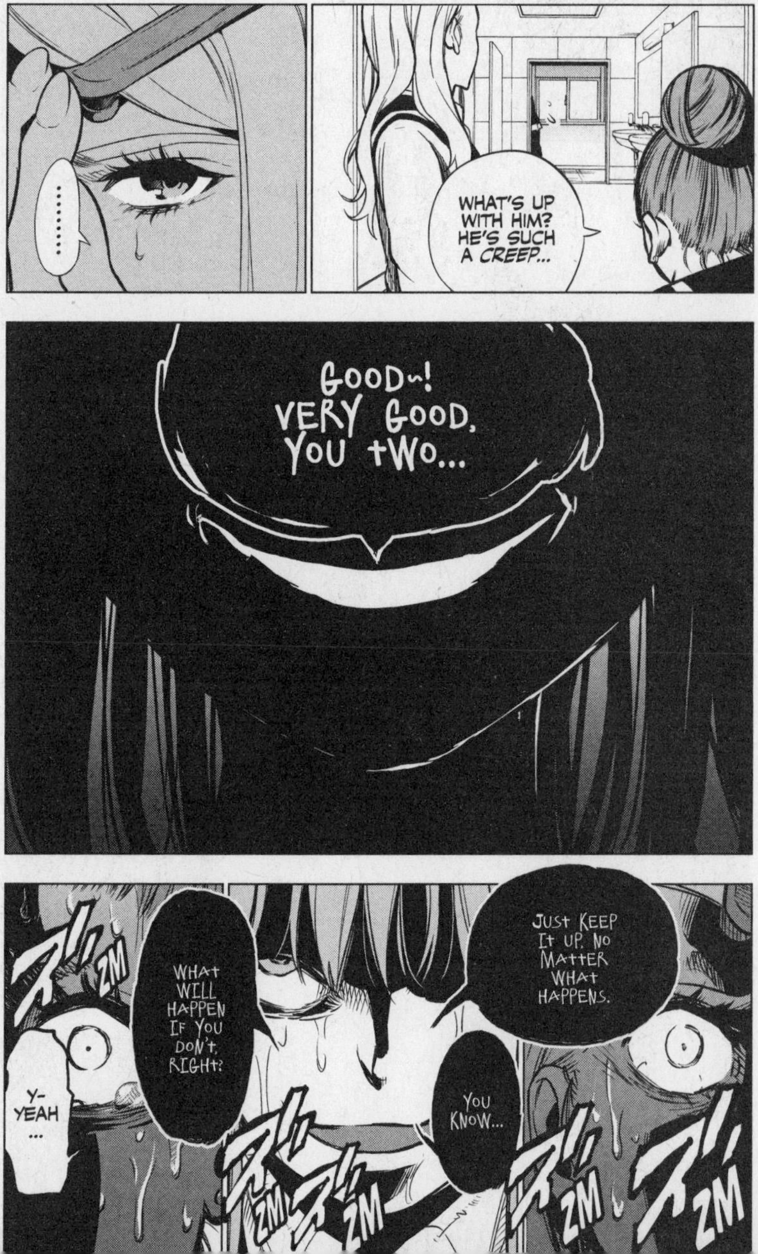
WHAT'S UP WITH HIM? HE'S SUCH A *CREEP*...
......
GOOD~! VERY GOOD, YOU TWO...
JUST KEEP IT UP, NO MATTER WHAT HAPPENS.
ZM
ZM
YOU KNOW...
WHAT WILL HAPPEN IF YOU DON'T, RIGHT?
ZM
ZM
ZM
Y-YEAH...

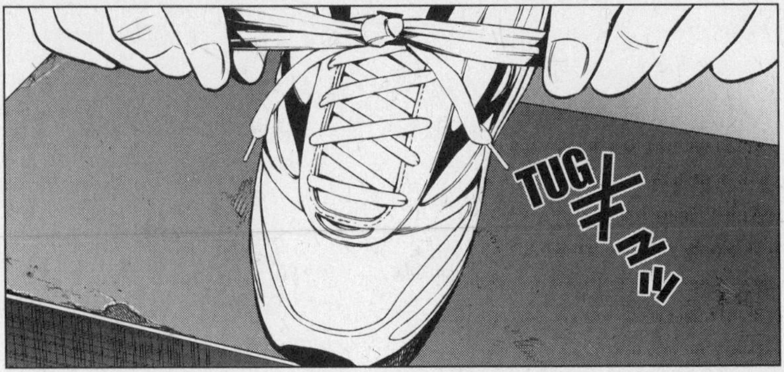
TUG
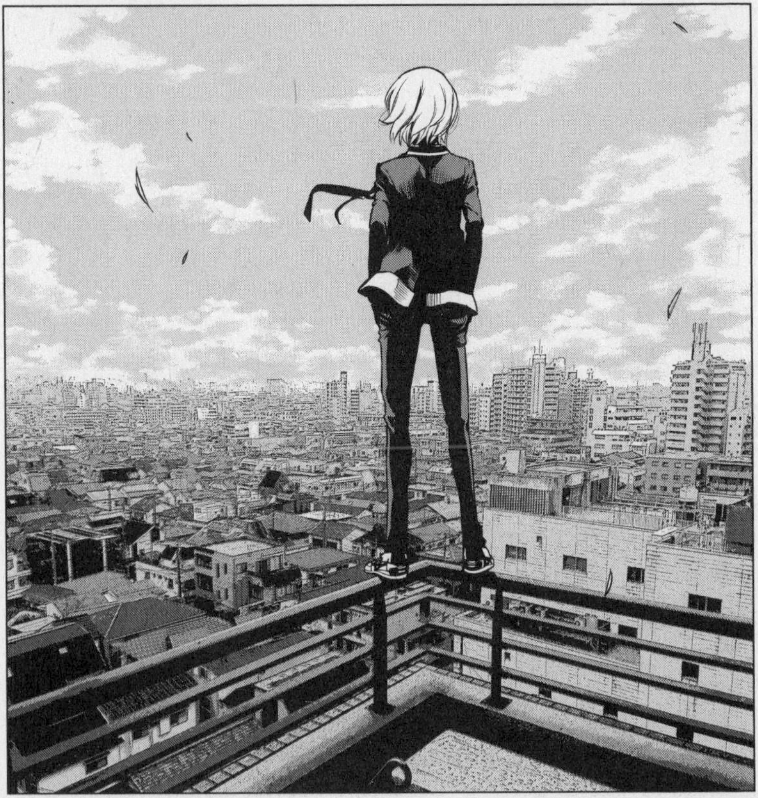

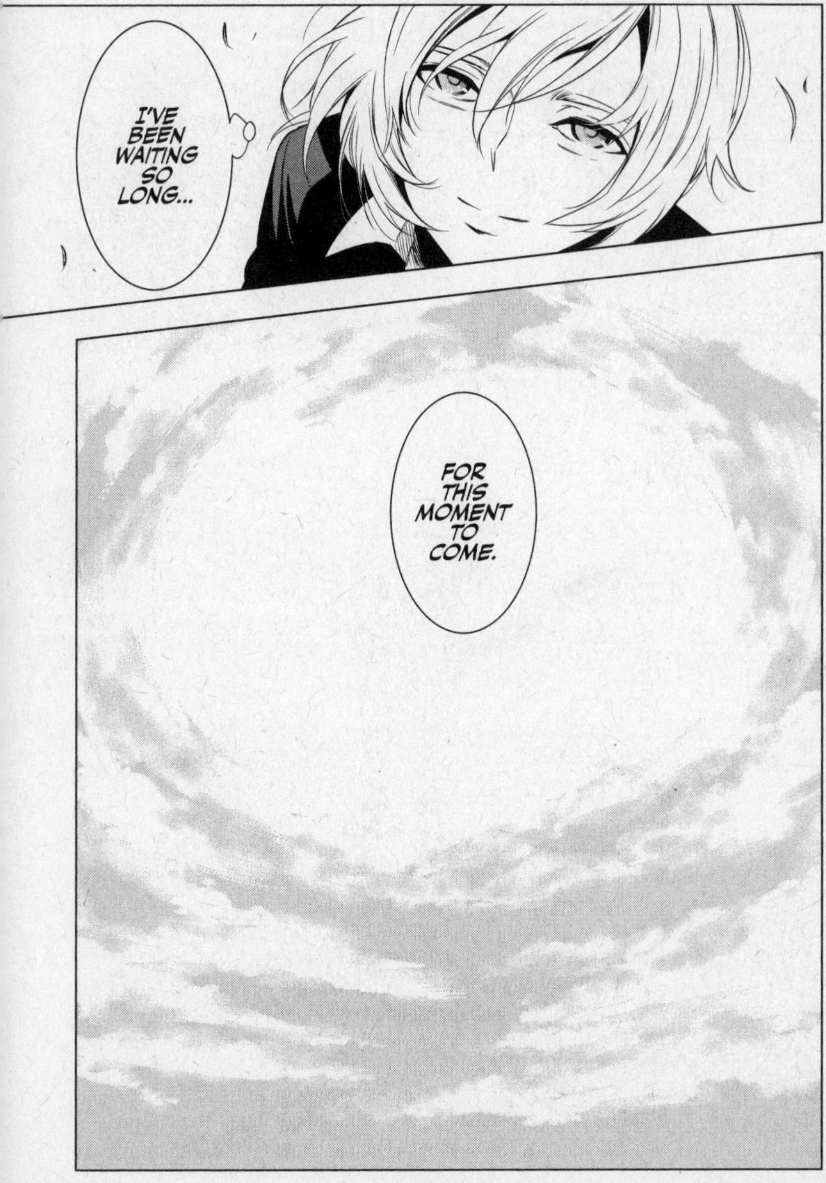
I'VE BEEN WAITING SO LONG...
FOR THIS MOMENT TO COME.

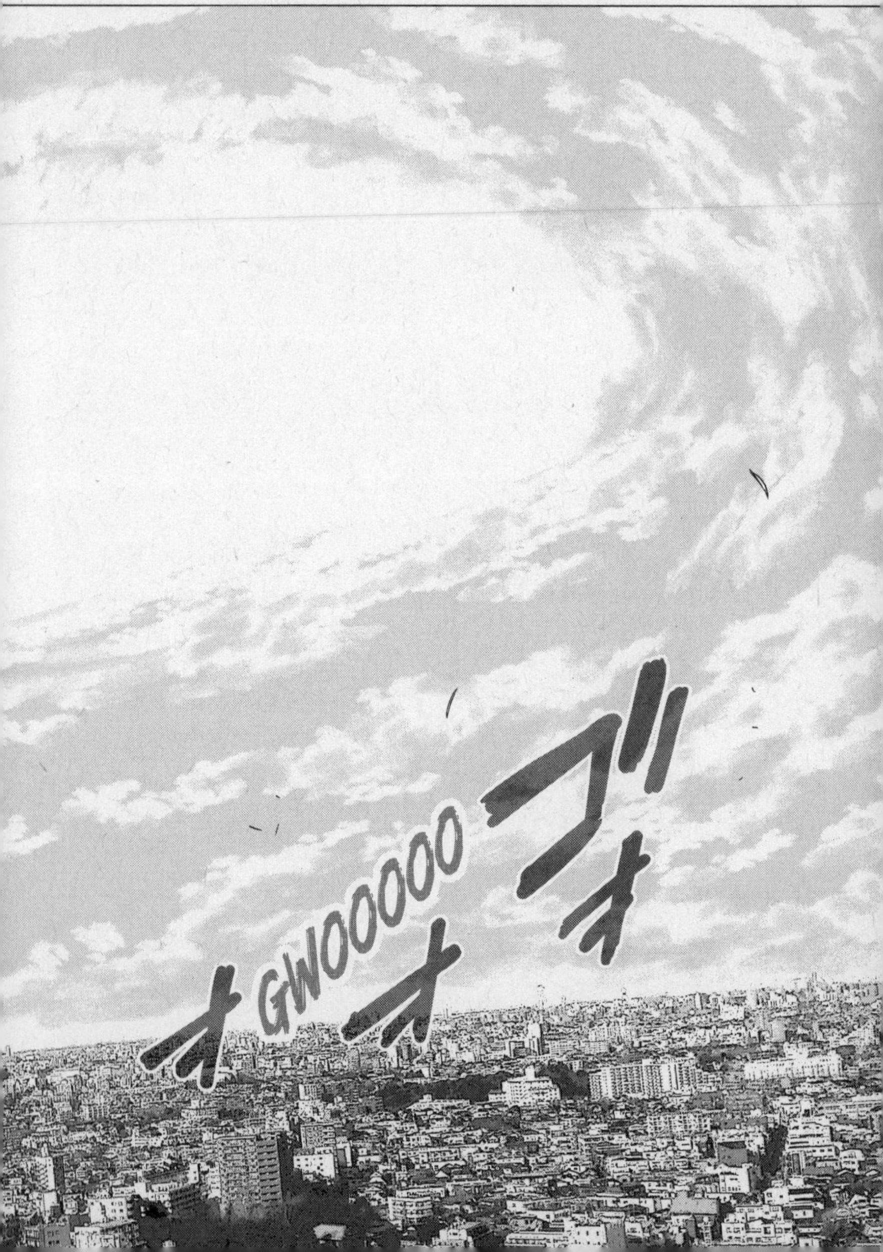
ゴォオオ
GWOOOOO

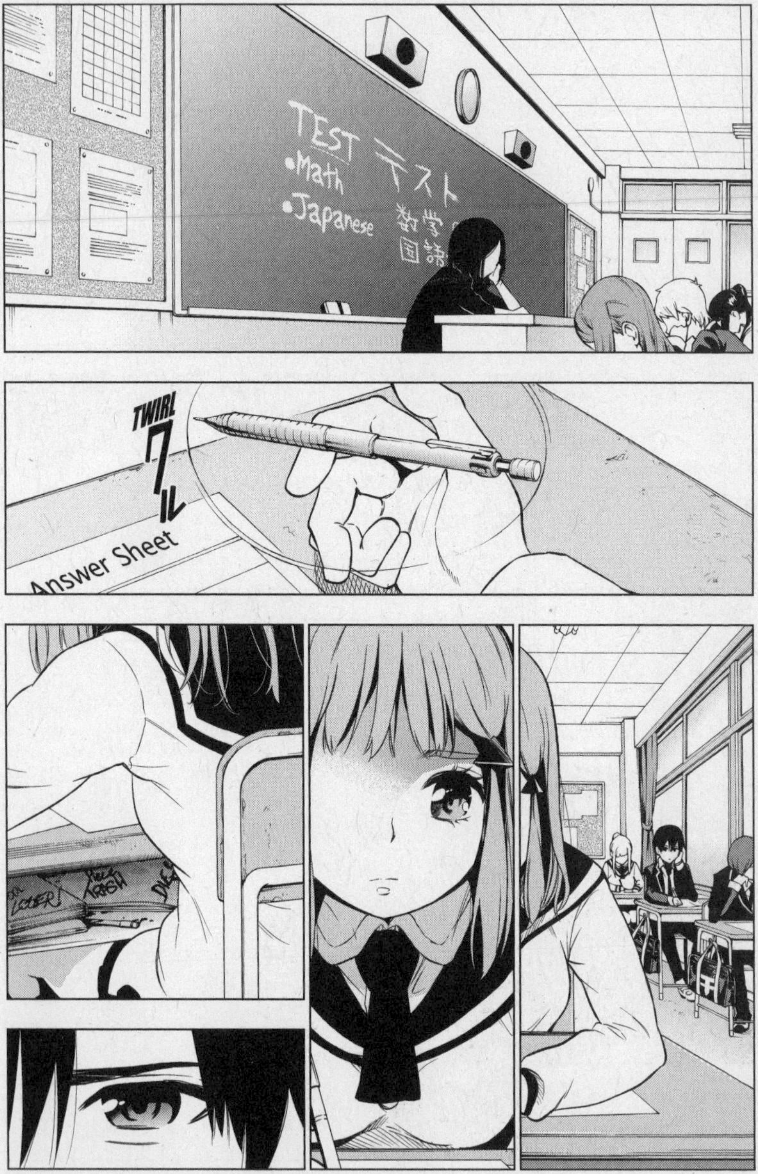
TEST テスト
•Math
•Japanese
数学
国語
TWIRL
クル
Answer Sheet
LOSER!
TRASH

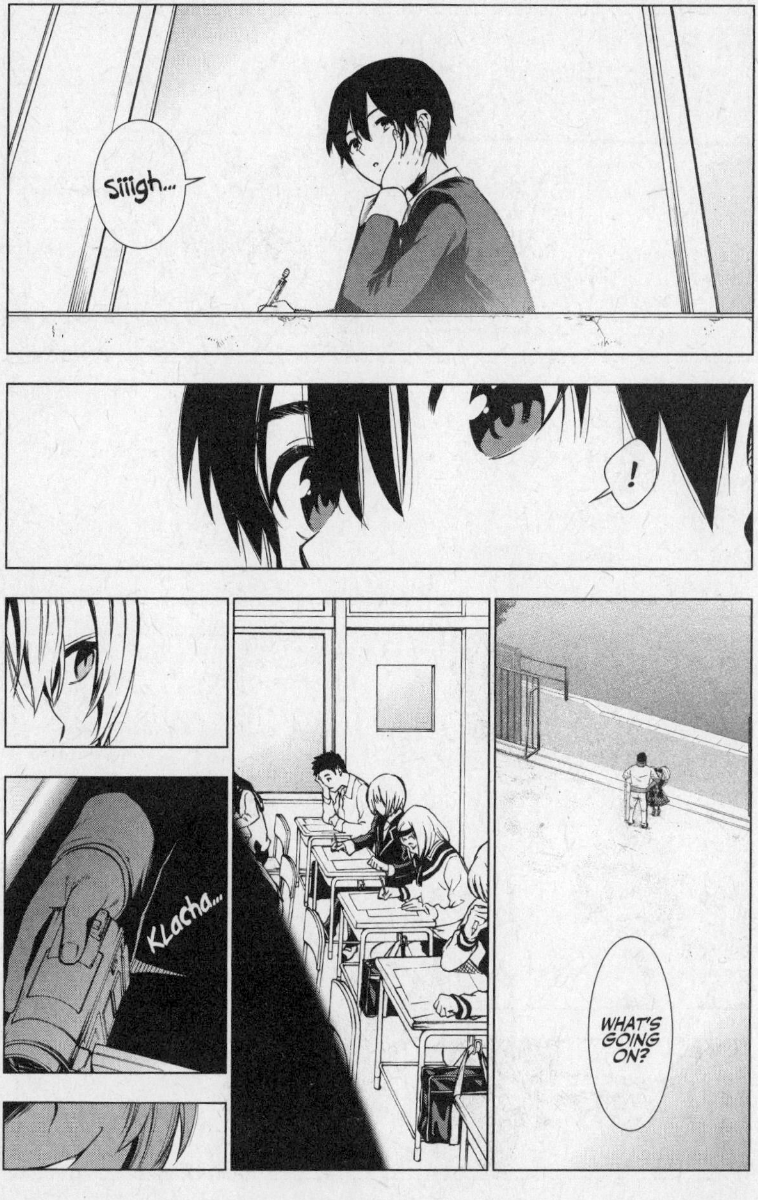
Siiigh...
!
WHAT'S GOING ON?
KLacha...

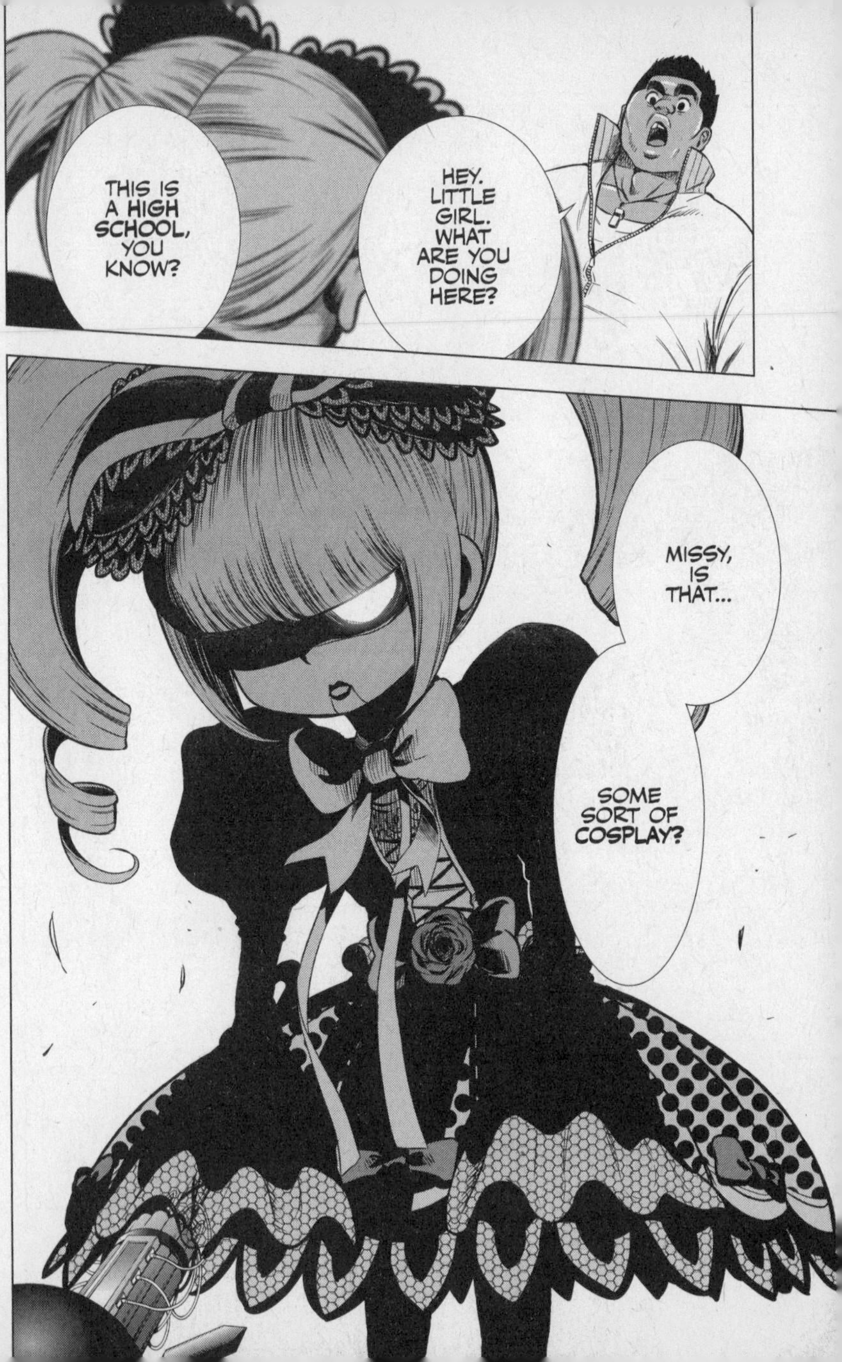
HEY. LITTLE GIRL. WHAT ARE YOU DOING HERE?
THIS IS A HIGH SCHOOL, YOU KNOW?
MISSY, IS THAT...
SOME SORT OF COSPLAY?

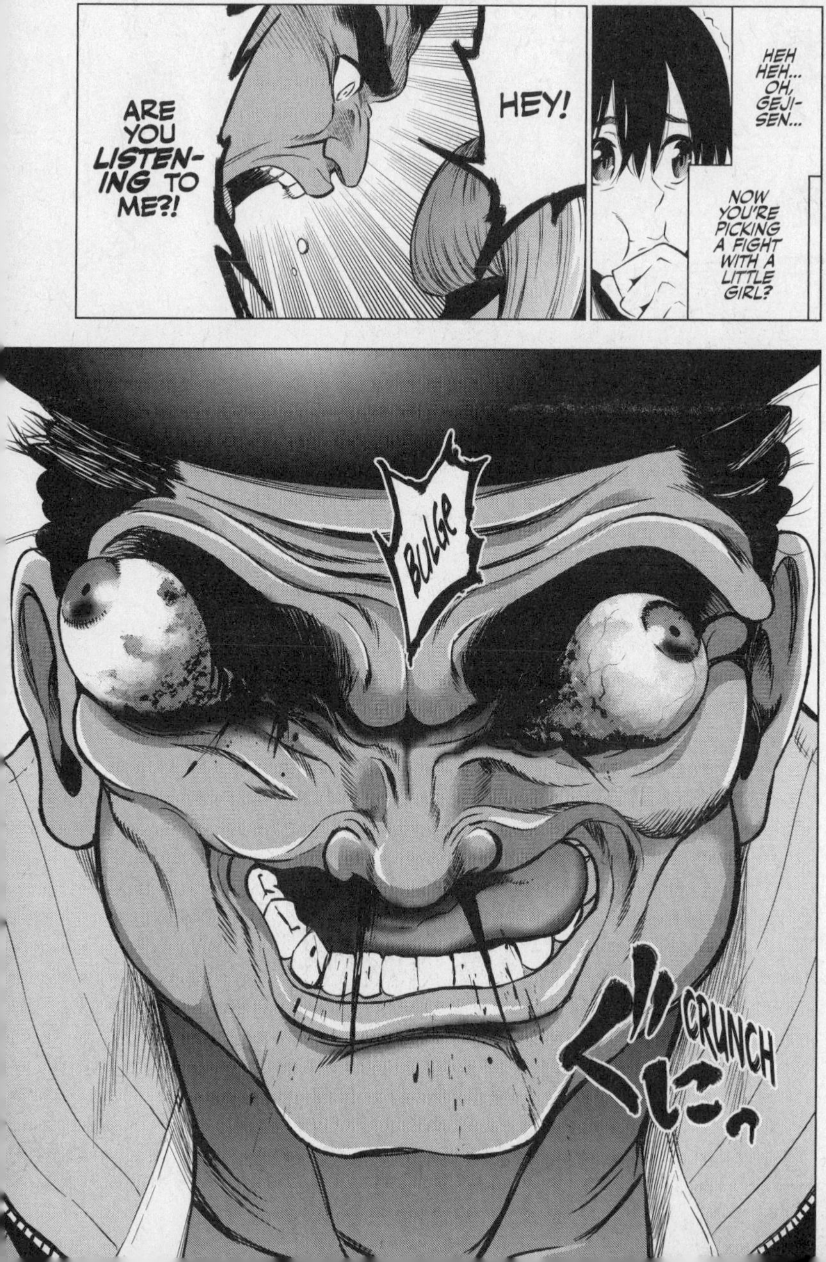
HEH HEH... OH, GEJI-SEN...
NOW YOU'RE PICKING A FIGHT WITH A LITTLE GIRL?
HEY!
ARE YOU LISTENING TO ME?!
BULGE
CRUNCH

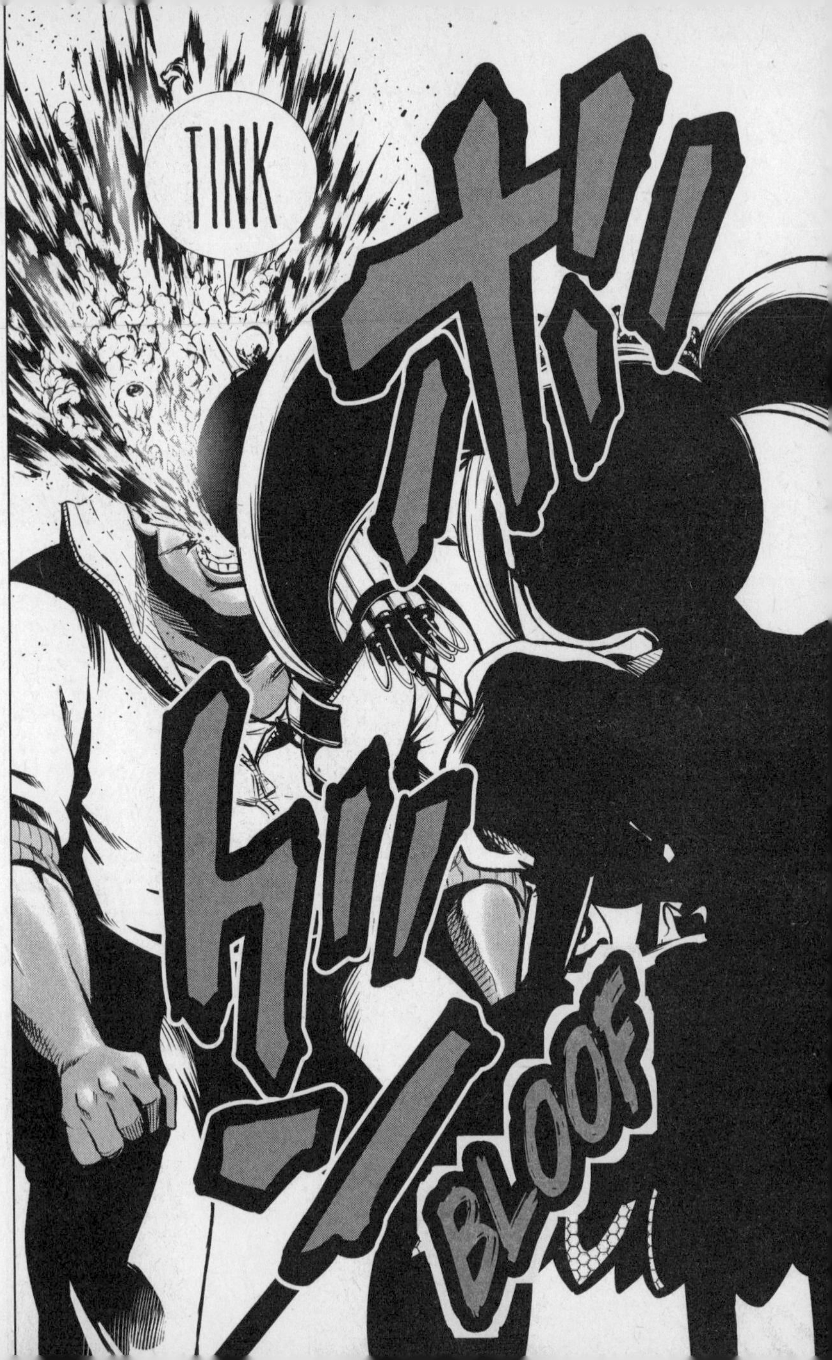
TINK
BLOOF

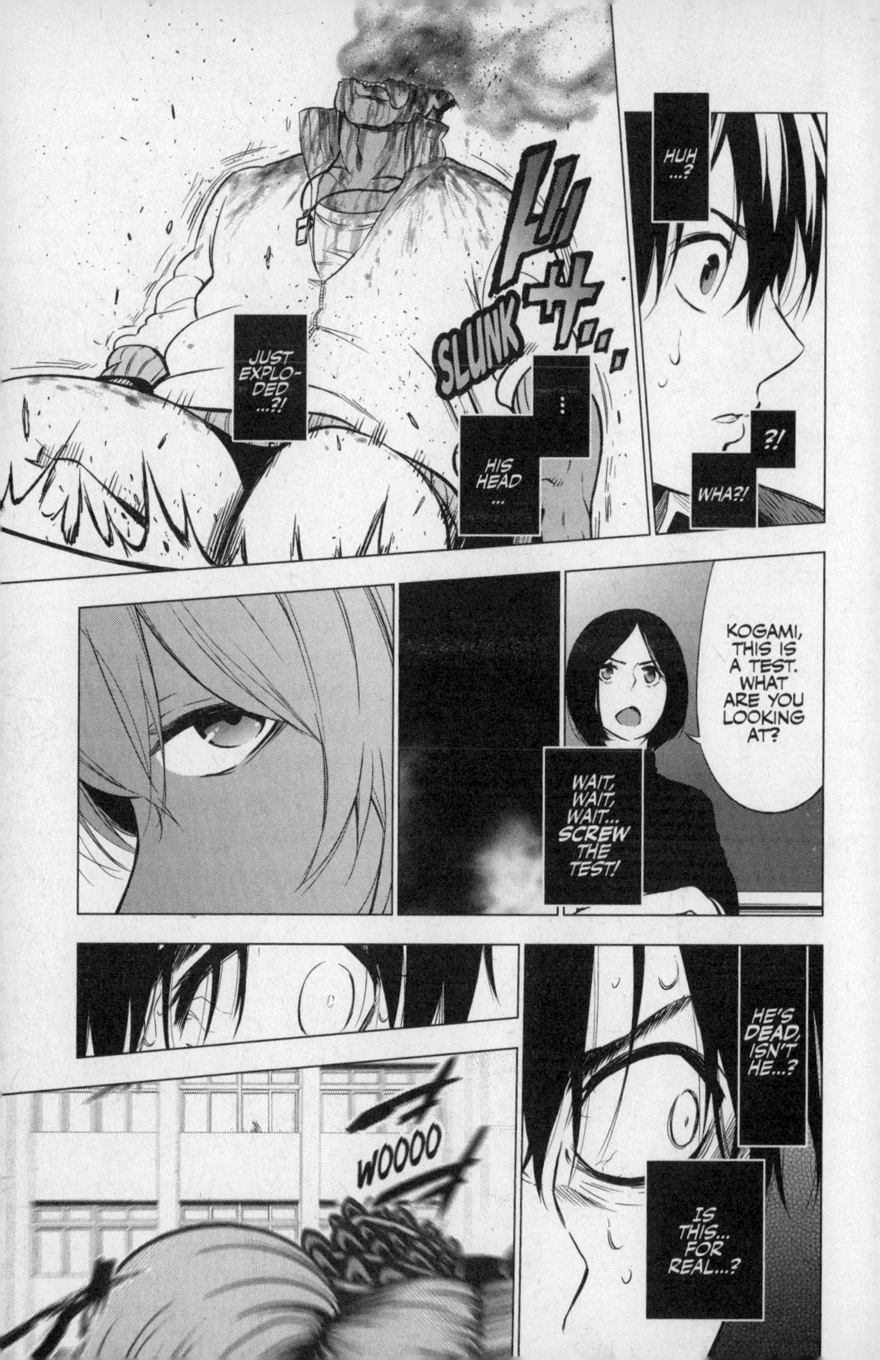
HUH ...?
?!
WHA?!
SLUNK
...
HIS HEAD ...
JUST EXPLO-DED ...?!
KOGAMI, THIS IS A TEST. WHAT ARE YOU LOOKING AT?
WAIT, WAIT, WAIT... SCREW THE TEST!
HE'S DEAD, ISN'T HE...?
IS THIS... FOR REAL...?
WOOOO

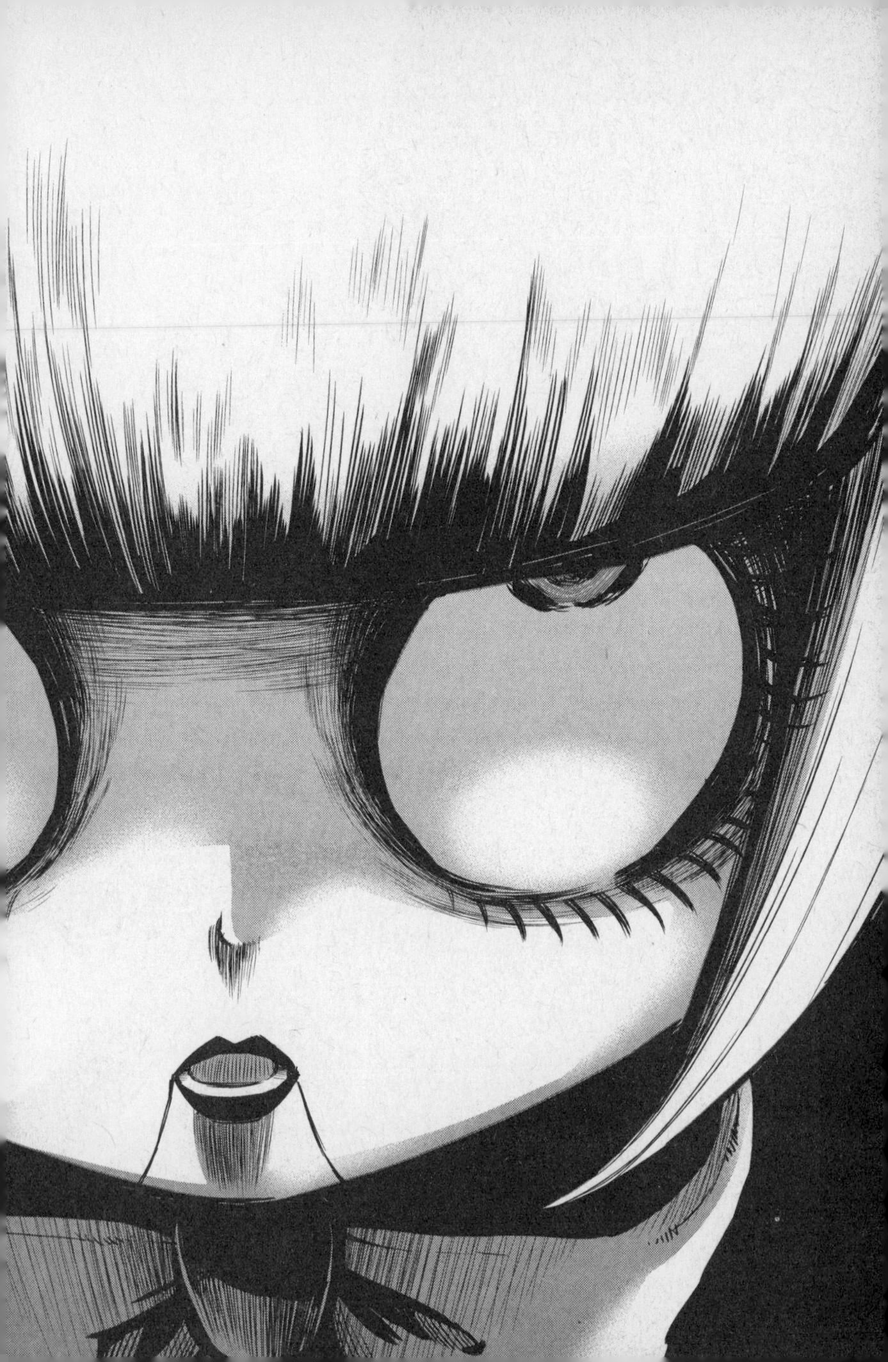

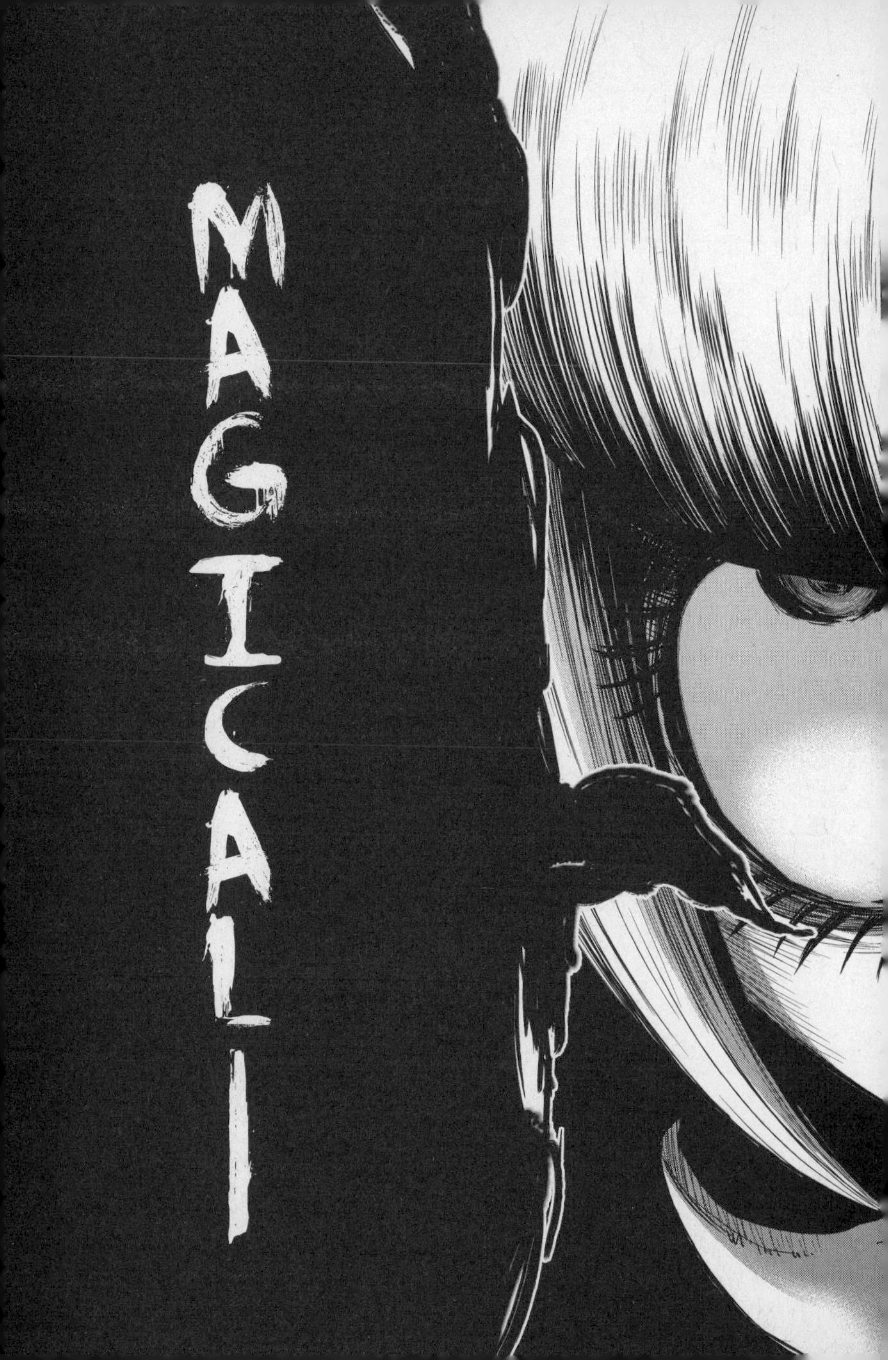
MAGICAL

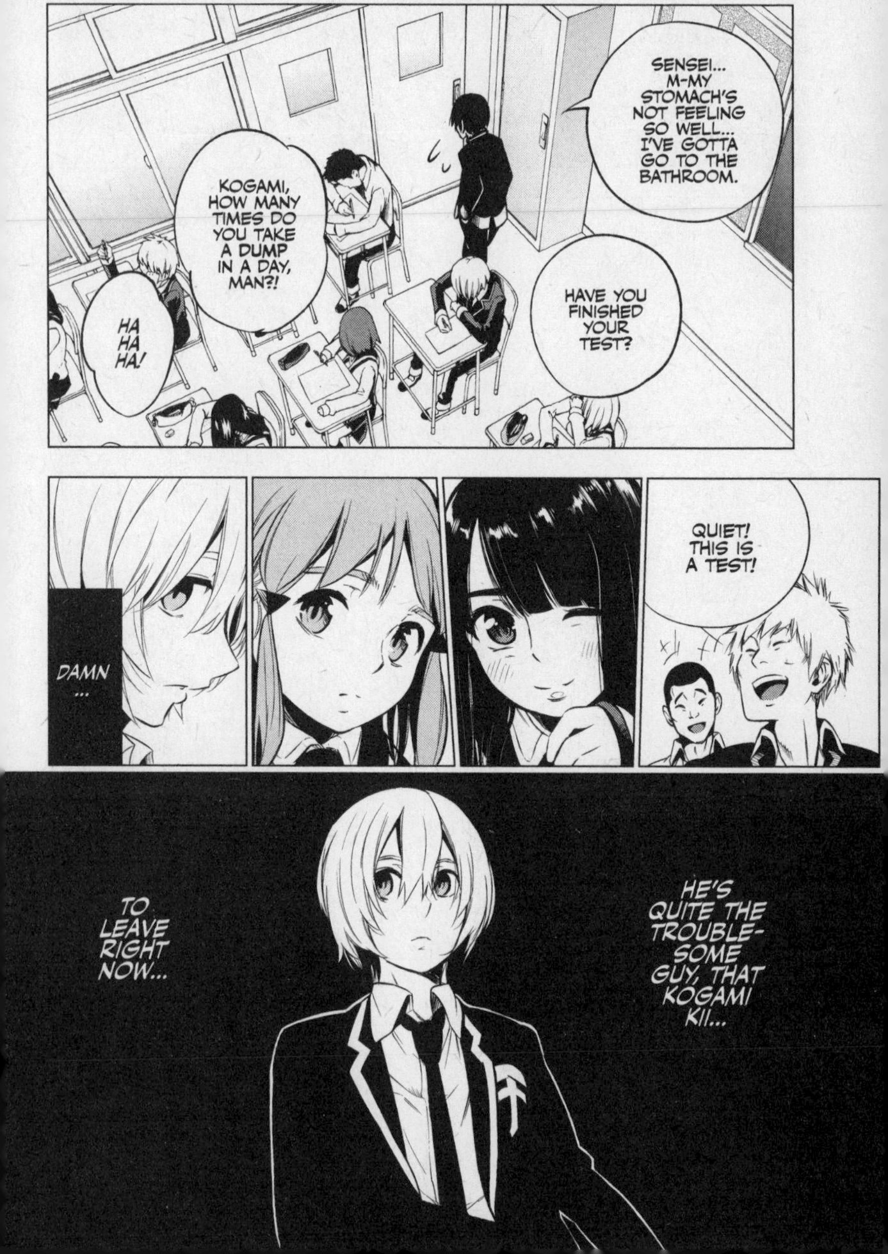
SENSEI... M-MY STOMACH'S NOT FEELING SO WELL... I'VE GOTTA GO TO THE BATHROOM.
HAVE YOU FINISHED YOUR TEST?
KOGAMI, HOW MANY TIMES DO YOU TAKE A DUMP IN A DAY, MAN?!
HA HA HA!
QUIET! THIS IS A TEST!
DAMN...
HE'S QUITE THE TROUBLE-SOME GUY, THAT KOGAMI KII...
TO LEAVE RIGHT NOW...

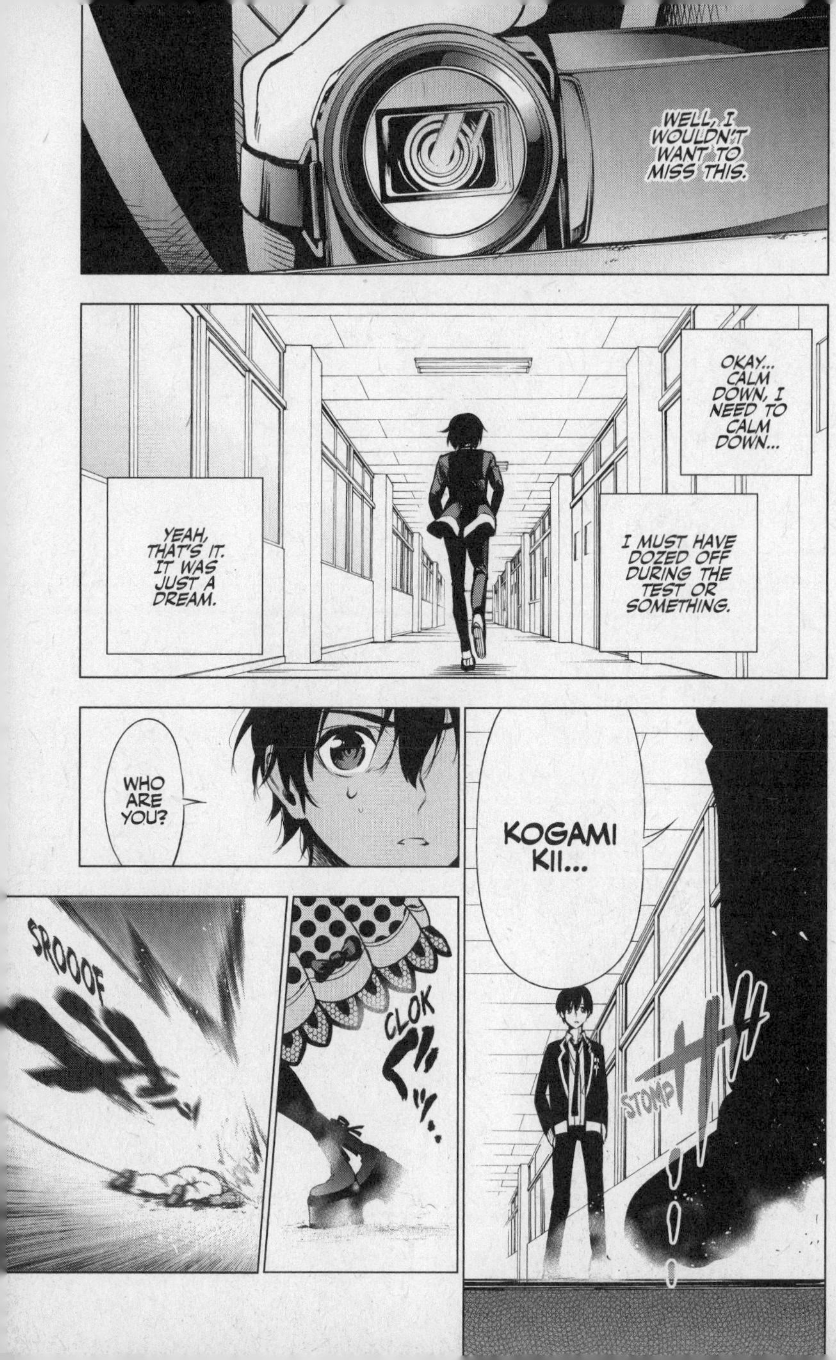
WELL, I WOULDN'T WANT TO MISS THIS.
OKAY... CALM DOWN, I NEED TO CALM DOWN...
I MUST HAVE DOZED OFF DURING THE TEST OR SOMETHING.
YEAH, THAT'S IT. IT WAS JUST A DREAM.
KOGAMI KII...
STOMP
WHO ARE YOU?
CLOK
SROOOF

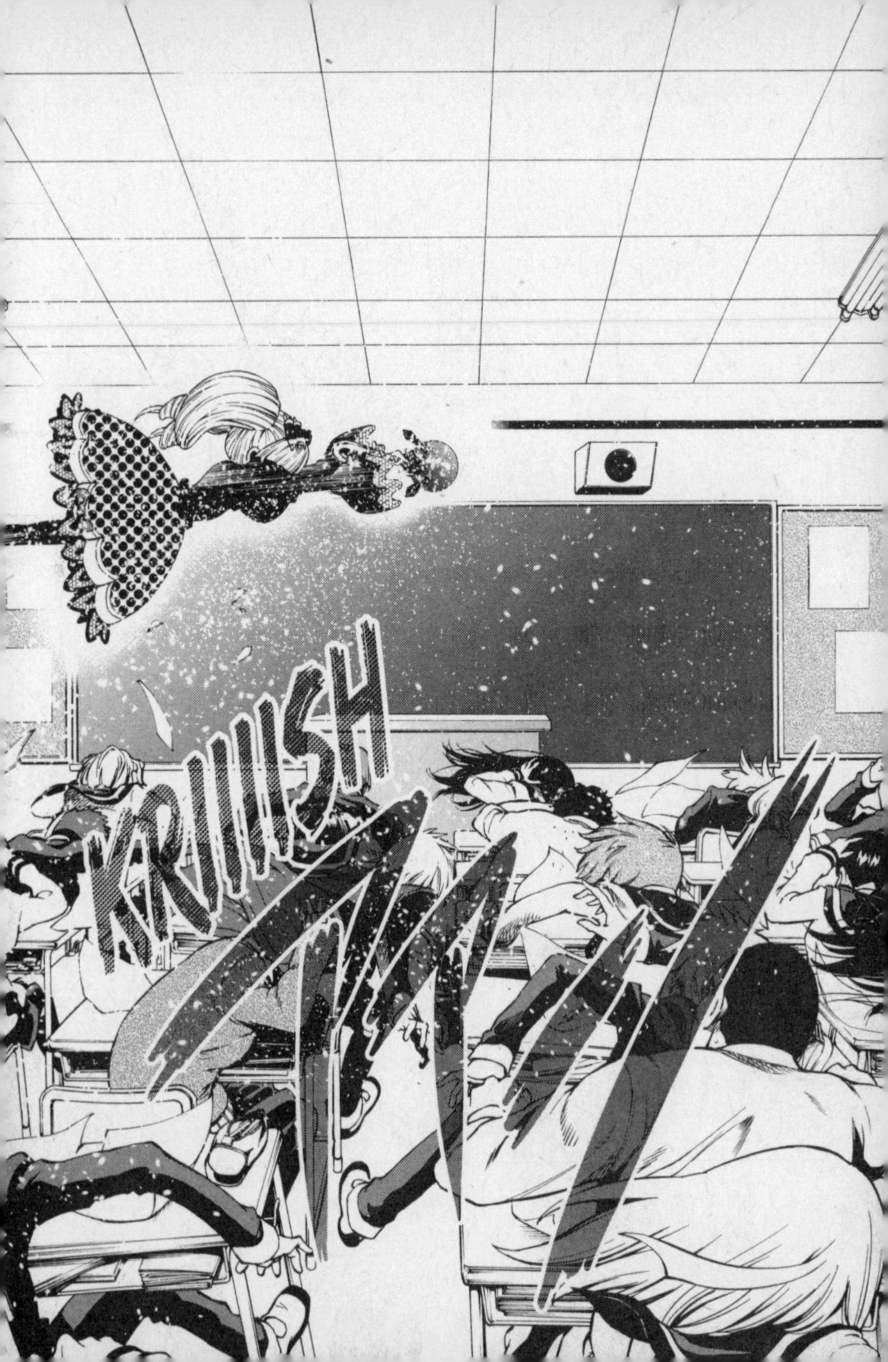
KRUUSH

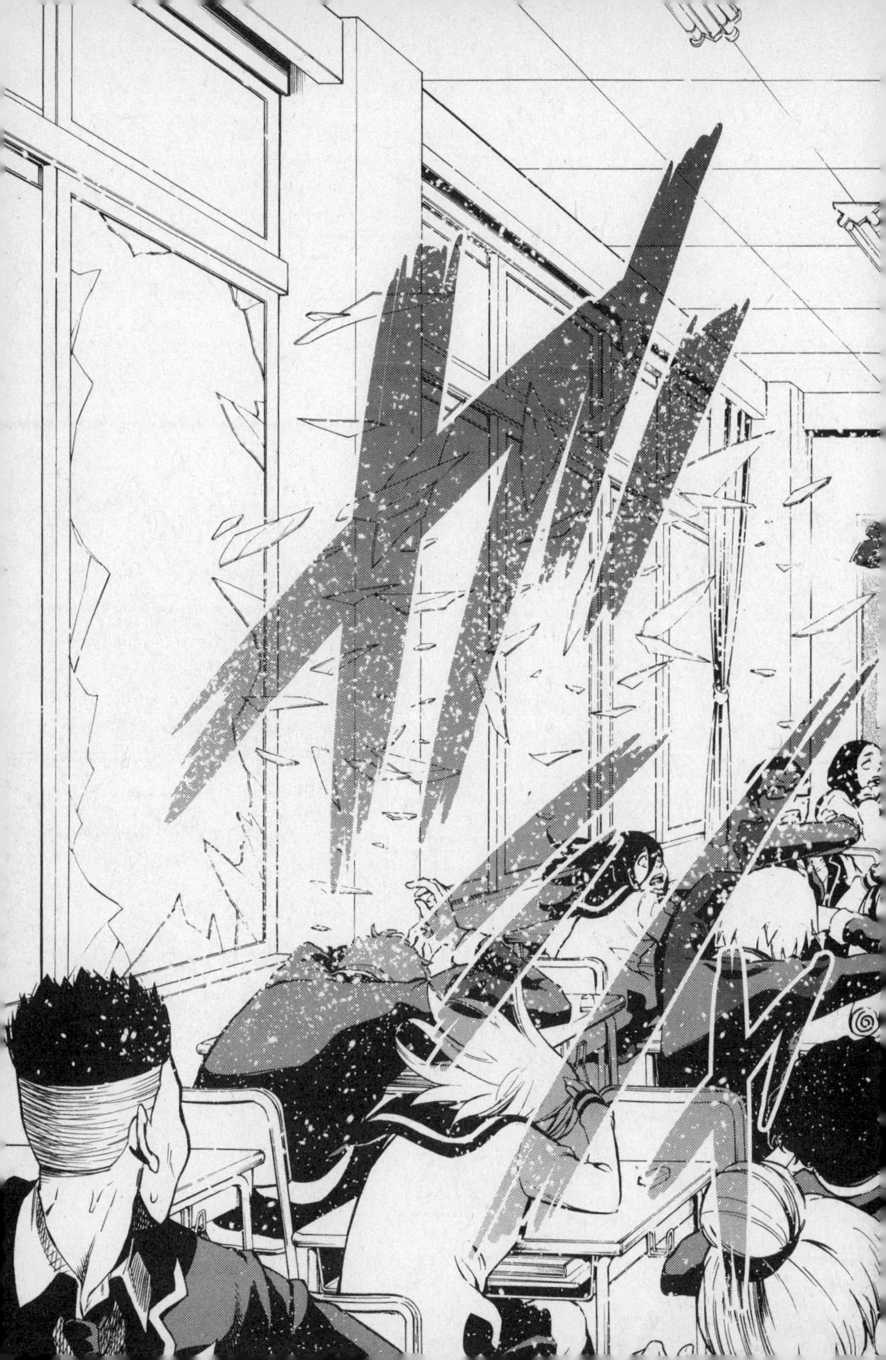

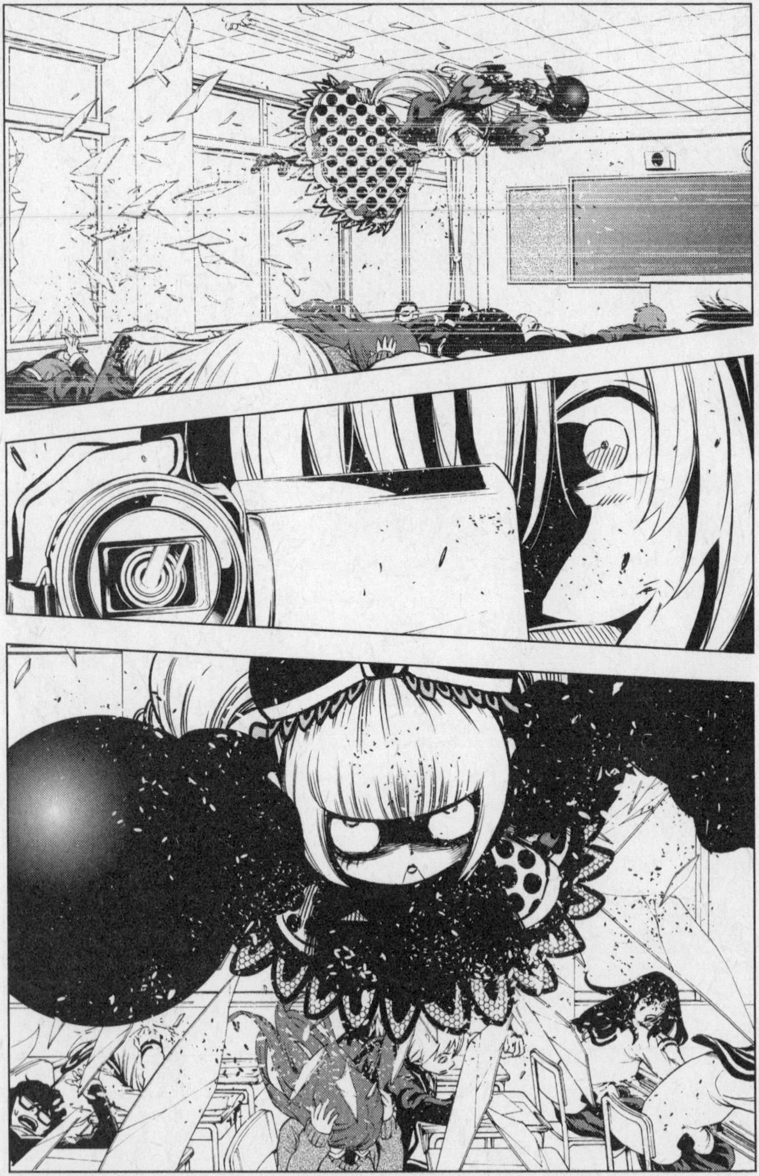

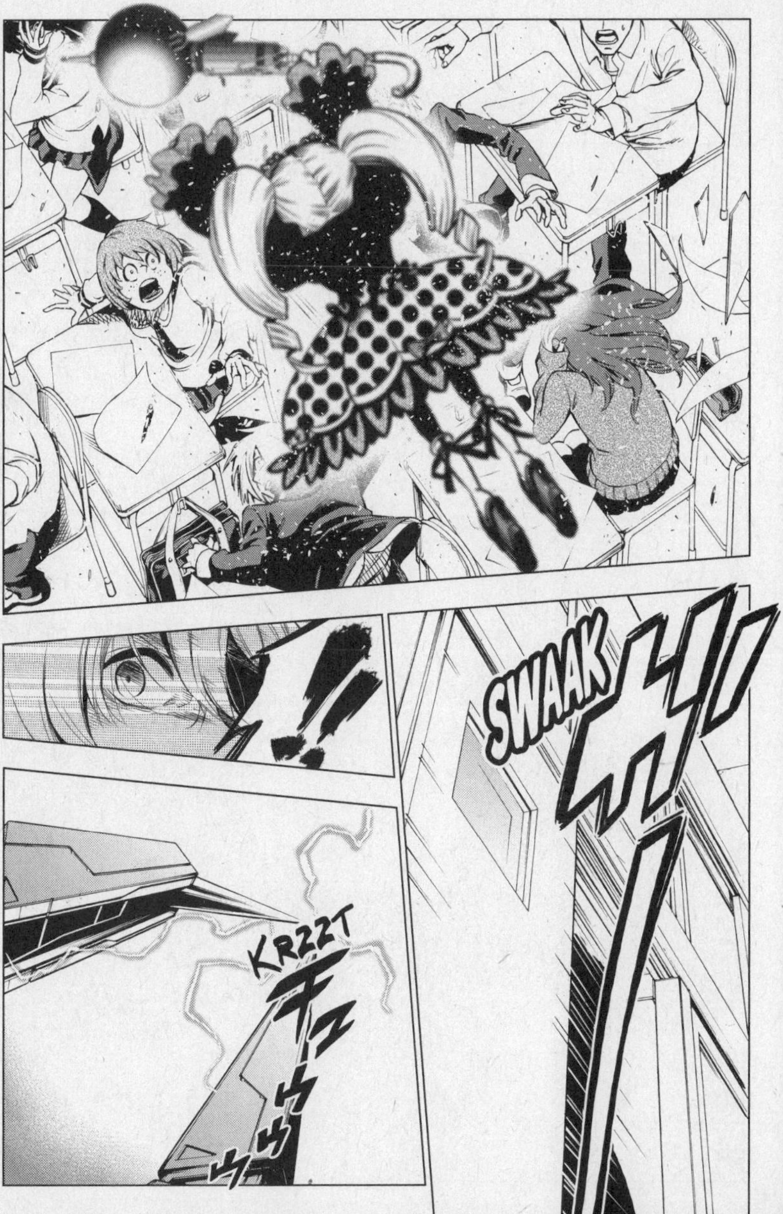
SWAAK
KRZZT

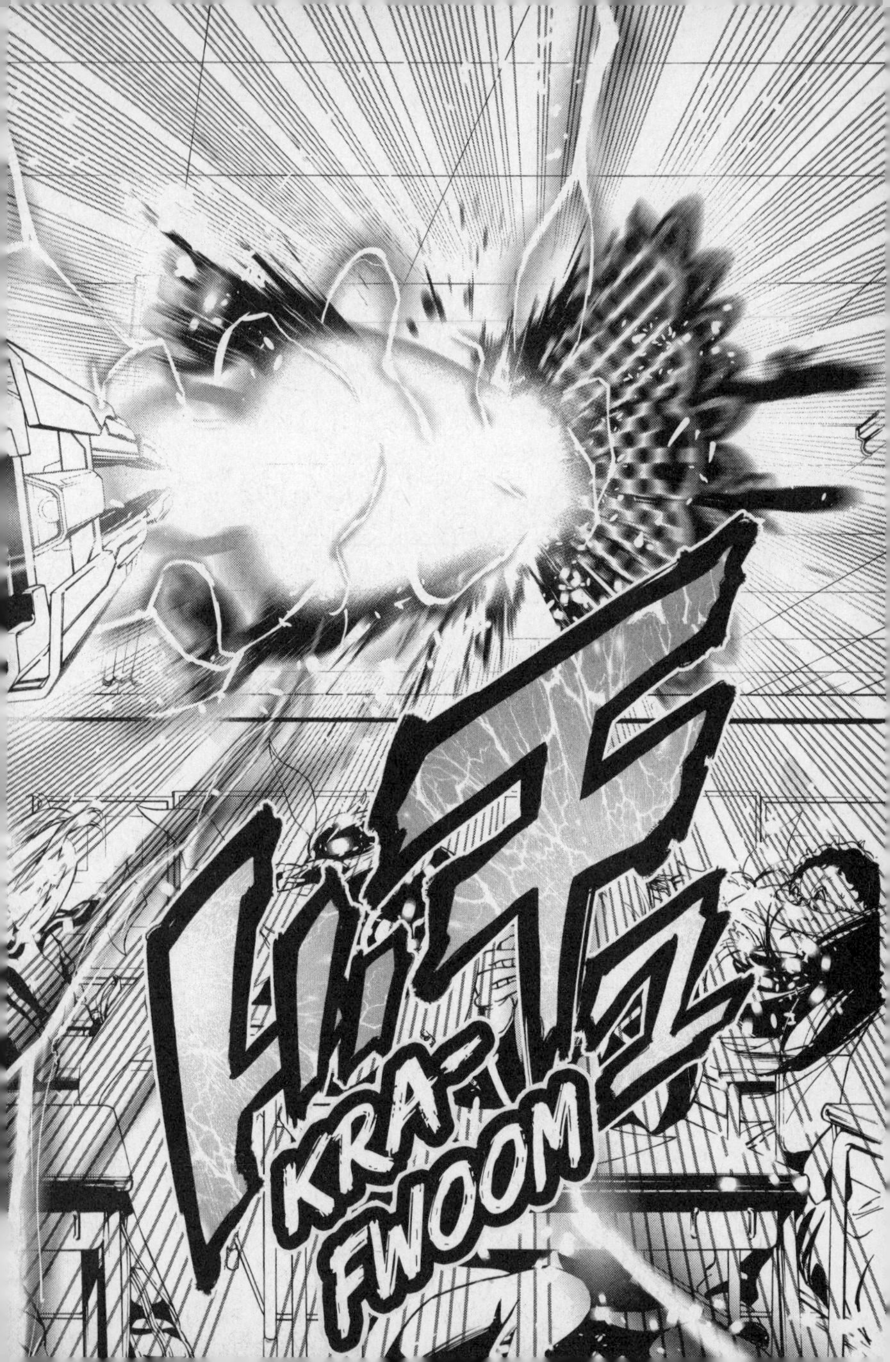
KRA-FWOOM

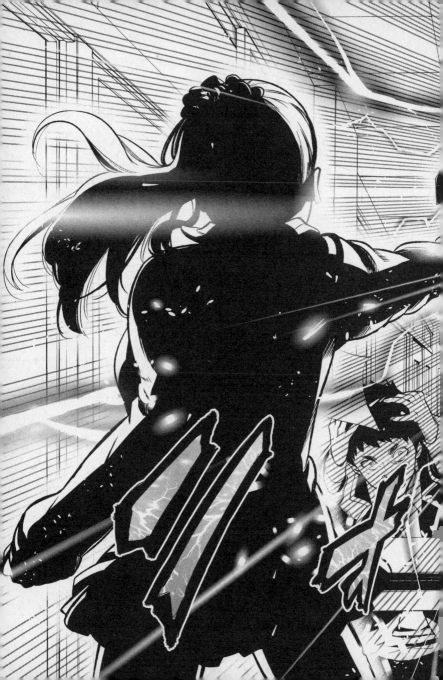

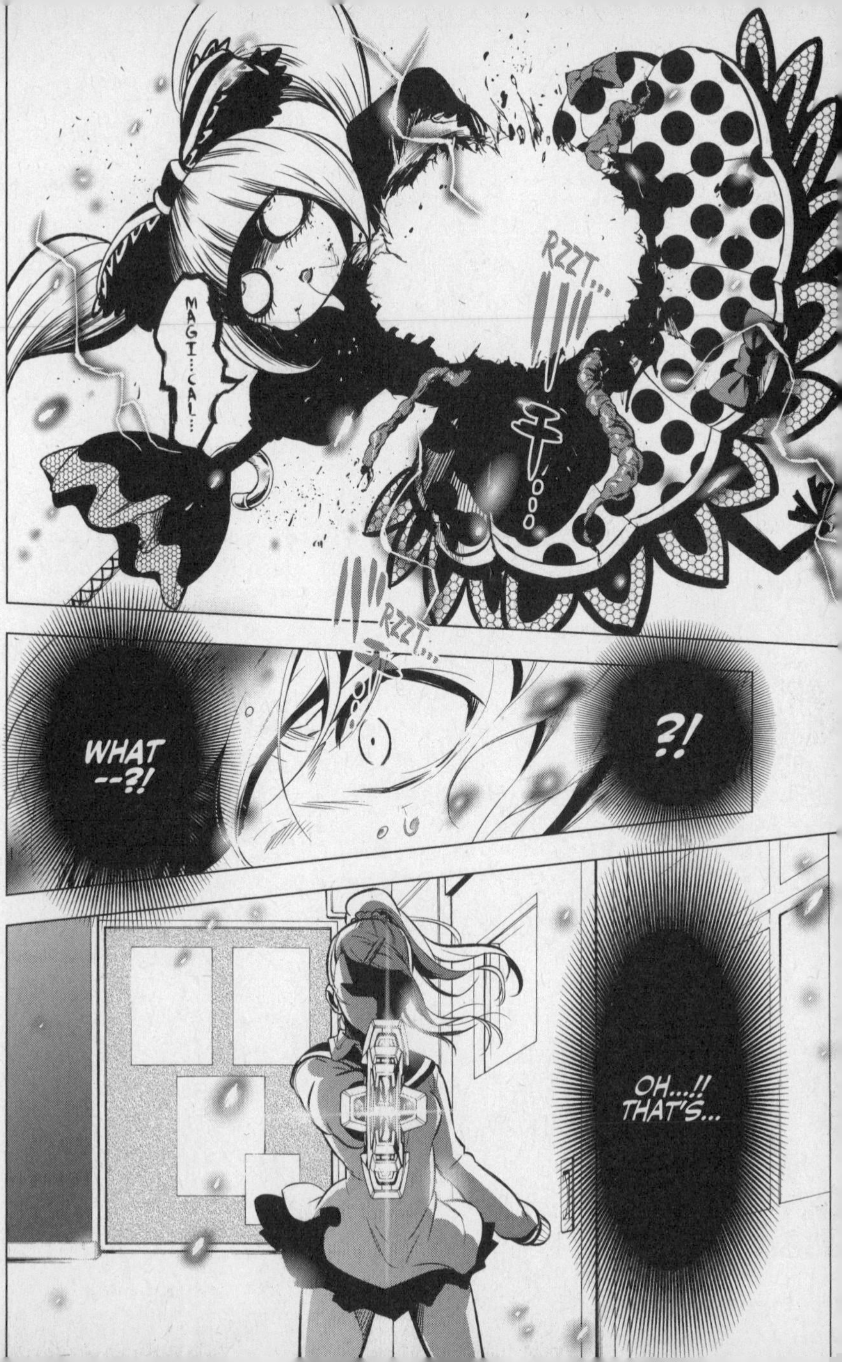
RZZT...
MAGI...CAL...
RZZT...
?!
WHAT --?!
OH...!! THAT'S...

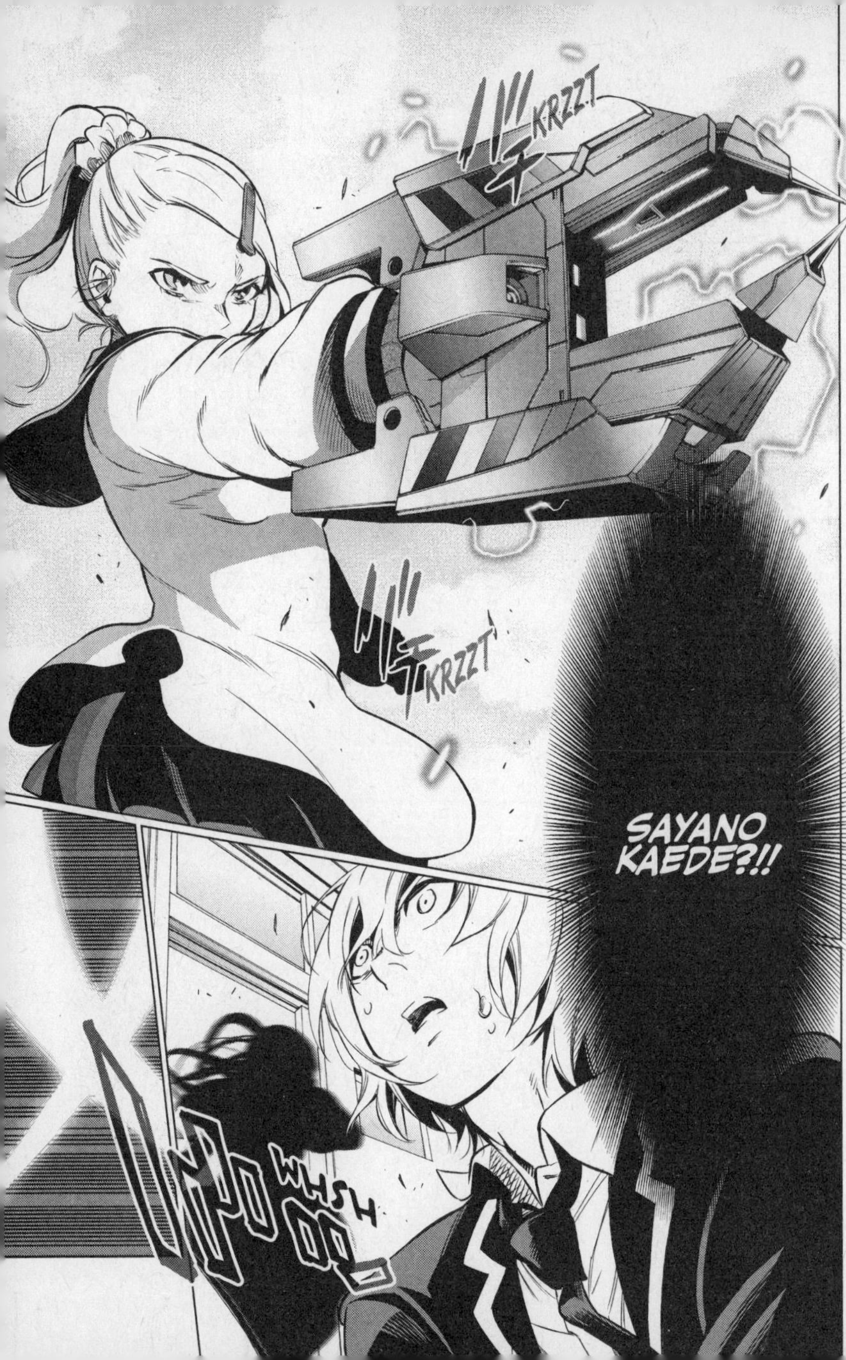
KRZZT
KRZZT
SAYANO KAEDE?!!
WHSH

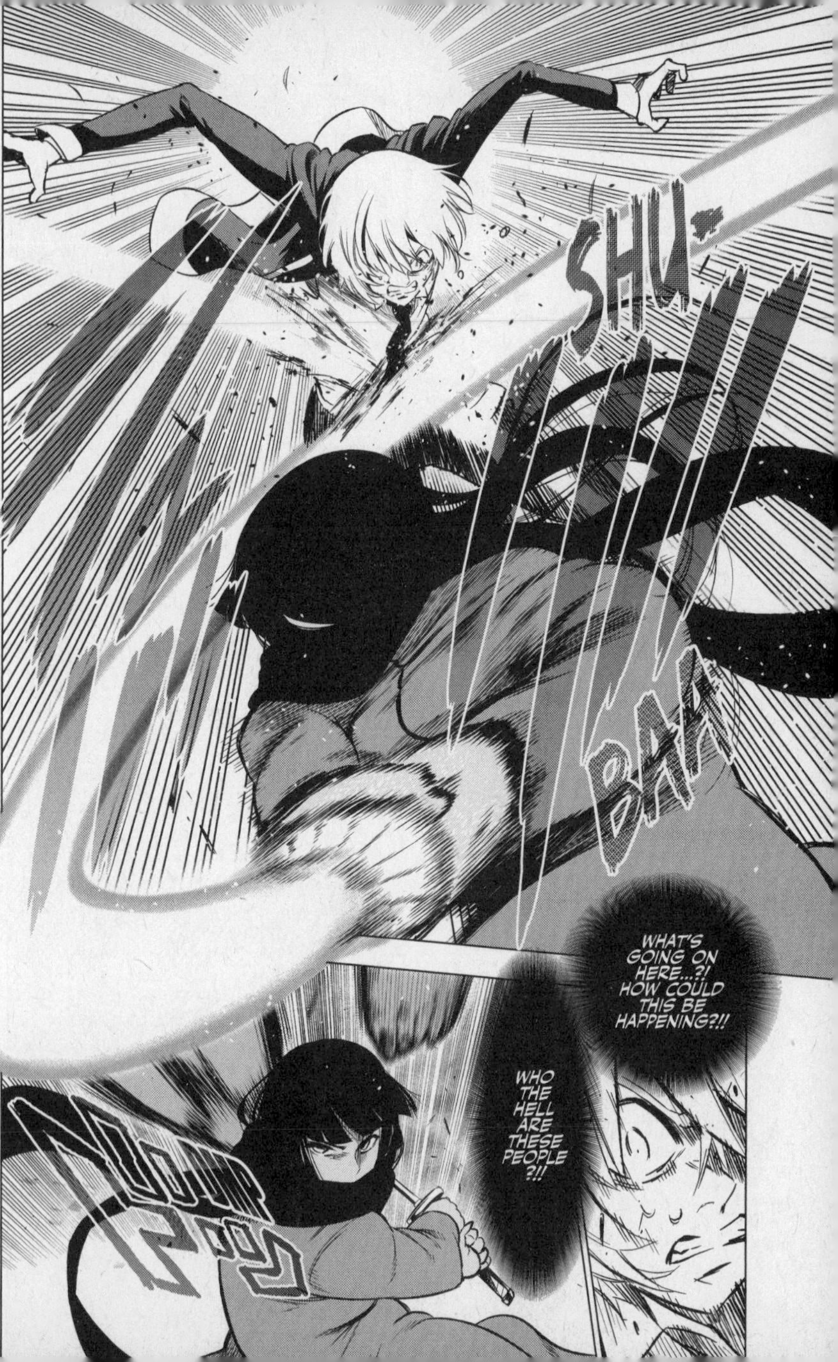
SHU-
BAA
WHAT'S GOING ON HERE...?! HOW COULD THIS BE HAPPENING?!!
WHO THE HELL ARE THESE PEOPLE ?!!

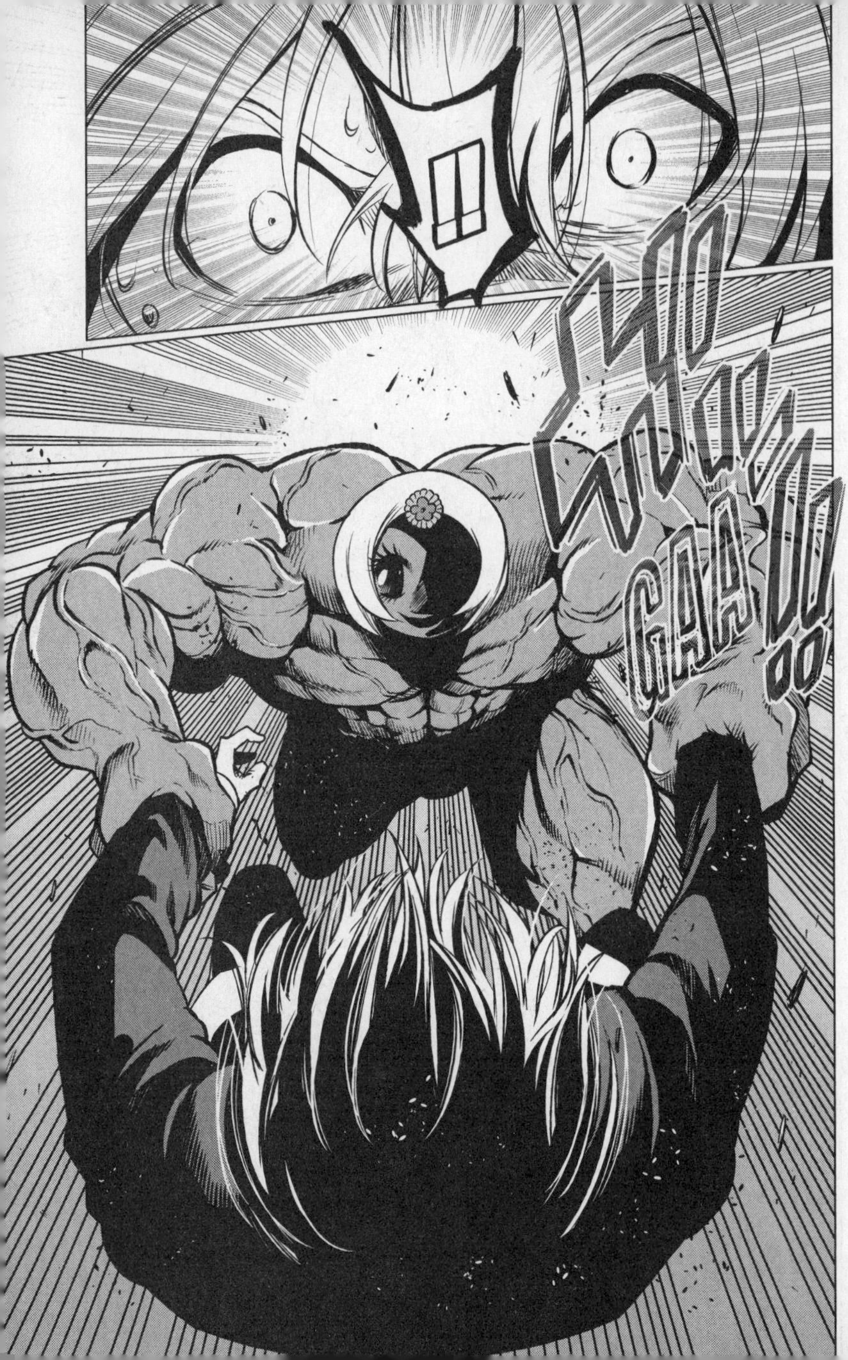
!!

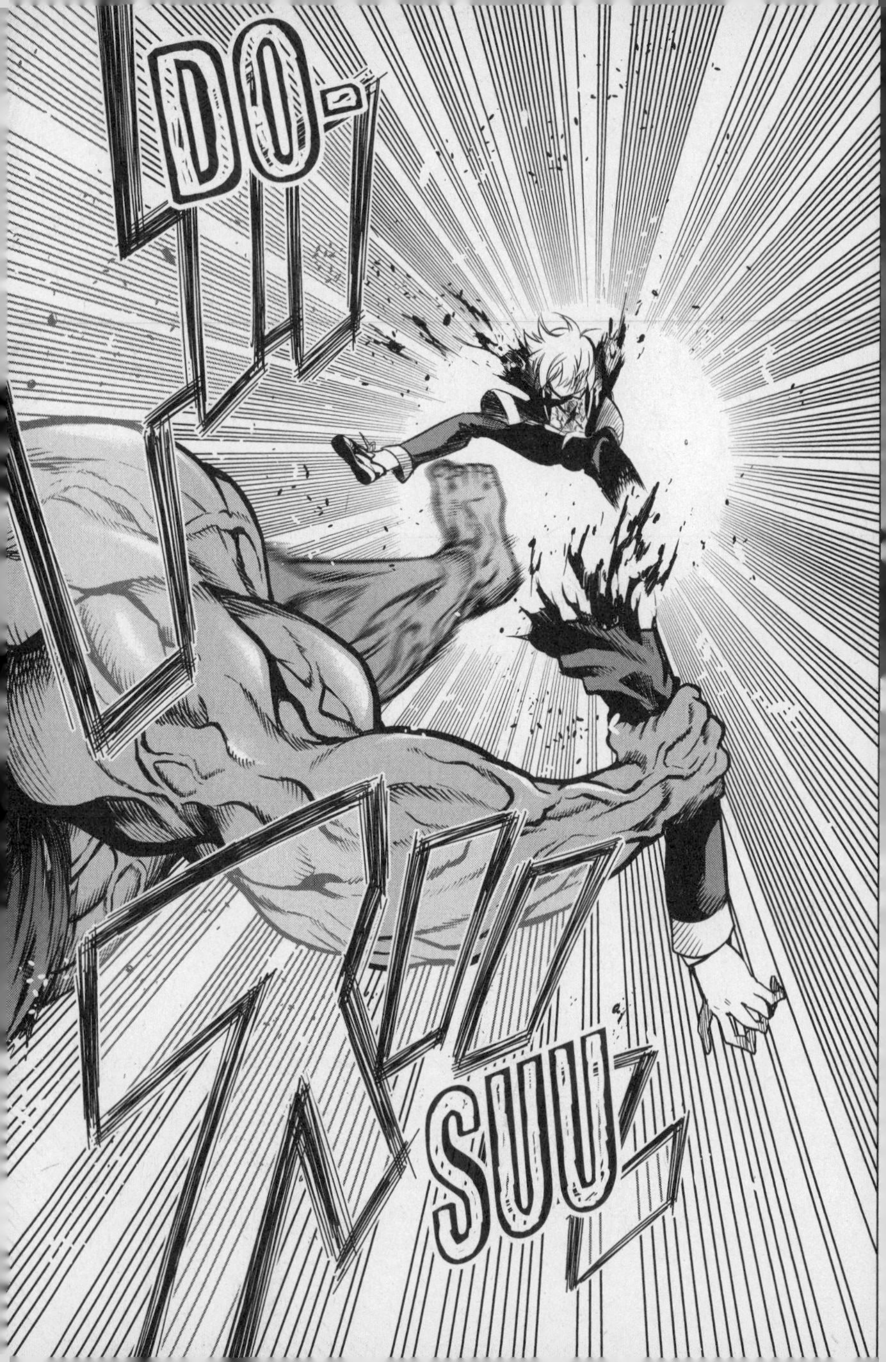
DO-
SUU

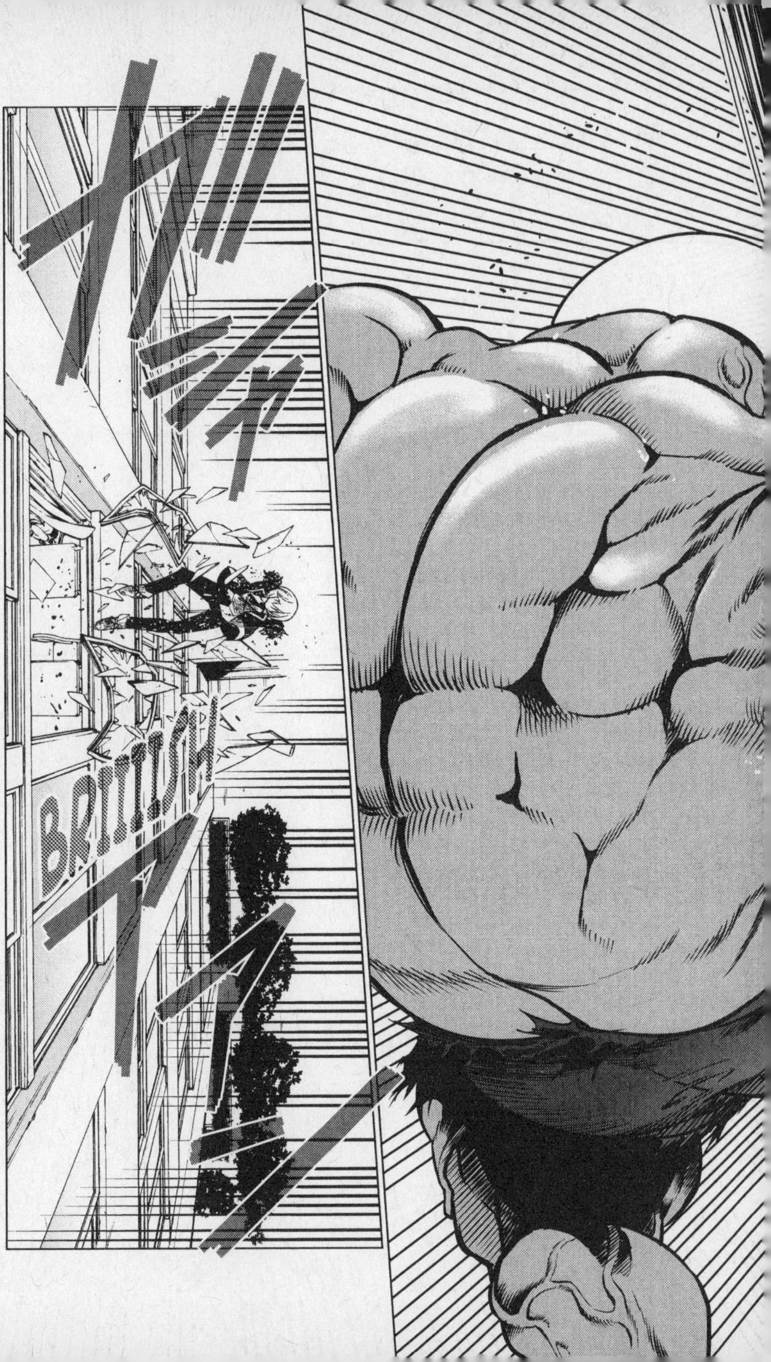
BRIIIISH!

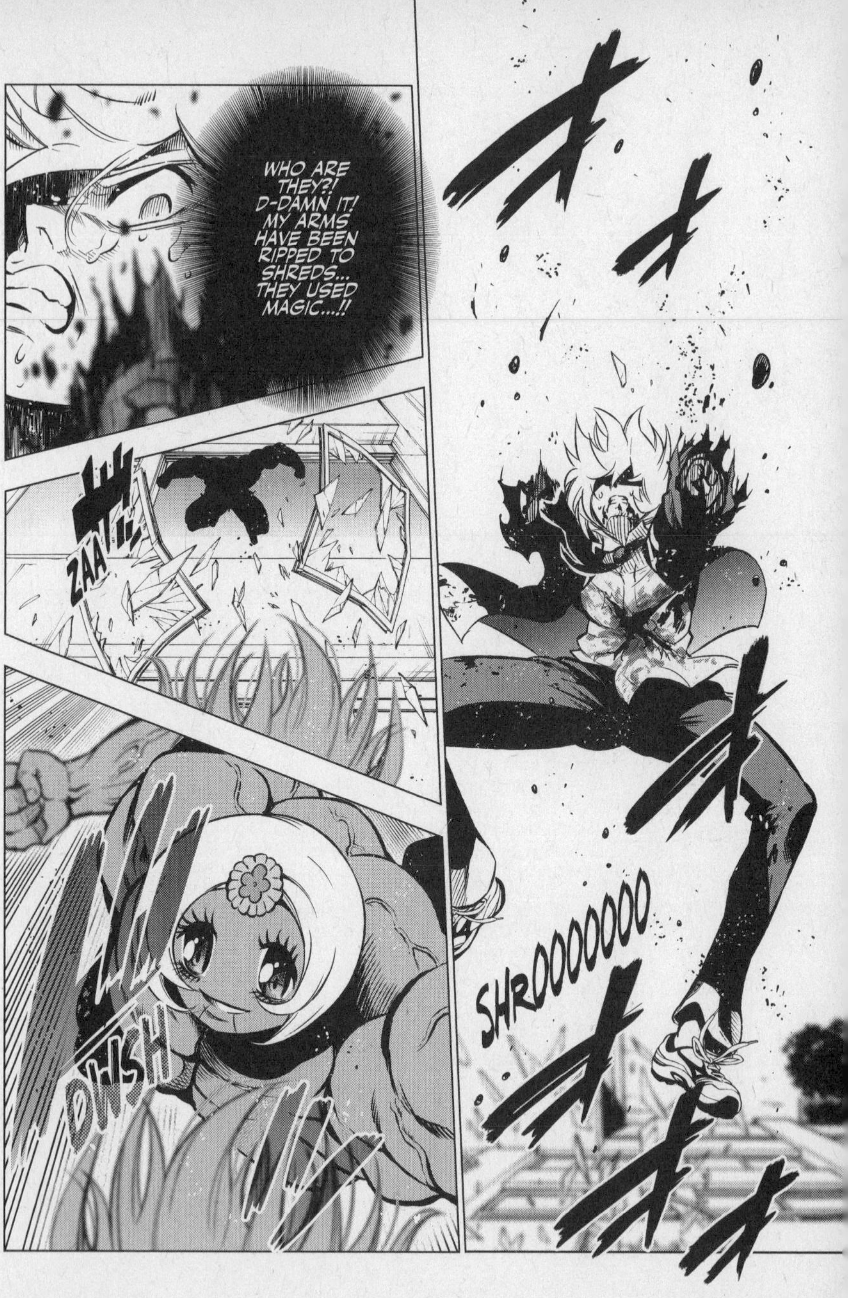
SHROOOOOOO
WHO ARE THEY?! D-DAMN IT! MY ARMS HAVE BEEN RIPPED TO SHREDS... THEY USED MAGIC...!!
ZAA
DWSH

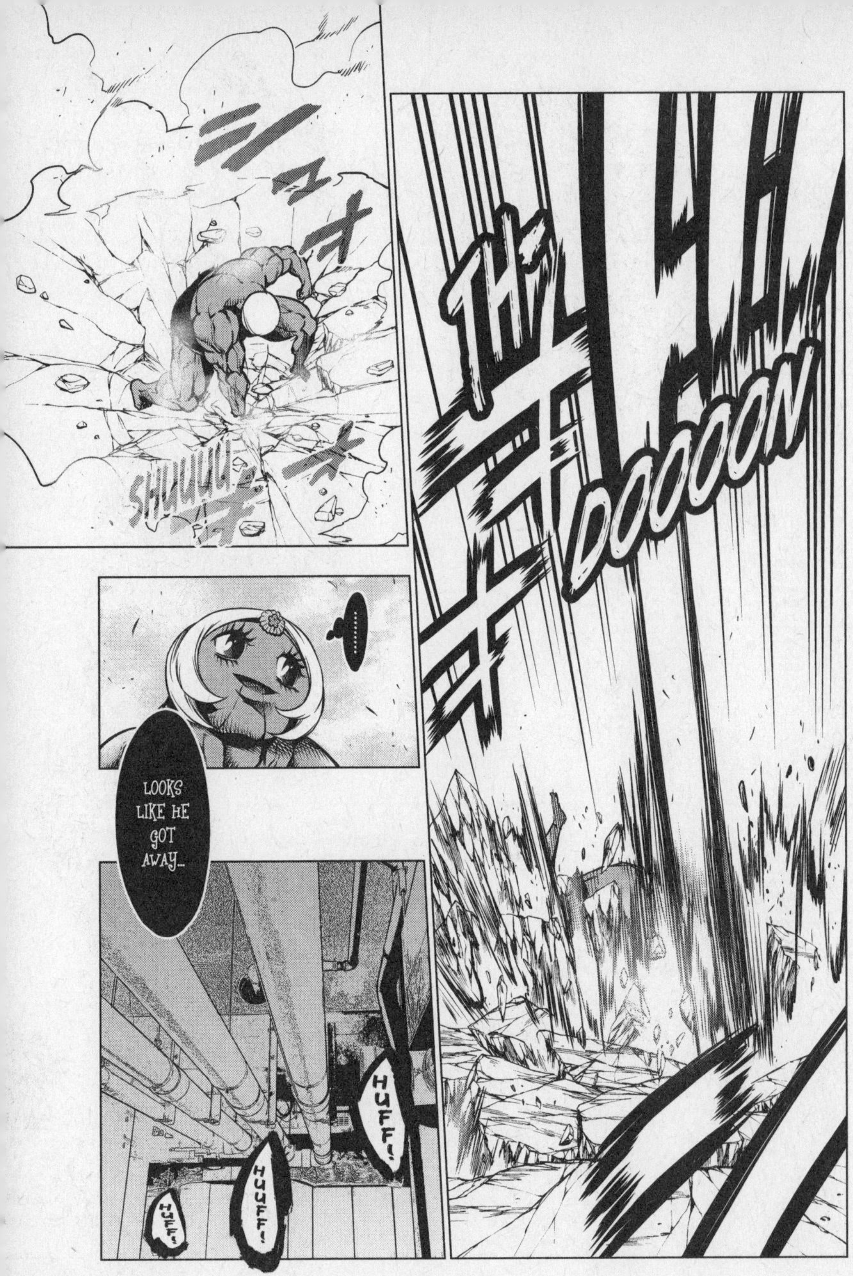
TH
DOOOON
SHUUUU
......
LOOKS LIKE HE GOT AWAY...
HUFF!
HUUFF!
HUFF!

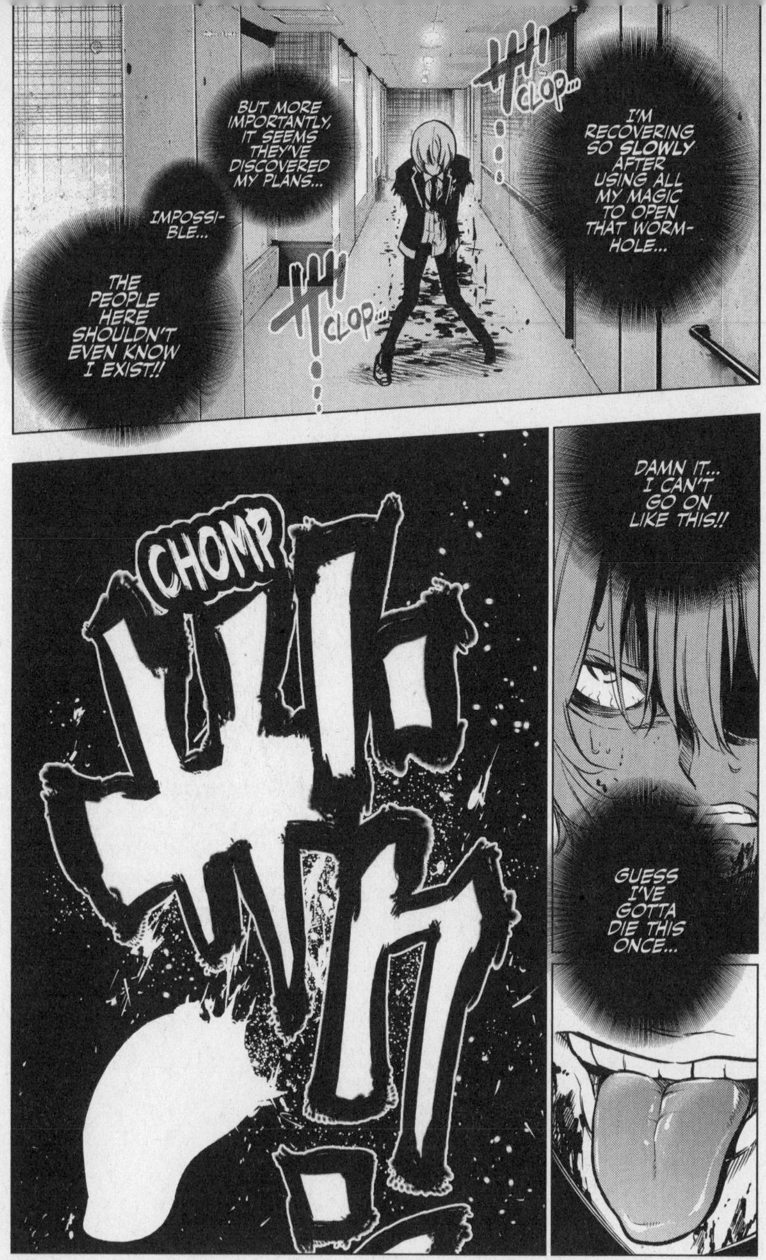
CLOP...
I'M RECOVERING SO SLOWLY AFTER USING ALL MY MAGIC TO OPEN THAT WORM-HOLE...
BUT MORE IMPORTANTLY, IT SEEMS THEY'VE DISCOVERED MY PLANS...
IMPOSSI-BLE...
THE PEOPLE HERE SHOULDN'T EVEN KNOW I EXIST!!
CLOP...
DAMN IT... I CAN'T GO ON LIKE THIS!!
GUESS I'VE GOTTA DIE THIS ONCE...
CHOMP

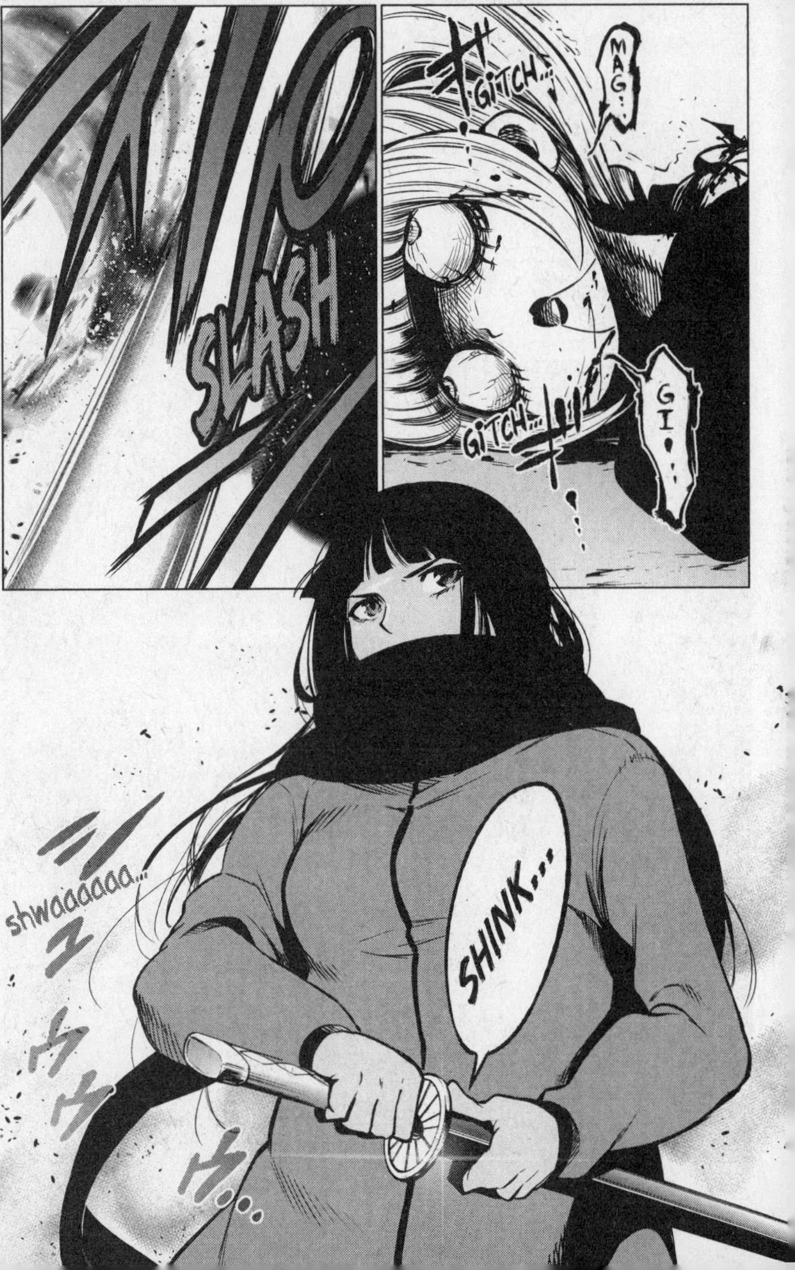
MAG...
GITCH...
GI...
GITCH...
SLASH
SHINK...
shwaaaaaa...

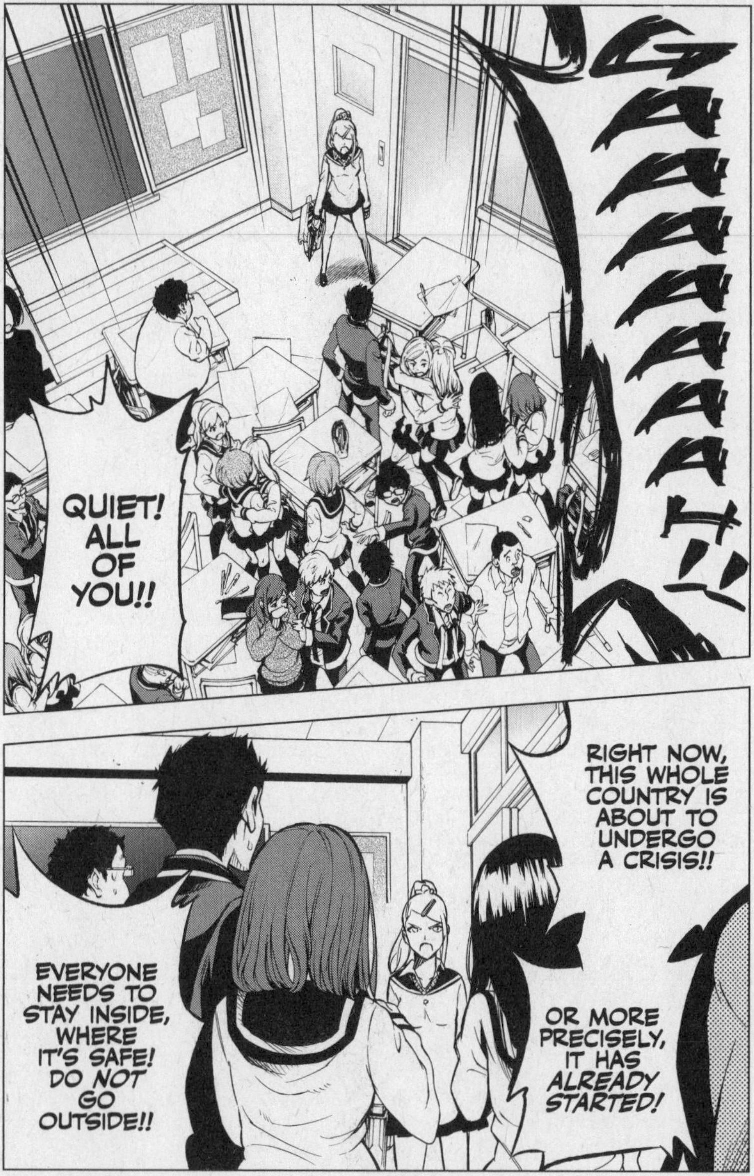
GAAAAAAAH!!
QUIET! ALL OF YOU!!
RIGHT NOW, THIS WHOLE COUNTRY IS ABOUT TO UNDERGO A CRISIS!!
OR MORE PRECISELY, IT HAS *ALREADY STARTED!*
EVERYONE NEEDS TO STAY INSIDE, WHERE IT'S SAFE! DO *NOT* GO OUTSIDE!!

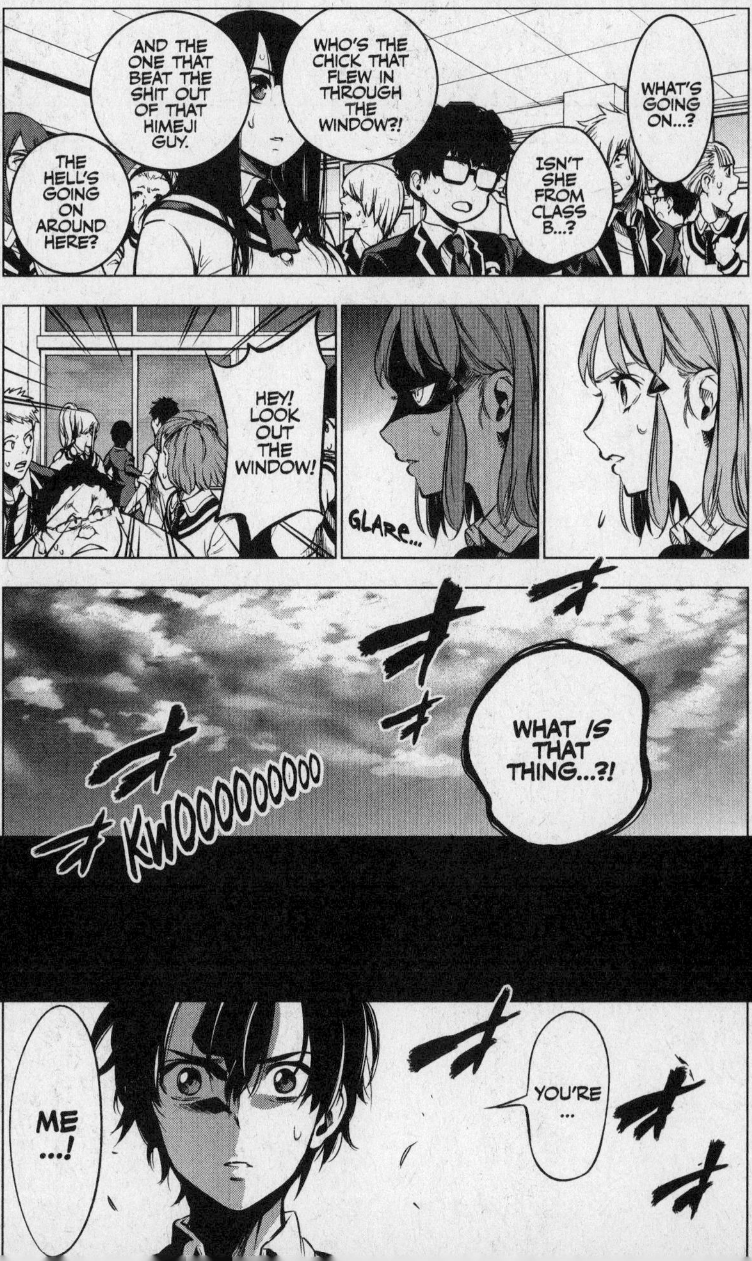
WHAT'S GOING ON...?
ISN'T SHE FROM CLASS B...?
WHO'S THE CHICK THAT FLEW IN THROUGH THE WINDOW?!
AND THE ONE THAT BEAT THE SHIT OUT OF THAT HIMEJI GUY.
THE HELL'S GOING ON AROUND HERE?
GLARE...
HEY! LOOK OUT THE WINDOW!
WHAT *IS* THAT THING...?!
KWOOOOOOOOO
[redacted]
YOU'RE ...
ME ...!

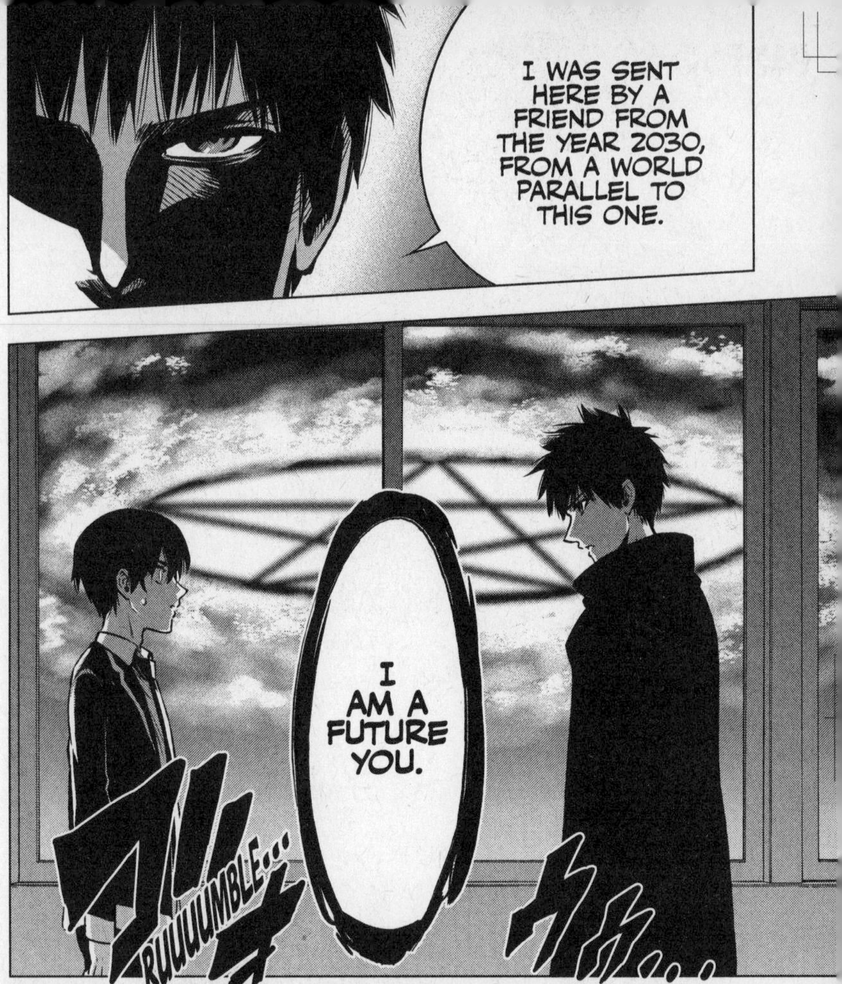
I WAS SENT HERE BY A FRIEND FROM THE YEAR 2030, FROM A WORLD PARALLEL TO THIS ONE.
I AM A FUTURE YOU.
RUUUUMBLE...
A FUTURE...
ME...?

# Final Season

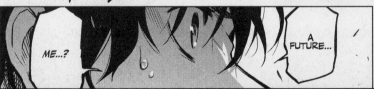

# 045.DUAL SAVIOR

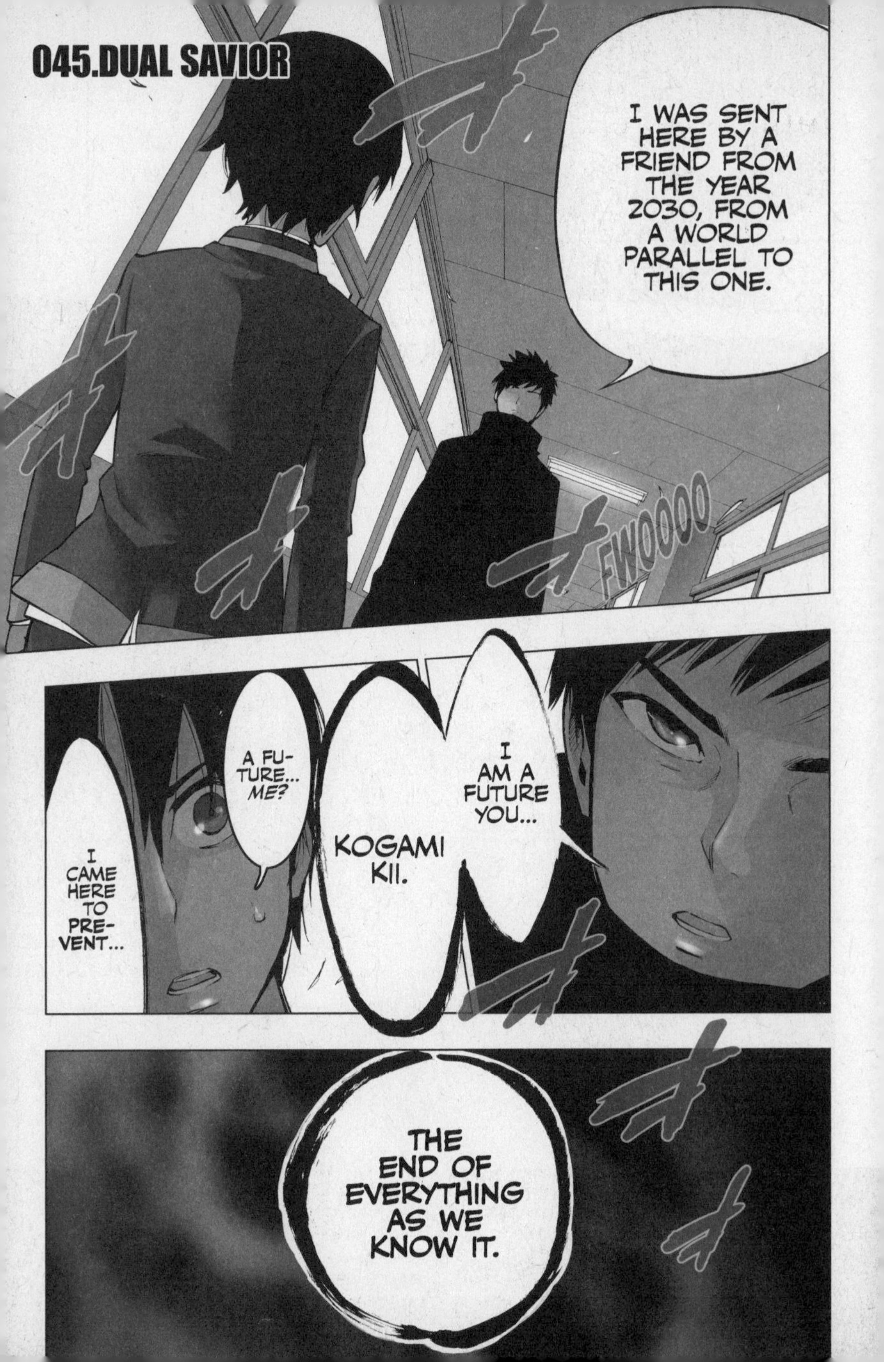

I WAS SENT HERE BY A FRIEND FROM THE YEAR 2030, FROM A WORLD PARALLEL TO THIS ONE.
FWOOOO
I AM A FUTURE YOU...
KOGAMI KII.
A FU-TURE... ME?
I CAME HERE TO PRE-VENT...
THE END OF EVERYTHING AS WE KNOW IT.

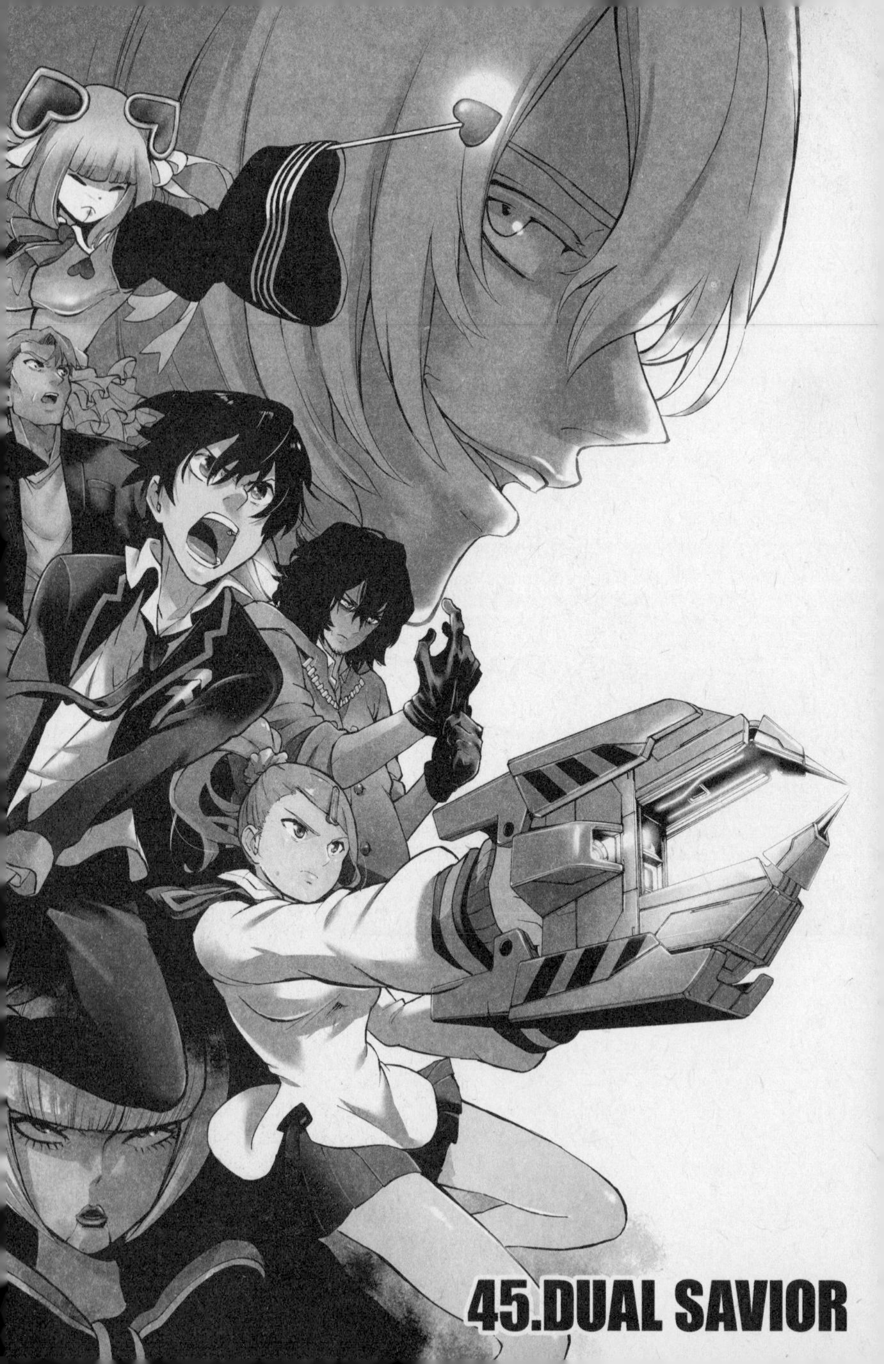
45.DUAL SAVIOR

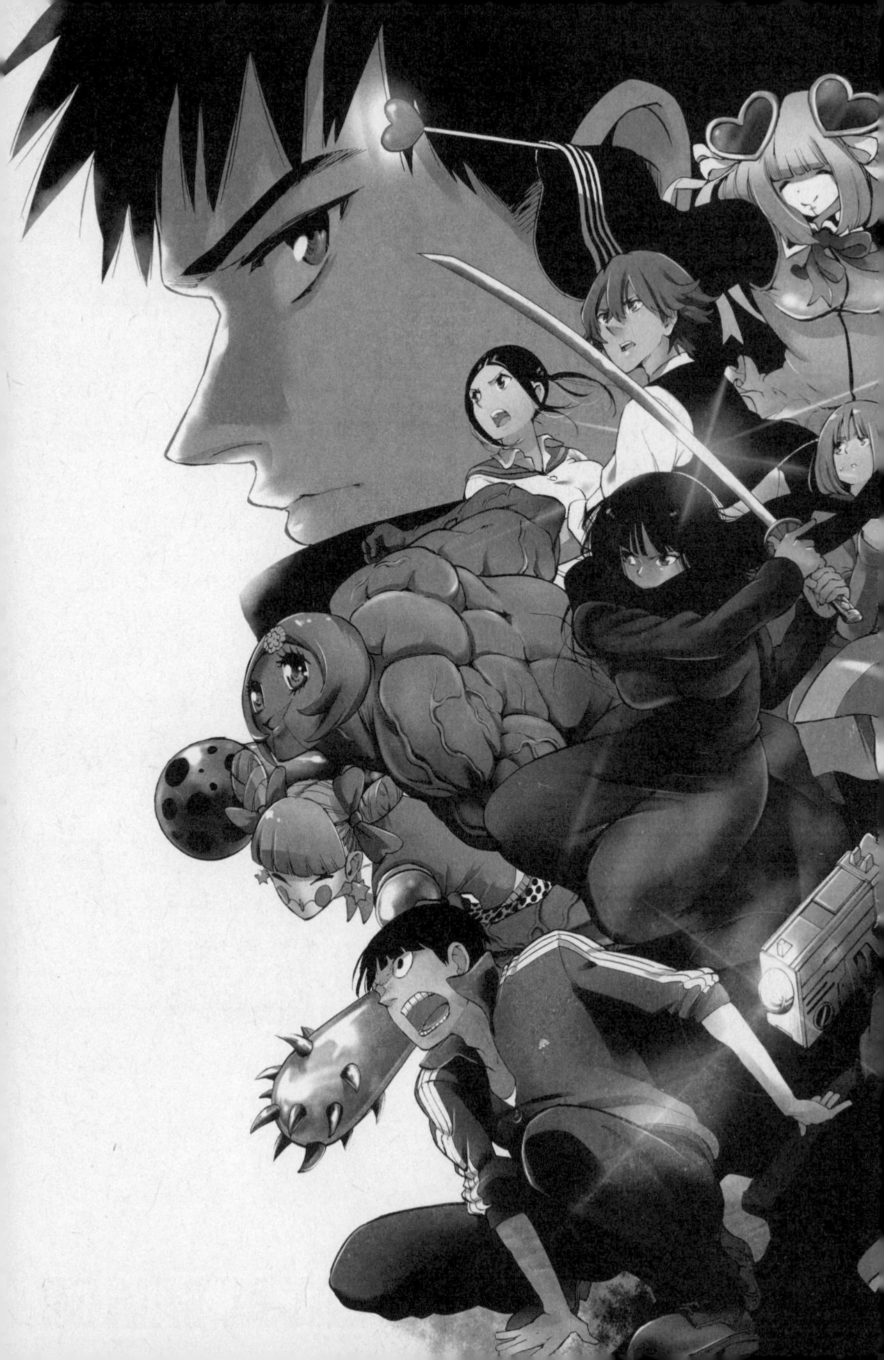

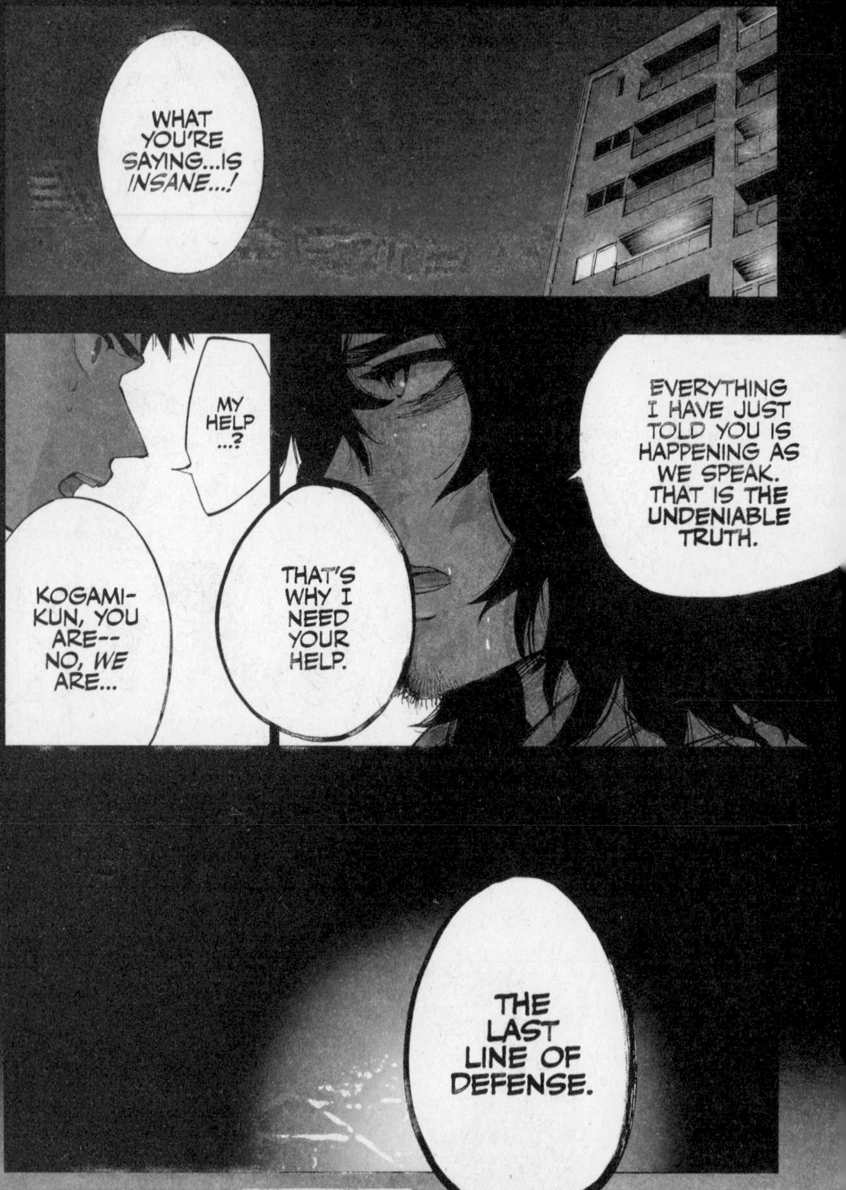
WHAT YOU'RE SAYING...IS INSANE...!
EVERYTHING I HAVE JUST TOLD YOU IS HAPPENING AS WE SPEAK. THAT IS THE UNDENIABLE TRUTH.
THAT'S WHY I NEED YOUR HELP.
MY HELP ...?
KOGAMI-KUN, YOU ARE-- NO, WE ARE...
THE LAST LINE OF DEFENSE.

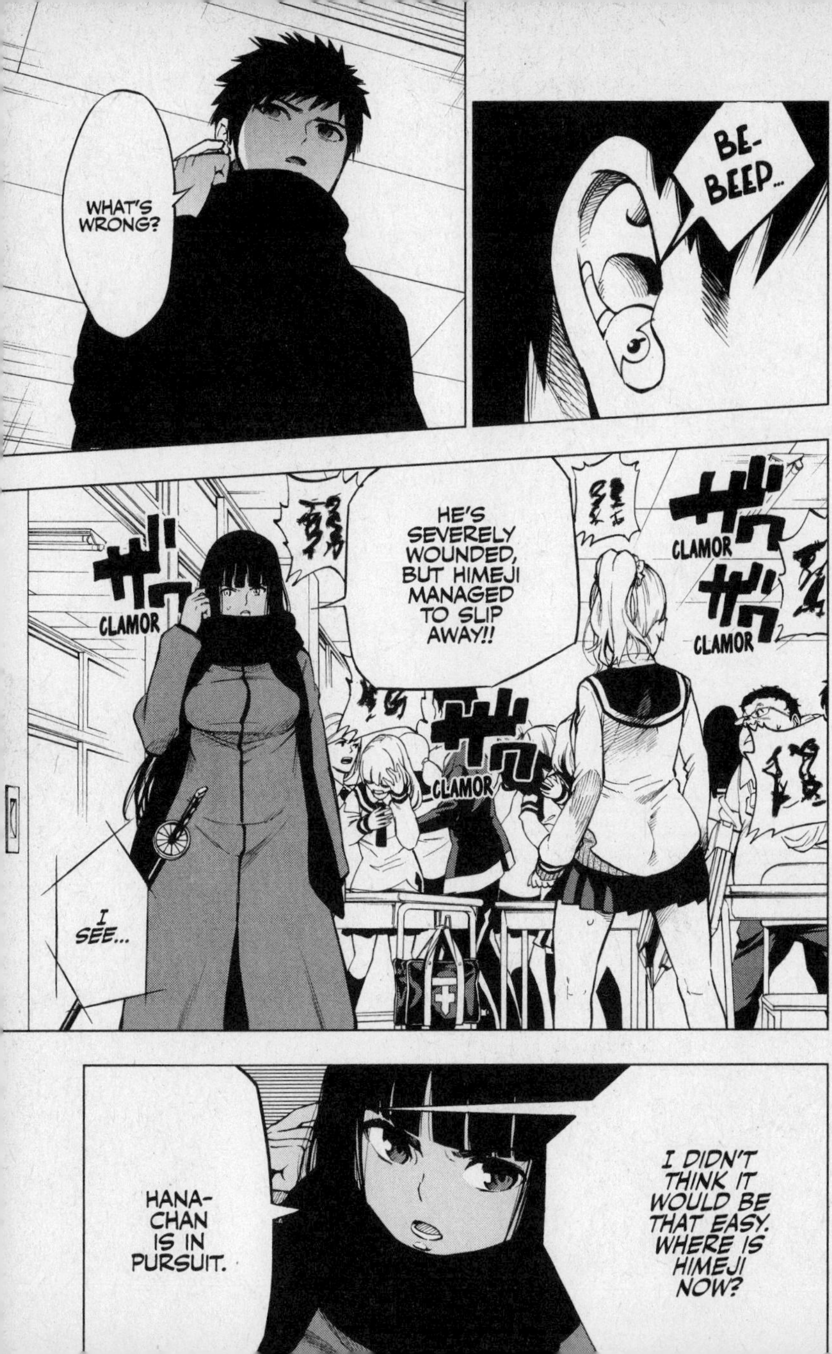
BE-BEEP...
WHAT'S WRONG?
CLAMOR
CLAMOR
HE'S SEVERELY WOUNDED, BUT HIMEJI MANAGED TO SLIP AWAY!!
CLAMOR
CLAMOR
I SEE...
I DIDN'T THINK IT WOULD BE THAT EASY. WHERE IS HIMEJI NOW?
HANA-CHAN IS IN PURSUIT.

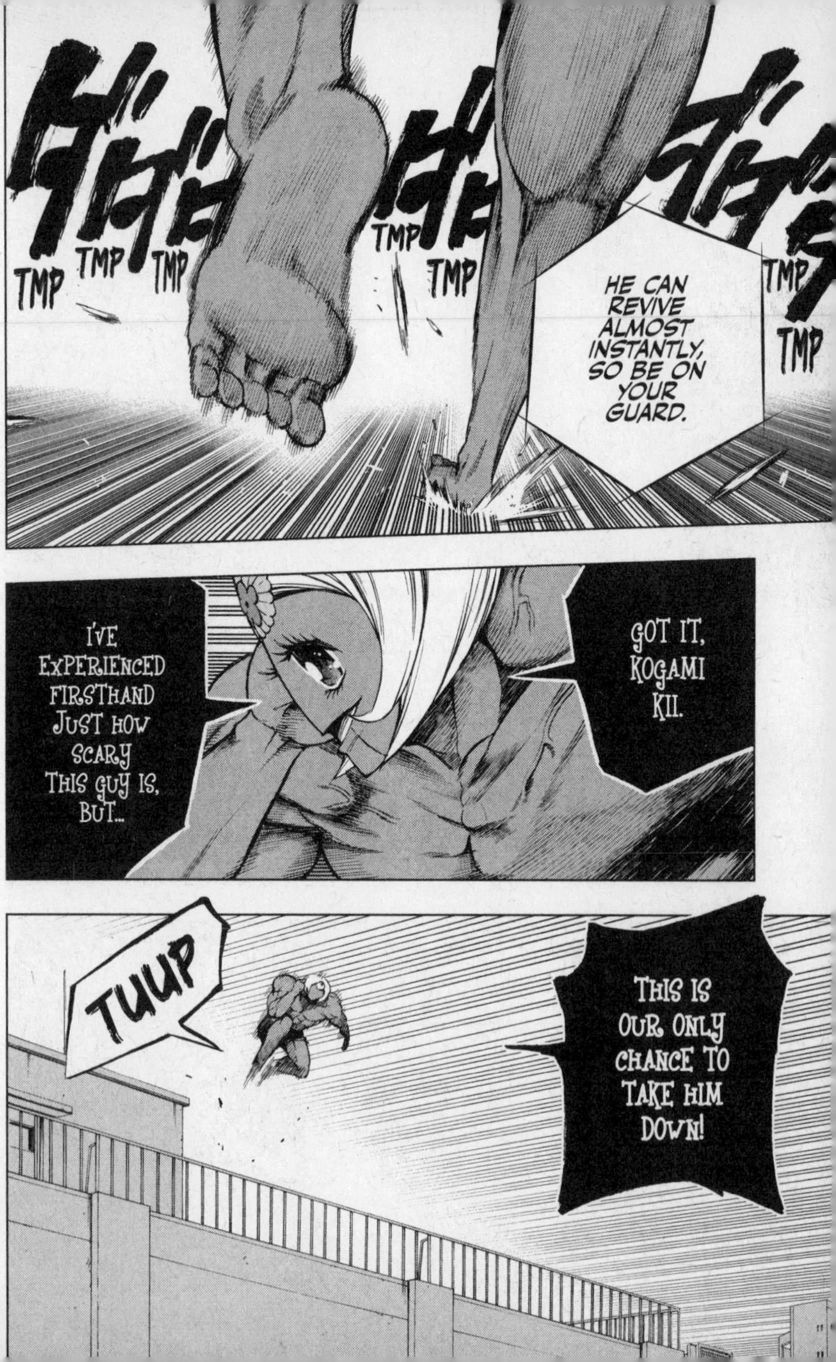
TMP
TMP
HE CAN REVIVE ALMOST INSTANTLY, SO BE ON YOUR GUARD.
TMP
TMP
TMP
TMP
TMP
GOT IT, KOGAMI KII.
I'VE EXPERIENCED FIRSTHAND JUST HOW SCARY THIS GUY IS, BUT...
THIS IS OUR ONLY CHANCE TO TAKE HIM DOWN!
TUUP

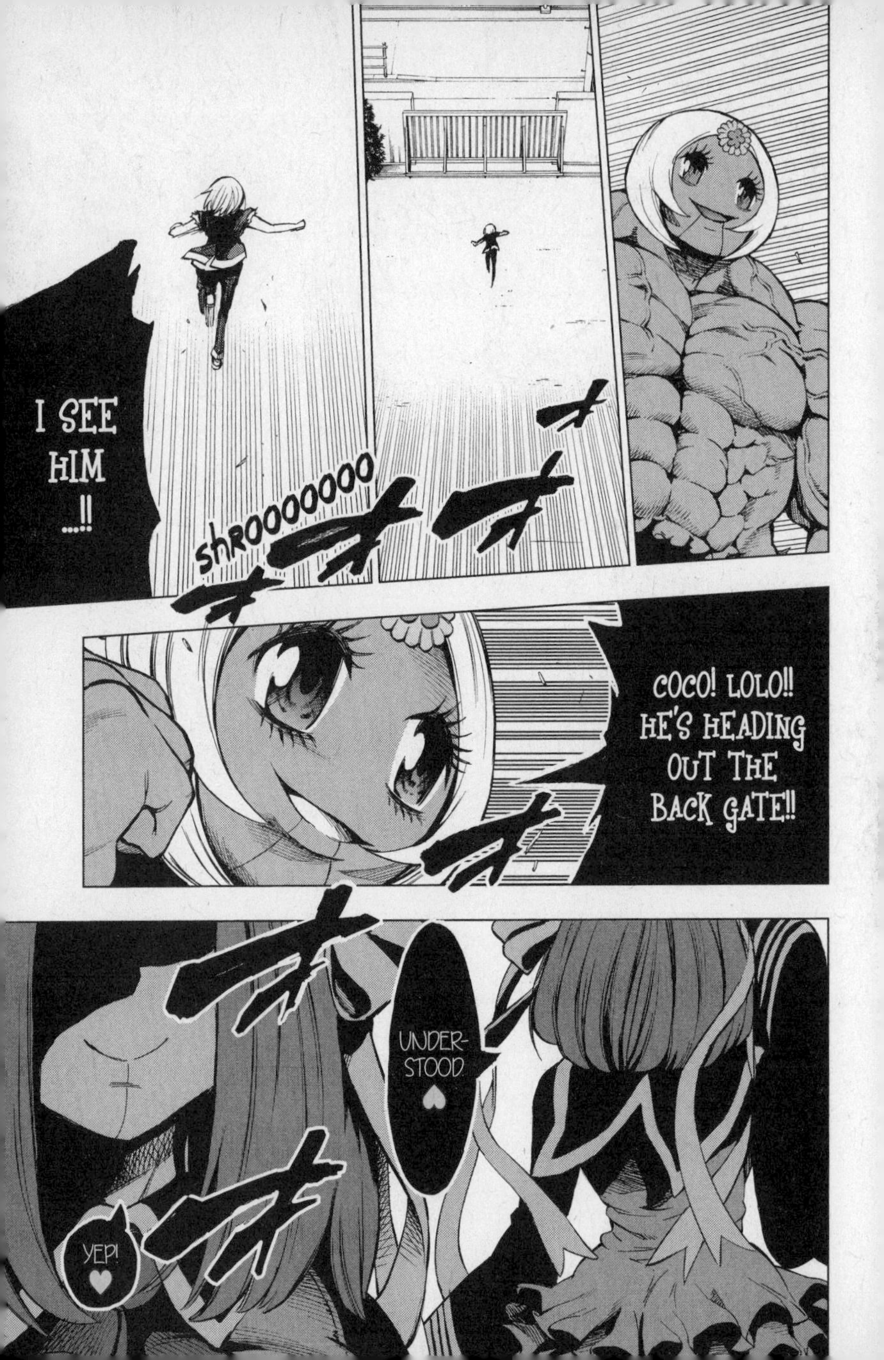
I SEE HIM ...!!
shROOOOOOO
COCO! LOLO!! HE'S HEADING OUT THE BACK GATE!!
UNDER-STOOD ♥
YEP! ♥

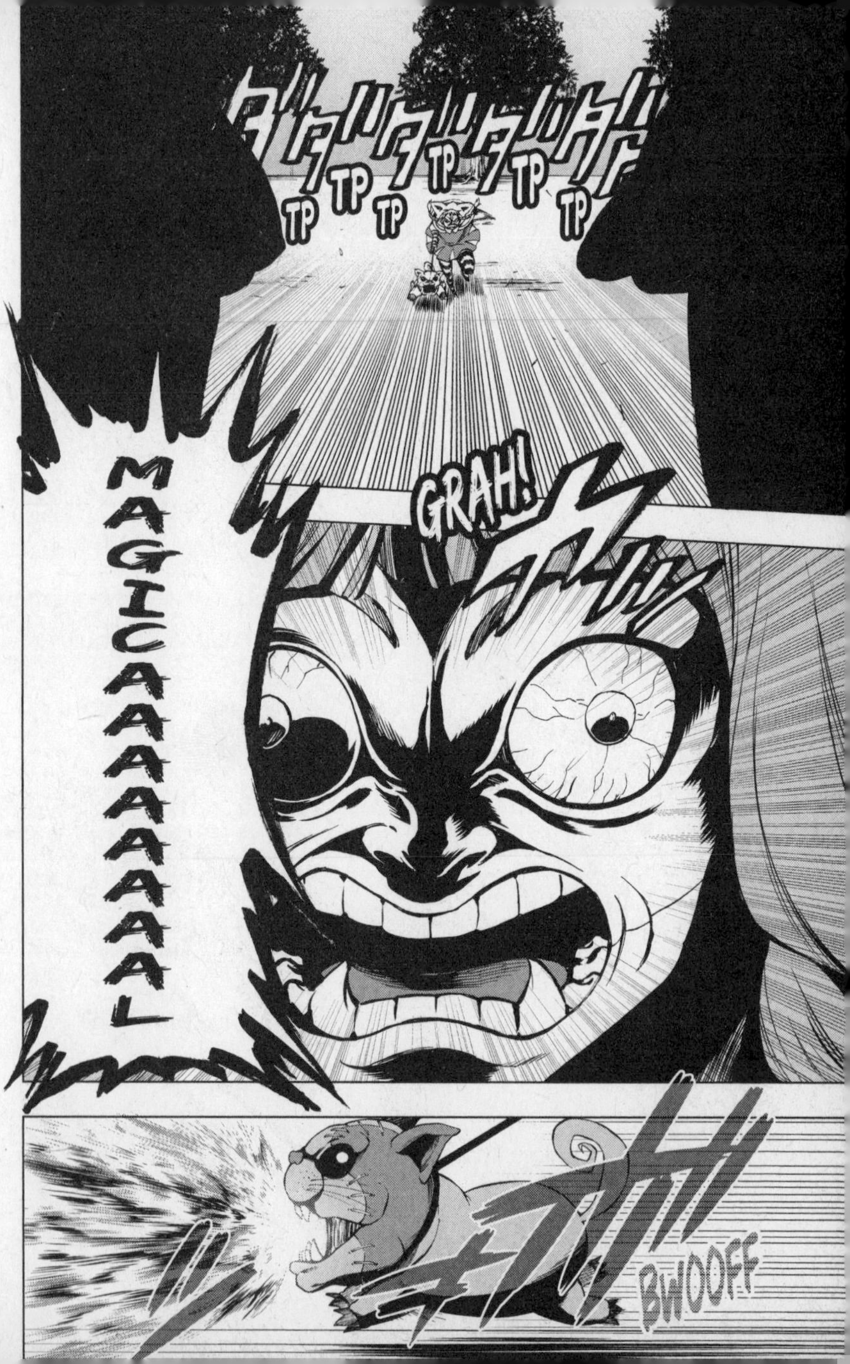
TP TP TP TP TP TP
MAGICAAAAAAAAL
GRAH!
BWOOFF

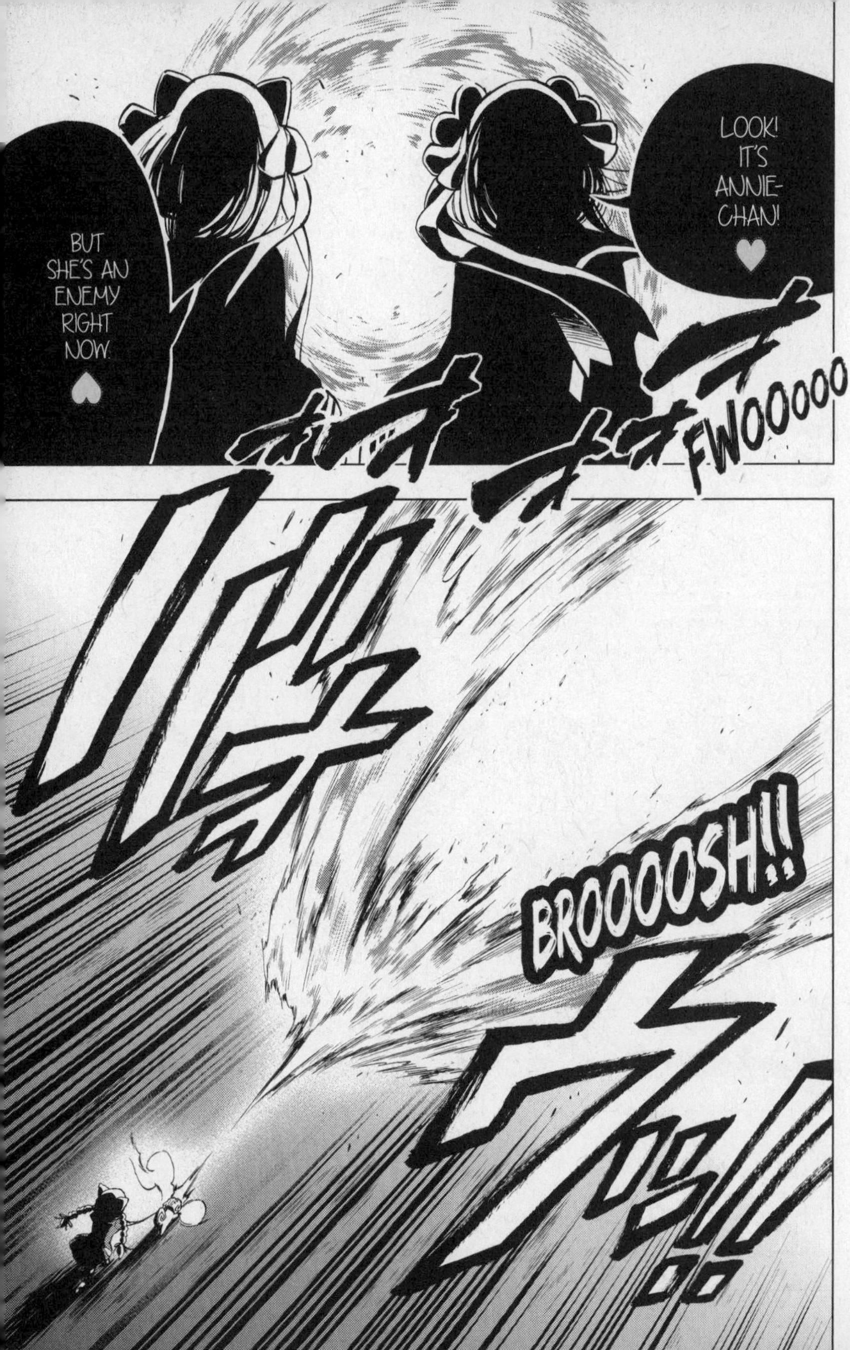
LOOK! IT'S ANNIE-CHAN! ♥
BUT SHE'S AN ENEMY RIGHT NOW. ♥
FWOOOOO
BROOOOSH!!

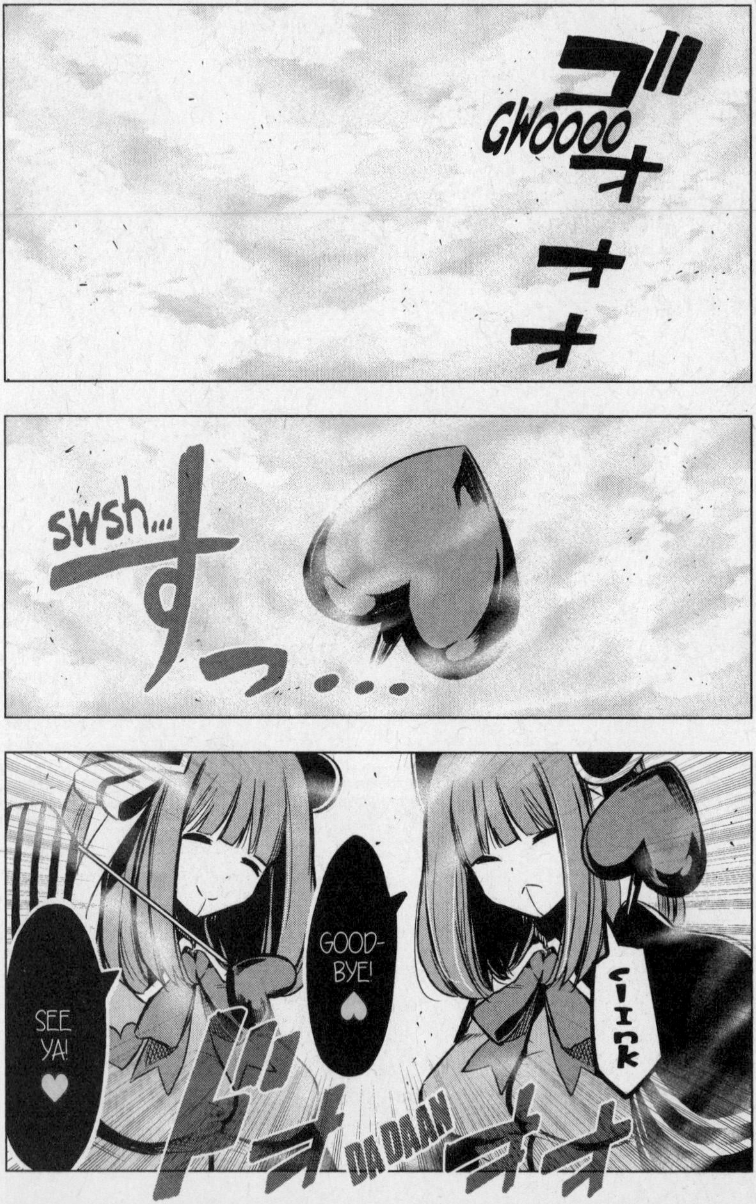
ゴオオオ
GWOOOO
swsh...
すっ...
CLINK
GOOD-BYE! ♥
SEE YA! ♥
DA DAAN

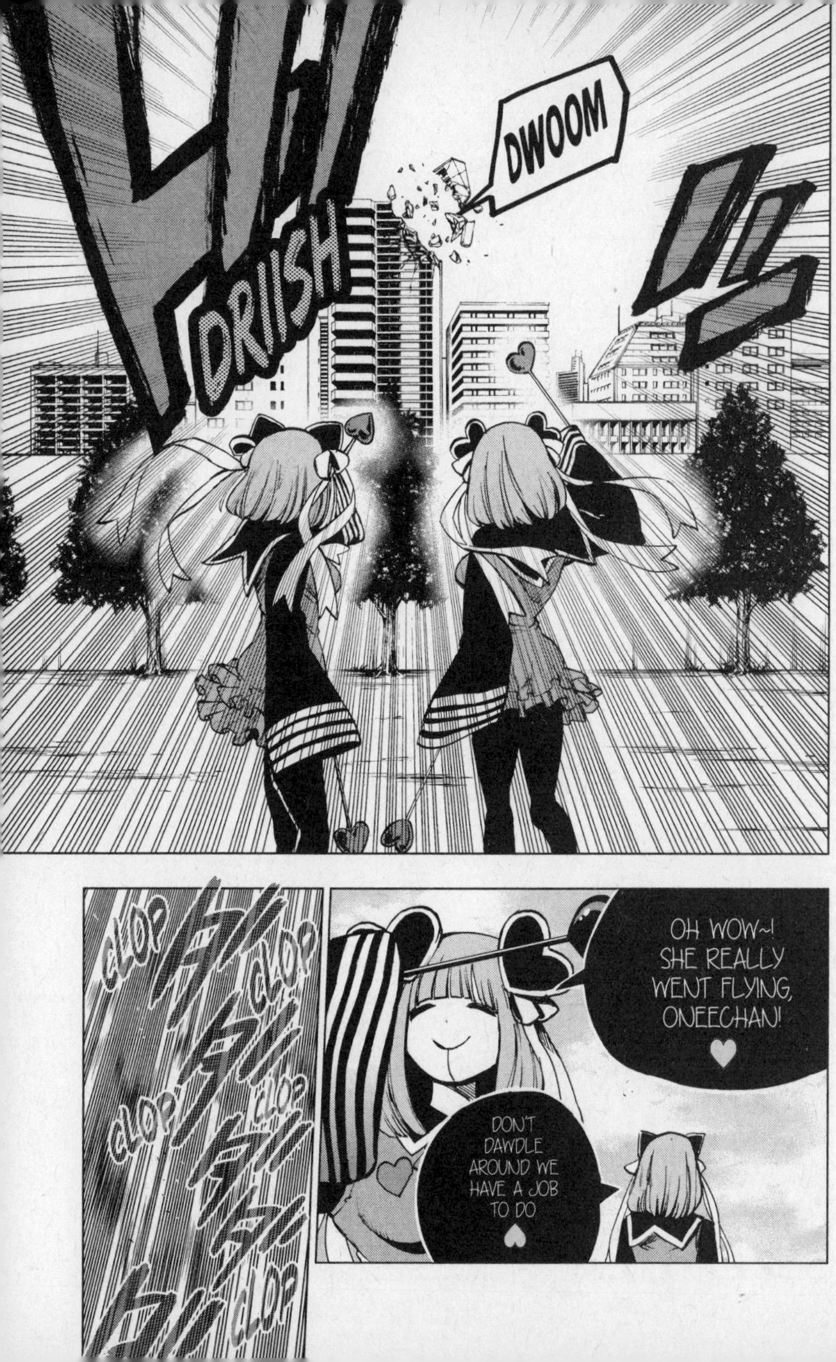
DWOOM
CRUSH
OH WOW~! SHE REALLY WENT FLYING, ONEECHAN! ♥
DON'T DAWDLE AROUND WE HAVE A JOB TO DO ♥
CLOP CLOP CLOP CLOP CLOP CLOP CLOP

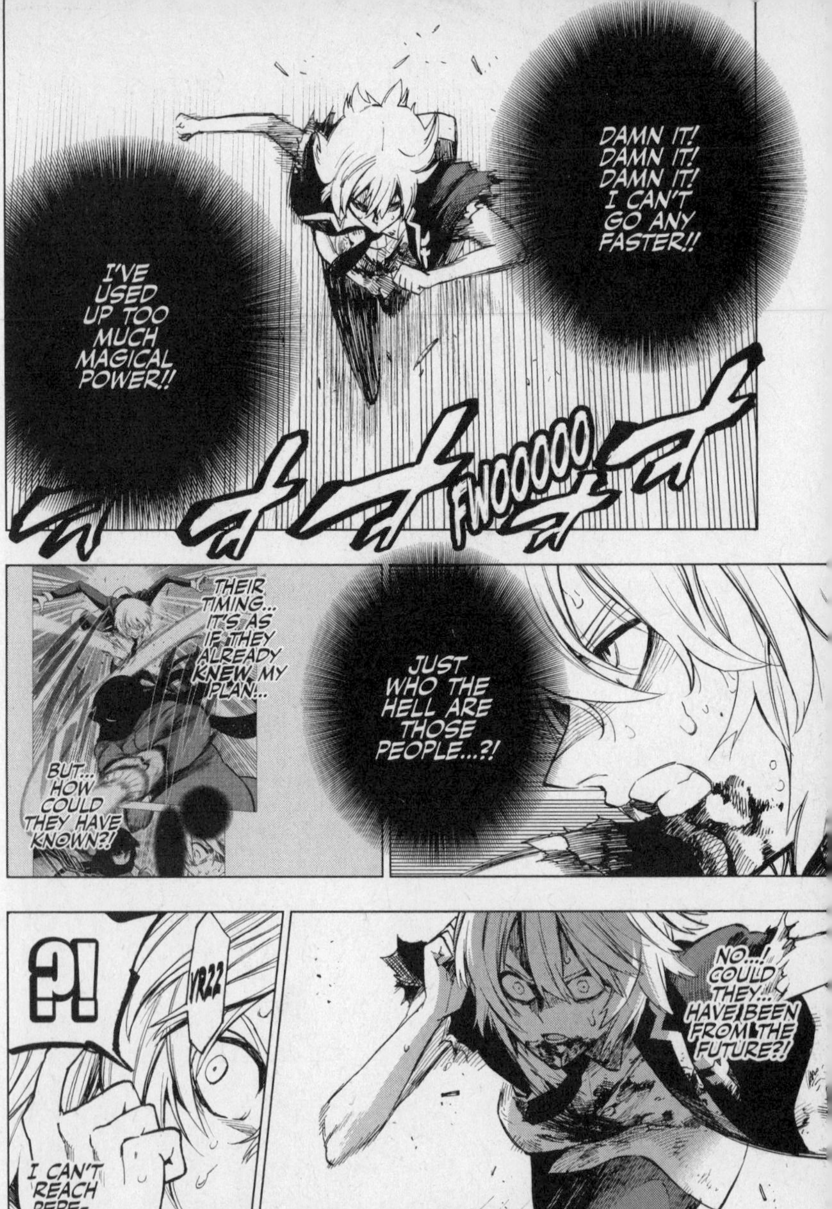
DAMN IT! DAMN IT! DAMN IT! I CAN'T GO ANY FASTER!!
I'VE USED UP TOO MUCH MAGICAL POWER!!
FWOOOOO
JUST WHO THE HELL ARE THOSE PEOPLE...?!
THEIR TIMING... IT'S AS IF THEY ALREADY KNEW MY PLAN...
BUT... HOW COULD THEY HAVE KNOWN?!
NO...! COULD THEY... HAVE BEEN FROM THE FUTURE?!
BUT WHO...?!
?!
I CAN'T REACH PEPE-CHAN...!

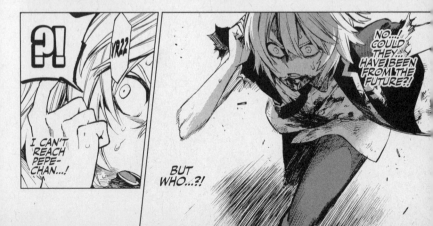

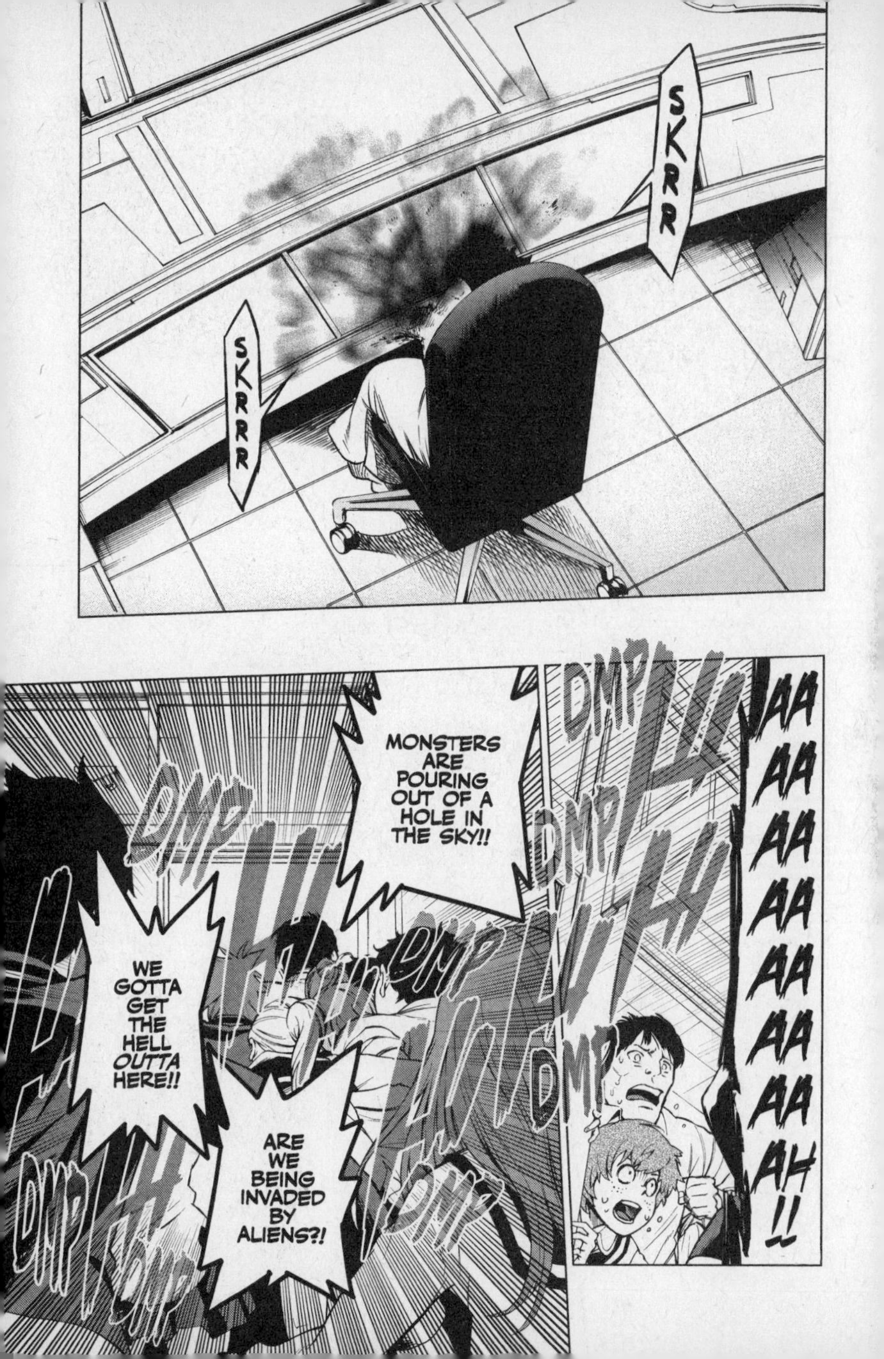
SKRR
SKRRR
AAAAAAAAAAAAAAAH!!
DMP
DMP
MONSTERS ARE POURING OUT OF A HOLE IN THE SKY!!
DMP
WE GOTTA GET THE HELL OUTTA HERE!!
ARE WE BEING INVADED BY ALIENS?!
DMP

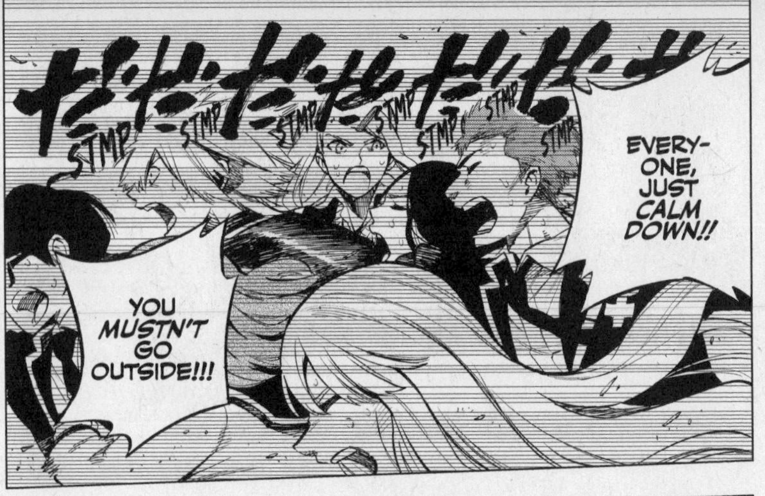
STMP STMP STMP STMP STMP STMP STMP
EVERY-ONE, JUST CALM DOWN!!
YOU MUSTN'T GO OUTSIDE!!!

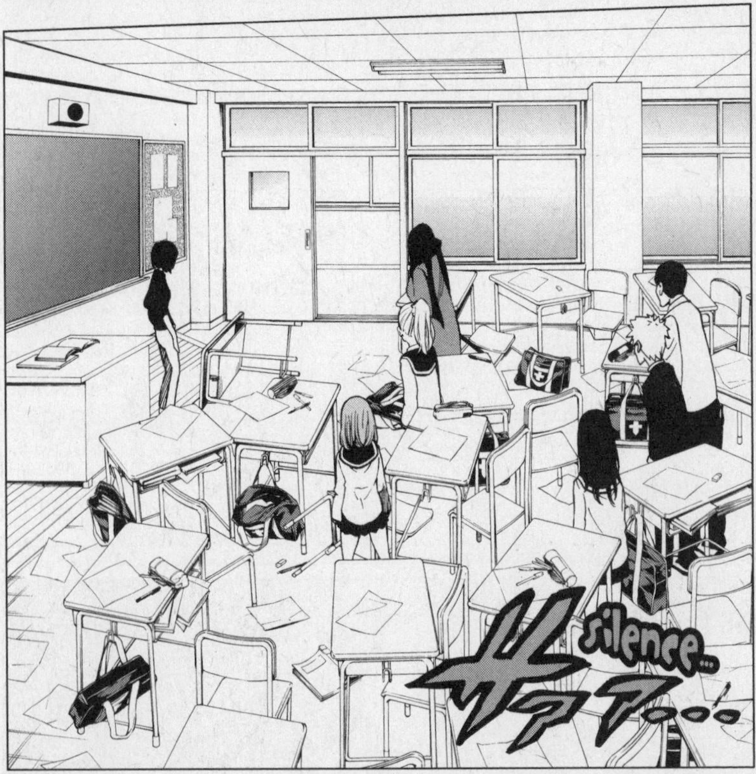
silence...

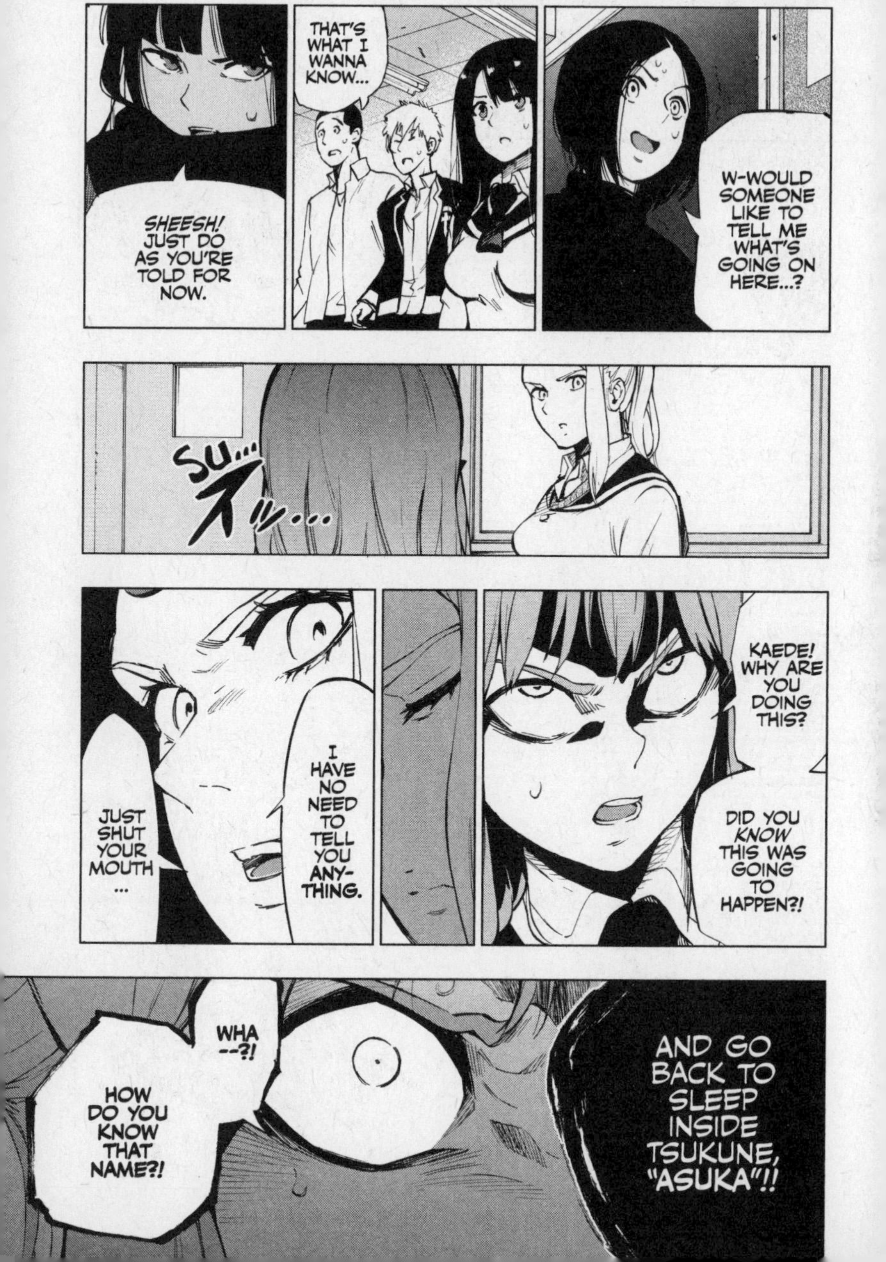
W-WOULD SOMEONE LIKE TO TELL ME WHAT'S GOING ON HERE...?
THAT'S WHAT I WANNA KNOW...
SHEESH! JUST DO AS YOU'RE TOLD FOR NOW.
SU...
KAEDE! WHY ARE YOU DOING THIS?
DID YOU *KNOW* THIS WAS GOING TO HAPPEN?!
I HAVE NO NEED TO TELL YOU ANY-THING.
JUST SHUT YOUR MOUTH...
AND GO BACK TO SLEEP INSIDE TSUKUNE, "ASUKA"!!
WHA--?!
HOW DO YOU KNOW THAT NAME?!

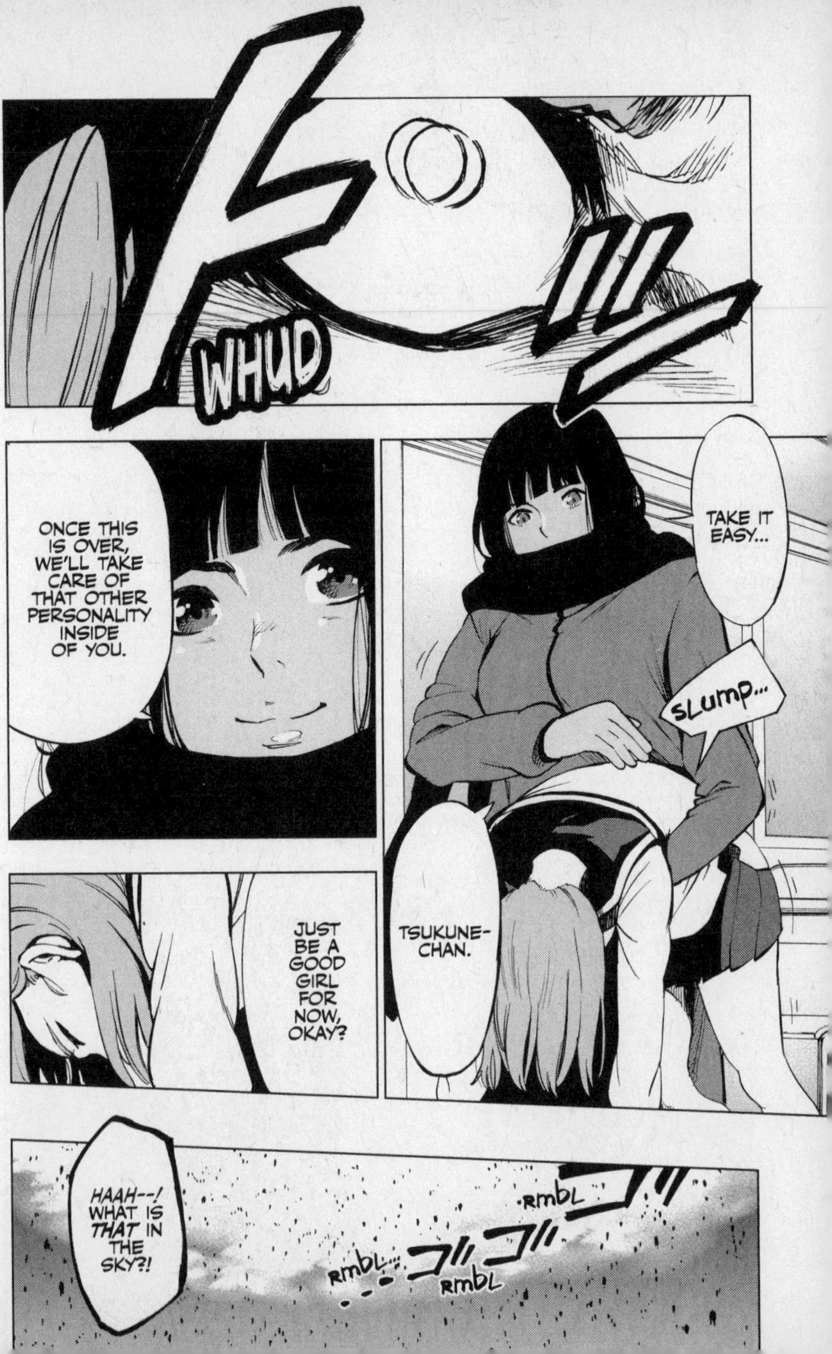
WHUD
TAKE IT EASY...
SLUMP...
TSUKUNE-CHAN.
ONCE THIS IS OVER, WE'LL TAKE CARE OF THAT OTHER PERSONALITY INSIDE OF YOU.
JUST BE A GOOD GIRL FOR NOW, OKAY?
RMBL
RMBL
RMBL
HAAH--! WHAT IS *THAT* IN THE SKY?!

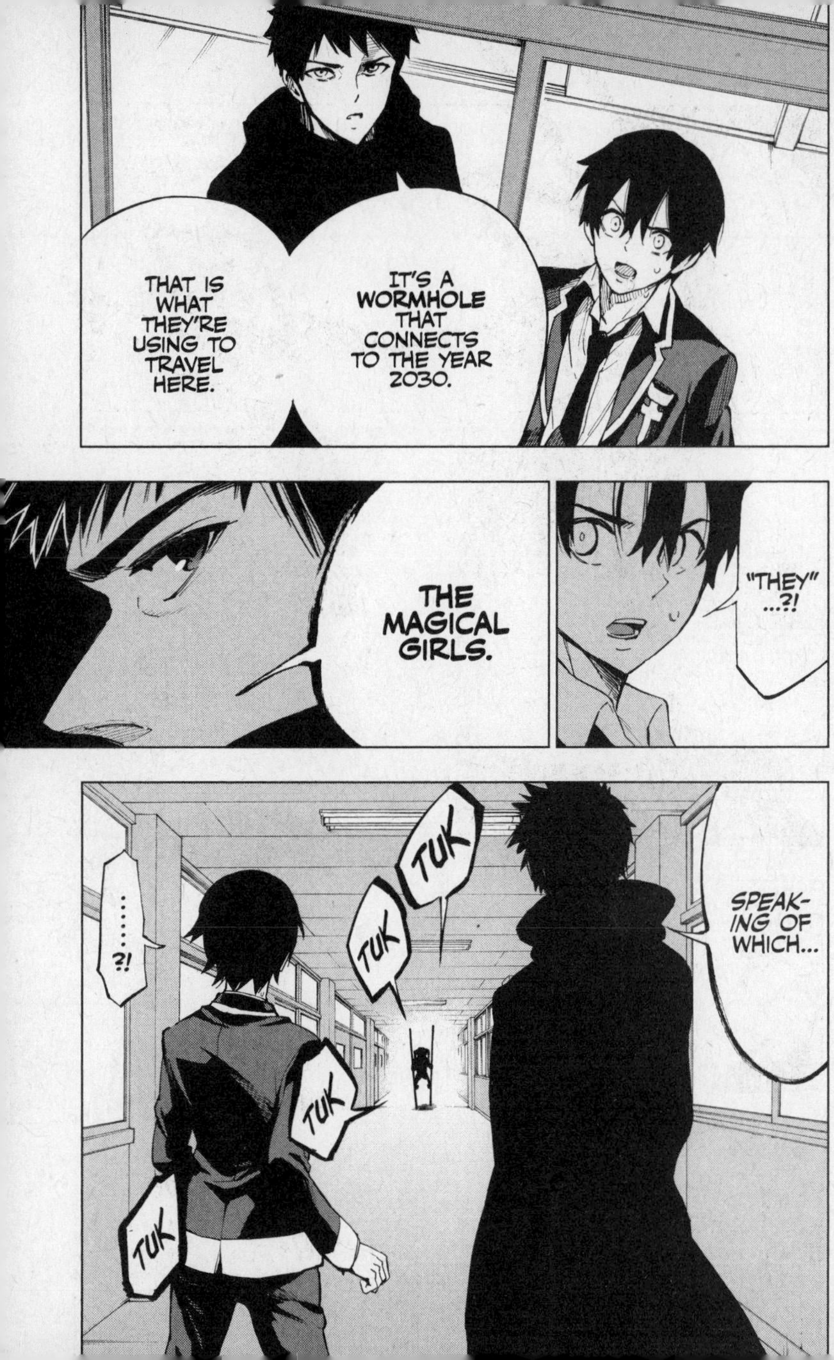
IT'S A WORMHOLE THAT CONNECTS TO THE YEAR 2030.
THAT IS WHAT THEY'RE USING TO TRAVEL HERE.
"THEY" ...?!
THE MAGICAL GIRLS.
SPEAK-ING OF WHICH...
TUK
TUK
TUK
TUK
......?!

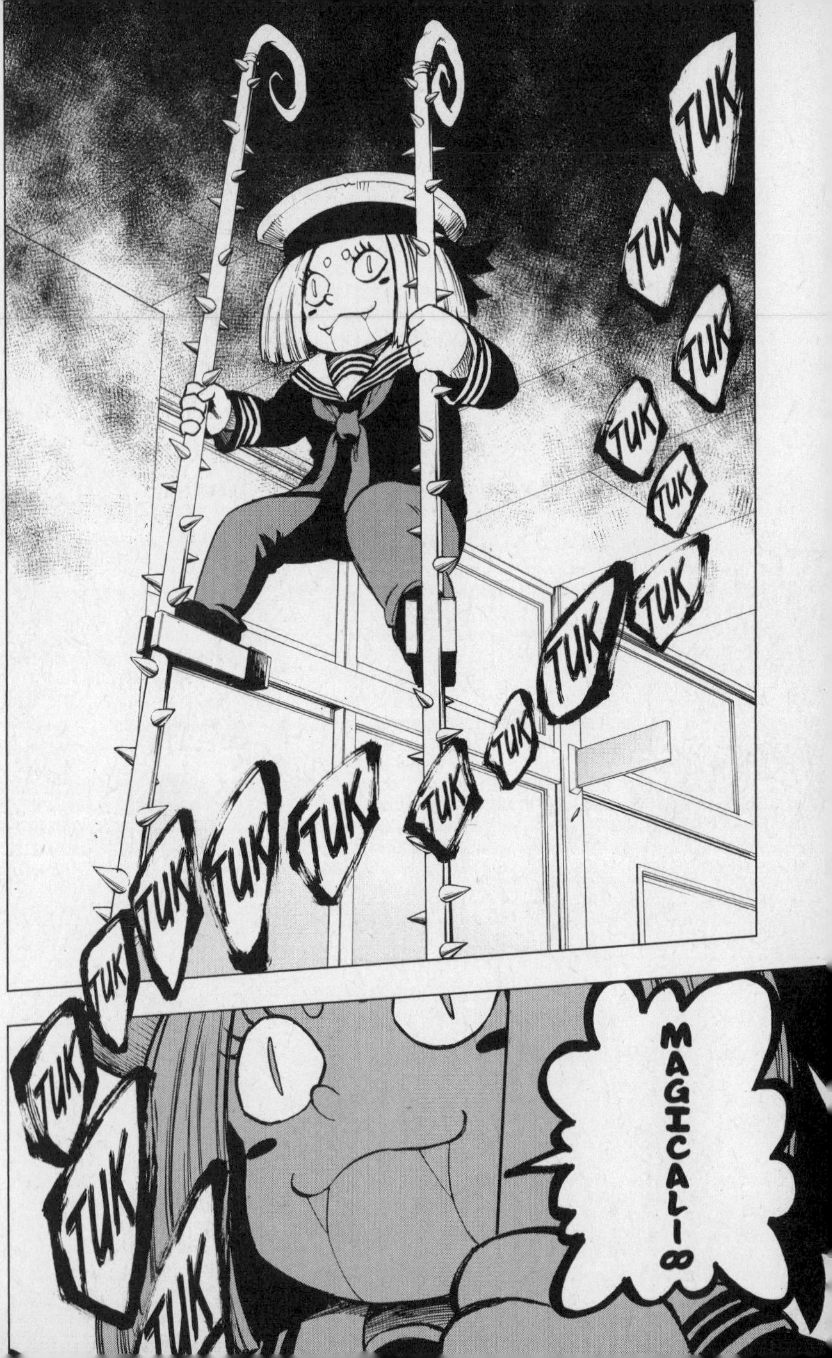
TUK
TUK
TUK
TUK
TUK
TUK
TUK
TUK
TUK
TUK
TUK
TUK
TUK
TUK
TUK
TUK
MAGICAL-∞

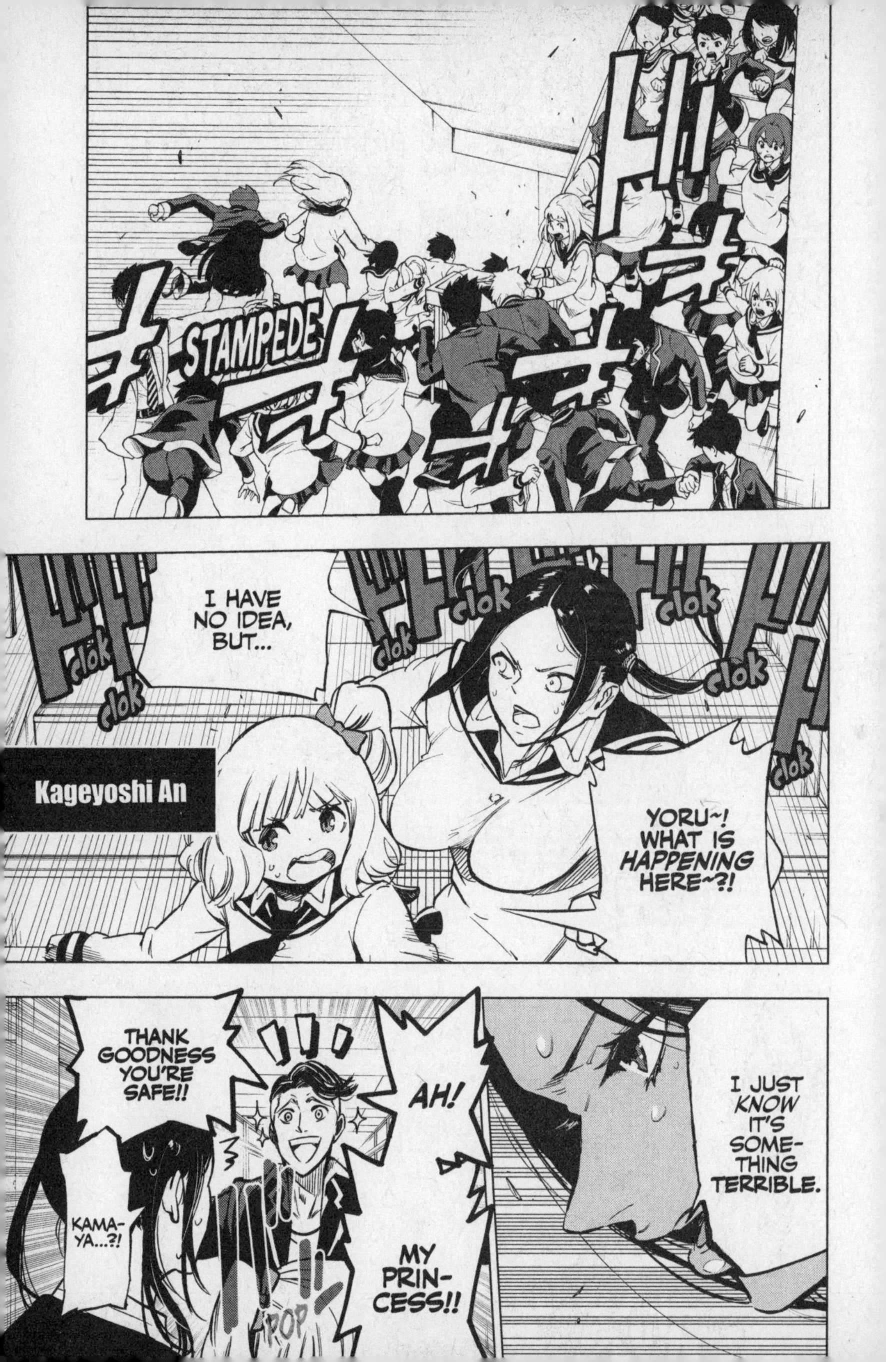
STAMPEDE
clok
clok
clok
YORU~! WHAT IS HAPPENING HERE~?!
I HAVE NO IDEA, BUT...
clok
clok
clok
Kageyoshi An
I JUST KNOW IT'S SOME-THING TERRIBLE.
AH!
MY PRIN-CESS!!
THANK GOODNESS YOU'RE SAFE!!
KAMA-YA...?!
POP

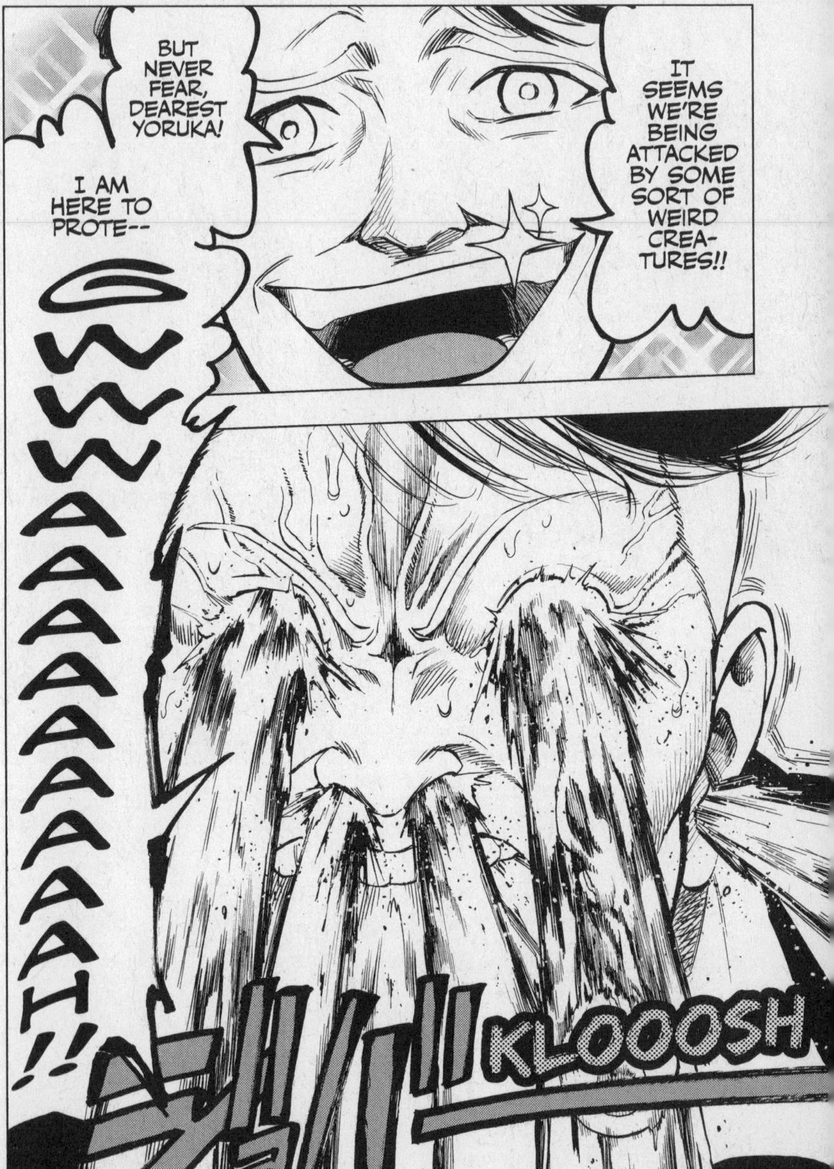
IT SEEMS WE'RE BEING ATTACKED BY SOME SORT OF WEIRD CREA-TURES!!
BUT NEVER FEAR, DEAREST YORUKA!
I AM HERE TO PROTE--
GWWWAAAAAAAAAH!!
KLOOOSH

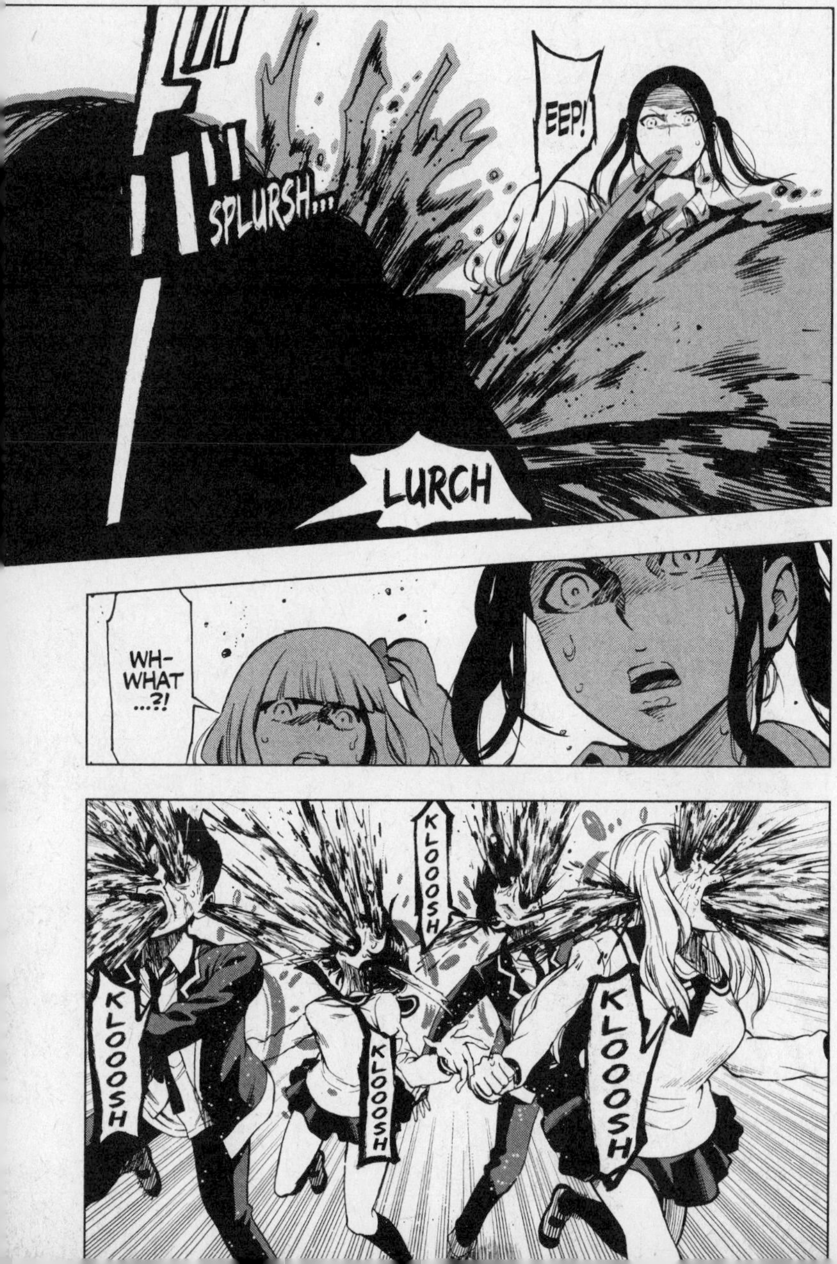
EEP!
SPLURSH...
LURCH
WH-WHAT...?!
KLOOOSH
KLOOOSH
KLOOOSH
KLOOOSH

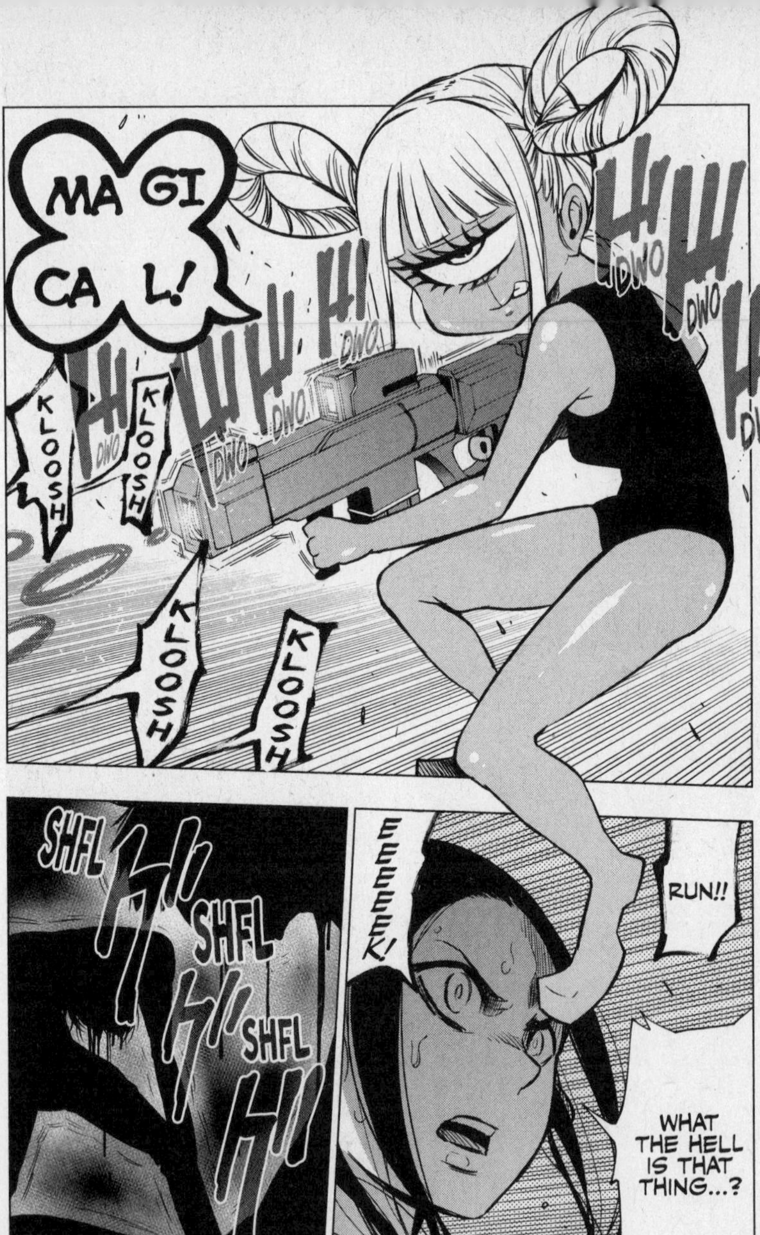
DWO
DWO
DWO
MAGICAL!
DWO
DWO
DWO
DWO
DWO
KLOOSH
KLOOSH
KLOOSH
KLOOSH
EEEEEK!
RUN!!
WHAT THE HELL IS THAT THING...?
SHFL
SHFL
SHFL

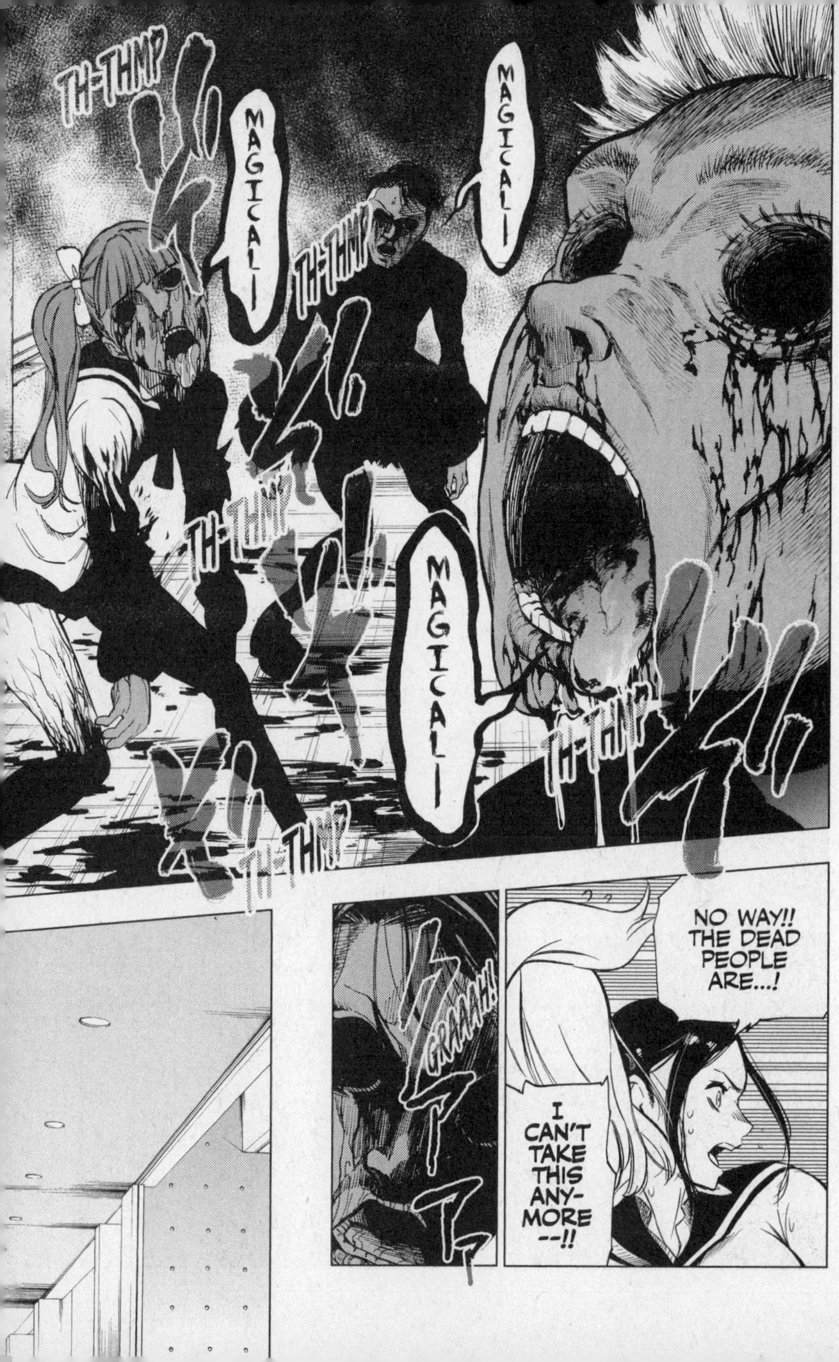

MAGICALI
TH-THMP
MAGICALI
TH-THMP
TH-THMP
MAGICALI
TH-THMP
TH-THMP
NO WAY!! THE DEAD PEOPLE ARE...!
I CAN'T TAKE THIS ANY-MORE --!!
GRAAAH!

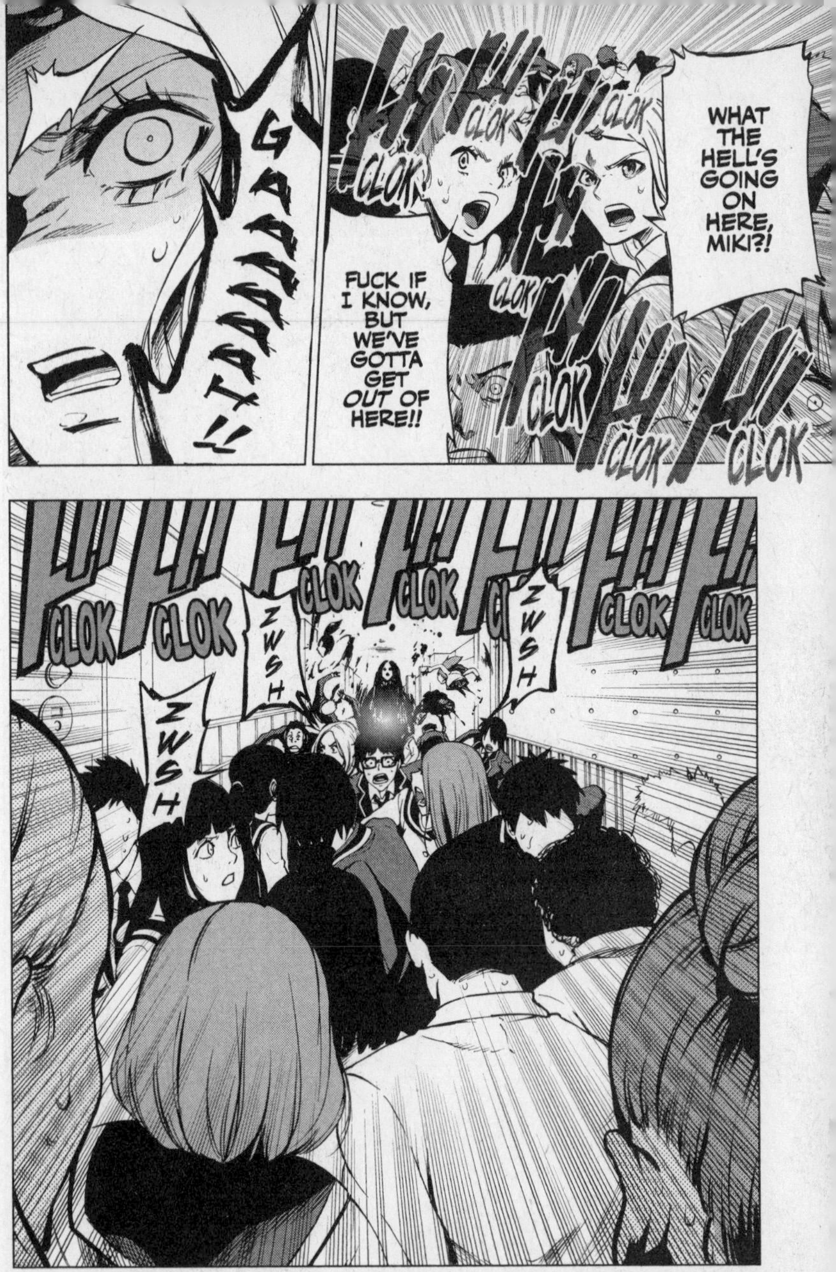
CLOK
CLOK
WHAT THE HELL'S GOING ON HERE, MIKI?!
CLOK
CLOK
FUCK IF I KNOW, BUT WE'VE GOTTA GET OUT OF HERE!!
CLOK
CLOK
CLOK
GAAAAAAH!!
CLOK
CLOK
CLOK
ZWSH
CLOK
CLOK
ZWSH
CLOK
CLOK
ZWSH

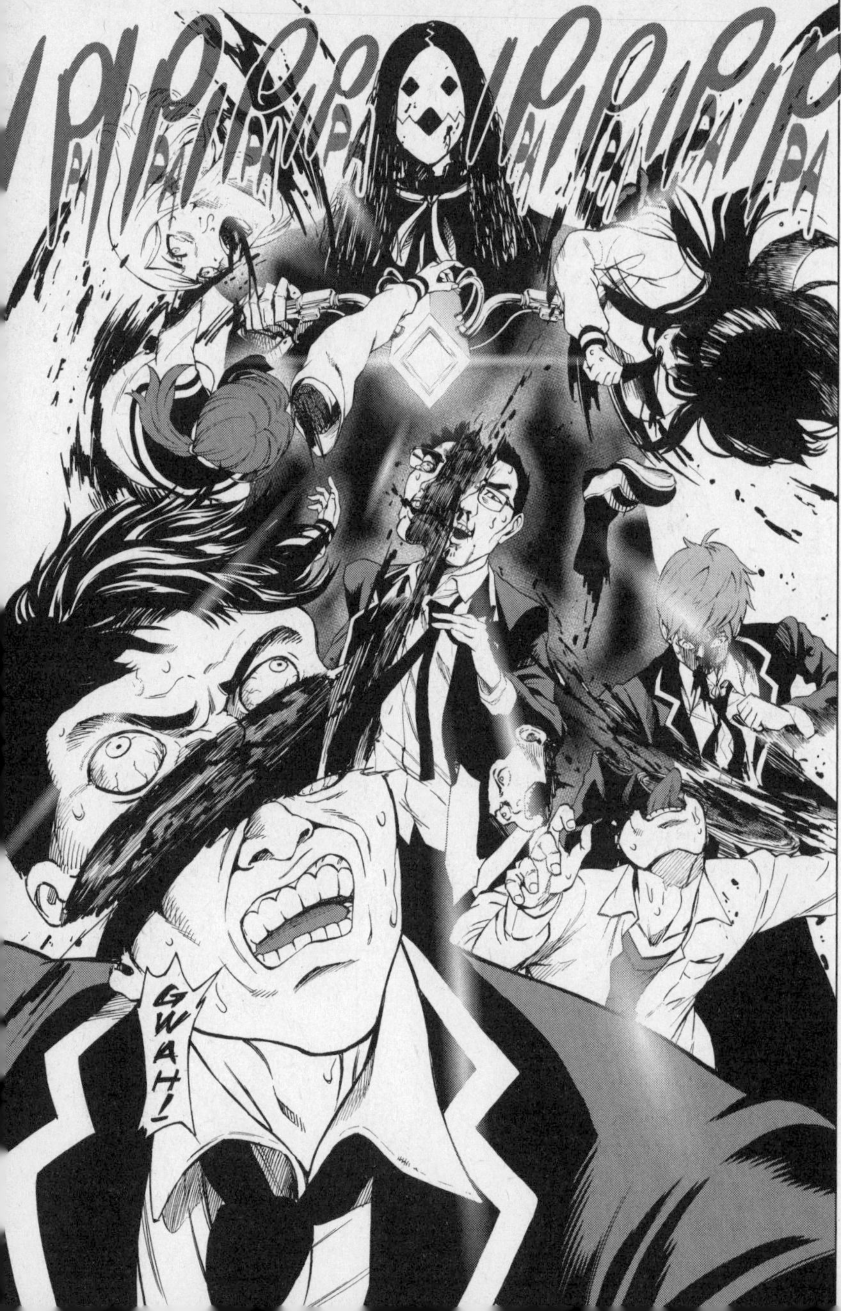
PA
GWAH!

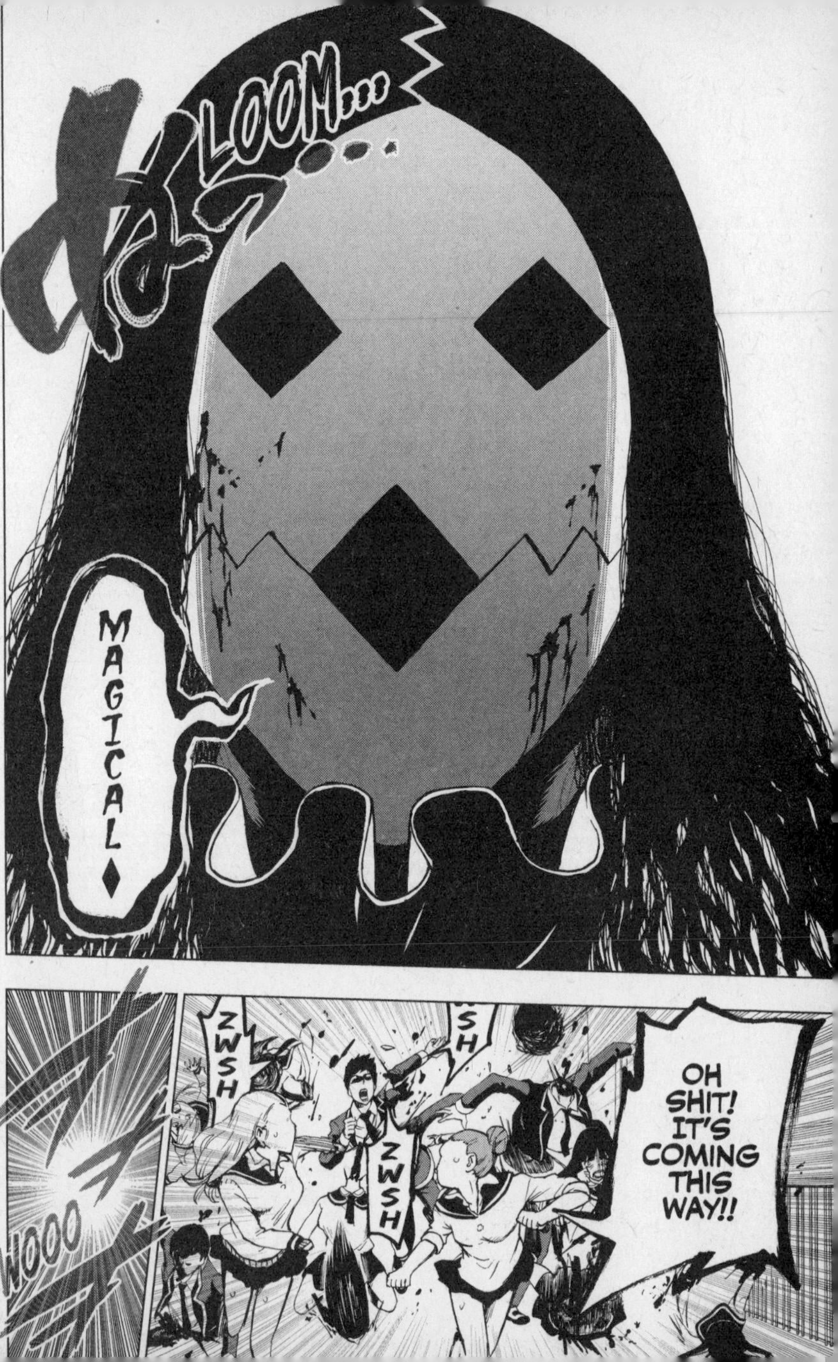
LOOM...
MAGICAL♦
OH SHIT! IT'S COMING THIS WAY!!
ZWSH
ZWSH
FWOOO

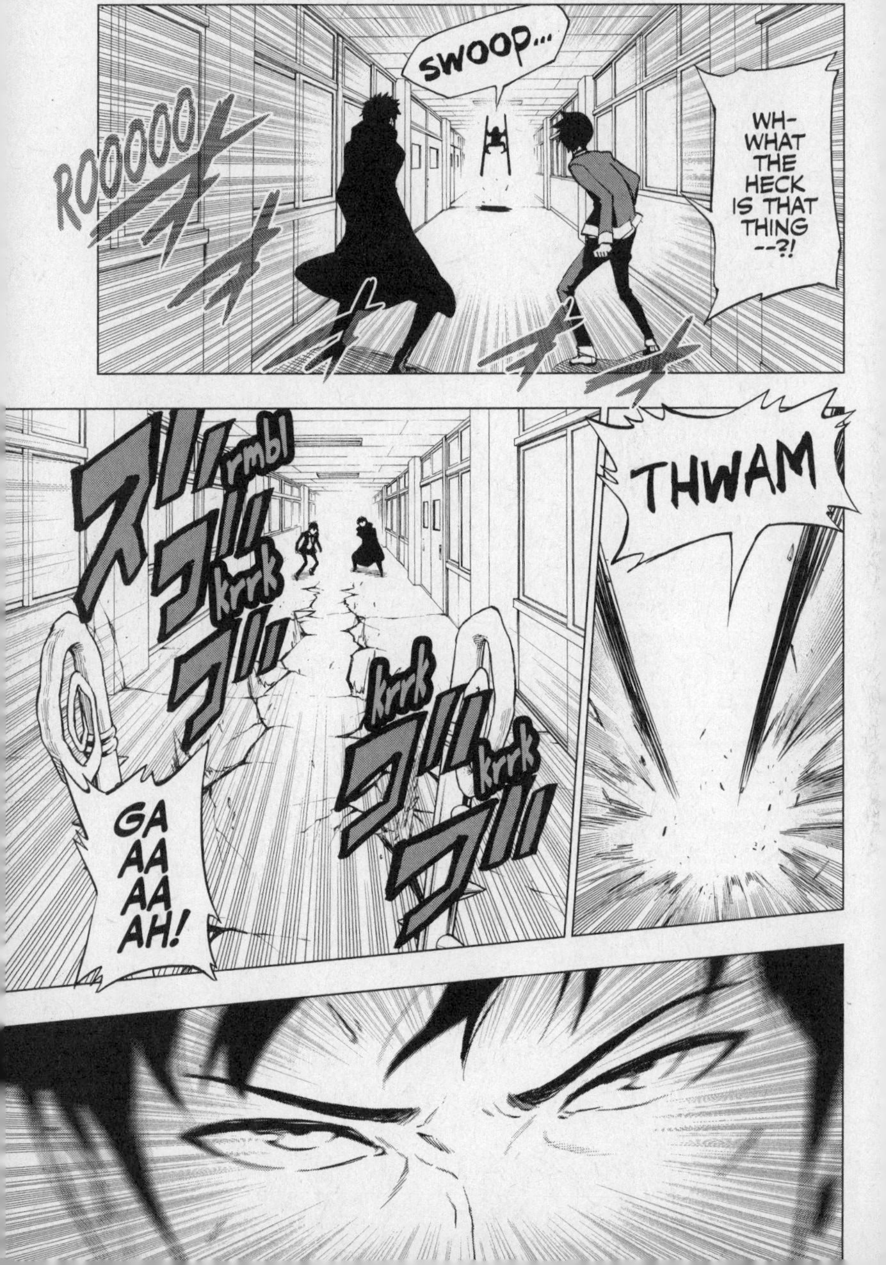
WH- WHAT THE HECK IS THAT THING--?!
SWOOP...
ROOOOO
THWAM
rmbl
krrk
krrk
krrk
GAAAAAAAH!

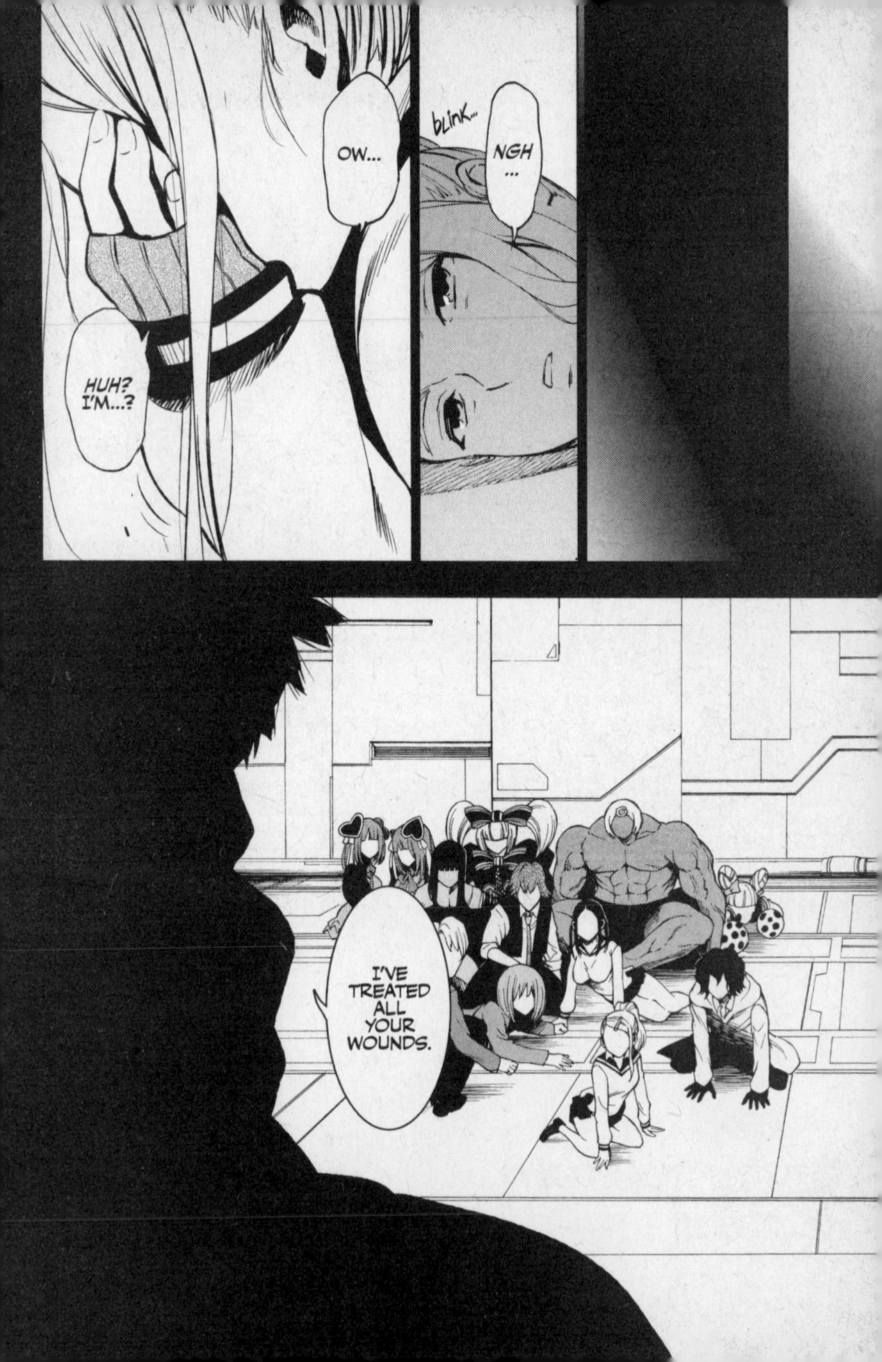

bLINK...
NGH ...
OW...
HUH? I'M...?
I'VE TREATED ALL YOUR WOUNDS.

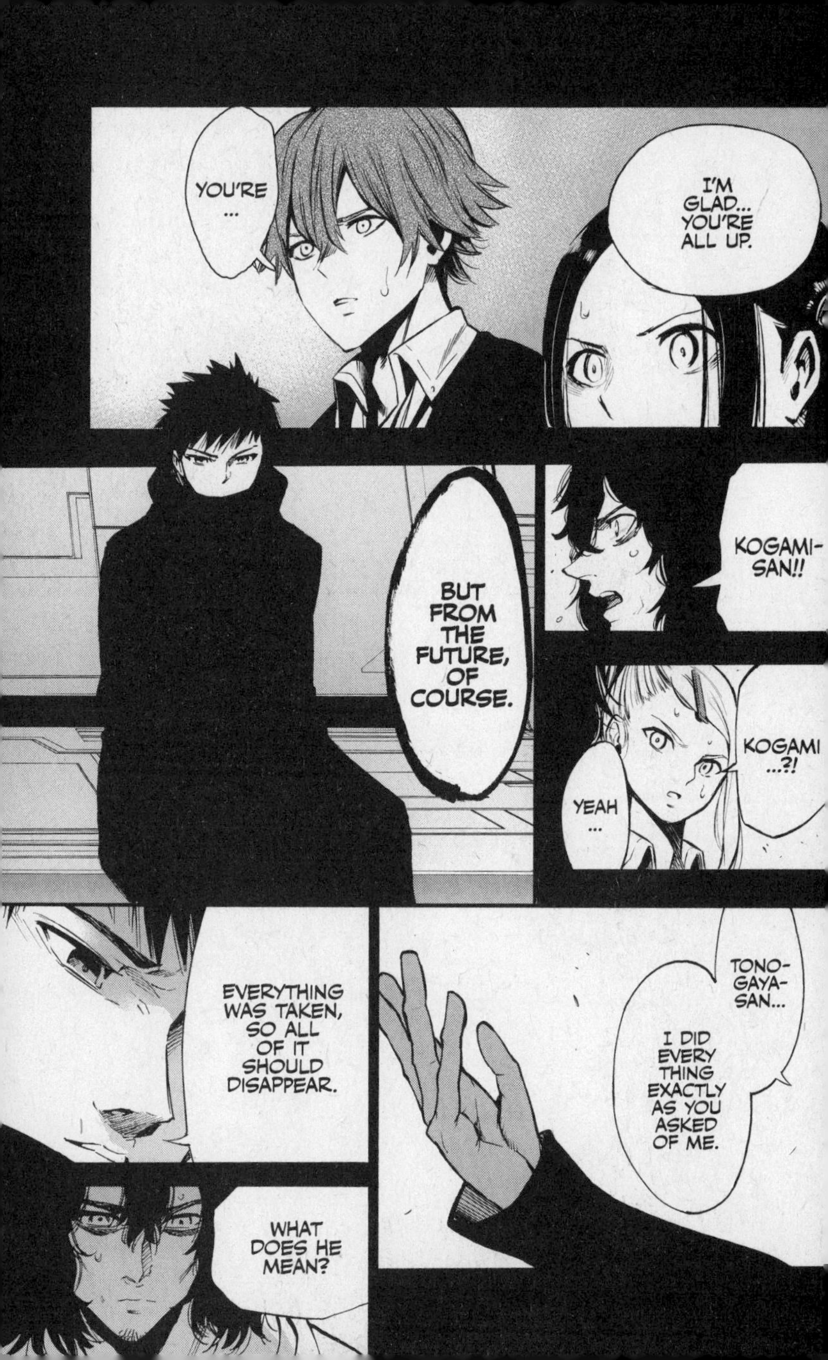
I'M GLAD... YOU'RE ALL UP.
YOU'RE ...
KOGAMI-SAN!!
KOGAMI ...?!
YEAH ...
BUT FROM THE FUTURE, OF COURSE.
TONO-GAYA-SAN...
I DID EVERY THING EXACTLY AS YOU ASKED OF ME.
EVERYTHING WAS TAKEN, SO ALL OF IT SHOULD DISAPPEAR.
WHAT DOES HE MEAN?

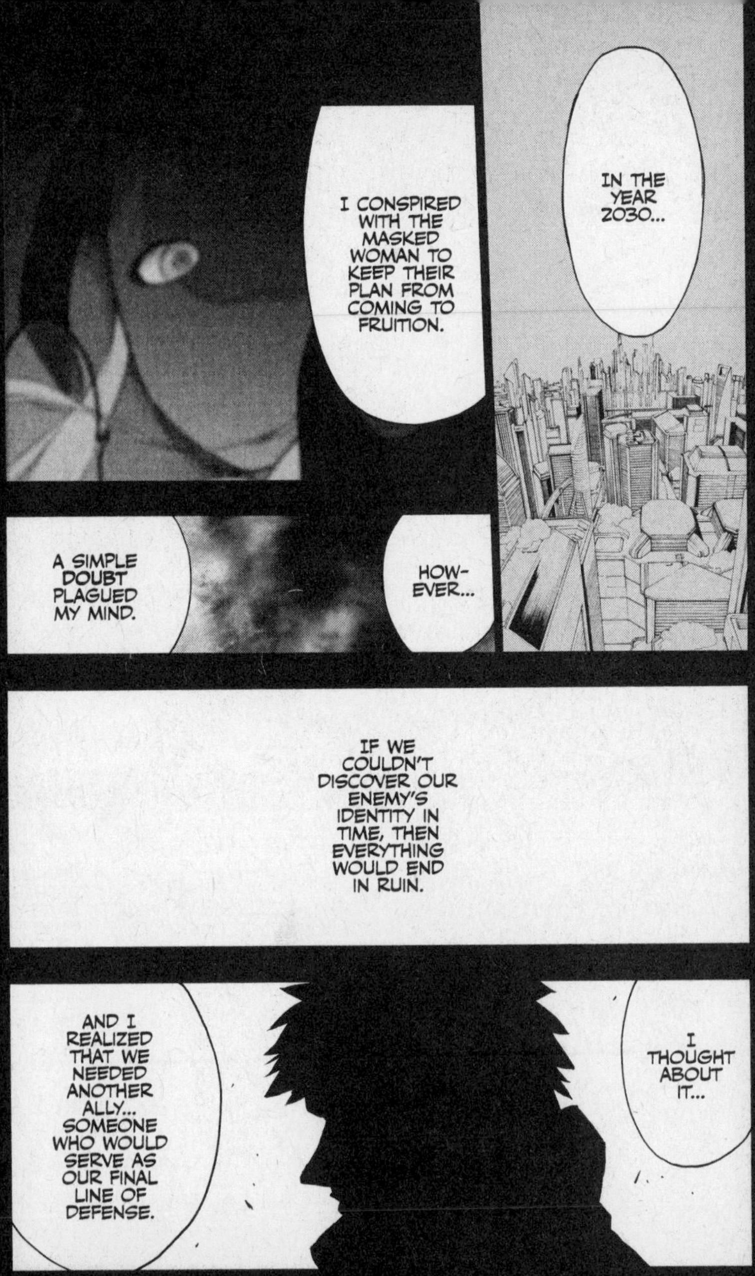
IN THE YEAR 2030...
I CONSPIRED WITH THE MASKED WOMAN TO KEEP THEIR PLAN FROM COMING TO FRUITION.
HOW-EVER...
A SIMPLE DOUBT PLAGUED MY MIND.
IF WE COULDN'T DISCOVER OUR ENEMY'S IDENTITY IN TIME, THEN EVERYTHING WOULD END IN RUIN.
I THOUGHT ABOUT IT...
AND I REALIZED THAT WE NEEDED ANOTHER ALLY... SOMEONE WHO WOULD SERVE AS OUR FINAL LINE OF DEFENSE.

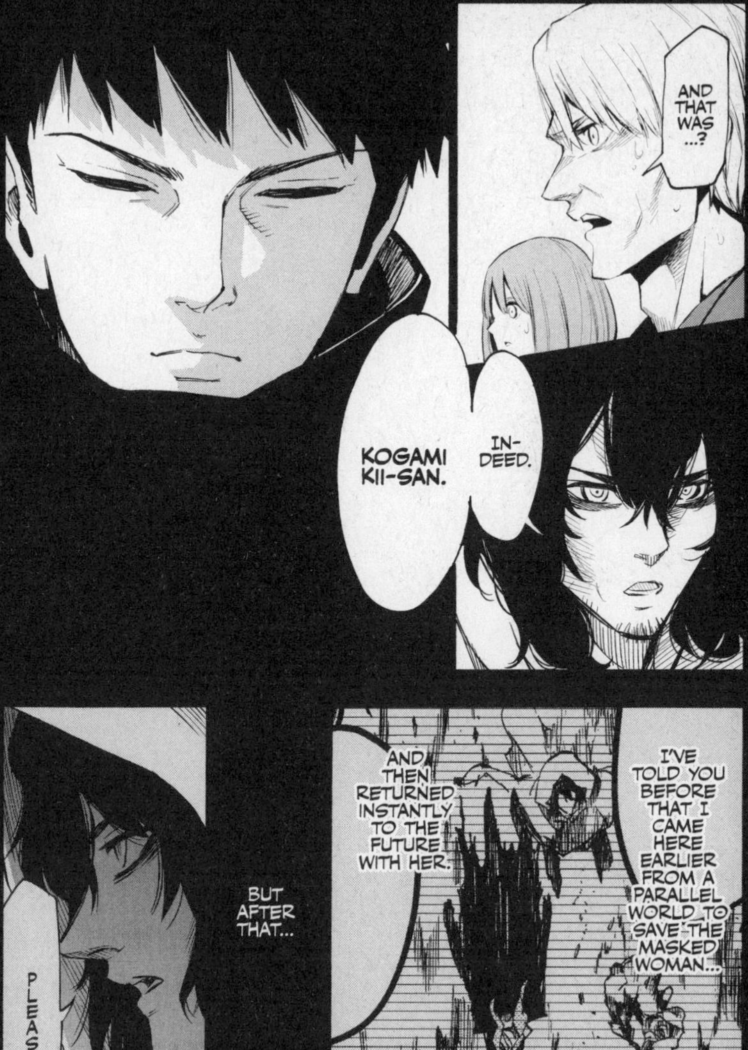
AND THAT WAS ...?
IN-DEED.
KOGAMI KII-SAN.
I'VE TOLD YOU BEFORE THAT I CAME HERE EARLIER FROM A PARALLEL WORLD TO SAVE THE MASKED WOMAN...
AND THEN RETURNED INSTANTLY TO THE FUTURE WITH HER.
BUT AFTER THAT...
PLEASE...

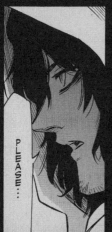

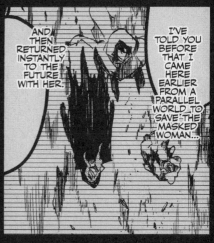

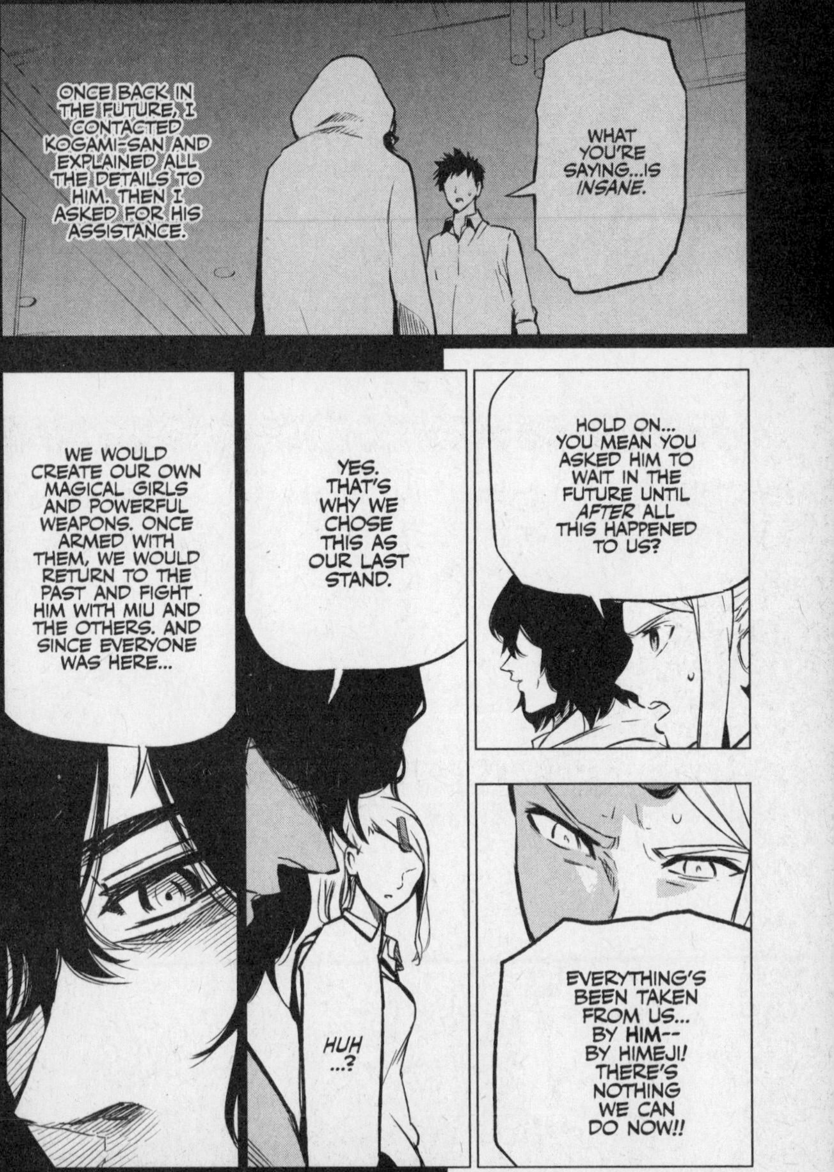
WHAT YOU'RE SAYING...IS *INSANE.*
ONCE BACK IN THE FUTURE, I CONTACTED KOGAMI-SAN AND EXPLAINED ALL THE DETAILS TO HIM. THEN I ASKED FOR HIS ASSISTANCE.
HOLD ON... YOU MEAN YOU ASKED HIM TO WAIT IN THE FUTURE UNTIL *AFTER* ALL THIS HAPPENED TO US?
EVERYTHING'S BEEN TAKEN FROM US... BY HIM-- BY HIMEJI! THERE'S NOTHING WE CAN DO NOW!!
YES. THAT'S WHY WE CHOSE THIS AS OUR LAST STAND.
*HUH ...?*
WE WOULD CREATE OUR OWN MAGICAL GIRLS AND POWERFUL WEAPONS. ONCE ARMED WITH THEM, WE WOULD RETURN TO THE PAST AND FIGHT HIM WITH MIU AND THE OTHERS. AND SINCE EVERYONE WAS HERE...

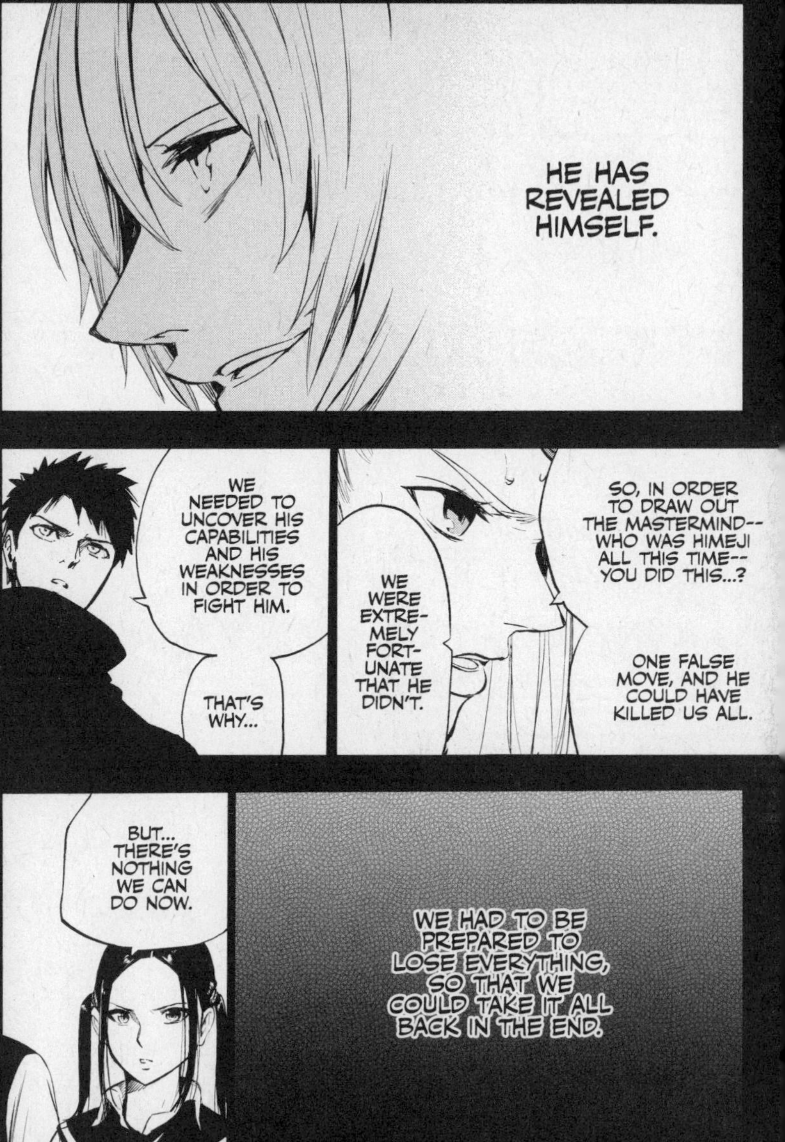
HE HAS REVEALED HIMSELF.
SO, IN ORDER TO DRAW OUT THE MASTERMIND-- WHO WAS HIMEJI ALL THIS TIME-- YOU DID THIS...?
ONE FALSE MOVE, AND HE COULD HAVE KILLED US ALL.
WE WERE EXTREMELY FORTUNATE THAT HE DIDN'T.
WE NEEDED TO UNCOVER HIS CAPABILITIES AND HIS WEAKNESSES IN ORDER TO FIGHT HIM.
THAT'S WHY...
WE HAD TO BE PREPARED TO LOSE EVERYTHING, SO THAT WE COULD TAKE IT ALL BACK IN THE END.
BUT... THERE'S NOTHING WE CAN DO NOW.

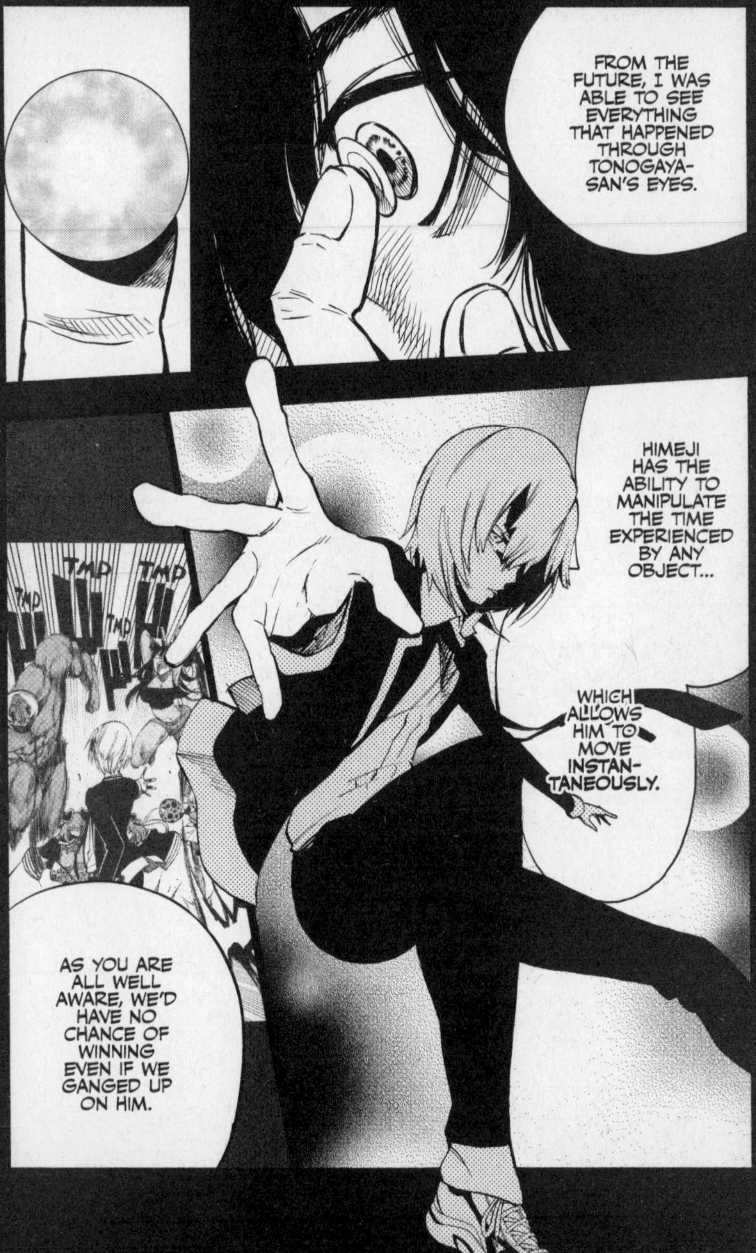
FROM THE FUTURE, I WAS ABLE TO SEE EVERYTHING THAT HAPPENED THROUGH TONOGAYA-SAN'S EYES.
HIMEJI HAS THE ABILITY TO MANIPULATE THE TIME EXPERIENCED BY ANY OBJECT...
WHICH ALLOWS HIM TO MOVE INSTAN-TANEOUSLY.
TMP
TMP
TMP
TMP
AS YOU ARE ALL WELL AWARE, WE'D HAVE NO CHANCE OF WINNING EVEN IF WE GANGED UP ON HIM.

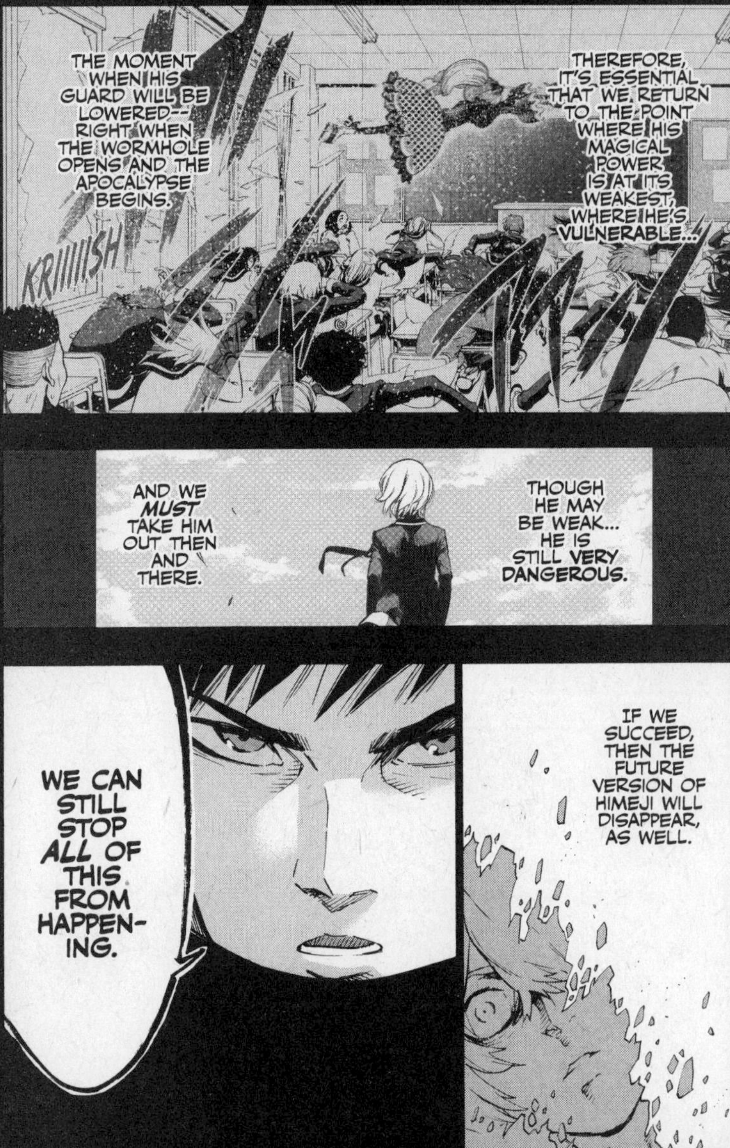
THEREFORE, IT'S ESSENTIAL THAT WE RETURN TO THE POINT WHERE HIS MAGICAL POWER IS AT ITS WEAKEST, WHERE HE'S VULNERABLE...
THE MOMENT WHEN HIS GUARD WILL BE LOWERED--RIGHT WHEN THE WORMHOLE OPENS AND THE APOCALYPSE BEGINS.
KRIIIIISH
THOUGH HE MAY BE WEAK... HE IS STILL VERY DANGEROUS.
AND WE MUST TAKE HIM OUT THEN AND THERE.
IF WE SUCCEED, THEN THE FUTURE VERSION OF HIMEJI WILL DISAPPEAR, AS WELL.
WE CAN STILL STOP ALL OF THIS FROM HAPPENING.

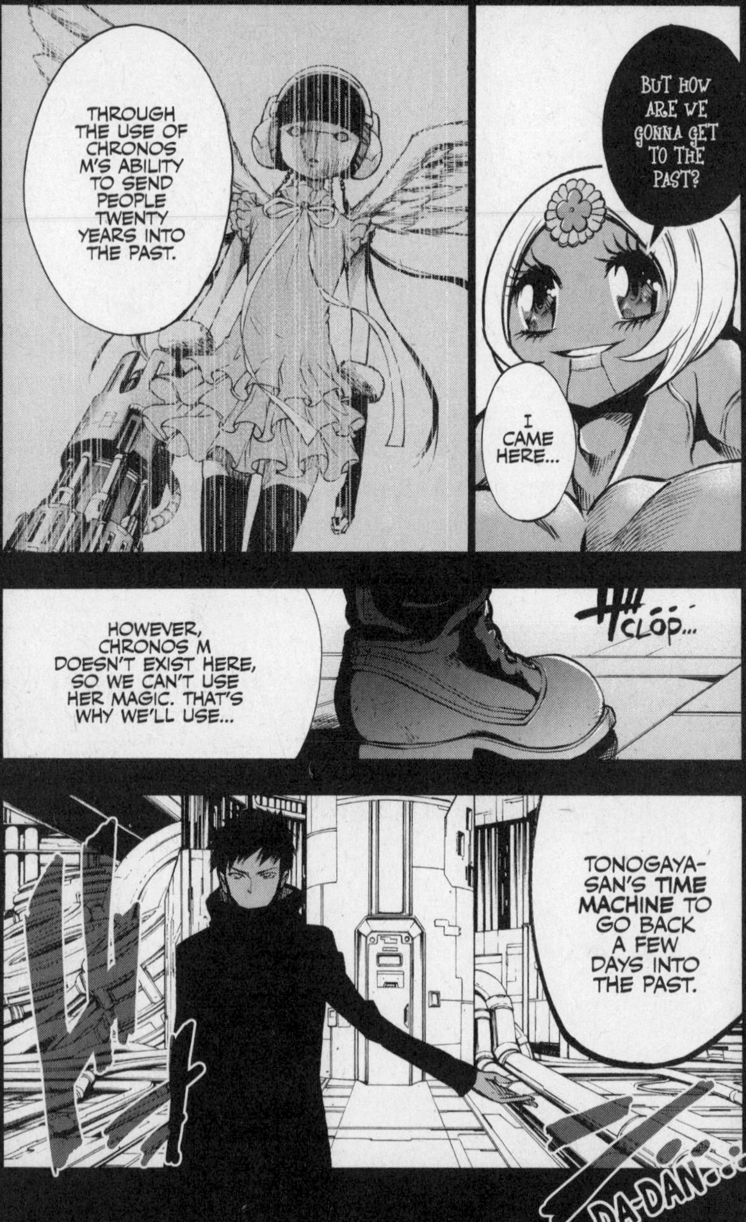
BUT HOW ARE WE GONNA GET TO THE PAST?
I CAME HERE...
THROUGH THE USE OF CHRONOS M'S ABILITY TO SEND PEOPLE TWENTY YEARS INTO THE PAST.
CLOP...
HOWEVER, CHRONOS M DOESN'T EXIST HERE, SO WE CAN'T USE HER MAGIC. THAT'S WHY WE'LL USE...
TONOGAYA-SAN'S TIME MACHINE TO GO BACK A FEW DAYS INTO THE PAST.
DA-DAN...

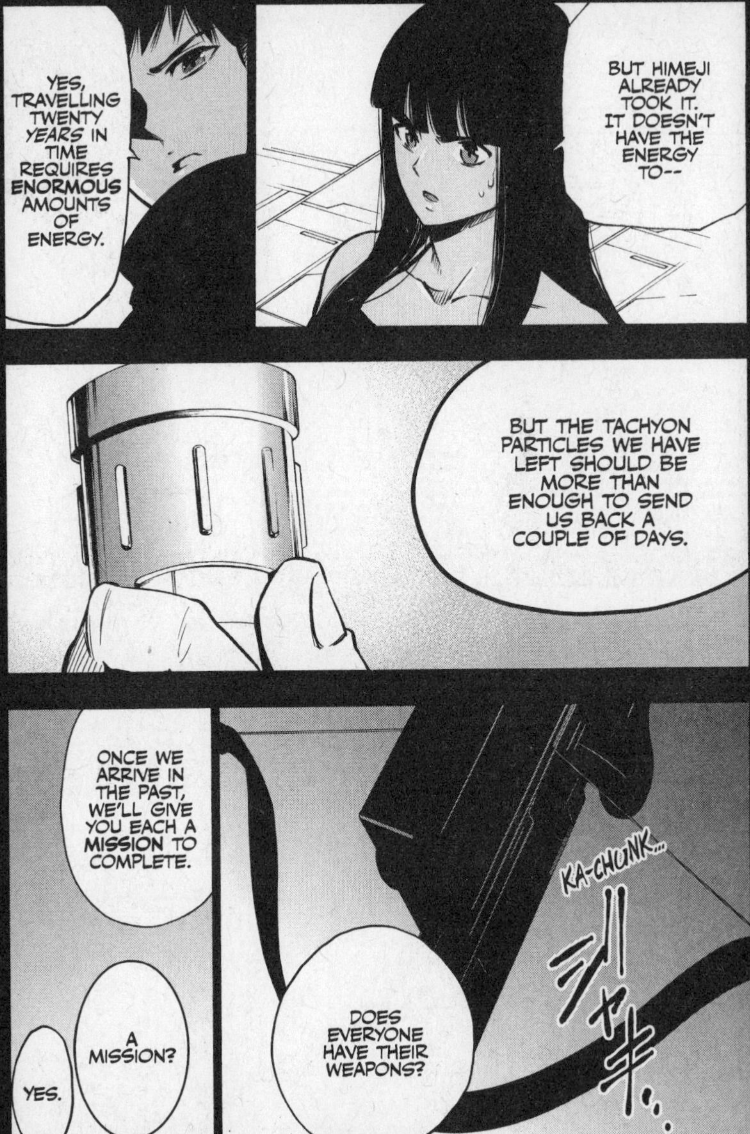
BUT HIMEJI ALREADY TOOK IT. IT DOESN'T HAVE THE ENERGY TO--
YES, TRAVELLING TWENTY *YEARS* IN TIME REQUIRES **ENORMOUS** AMOUNTS OF ENERGY.
BUT THE TACHYON PARTICLES WE HAVE LEFT SHOULD BE MORE THAN ENOUGH TO SEND US BACK A COUPLE OF DAYS.
KA-CHUNK...
ジャキ..
DOES EVERYONE HAVE THEIR WEAPONS?
ONCE WE ARRIVE IN THE PAST, WE'LL GIVE YOU EACH A **MISSION** TO COMPLETE.
A MISSION?
YES.

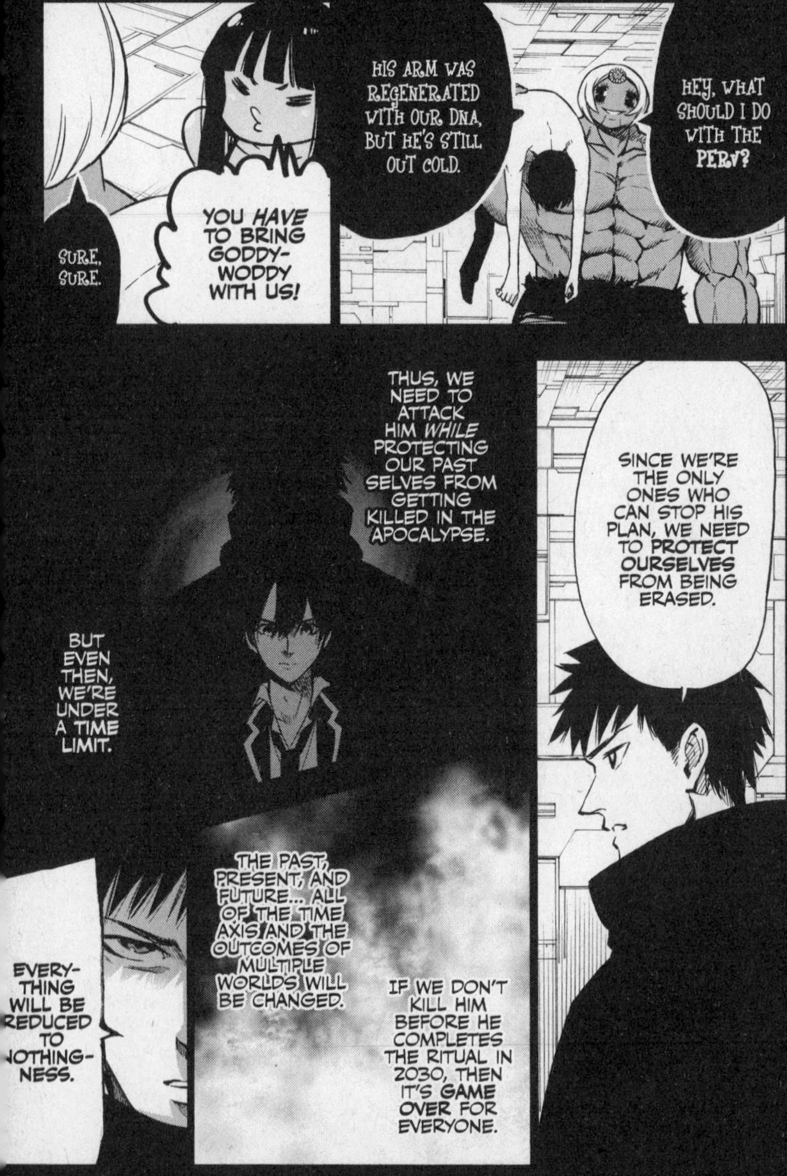
HEY, WHAT SHOULD I DO WITH THE PERV?
HIS ARM WAS REGENERATED WITH OUR DNA, BUT HE'S STILL OUT COLD.
YOU *HAVE* TO BRING GODDY-WODDY WITH US!
SURE, SURE.
SINCE WE'RE THE ONLY ONES WHO CAN STOP HIS PLAN, WE NEED TO PROTECT OURSELVES FROM BEING ERASED.
THUS, WE NEED TO ATTACK HIM *WHILE* PROTECTING OUR PAST SELVES FROM GETTING KILLED IN THE APOCALYPSE.
BUT EVEN THEN, WE'RE UNDER A TIME LIMIT.
IF WE DON'T KILL HIM BEFORE HE COMPLETES THE RITUAL IN 2030, THEN IT'S GAME OVER FOR EVERYONE.
THE PAST, PRESENT, AND FUTURE... ALL OF THE TIME AXIS AND THE OUTCOMES OF MULTIPLE WORLDS WILL BE CHANGED.
EVERY-THING WILL BE REDUCED TO NOTHING-NESS.

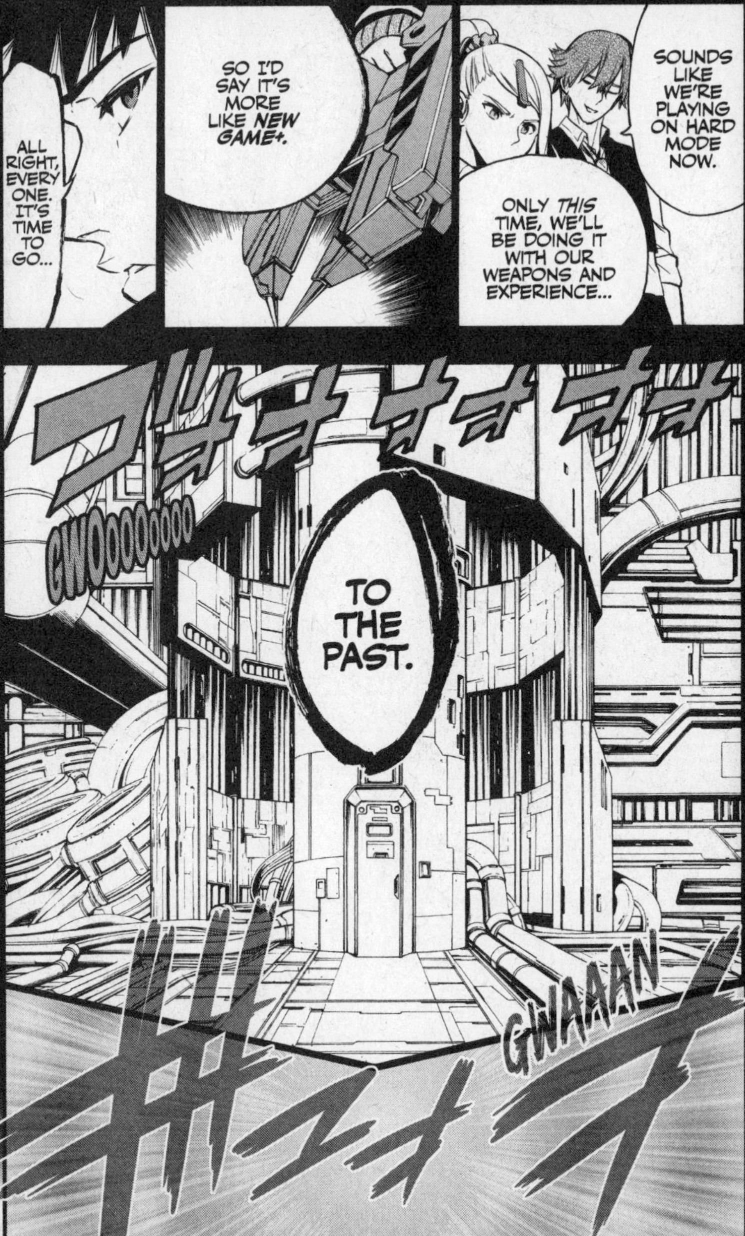
SOUNDS LIKE WE'RE PLAYING ON HARD MODE NOW.
ONLY THIS TIME, WE'LL BE DOING IT WITH OUR WEAPONS AND EXPERIENCE...
SO I'D SAY IT'S MORE LIKE NEW GAME+.
ALL RIGHT, EVERY ONE. IT'S TIME TO GO...
GWOOOOOOO
TO THE PAST.
GWAAAN

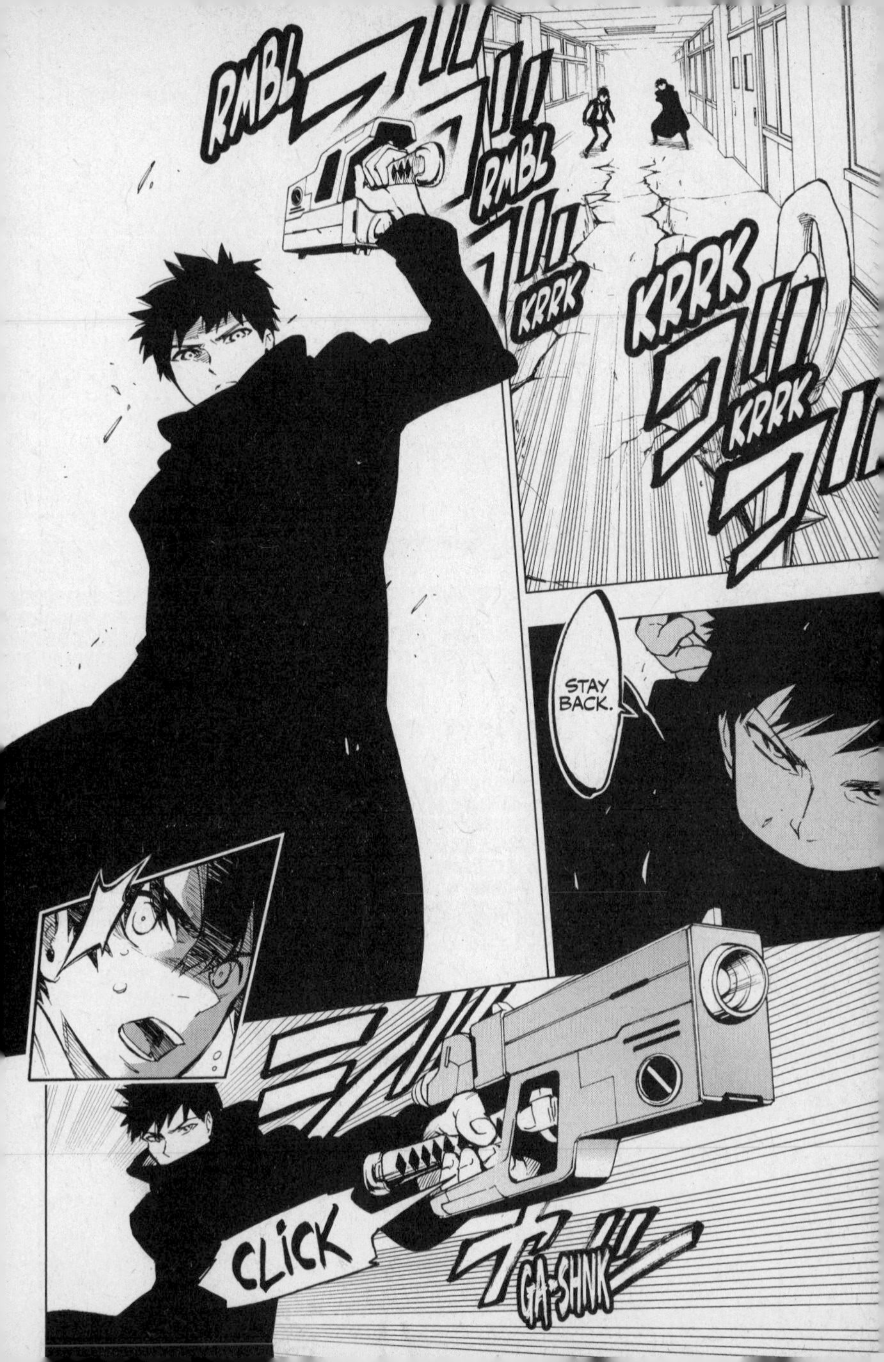
KRRK
KRRK
STAY BACK.
RMBL
RMBL
KRRK
GA-SHNK
CLICK

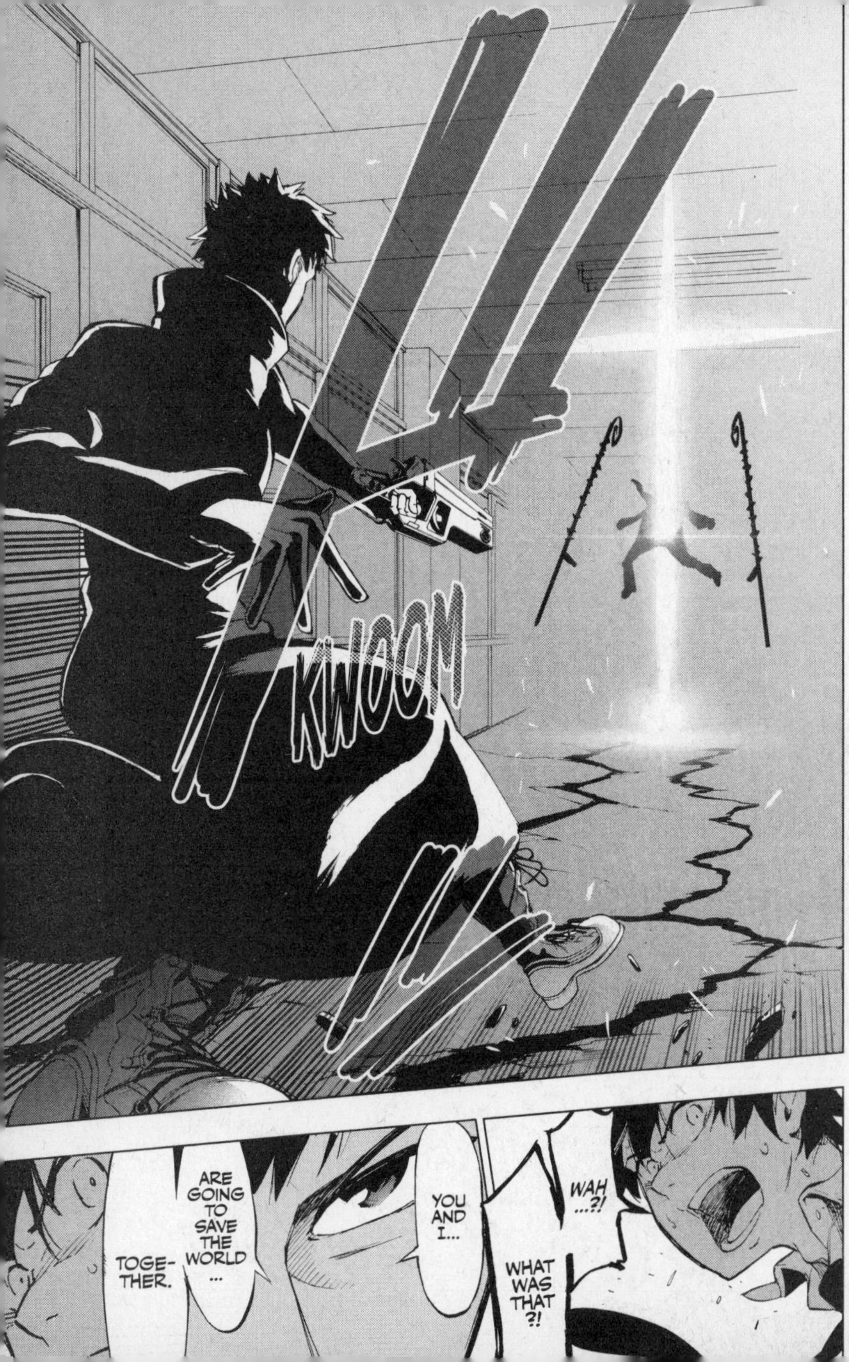
KWOOM
WAH ...?!
WHAT WAS THAT ?!
YOU AND I...
ARE GOING TO SAVE THE WORLD ...
TOGE-THER.

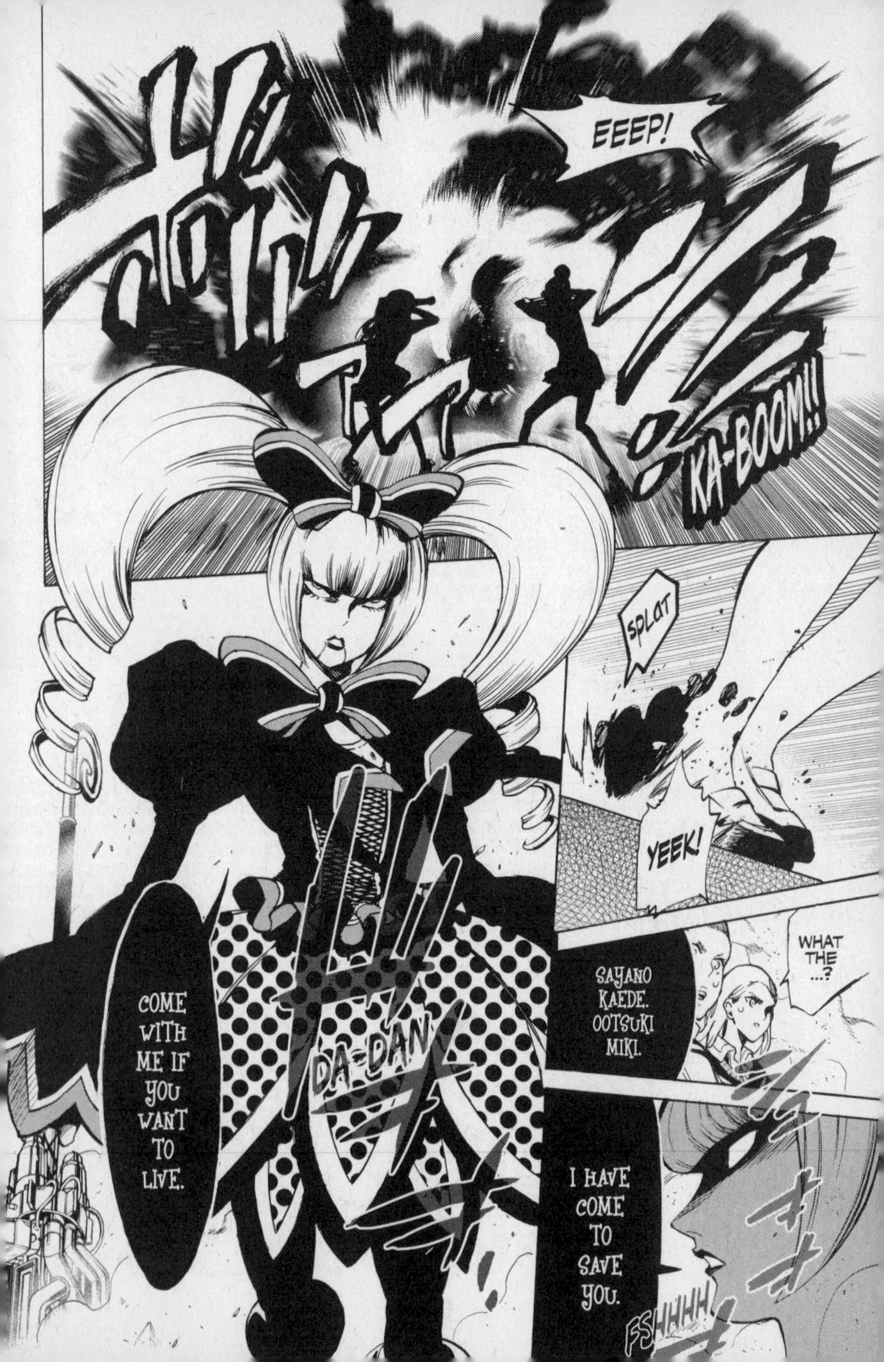
EEEP!
KA-BOOM!!
SPLAT
YEEK!
WHAT THE ...?
SAYANO KAEDE. OOTSUKI MIKI.
I HAVE COME TO SAVE YOU.
FSHHHH
COME WITH ME IF YOU WANT TO LIVE.
DA-DAN

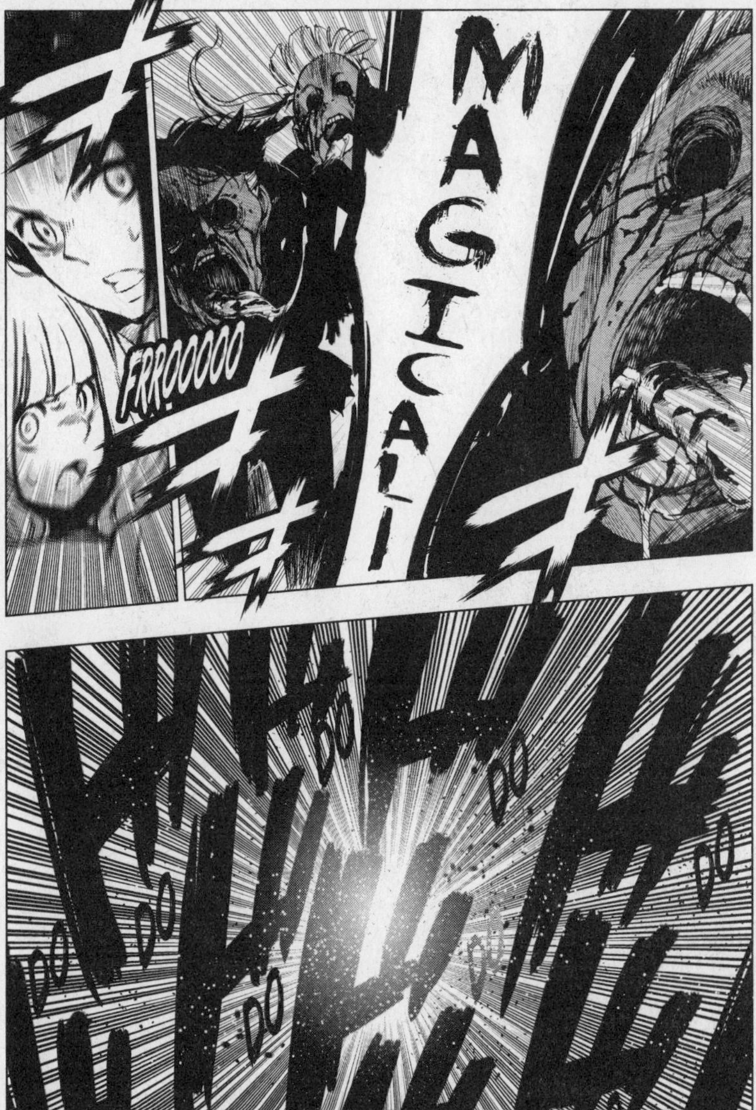
MAGICAL!
FRROOOOO
DO
DO
DO
DO
DO
DO
DO
DO
DO
DO
DO

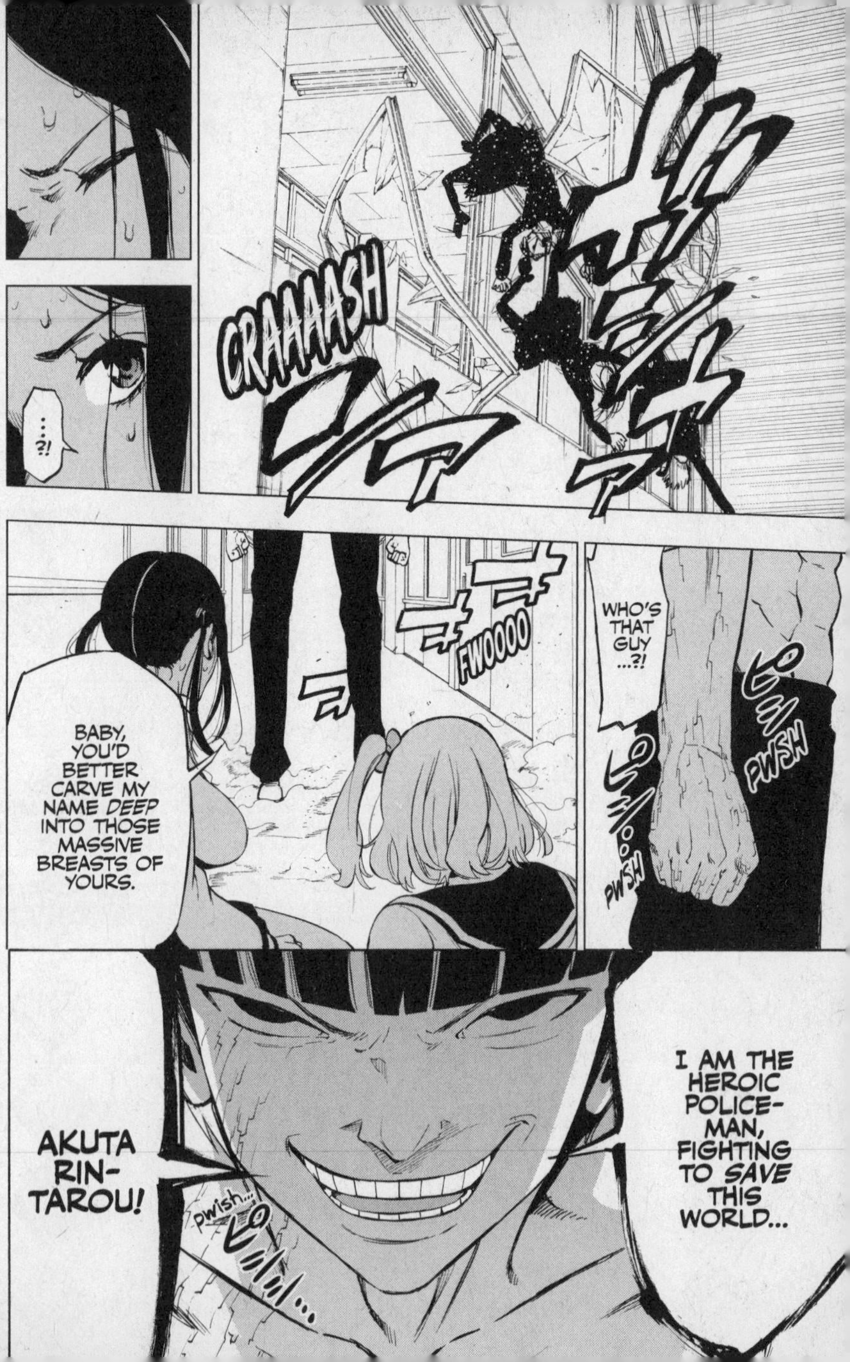
CRAAAASH
...?!
WHO'S THAT GUY ...?!
PWSH
PWSH
FWOOOO
BABY, YOU'D BETTER CARVE MY NAME DEEP INTO THOSE MASSIVE BREASTS OF YOURS.
I AM THE HEROIC POLICE-MAN, FIGHTING TO SAVE THIS WORLD...
AKUTA RIN-TAROU!
pwish...

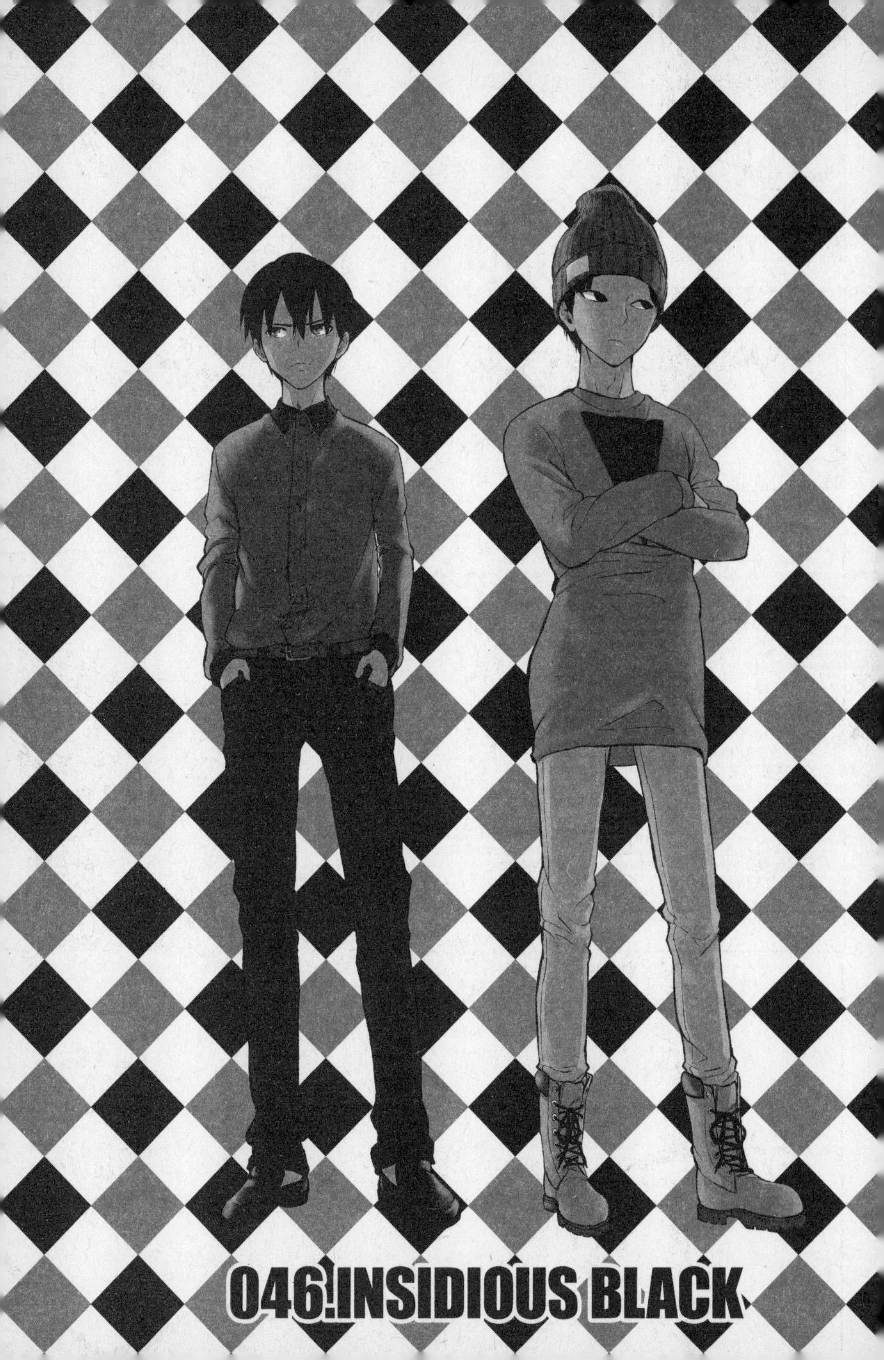

# 046.INSIDIOUS BLACK

MAGICAL GIRL
APOCALYPSE

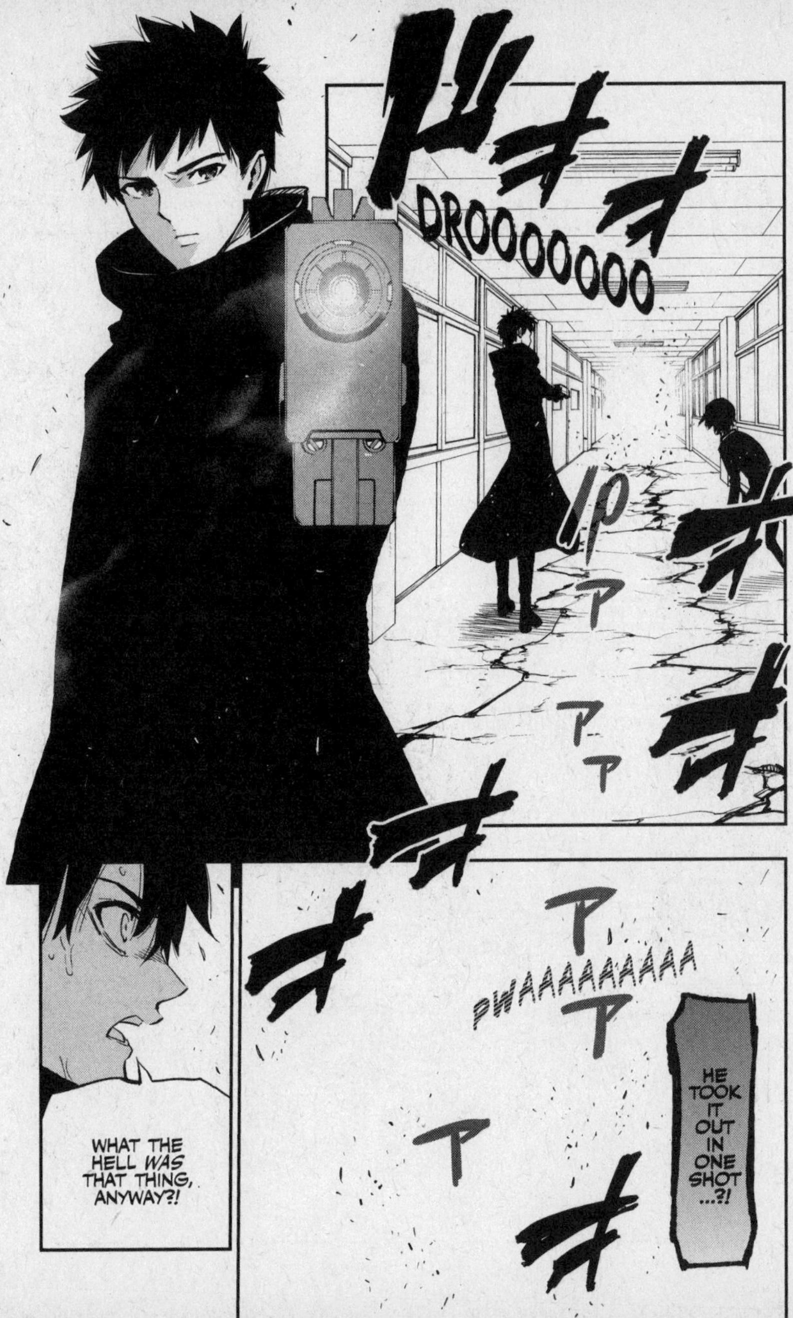

DROOOOOOOO
PWAAAAAAAAA
HE TOOK IT OUT IN ONE SHOT ...?!
WHAT THE HELL *WAS* THAT THING, ANYWAY?!

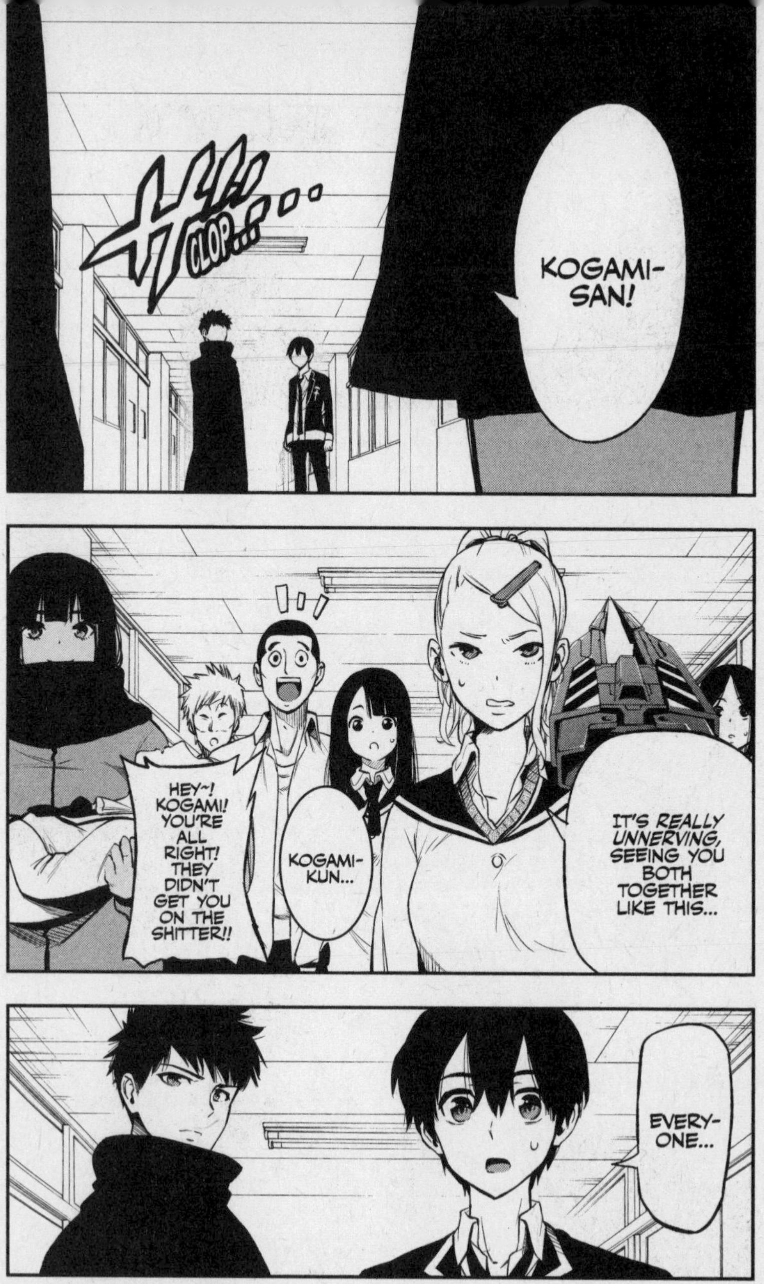
KOGAMI-SAN!
CLOP...
IT'S *REALLY* UNNERVING, SEEING YOU BOTH TOGETHER LIKE THIS...
KOGAMI-KUN...
HEY~! KOGAMI! YOU'RE ALL RIGHT! THEY DIDN'T GET YOU ON THE SHITTER!!
EVERY-ONE...

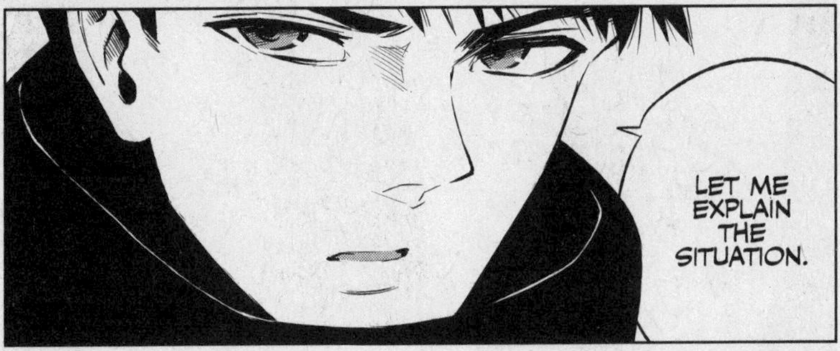
LET ME EXPLAIN THE SITUATION.

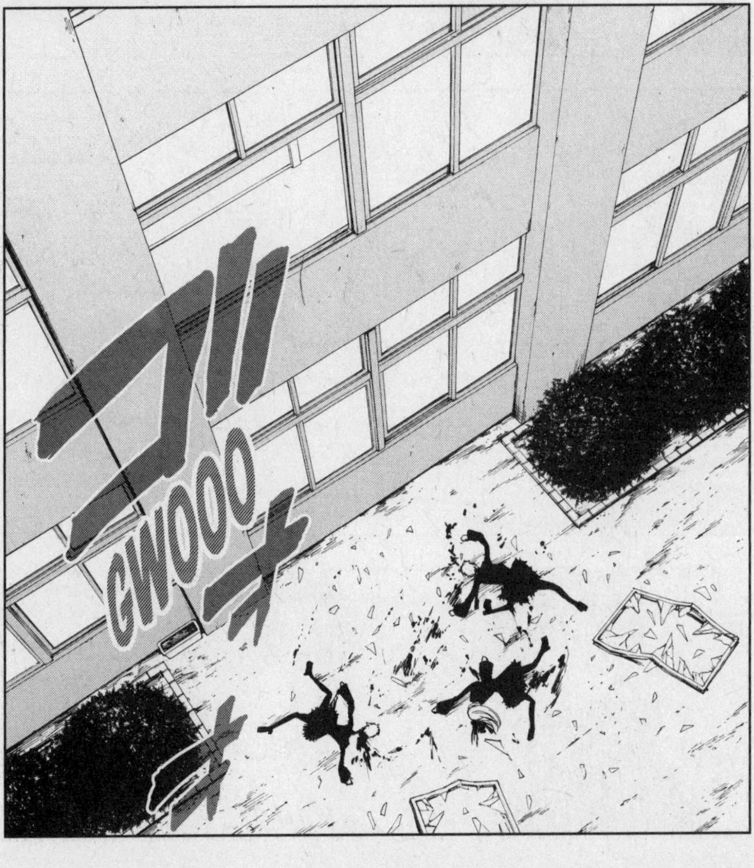
GWOOO

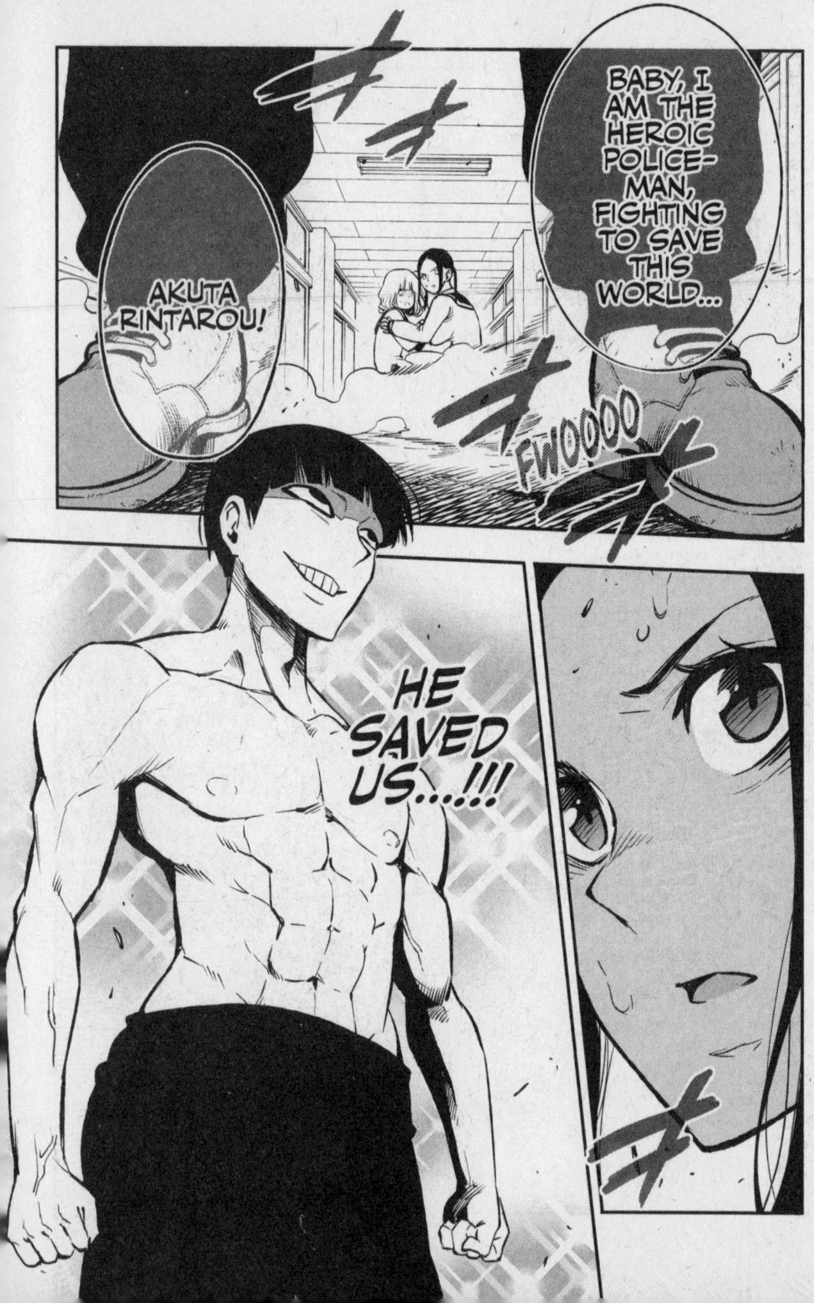
BABY, I AM THE HEROIC POLICE-MAN, FIGHTING TO SAVE THIS WORLD...
AKUTA RINTAROU!
FWOOOO
HE SAVED US...!!!

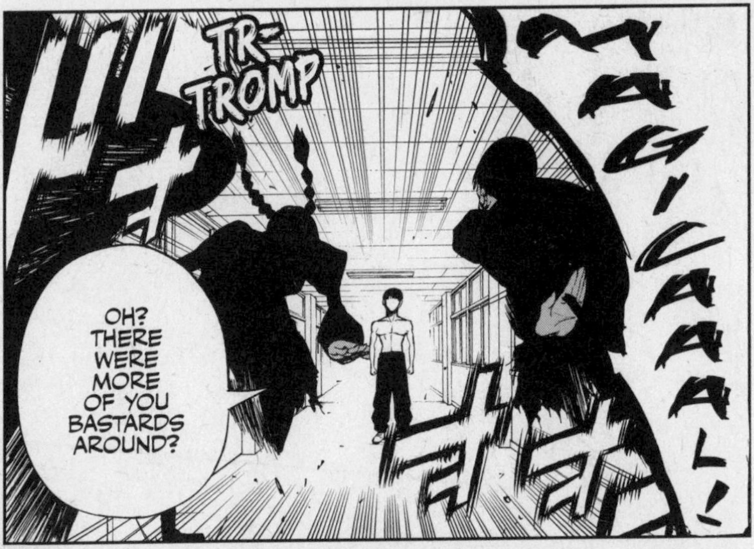
MAGICAAAL!
TR-
TROMP
OH? THERE WERE MORE OF YOU BASTARDS AROUND?
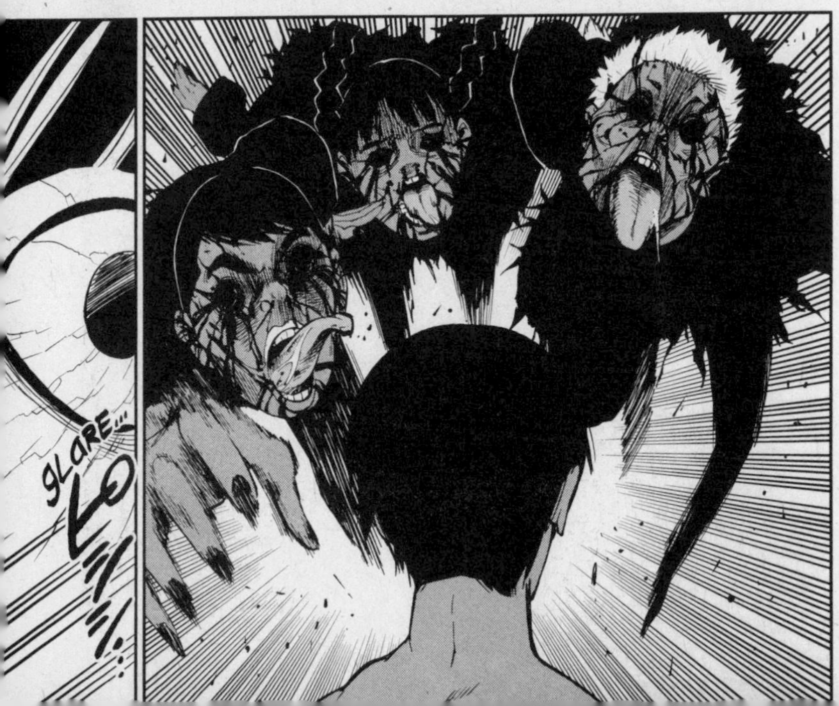
GLARE...

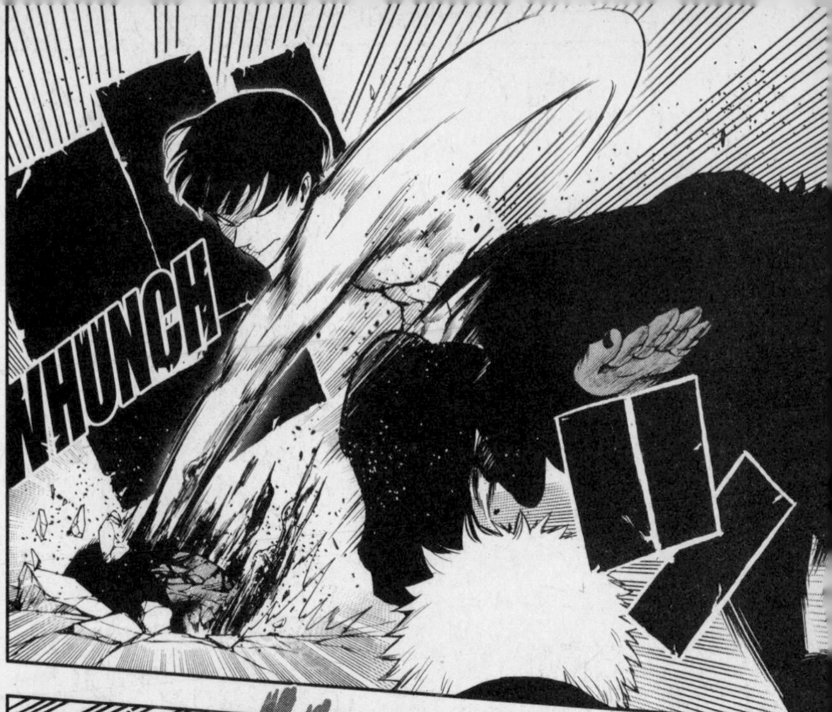
WHUNCH
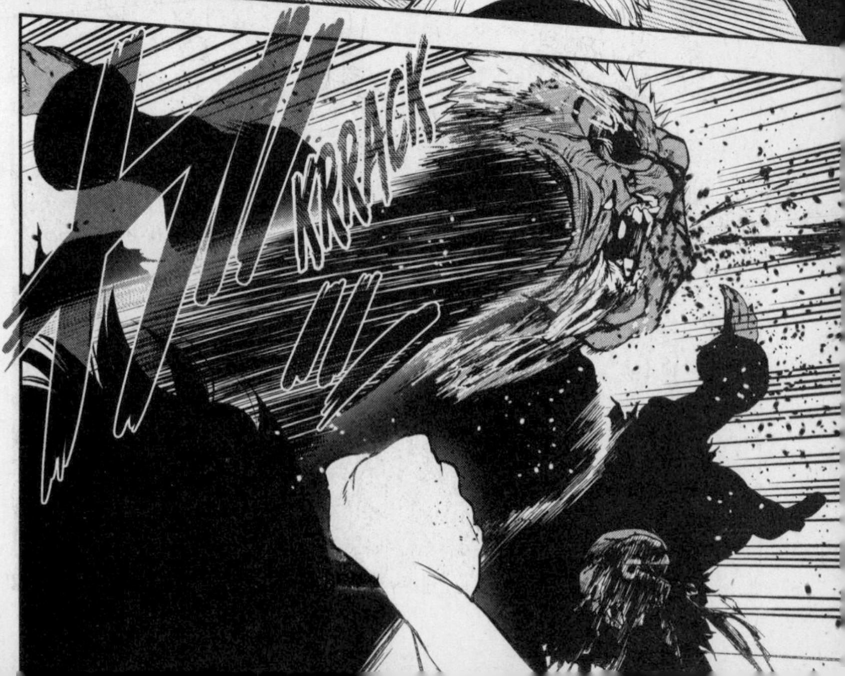
KRRACK

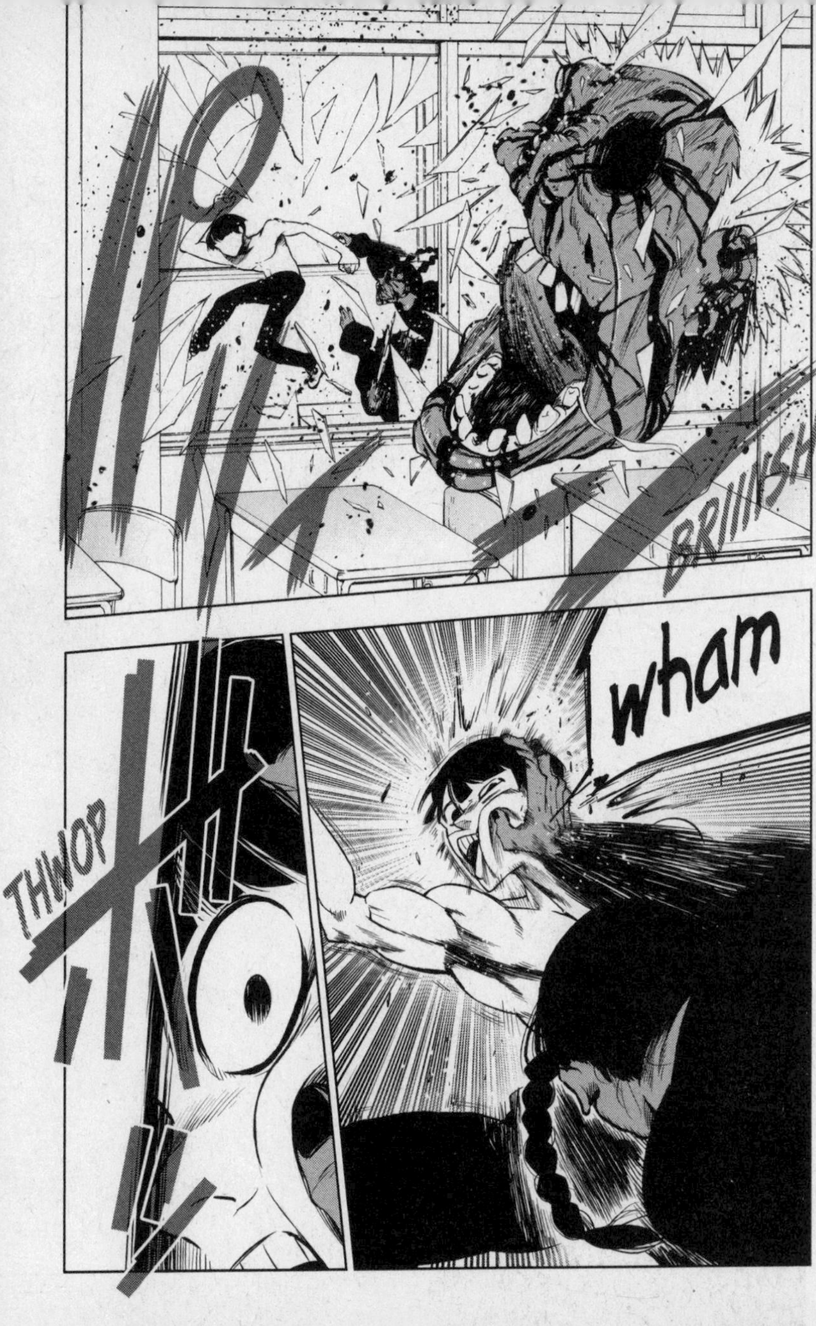
BRIIISH
wham
THWOP

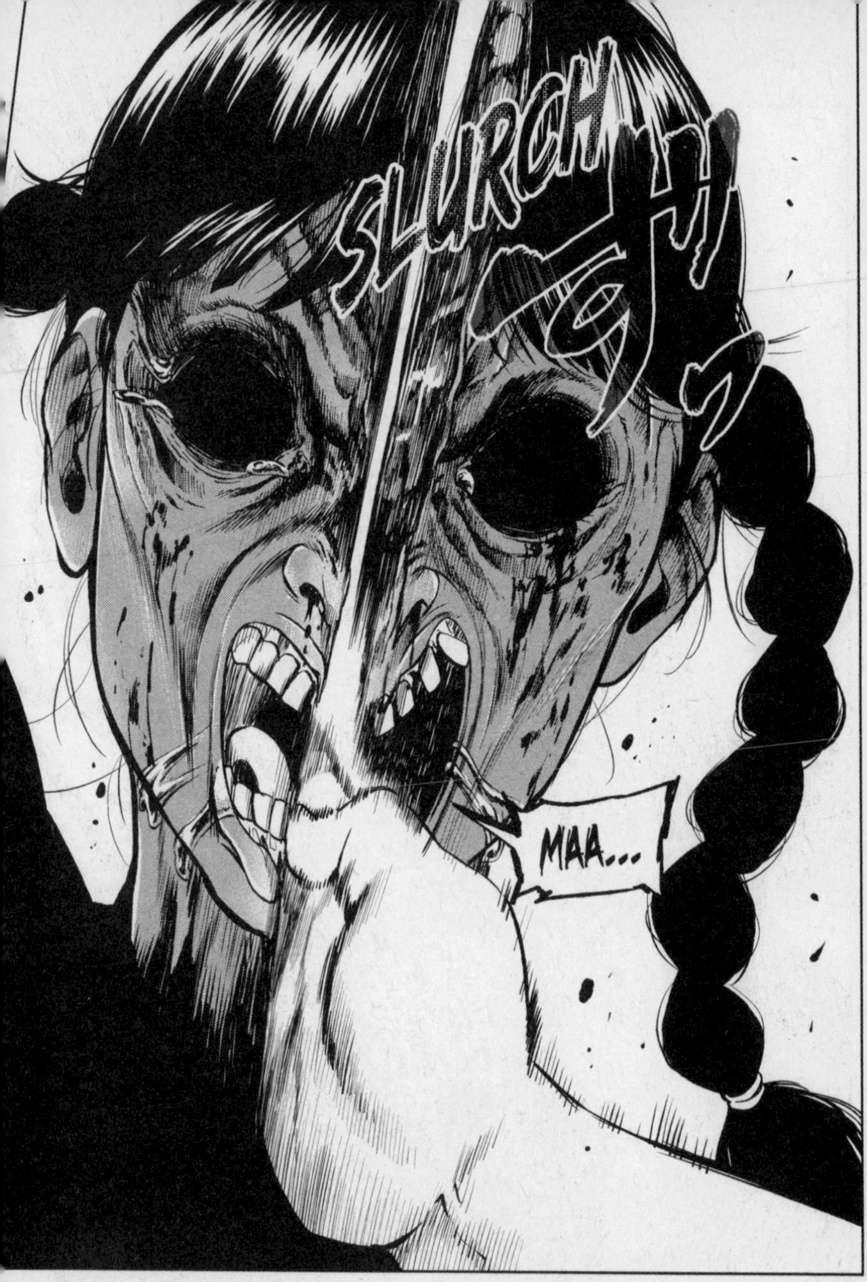
SLURCH
MAA...

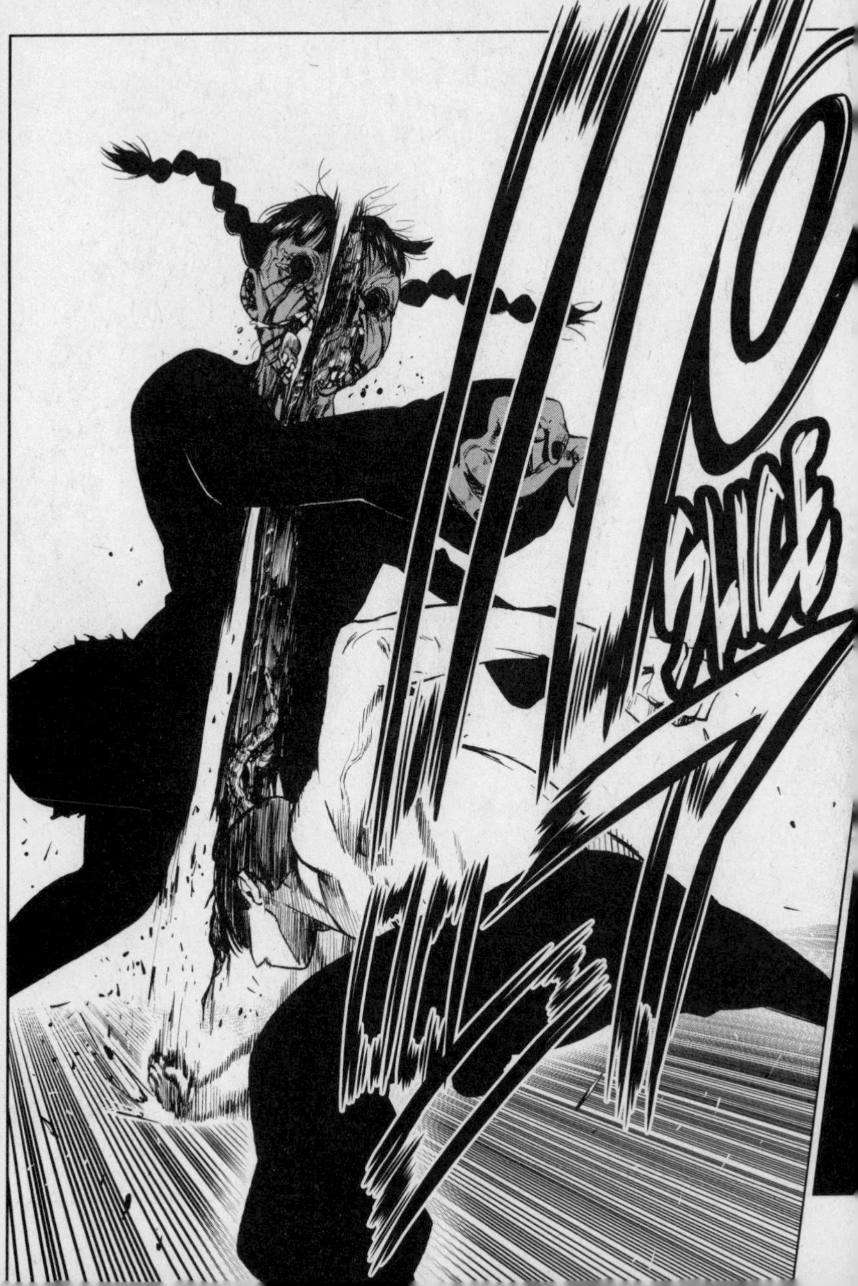
SLICE

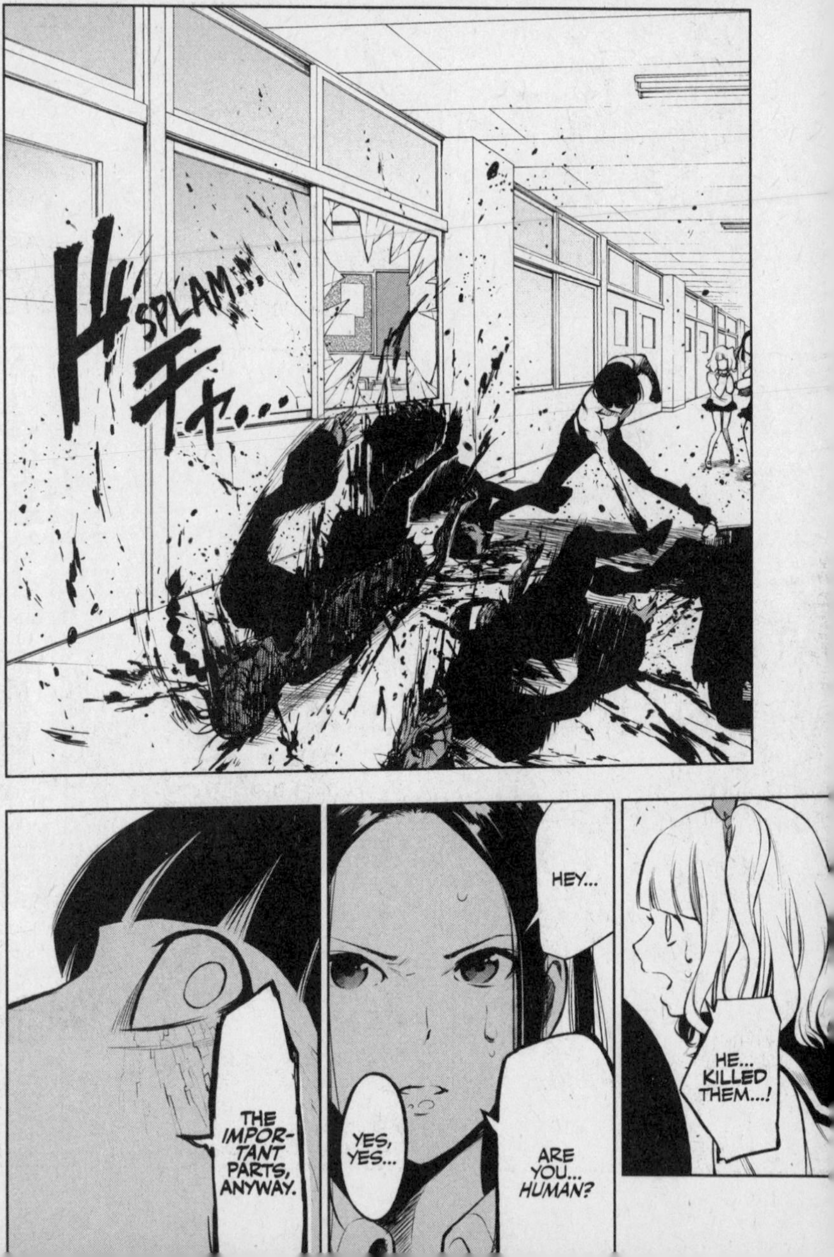
ドチャ...
SPLAM...!!
HE... KILLED THEM...!
HEY...
ARE YOU... HUMAN?
YES, YES...
THE IMPORTANT PARTS, ANYWAY.

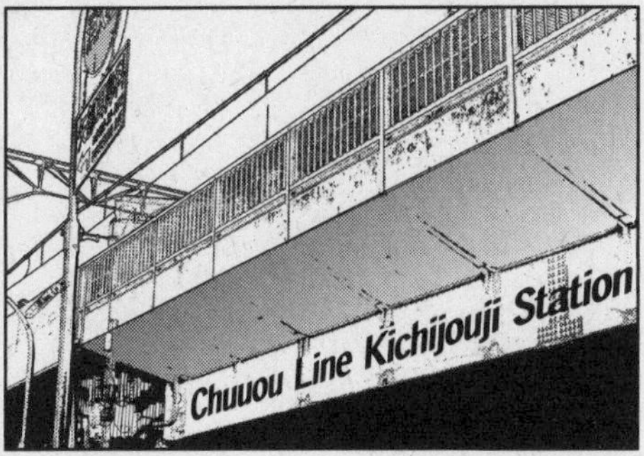
Chuuou Line Kichijouji Station
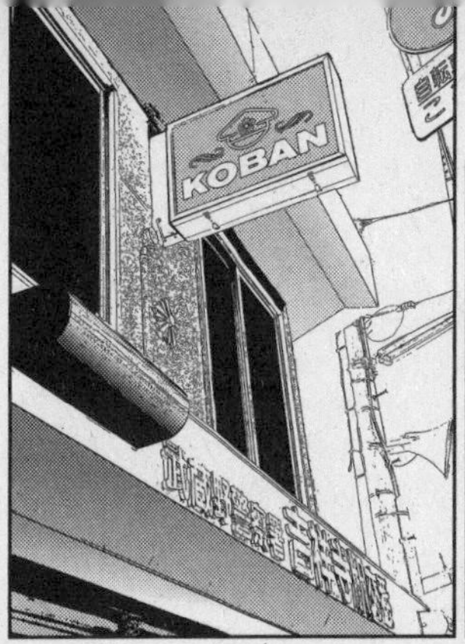
KOBAN
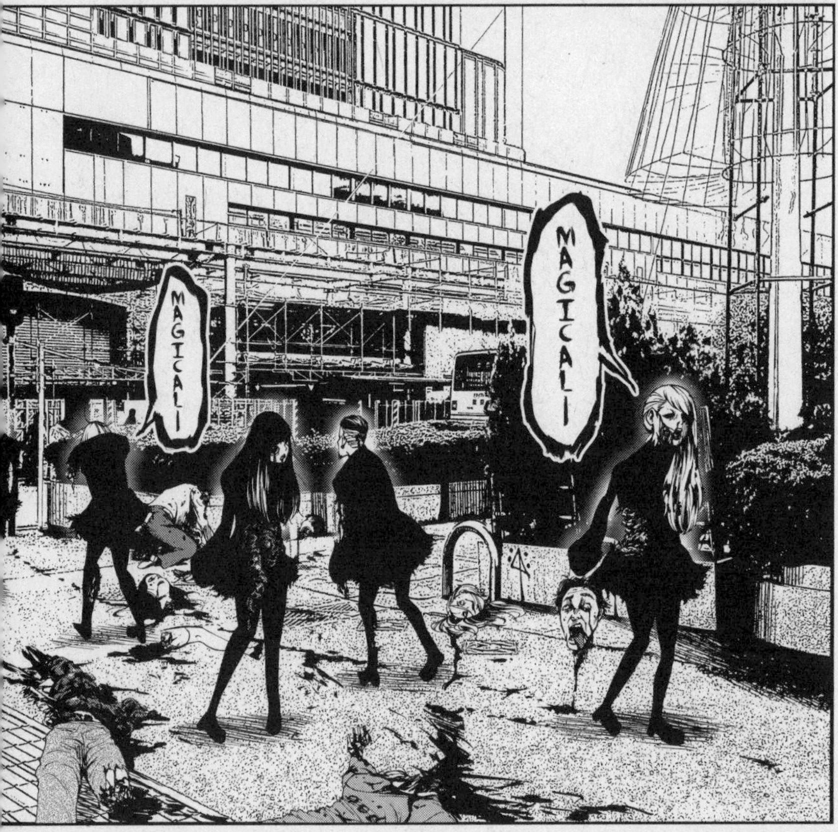
MAGICALI
MAGICALI

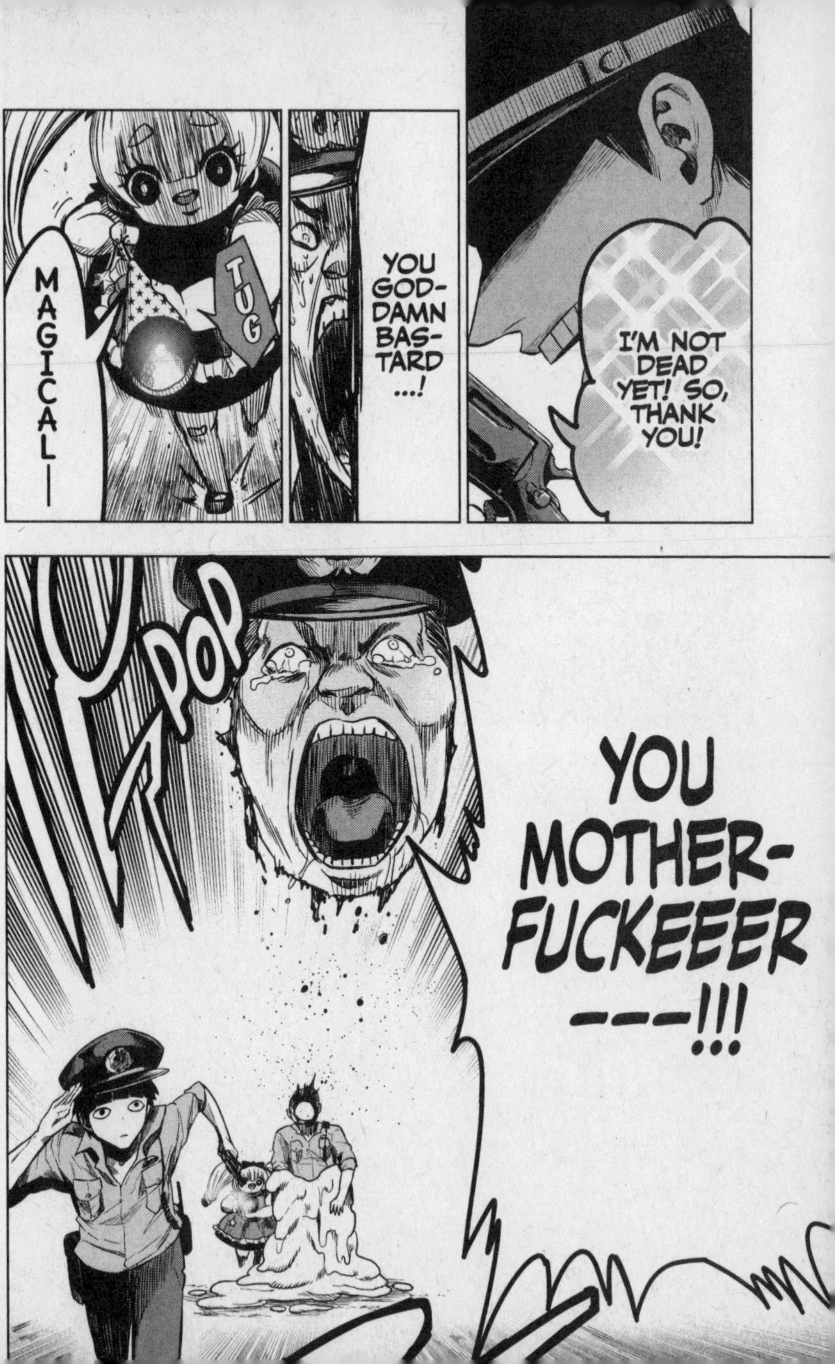
I'M NOT DEAD YET! SO, THANK YOU!
YOU GOD-DAMN BAS-TARD ....!
TUG
MAGICAL—
POP
YOU MOTHER-FUCKEEER ---!!!

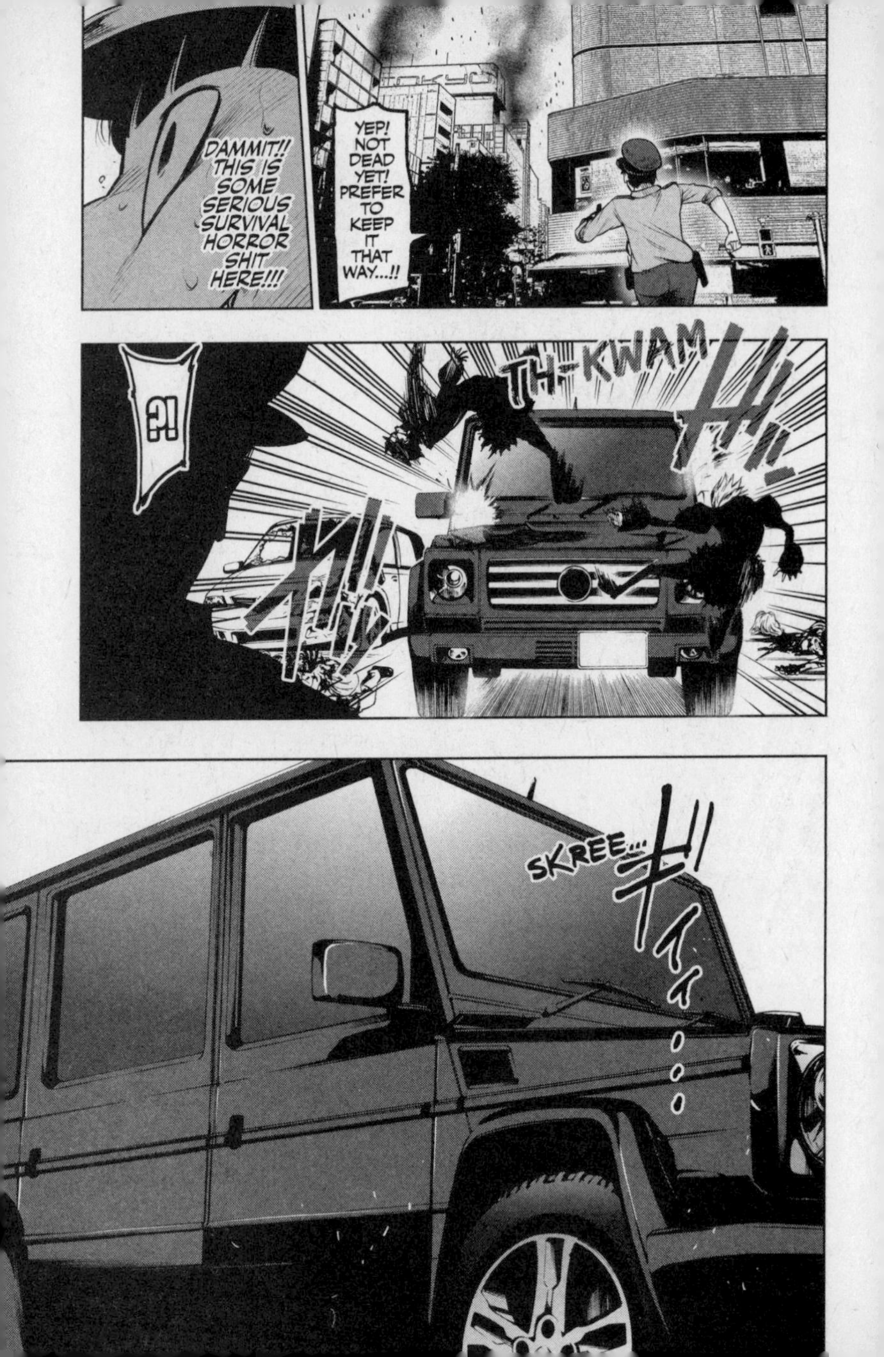
YEP! NOT DEAD YET! PREFER TO KEEP IT THAT WAY...!!
DAMMIT!! THIS IS SOME SERIOUS SURVIVAL HORROR SHIT HERE!!!
?!
TH-KWAM
SKREE...

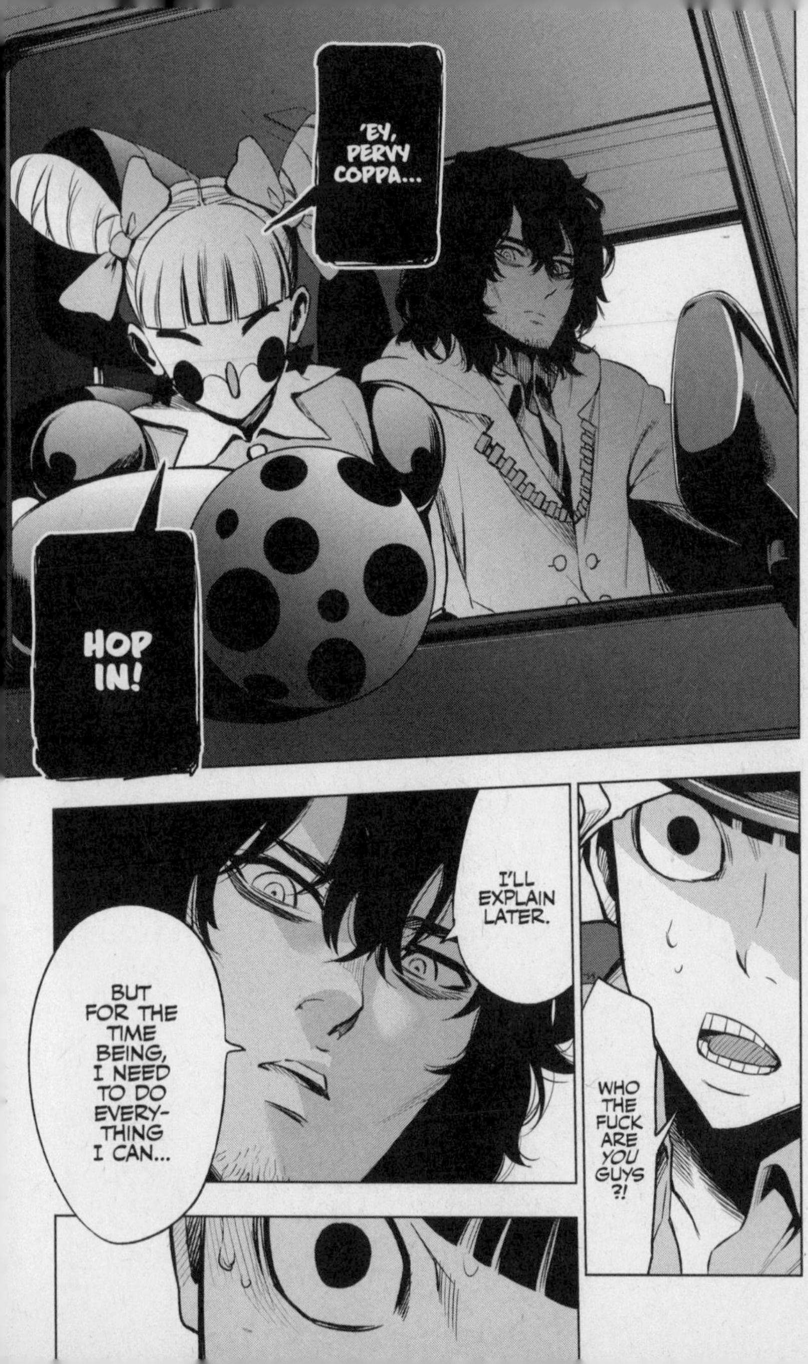
'EY, PERVY COPPA...
HOP IN!
WHO THE FUCK ARE YOU GUYS?!
I'LL EXPLAIN LATER.
BUT FOR THE TIME BEING, I NEED TO DO EVERY-THING I CAN...

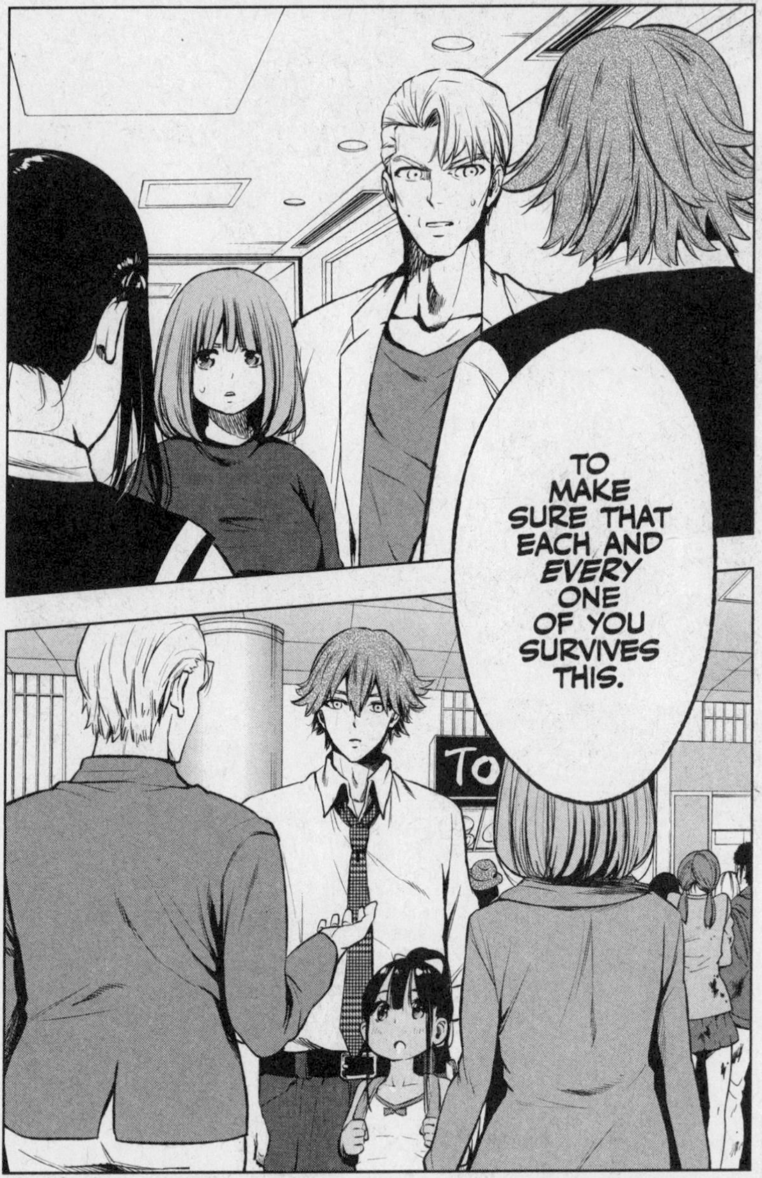
TO MAKE SURE THAT EACH AND *EVERY* ONE OF YOU SURVIVES THIS.
TO

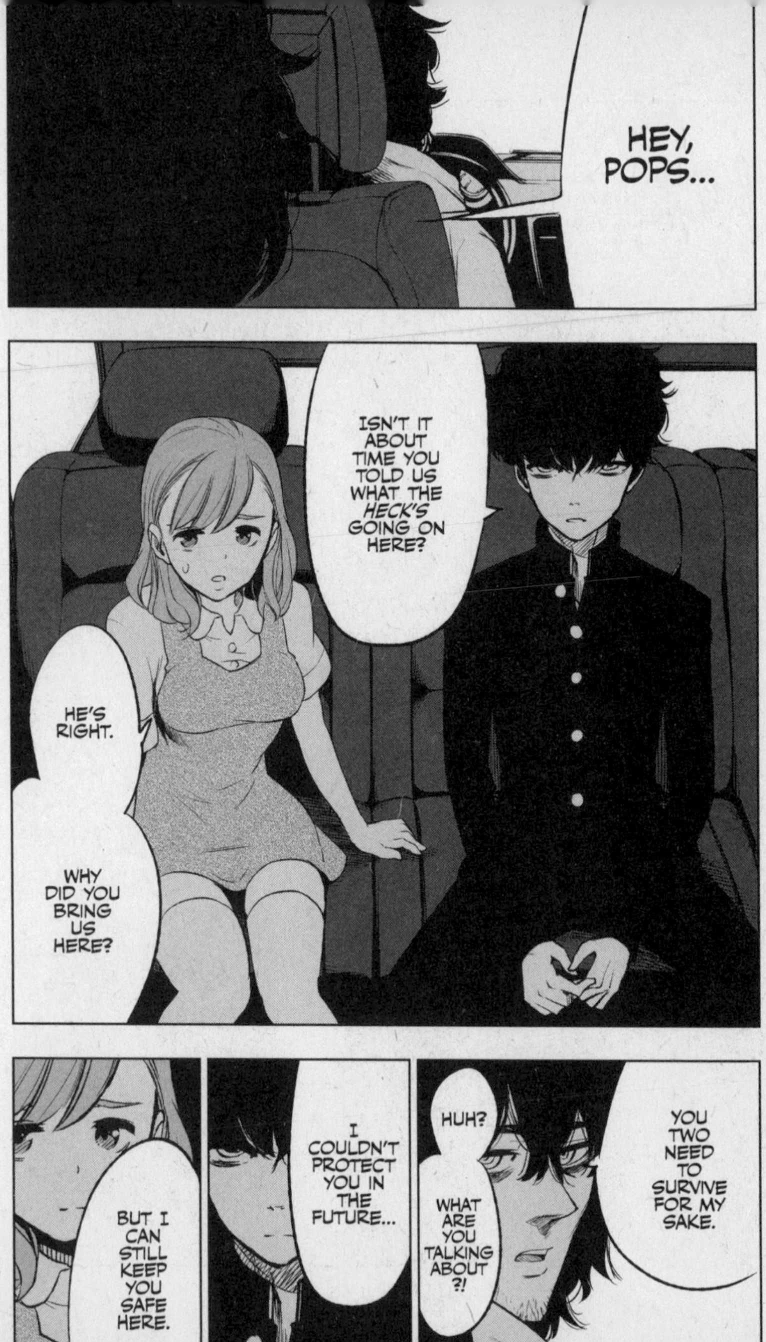
HEY, POPS...
ISN'T IT ABOUT TIME YOU TOLD US WHAT THE *HECK'S* GOING ON HERE?
HE'S RIGHT.
WHY DID YOU BRING US HERE?
YOU TWO NEED TO SURVIVE FOR MY SAKE.
HUH?
WHAT ARE YOU TALKING ABOUT?!
I COULDN'T PROTECT YOU IN THE FUTURE...
BUT I CAN STILL KEEP YOU SAFE HERE.

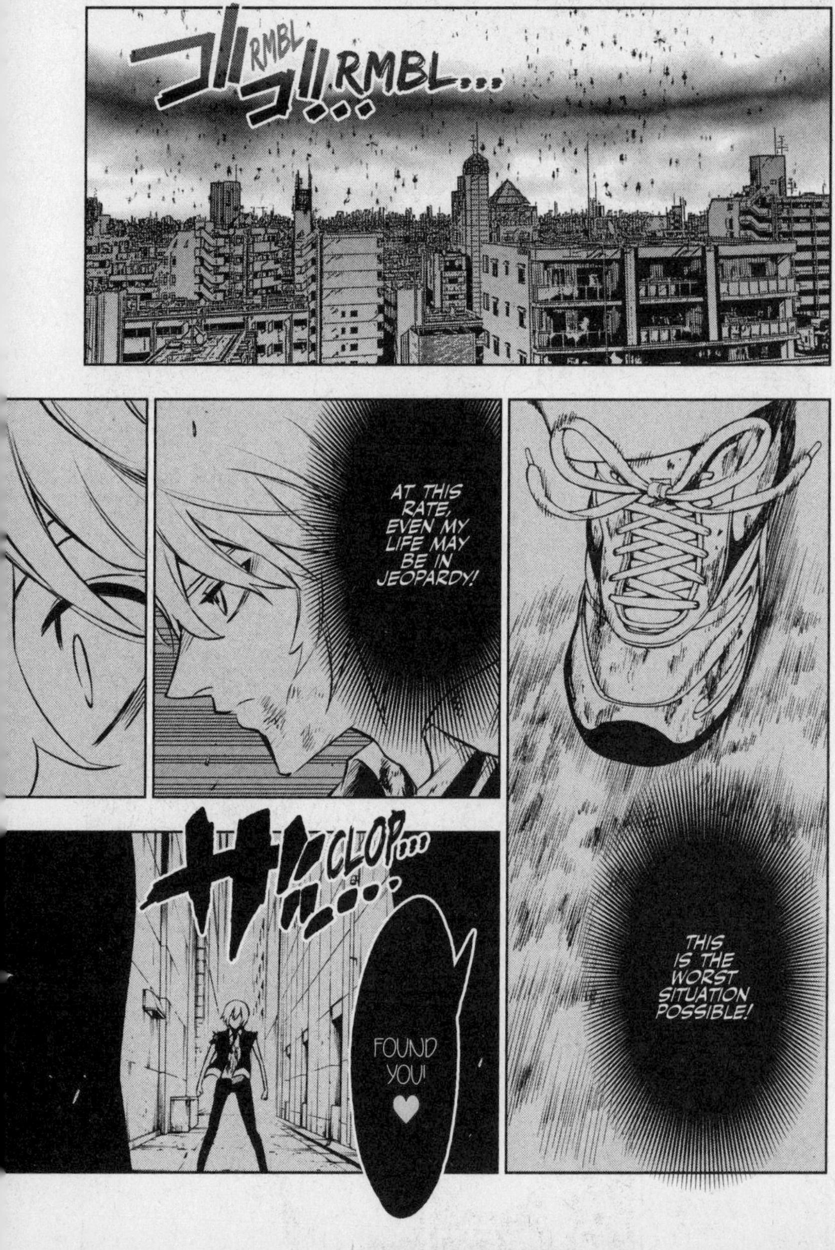
RMBL
RMBL...
THIS IS THE WORST SITUATION POSSIBLE!
AT THIS RATE, EVEN MY LIFE MAY BE IN JEOPARDY!
CLOP...
FOUND YOU! ♥

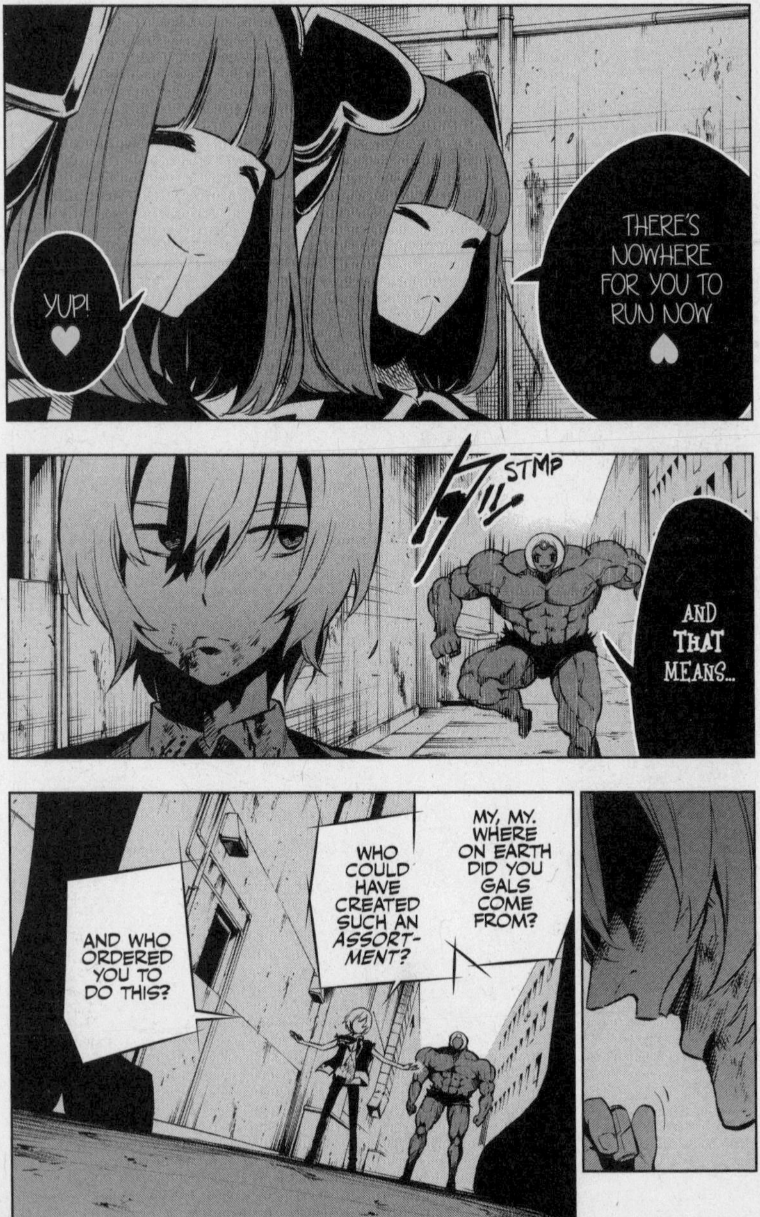
THERE'S NOWHERE FOR YOU TO RUN NOW ♥
YUP! ♥
STMP
AND THAT MEANS...
MY, MY. WHERE ON EARTH DID YOU GALS COME FROM?
WHO COULD HAVE CREATED SUCH AN ASSORT-MENT?
AND WHO ORDERED YOU TO DO THIS?

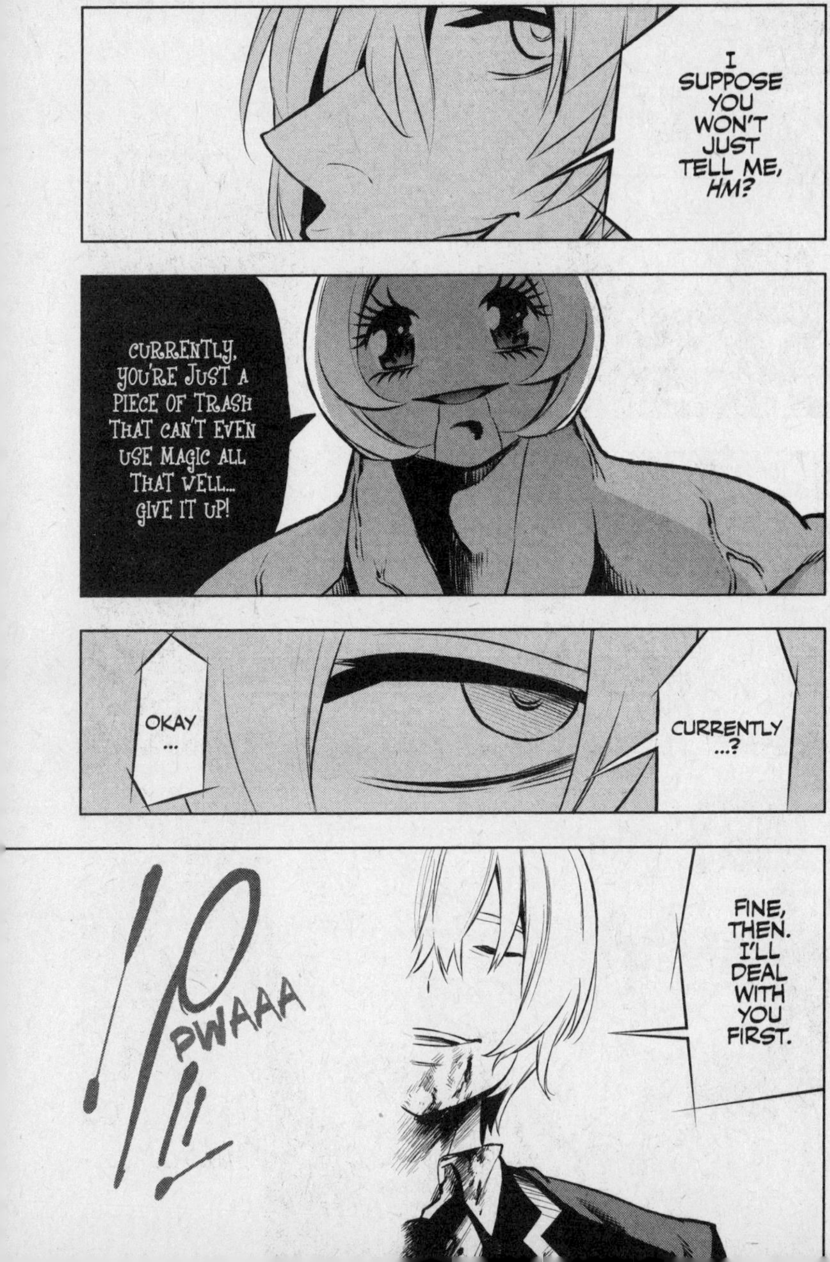
I SUPPOSE YOU WON'T JUST TELL ME, HM?
CURRENTLY, YOU'RE JUST A PIECE OF TRASH THAT CAN'T EVEN USE MAGIC ALL THAT WELL... GIVE IT UP!
CURRENTLY ...?
OKAY ...
FINE, THEN. I'LL DEAL WITH YOU FIRST.
PWAAA !!

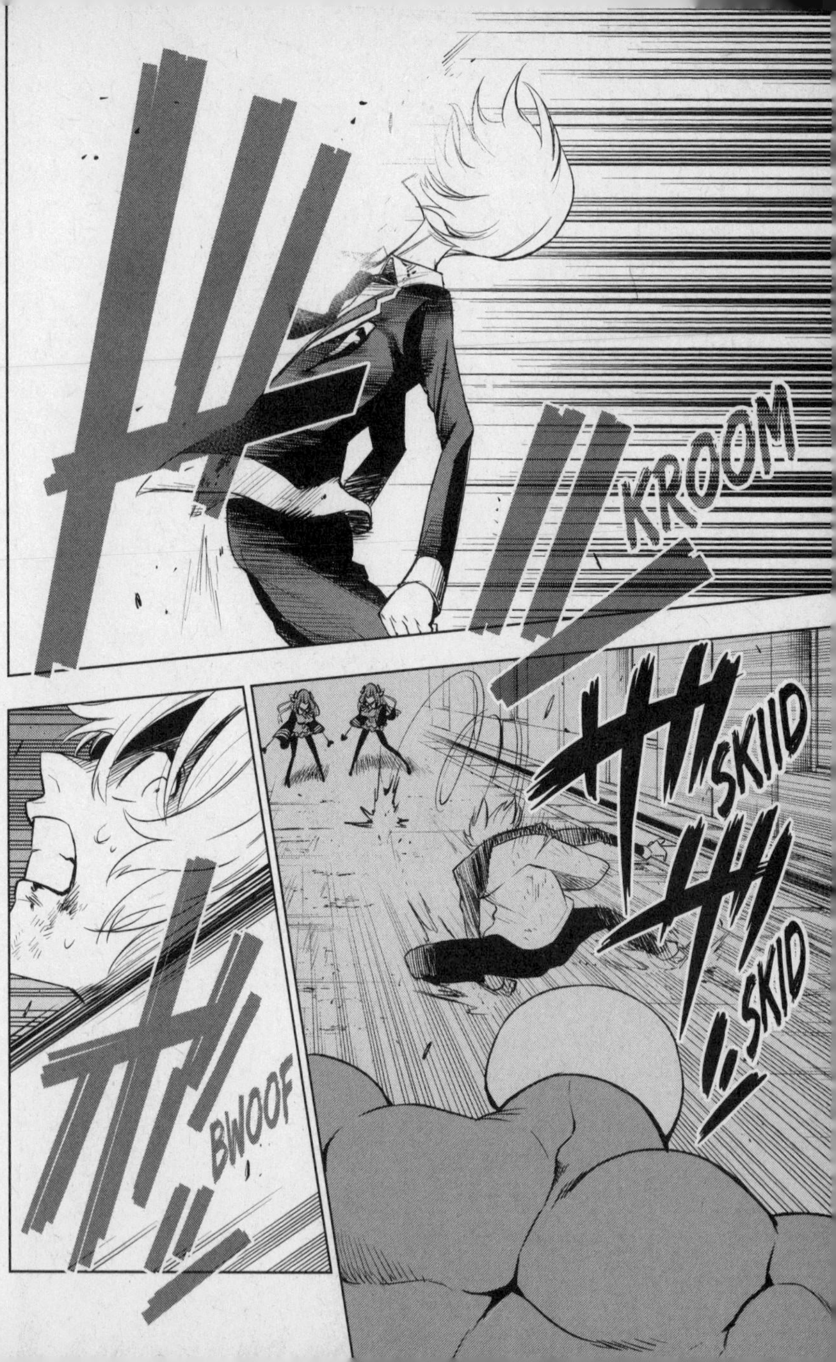
KROOM
SKIID
SKID
BWOOF

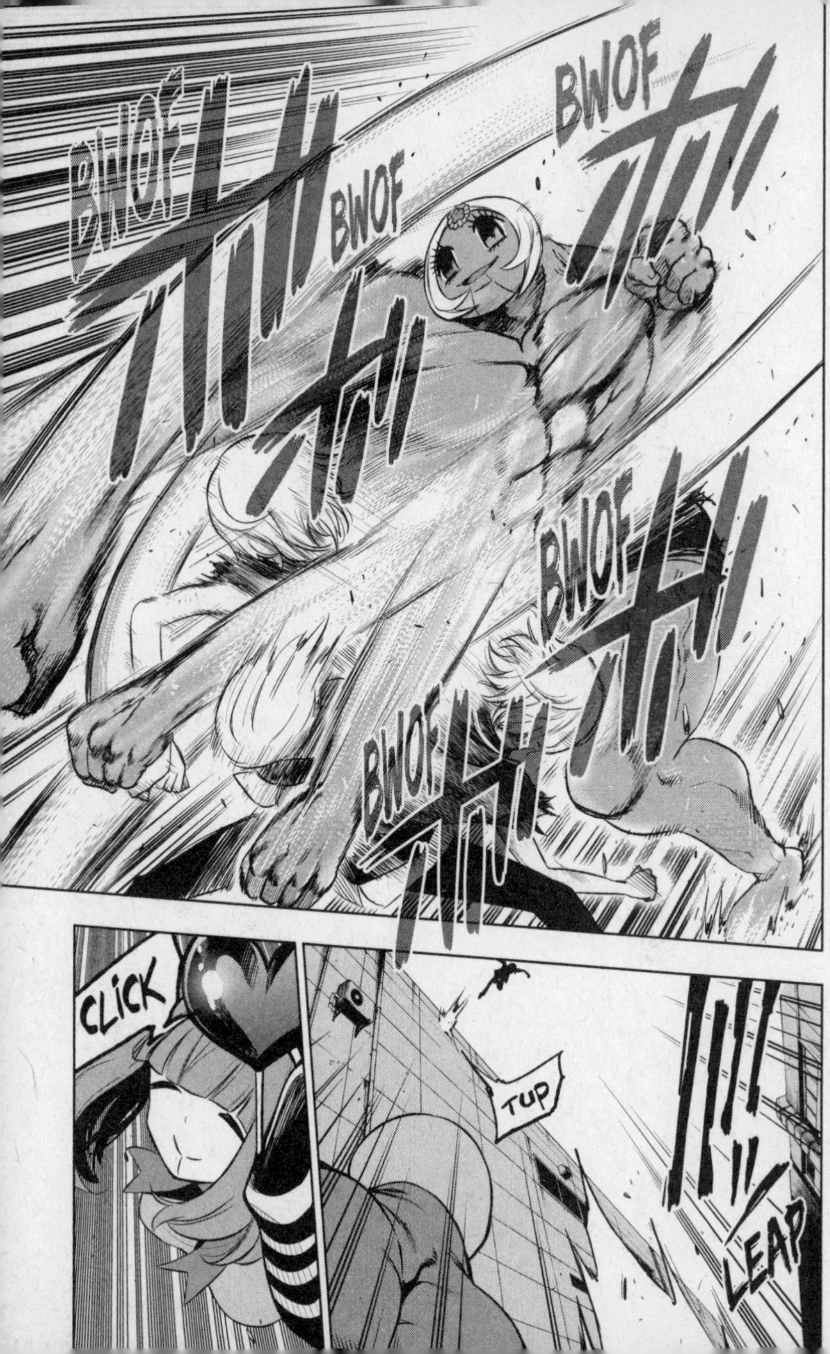
BWOF
BWOF
BWOF
BWOF
BWOF
TUP
LEAP
CLICK

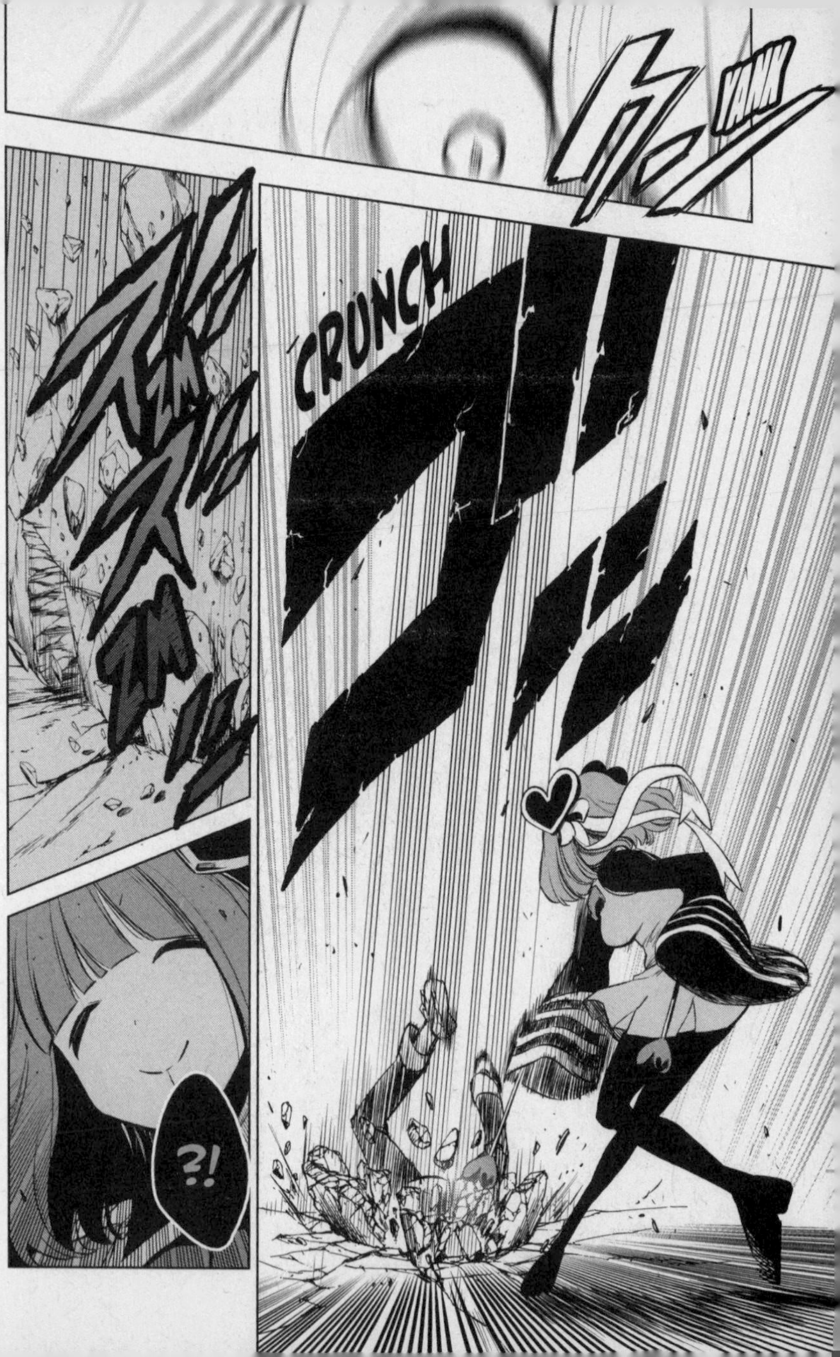

YANK
CRUNCH
?!

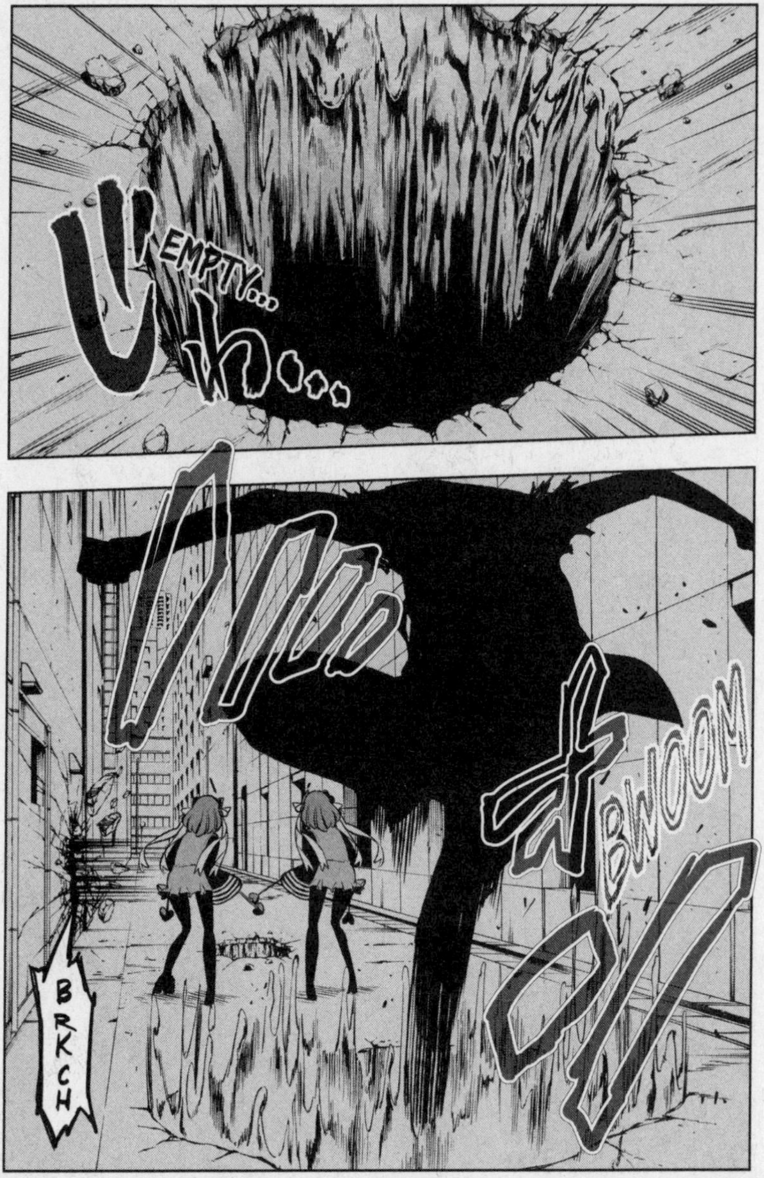
EMPTY...
BWOOM
BRKCH

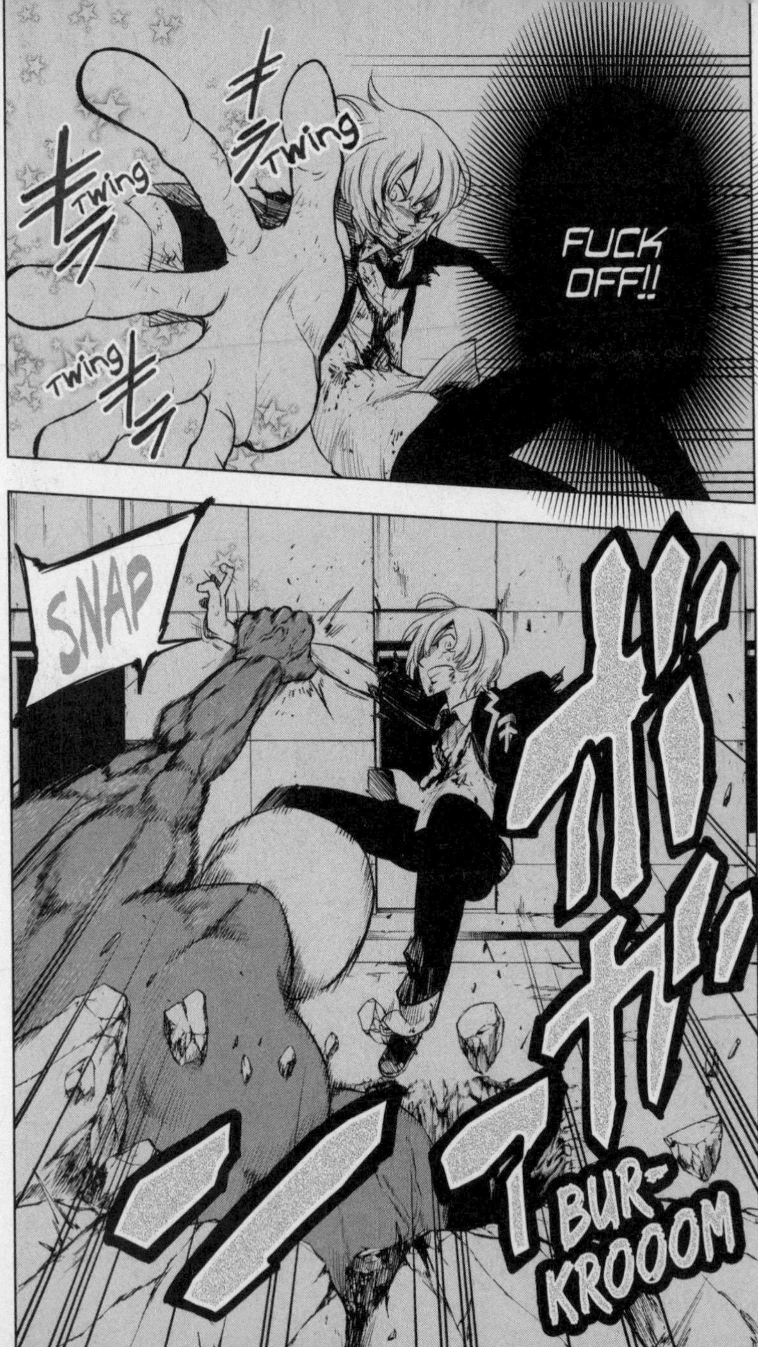
FUCK OFF!!
Twing
Twing
Twing
BUR-KROOOM
SNAP

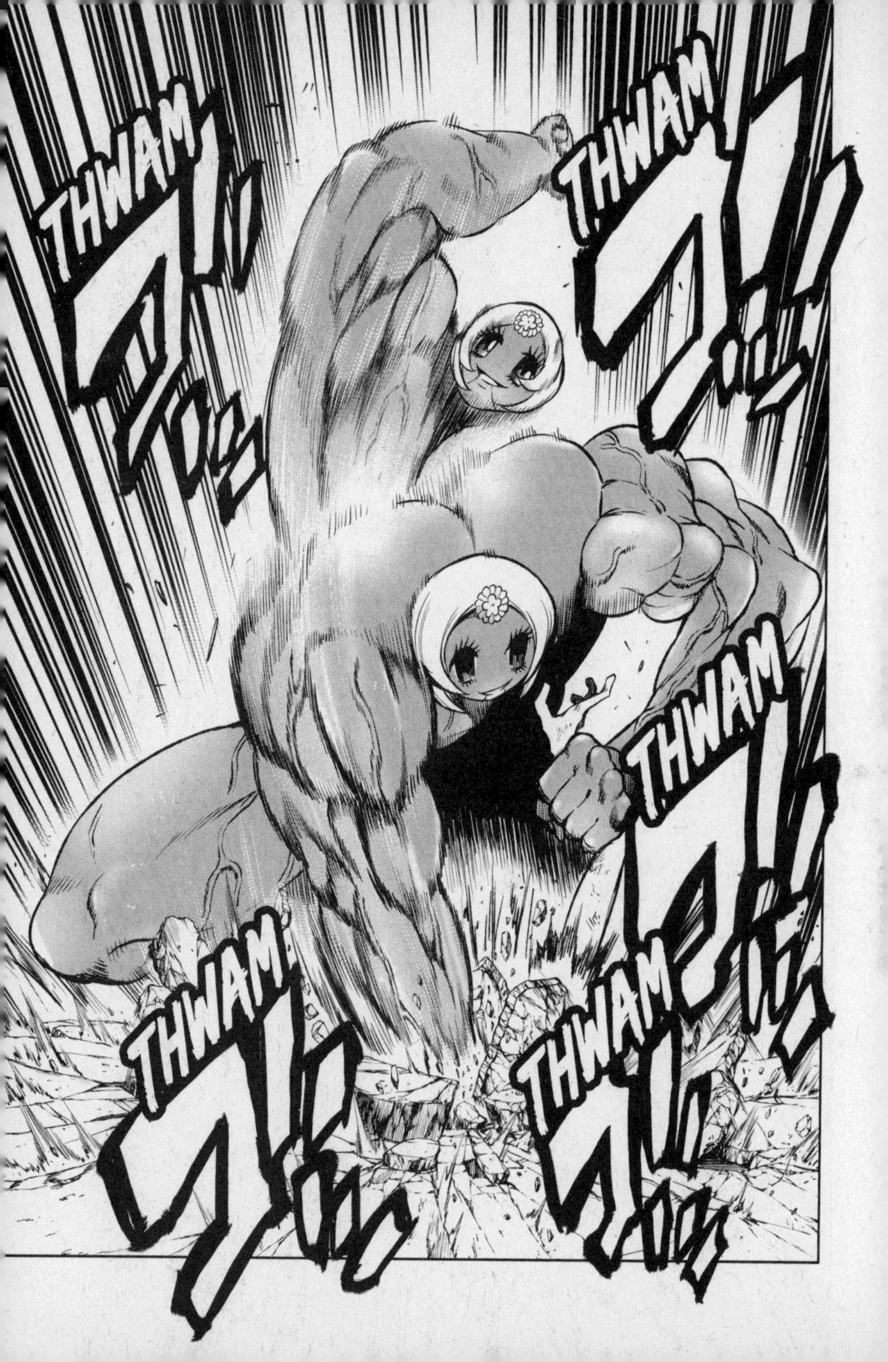
THWAM
THWAM
THWAM
THWAM
THWAM

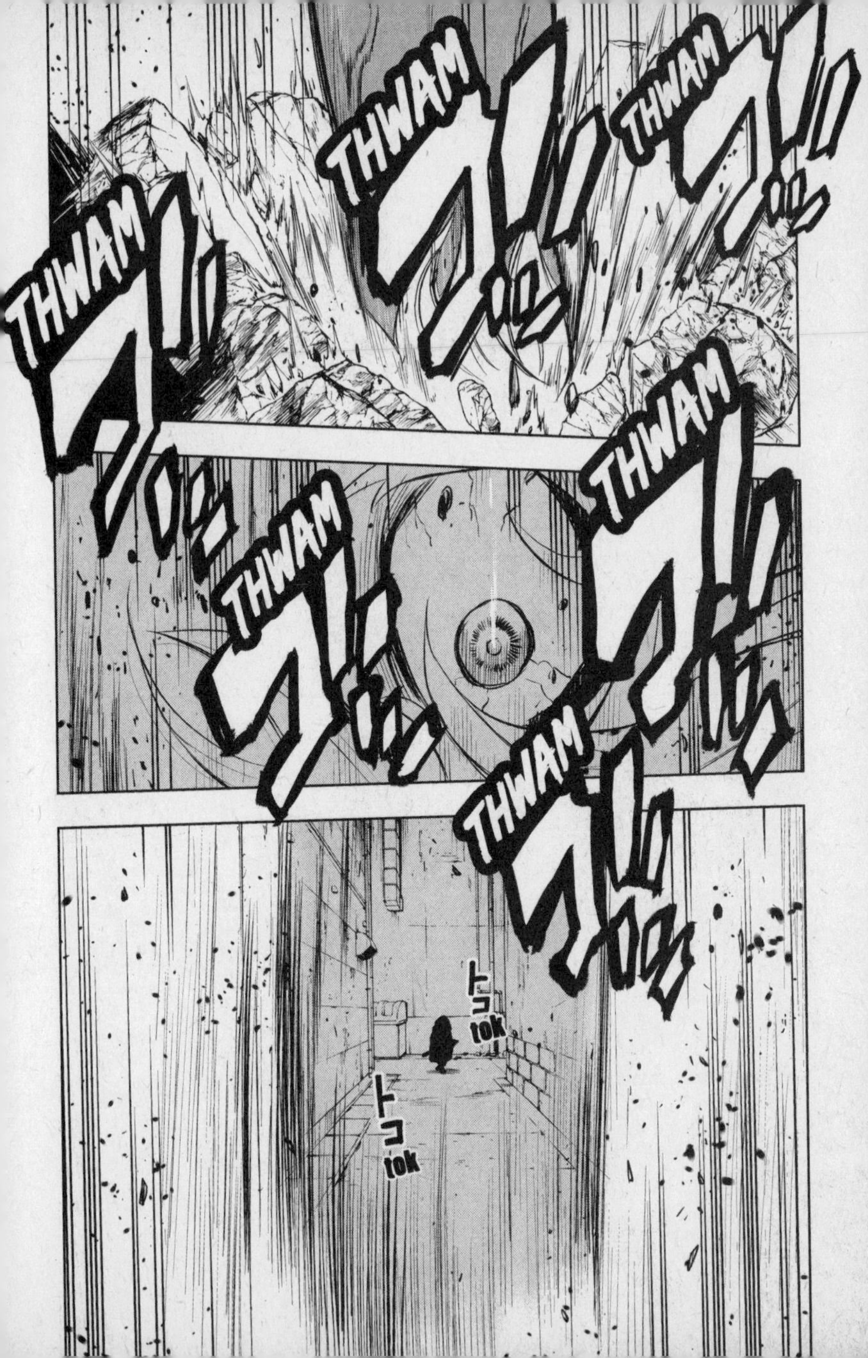
THWAM
THWAM
THWAM
THWAM
THWAM
THWAM
トコ tok
トコ tok

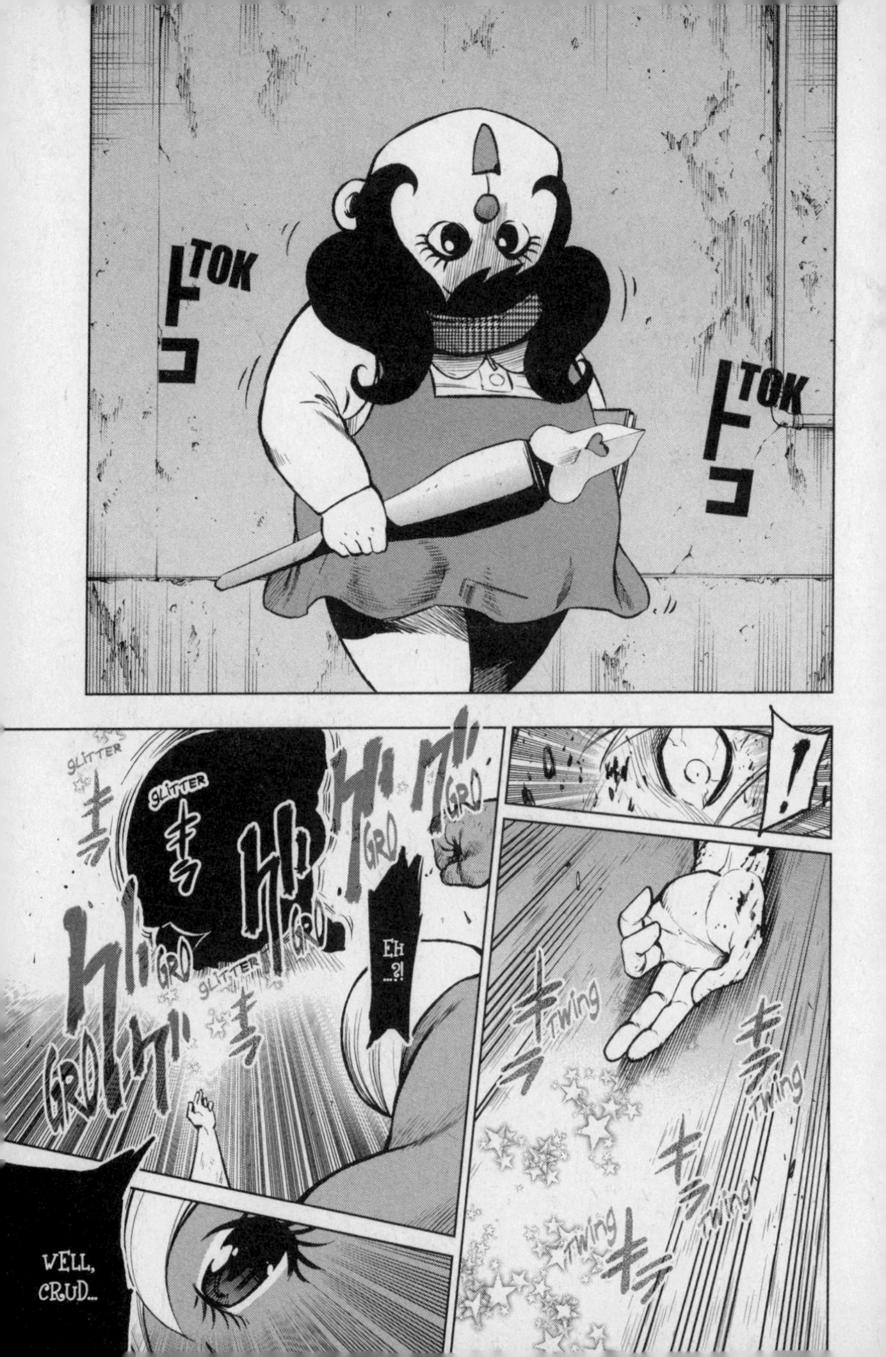

TOK
TOK
!
TWING
TWING
TWING
TWING
GRO
GRO
GRO
GRO
GRO
GLITTER
GLITTER
GLITTER
EH ...?!
WELL, CRUD...

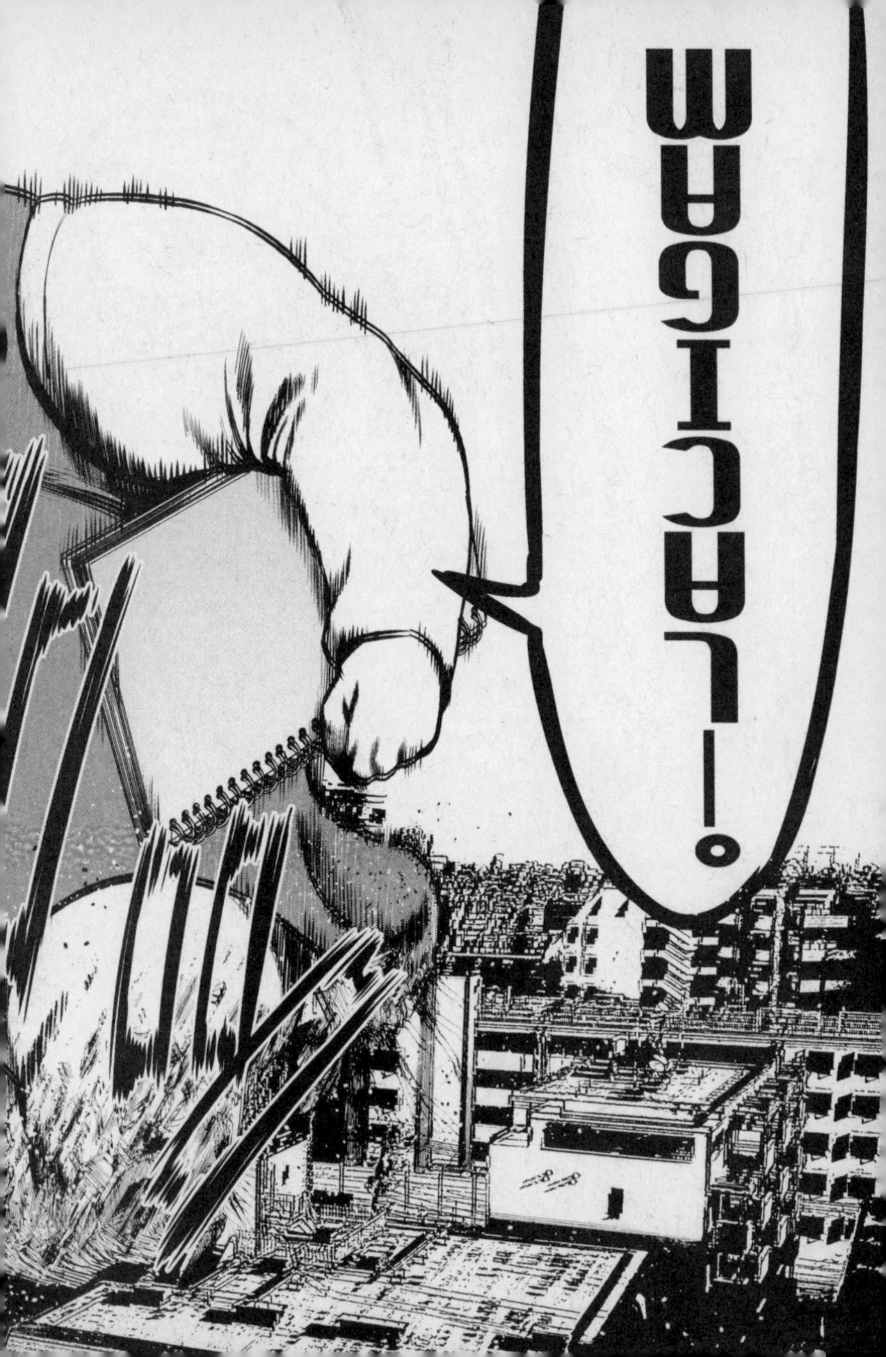
MAGICAL!

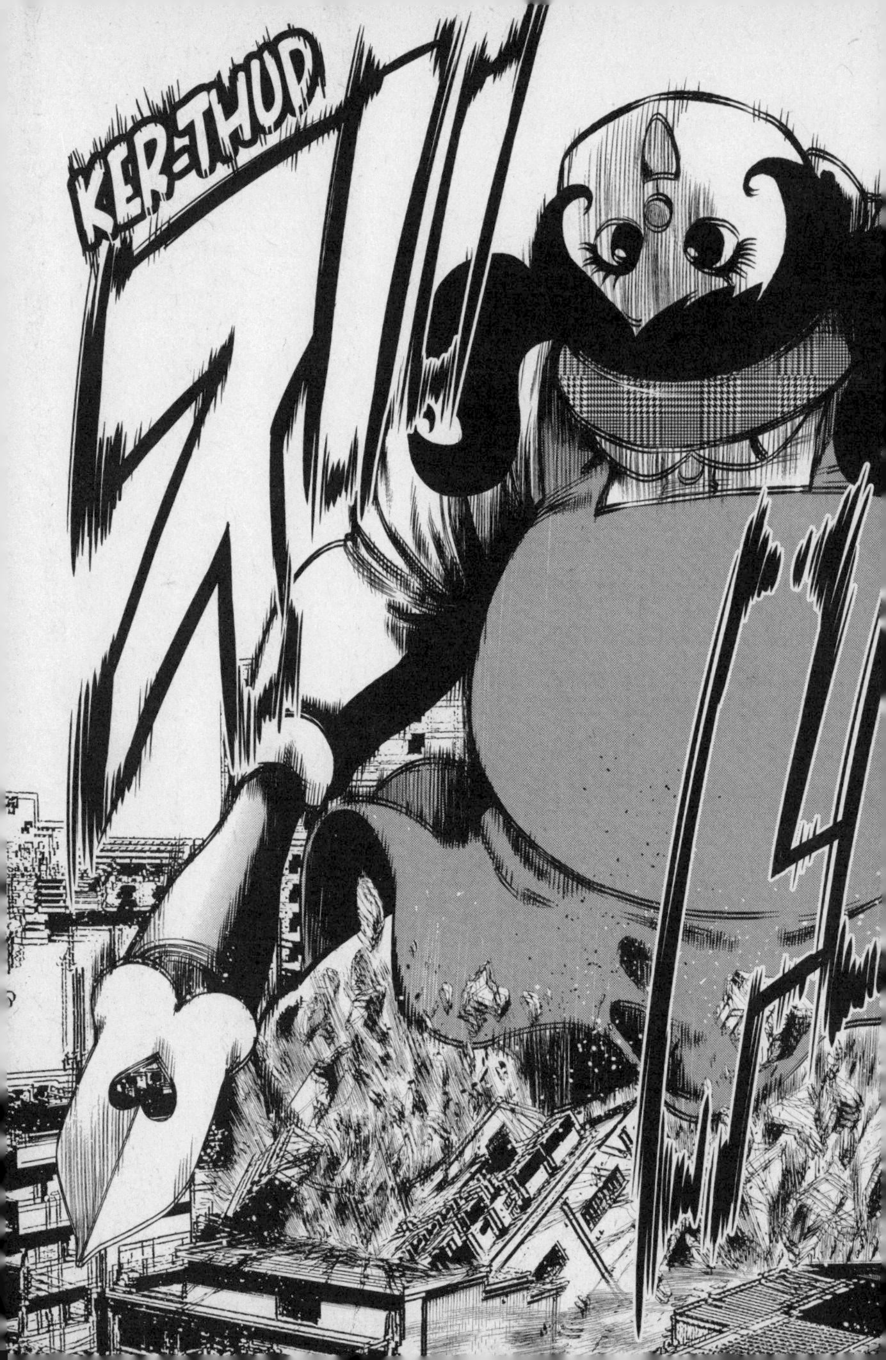
KER-THUD

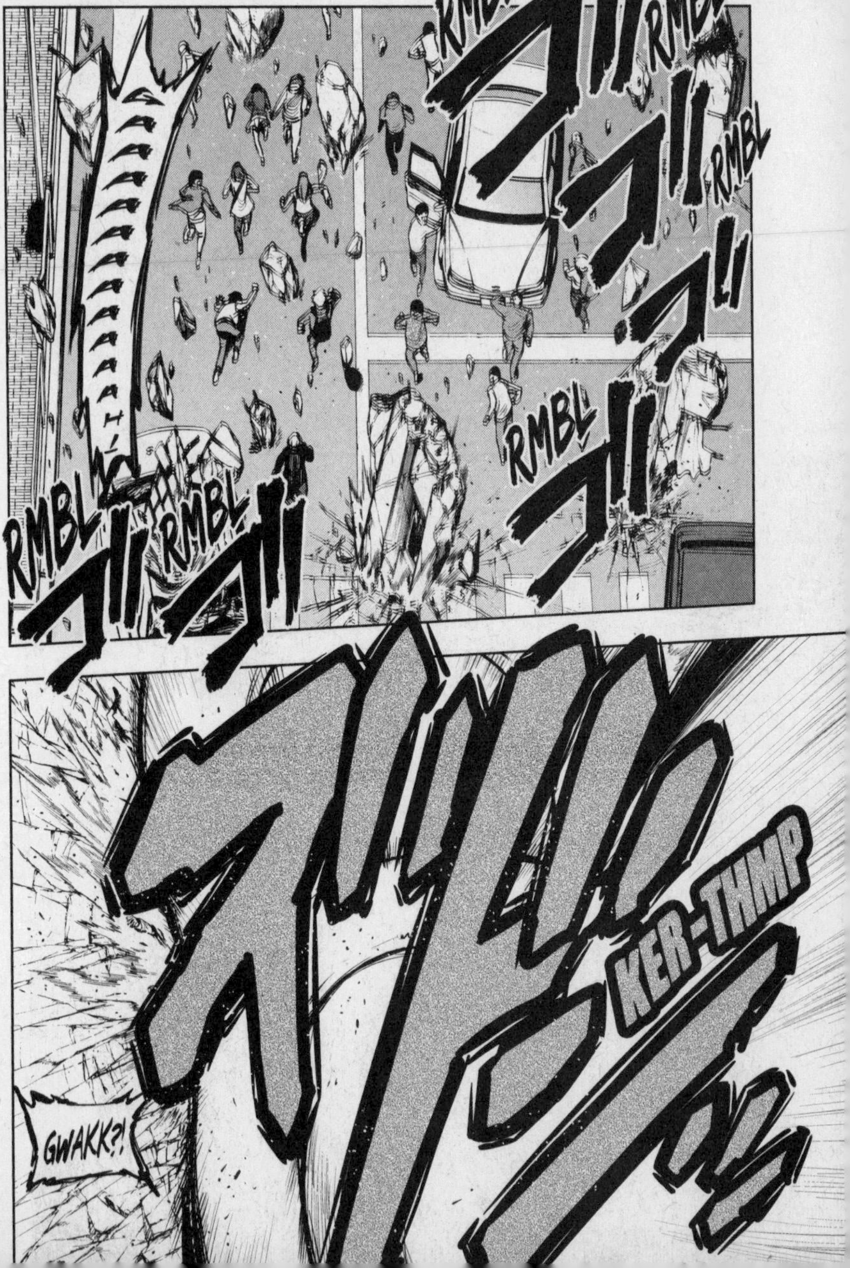
RMBL
RMBL
RMBL
RMBL
AAAAAAAAAAAAH!
RMBL
RMBL
KER-THMP
GWAKK?!

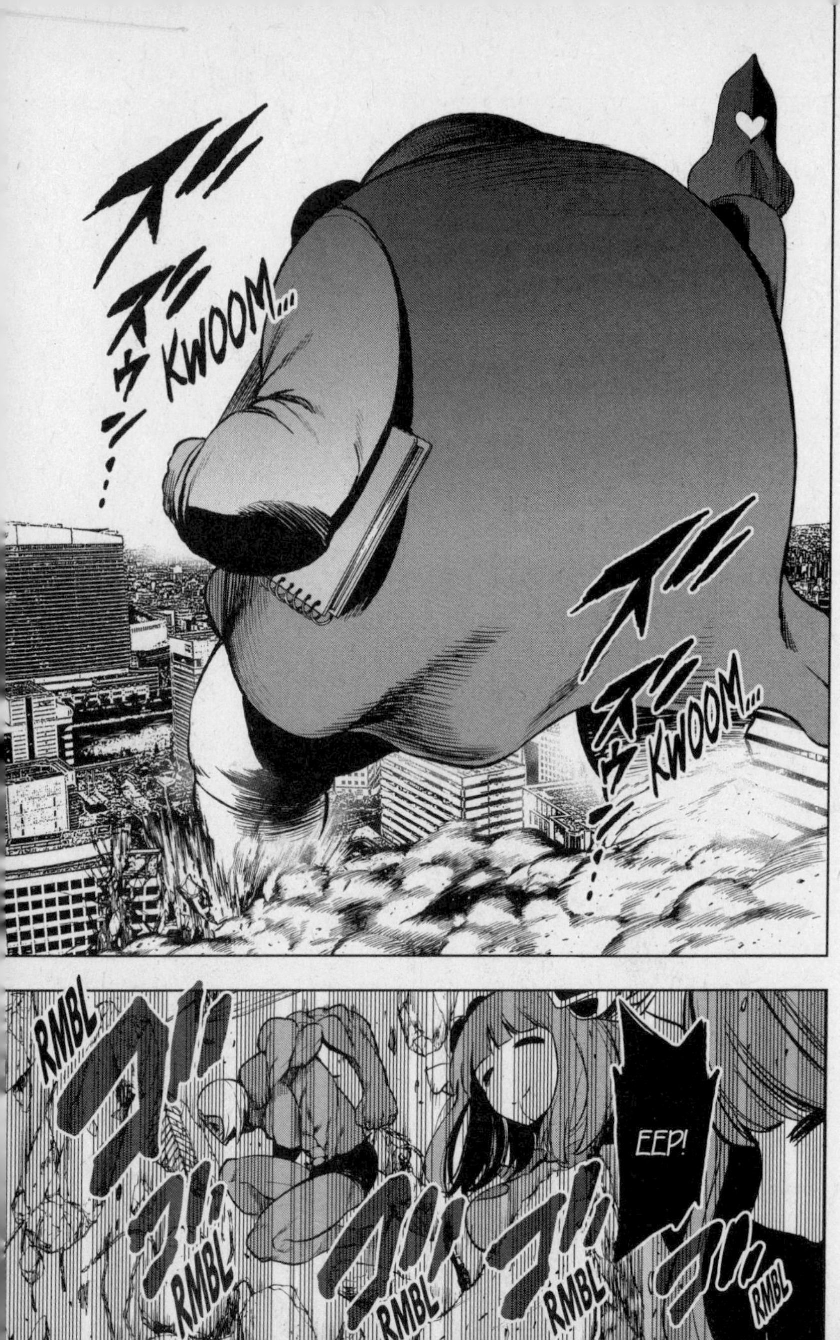
KWOOM...
KWOOM...
EEP!
RMBL
RMBL
RMBL
RMBL
RMBL
RMBL

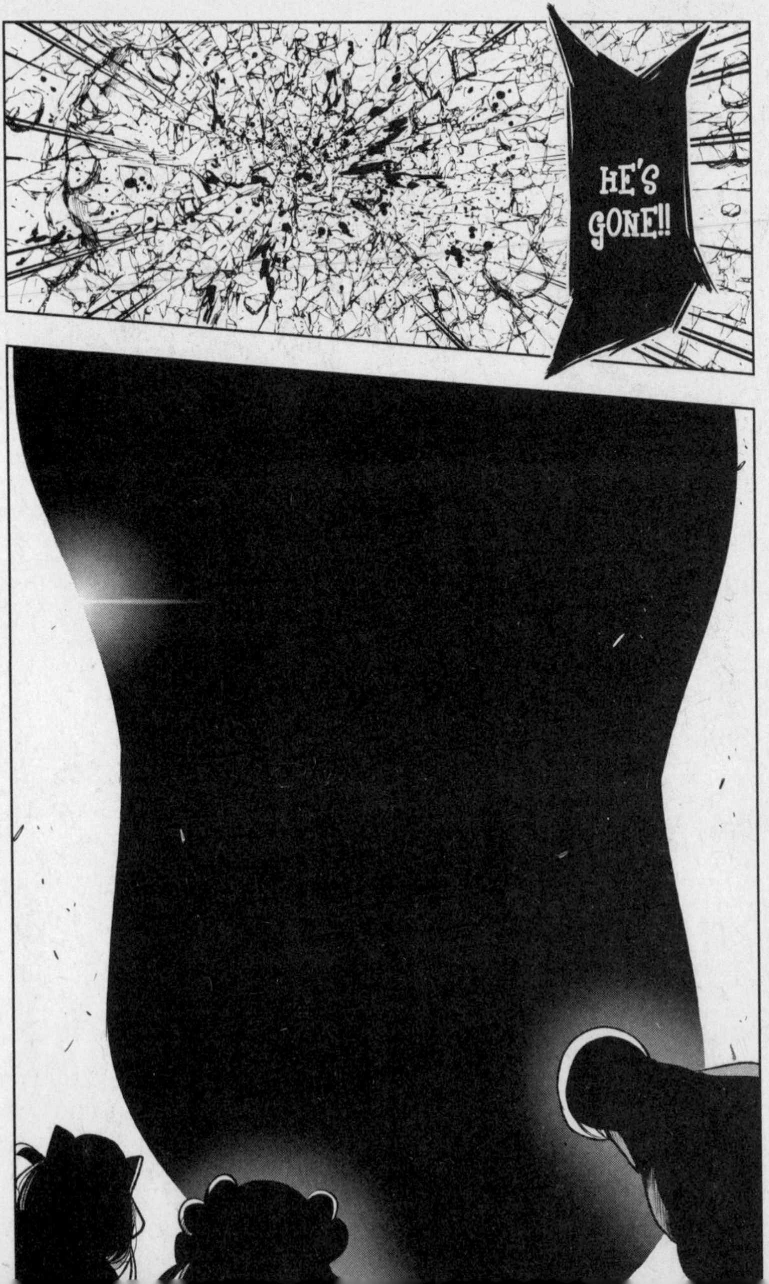
HE'S GONE!!

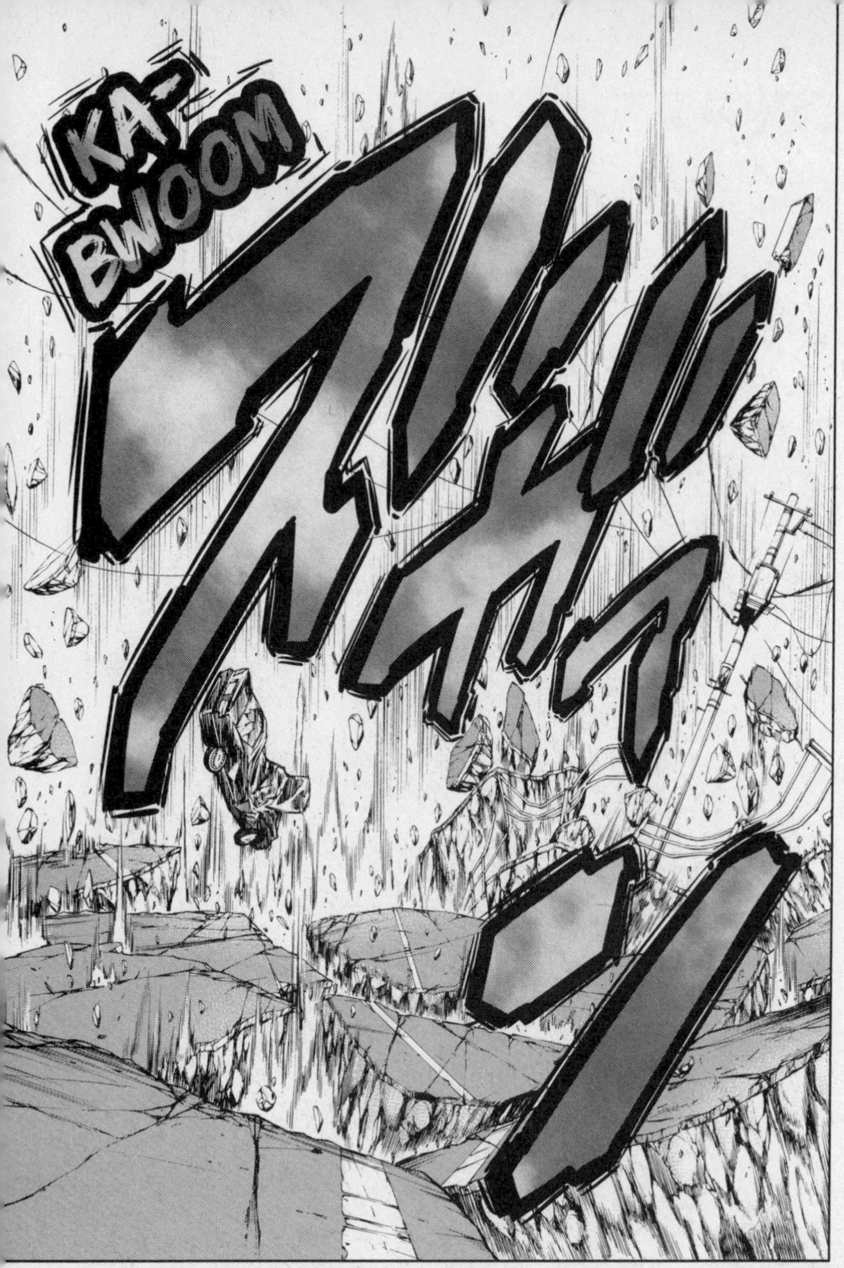
KA-BWOOM

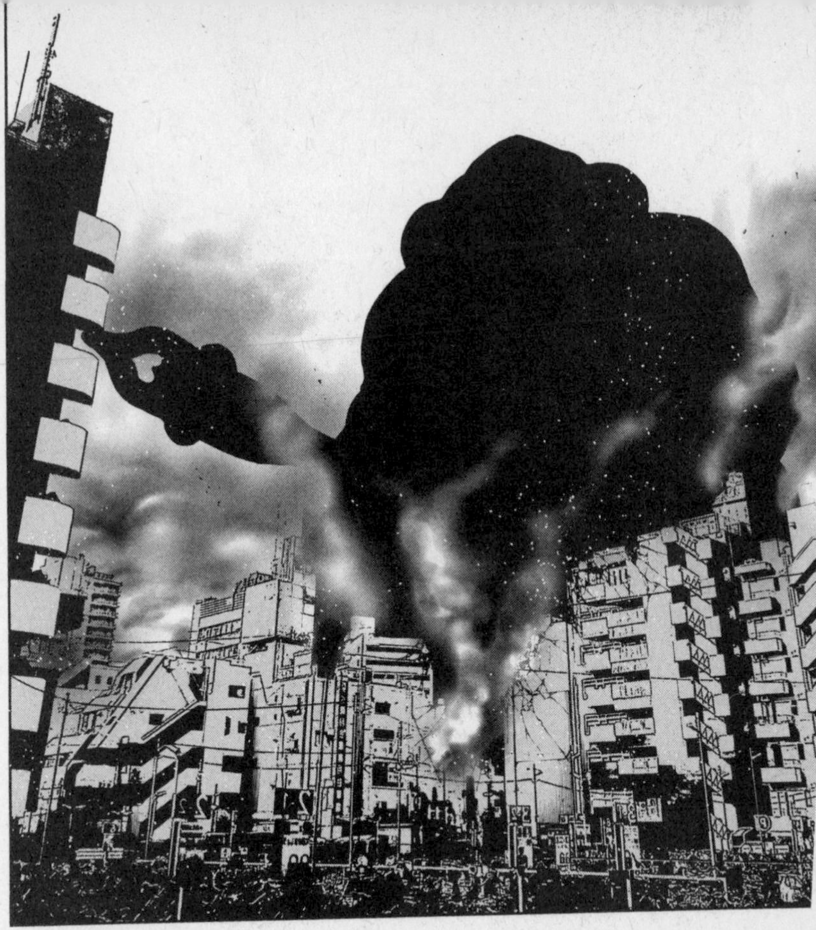

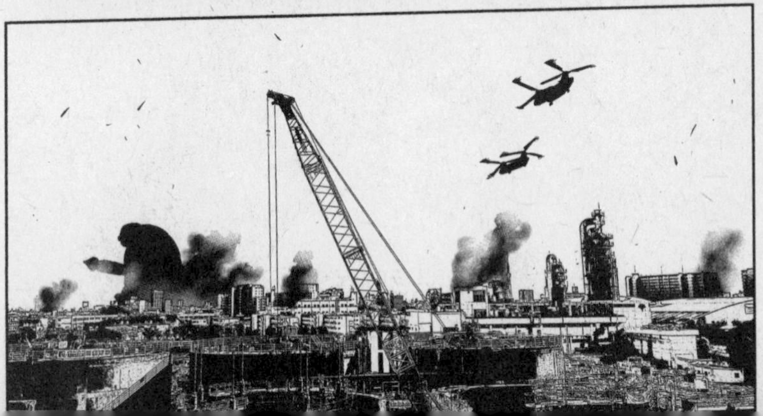

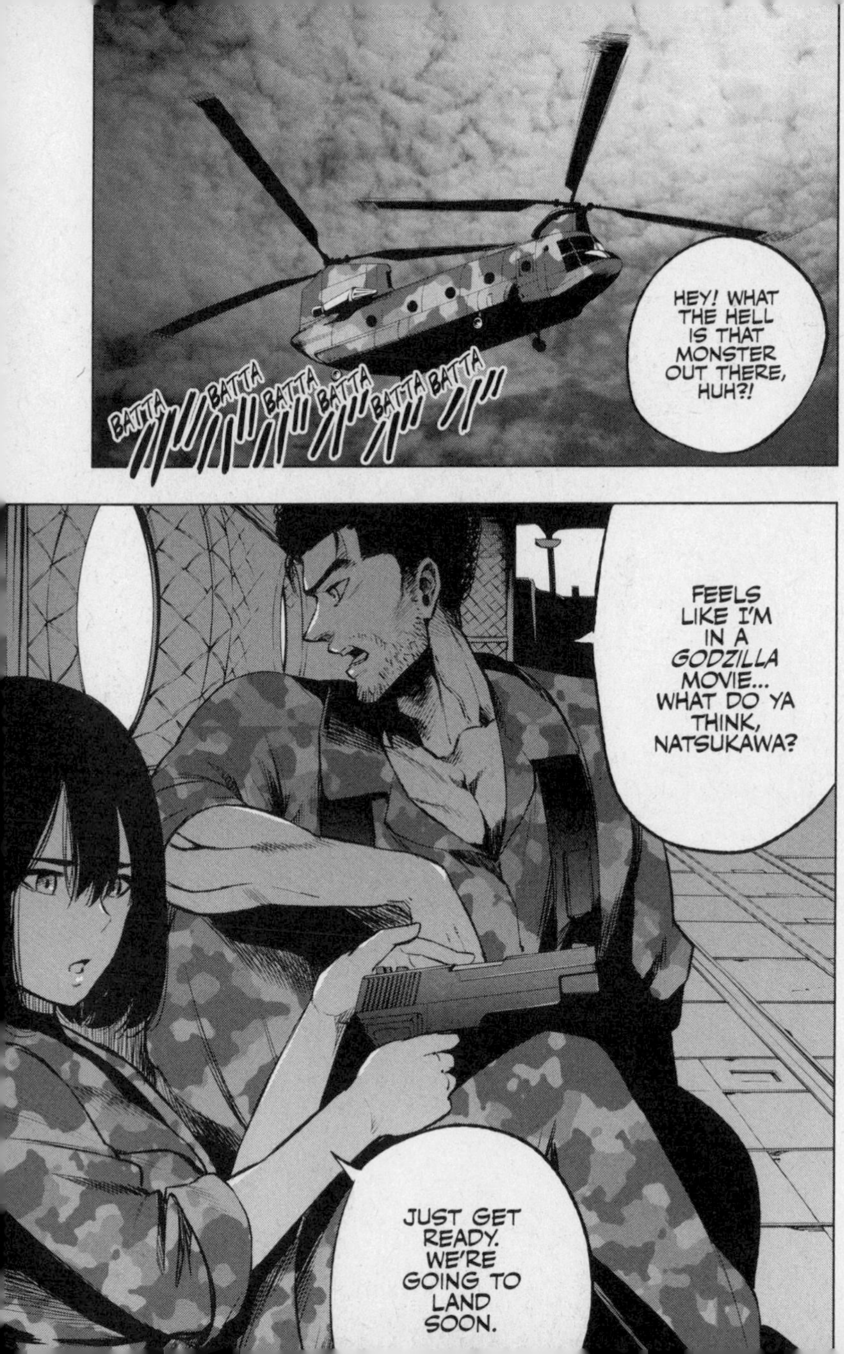
HEY! WHAT THE HELL IS THAT MONSTER OUT THERE, HUH?!
BATTA BATTA BATTA BATTA BATTA BATTA
FEELS LIKE I'M IN A *GODZILLA* MOVIE... WHAT DO YA THINK, NATSUKAWA?
JUST GET READY. WE'RE GOING TO LAND SOON.

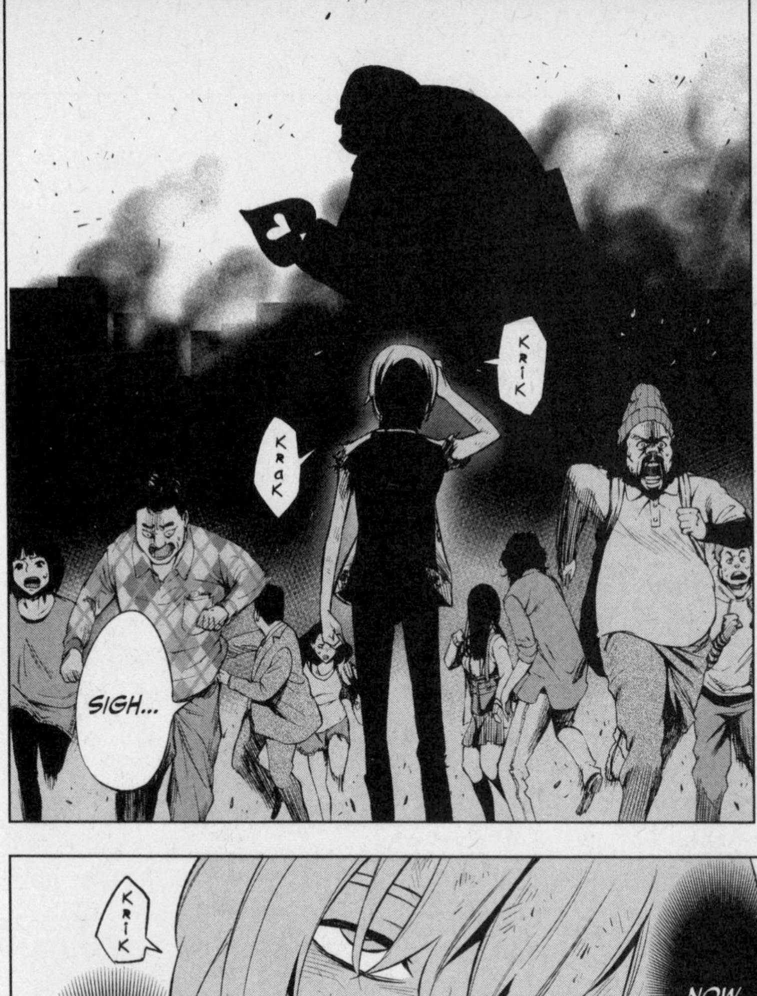
KRIK
KRAK
SIGH...
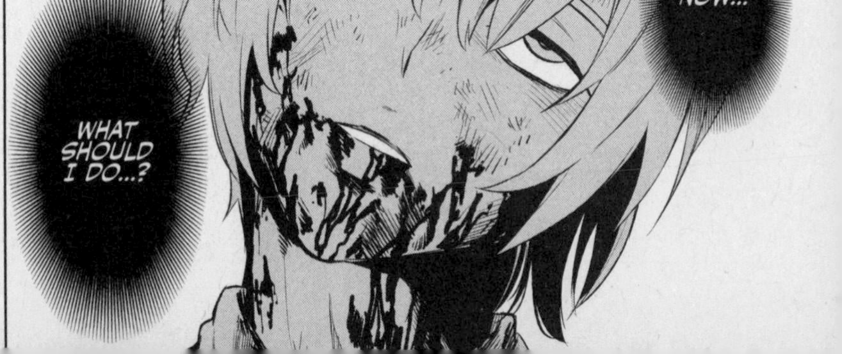
NOW...
KRIK
WHAT SHOULD I DO...?

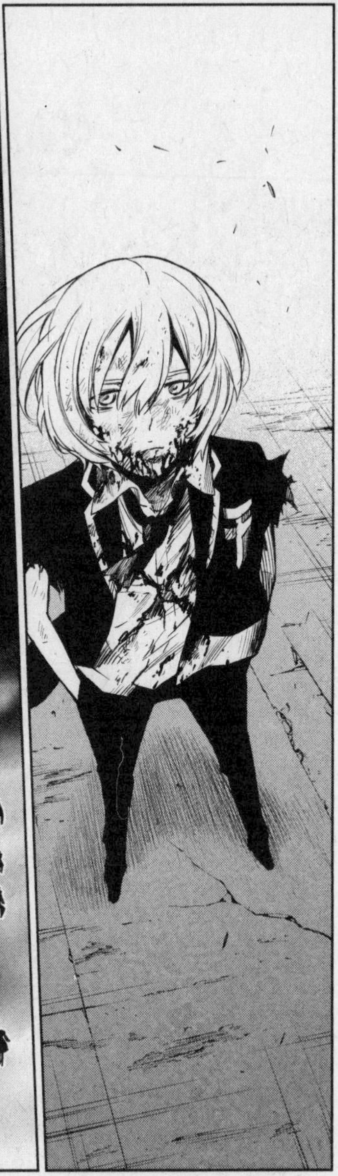
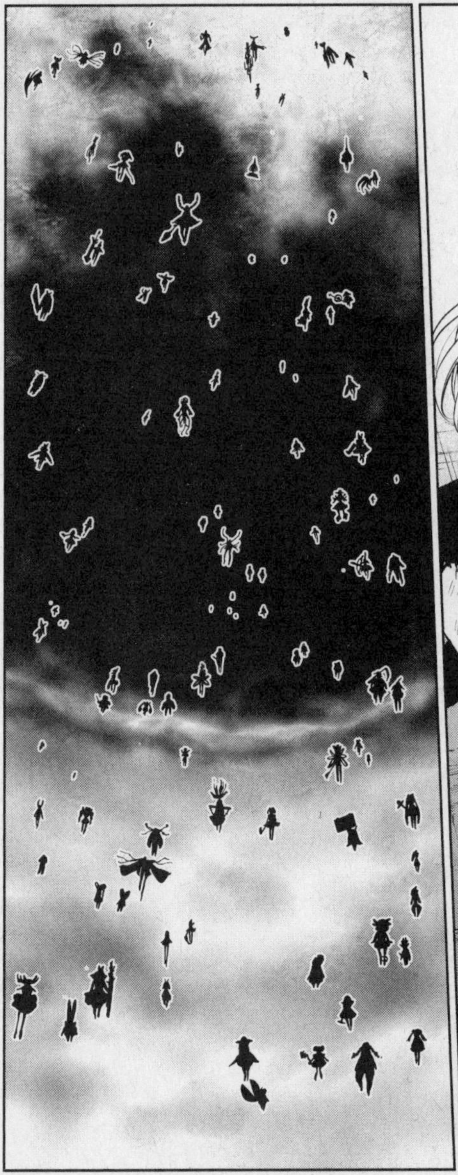

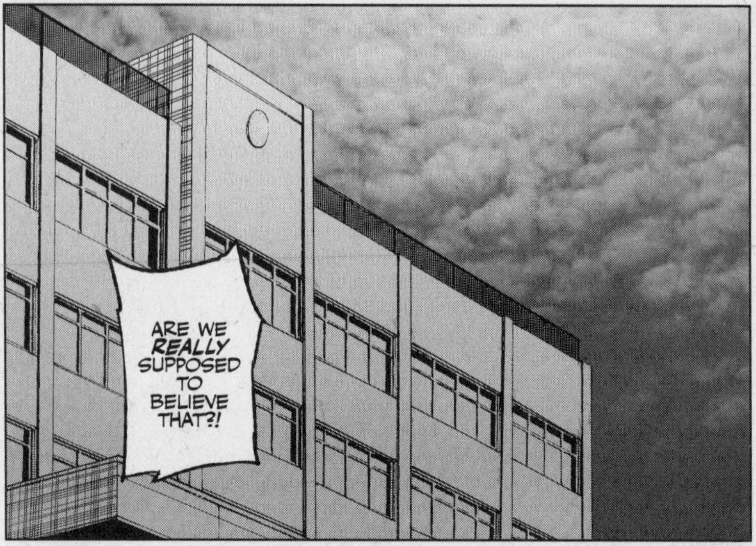
ARE WE *REALLY* SUPPOSED TO BELIEVE THAT?!

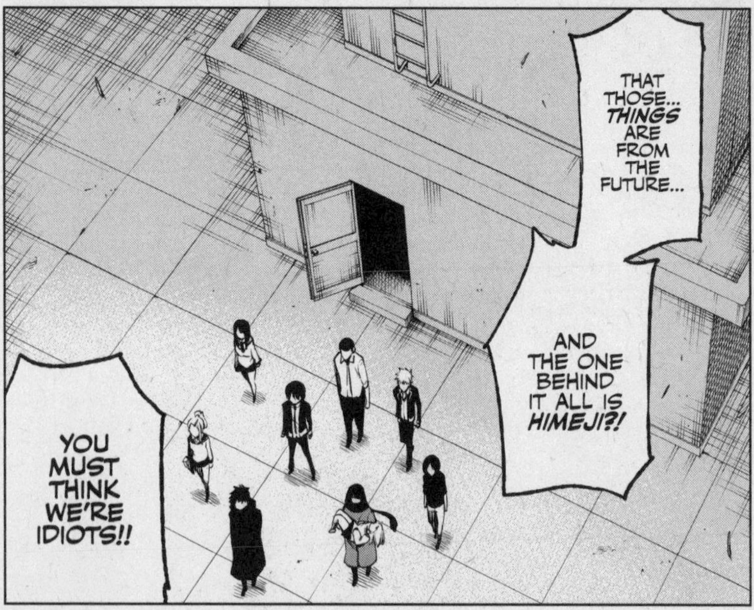
THAT THOSE... *THINGS* ARE FROM THE FUTURE...
AND THE ONE BEHIND IT ALL IS *HIMEJI*?!
YOU MUST THINK WE'RE IDIOTS!!

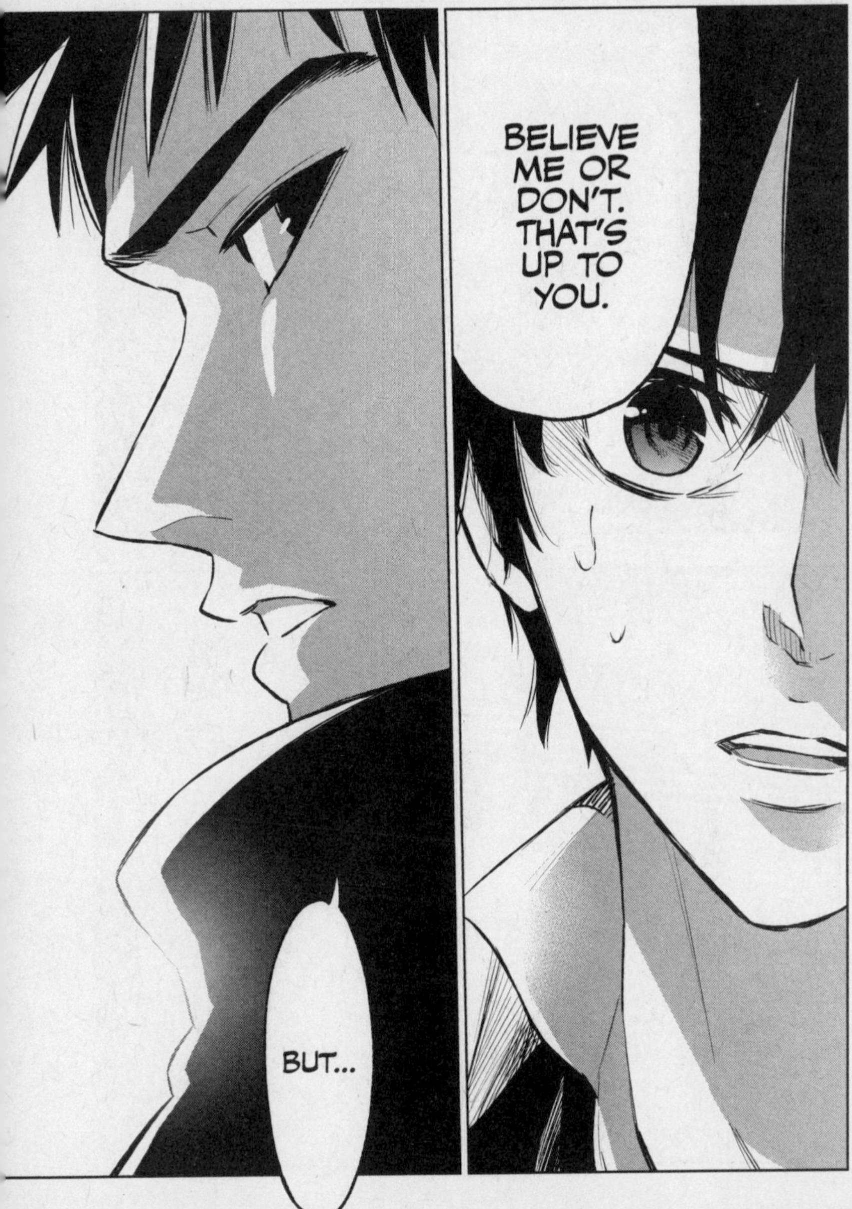
BELIEVE ME OR DON'T. THAT'S UP TO YOU.
BUT...

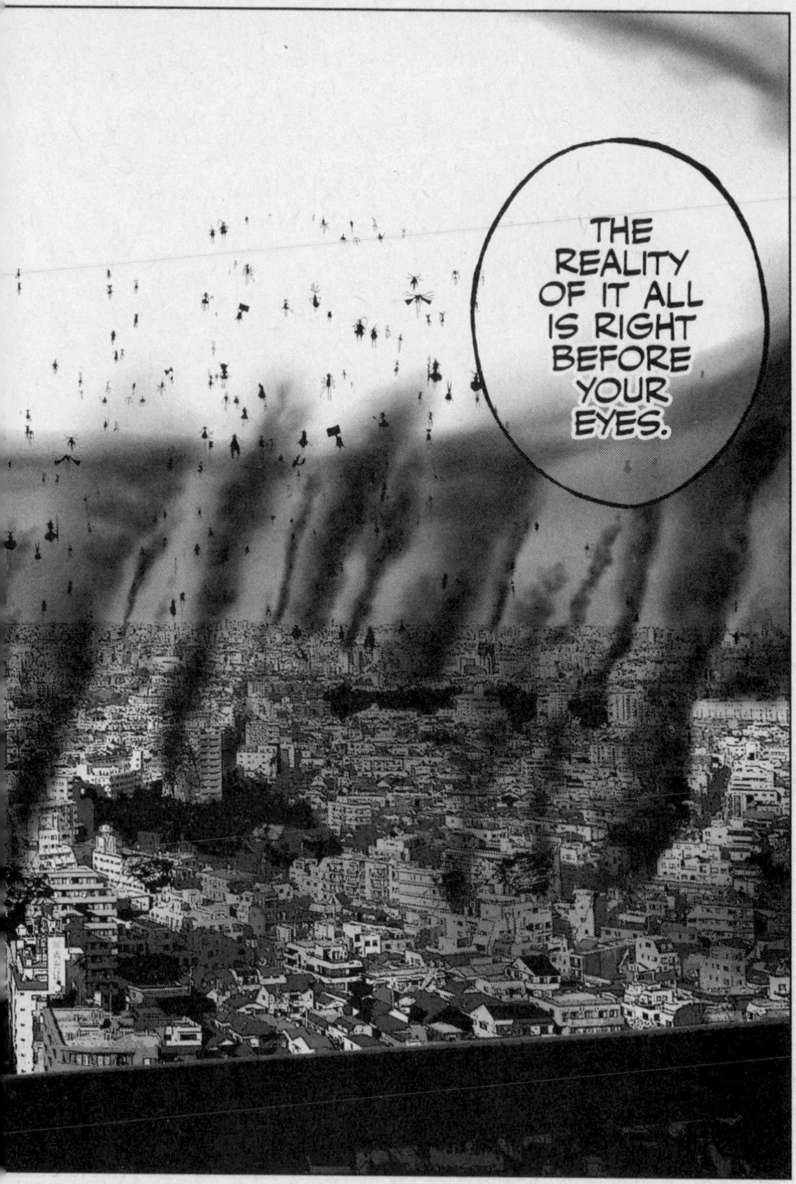
THE REALITY OF IT ALL IS RIGHT BEFORE YOUR EYES.

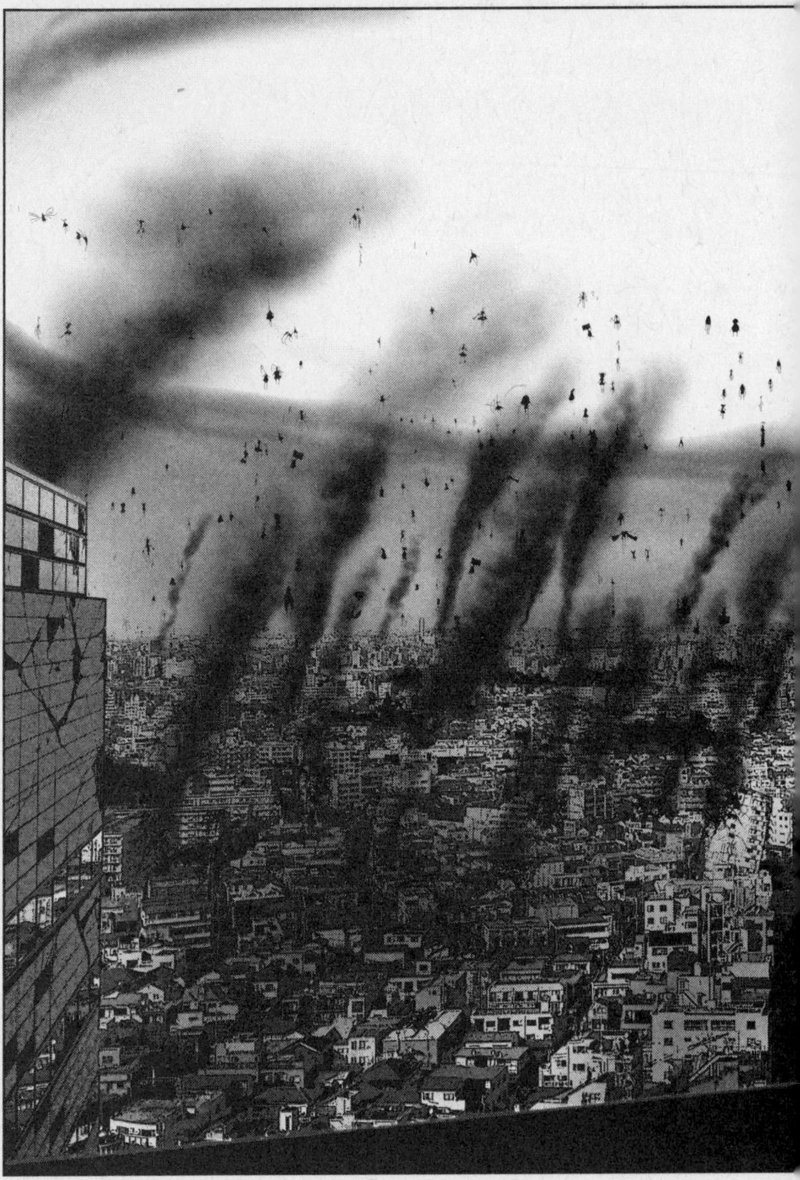

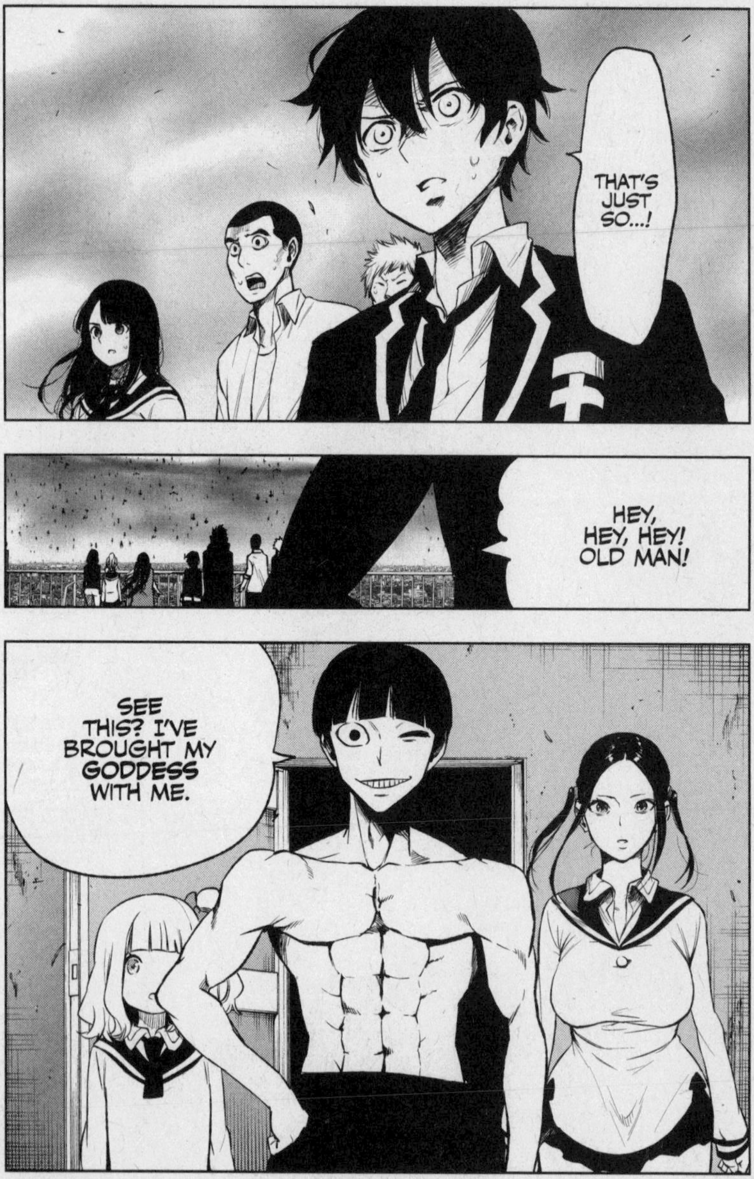
THAT'S JUST SO...!
HEY, HEY, HEY! OLD MAN!
SEE THIS? I'VE BROUGHT MY GODDESS WITH ME.

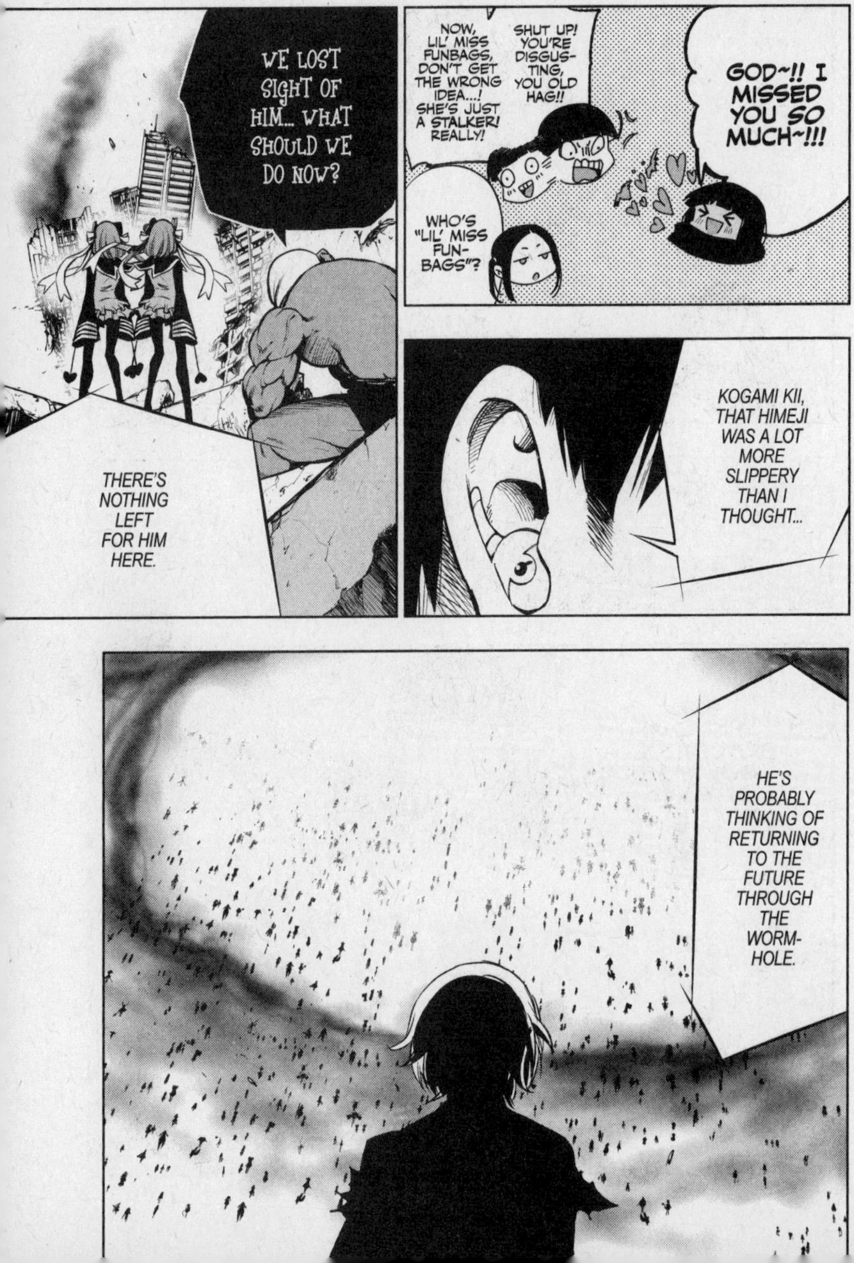
GOD~!! I MISSED YOU SO MUCH~!!!
SHUT UP! YOU'RE DISGUS-TING, YOU OLD HAG!!
NOW, LIL' MISS FUNBAGS, DON'T GET THE WRONG IDEA...! SHE'S JUST A STALKER! REALLY!
WHO'S "LIL' MISS FUN-BAGS"?
KOGAMI KII, THAT HIMEJI WAS A LOT MORE SLIPPERY THAN I THOUGHT...
WE LOST SIGHT OF HIM... WHAT SHOULD WE DO NOW?
THERE'S NOTHING LEFT FOR HIM HERE.
HE'S PROBABLY THINKING OF RETURNING TO THE FUTURE THROUGH THE WORM-HOLE.

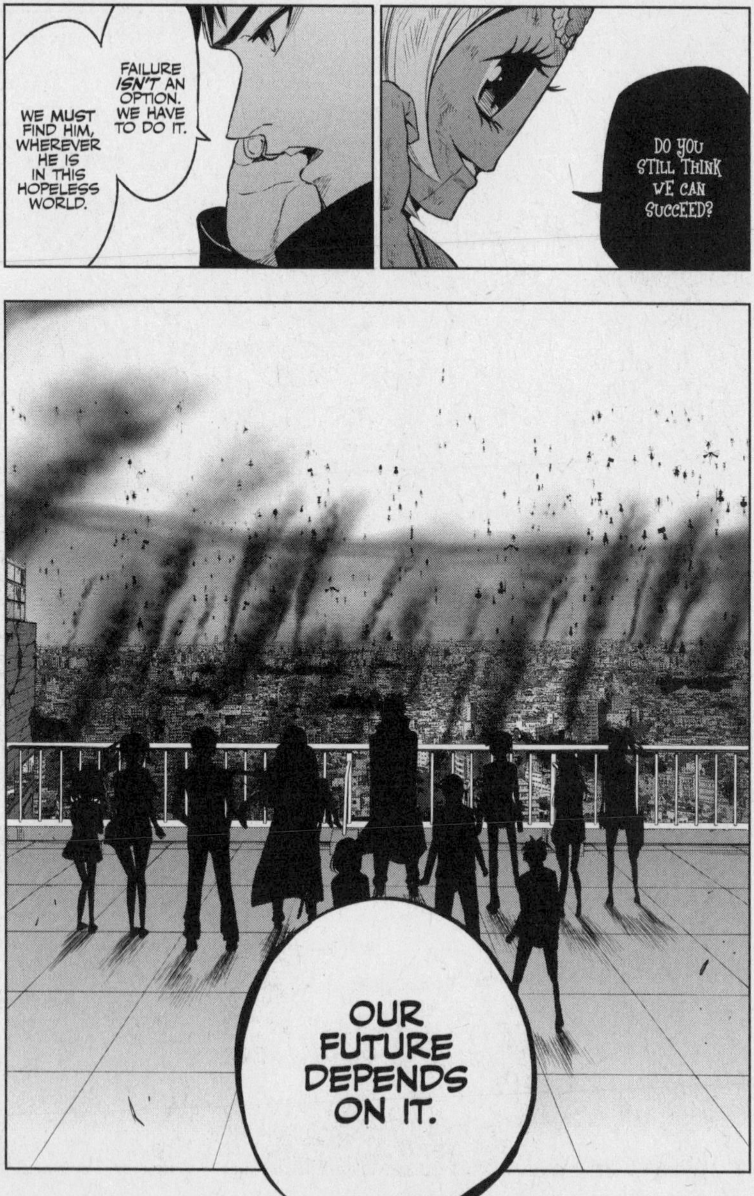
DO YOU STILL THINK WE CAN SUCCEED?
FAILURE ISN'T AN OPTION. WE HAVE TO DO IT.
WE MUST FIND HIM, WHEREVER HE IS IN THIS HOPELESS WORLD.
OUR FUTURE DEPENDS ON IT.

# 047.Last mission

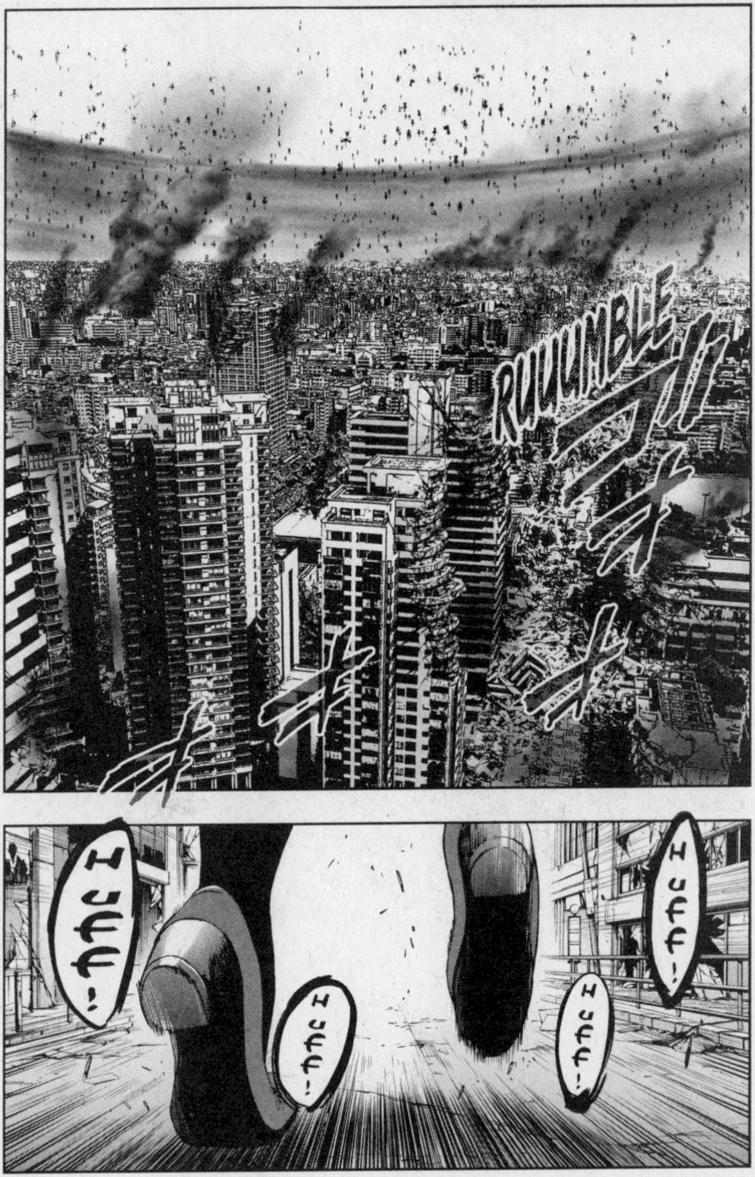
RUUUMBLE
HUFF!
HUFF!
HUFF!
HUFF!

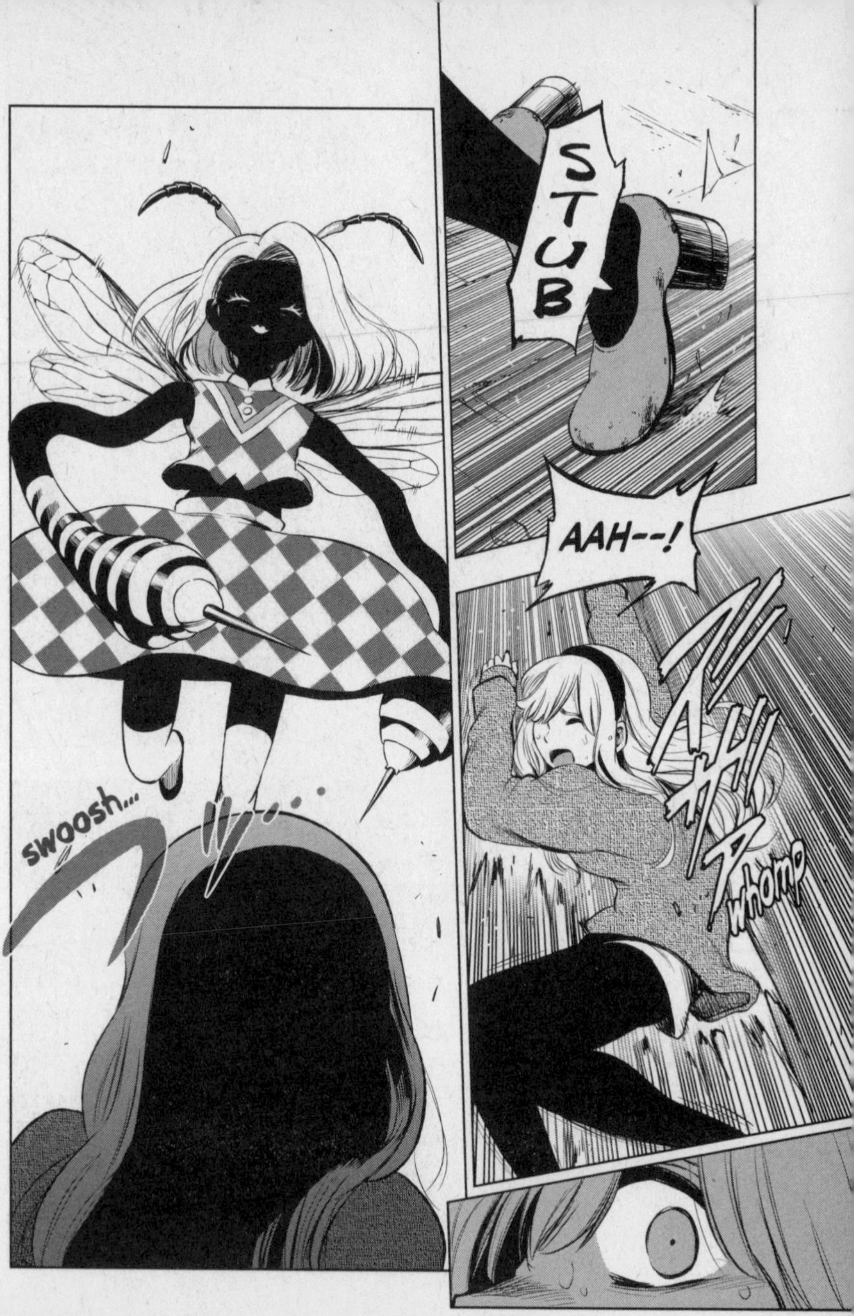
STUB
AAH--!
AHHA
whomp
swoosh...

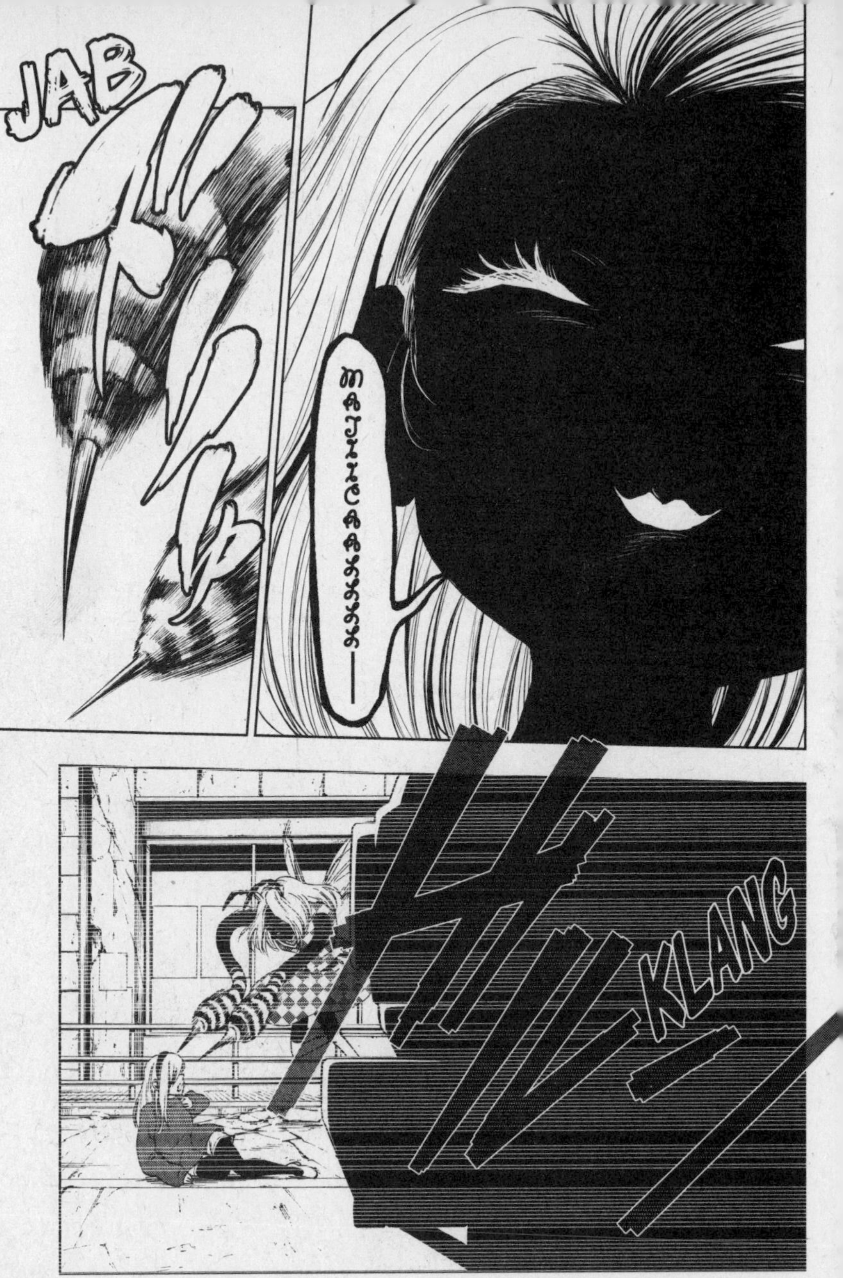
MAJIICAAKKKK—
JAB
KLANG

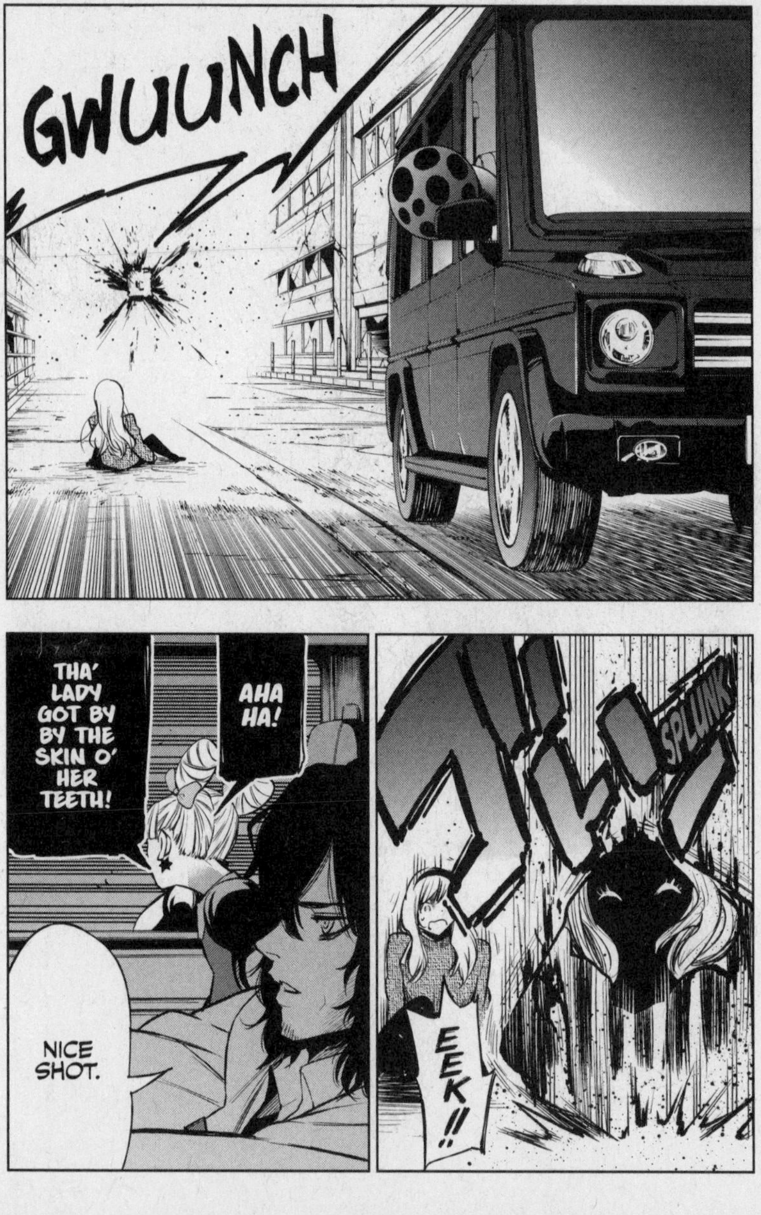
GWUUNCH
SPLUNK
EEK!!
AHA HA!
THA' LADY GOT BY BY THE SKIN O' HER TEETH!
NICE SHOT.

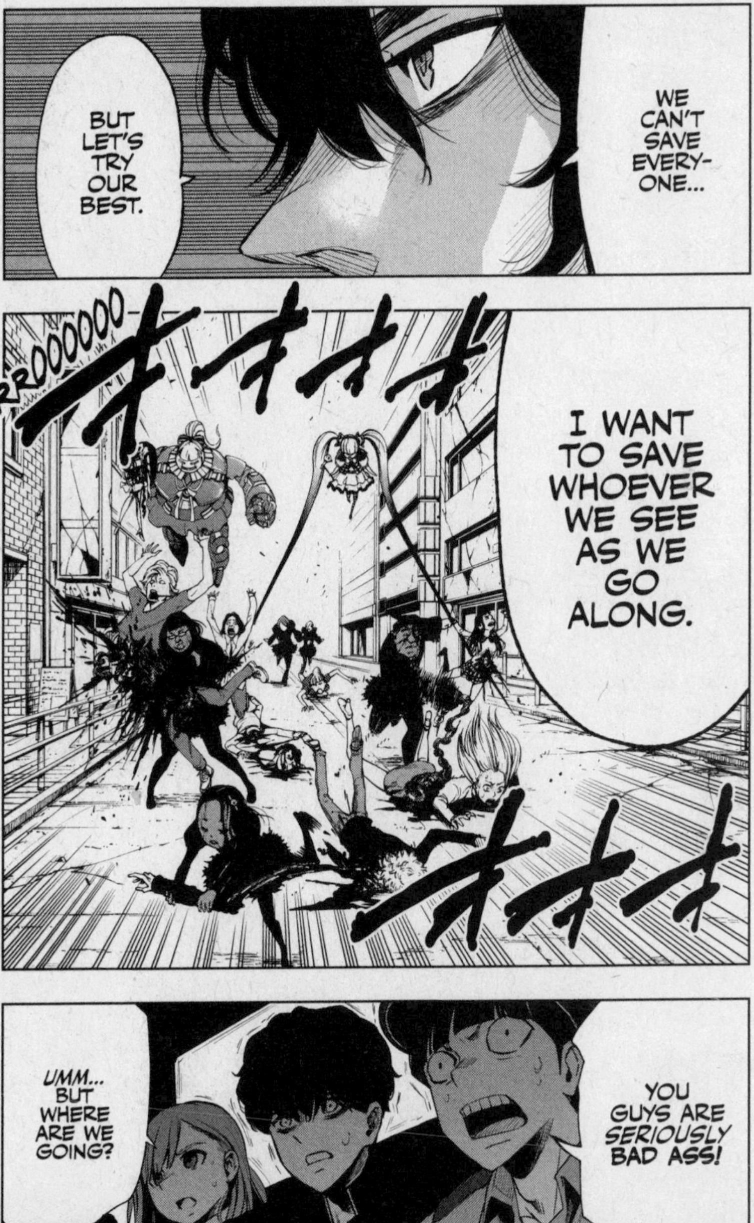
WE CAN'T SAVE EVERY-ONE...
BUT LET'S TRY OUR BEST.
I WANT TO SAVE WHOEVER WE SEE AS WE GO ALONG.
FRROOOOOO
YOU GUYS ARE SERIOUSLY BAD ASS!
UMM... BUT WHERE ARE WE GOING?

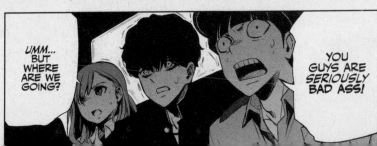

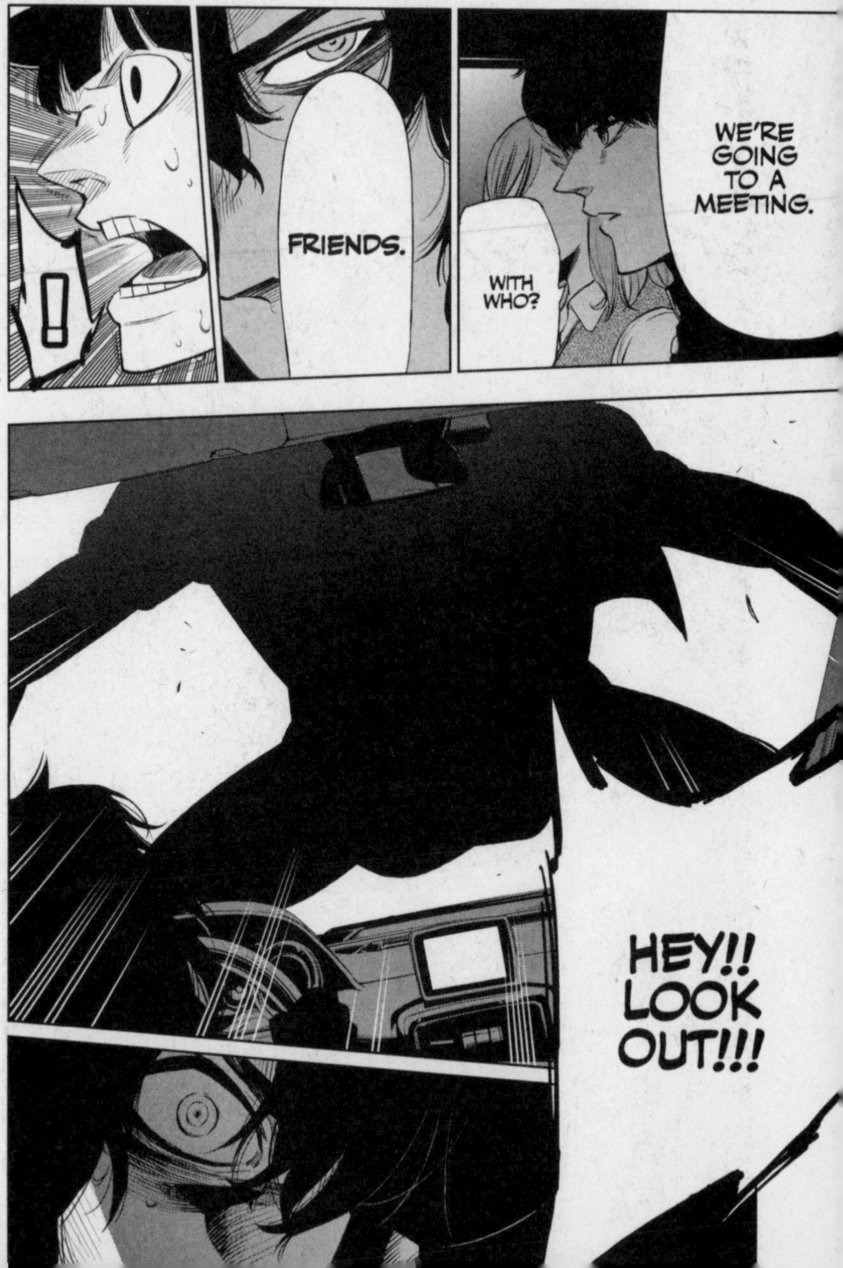
WE'RE GOING TO A MEETING.
WITH WHO?
FRIENDS.
!
HEY!! LOOK OUT!!!

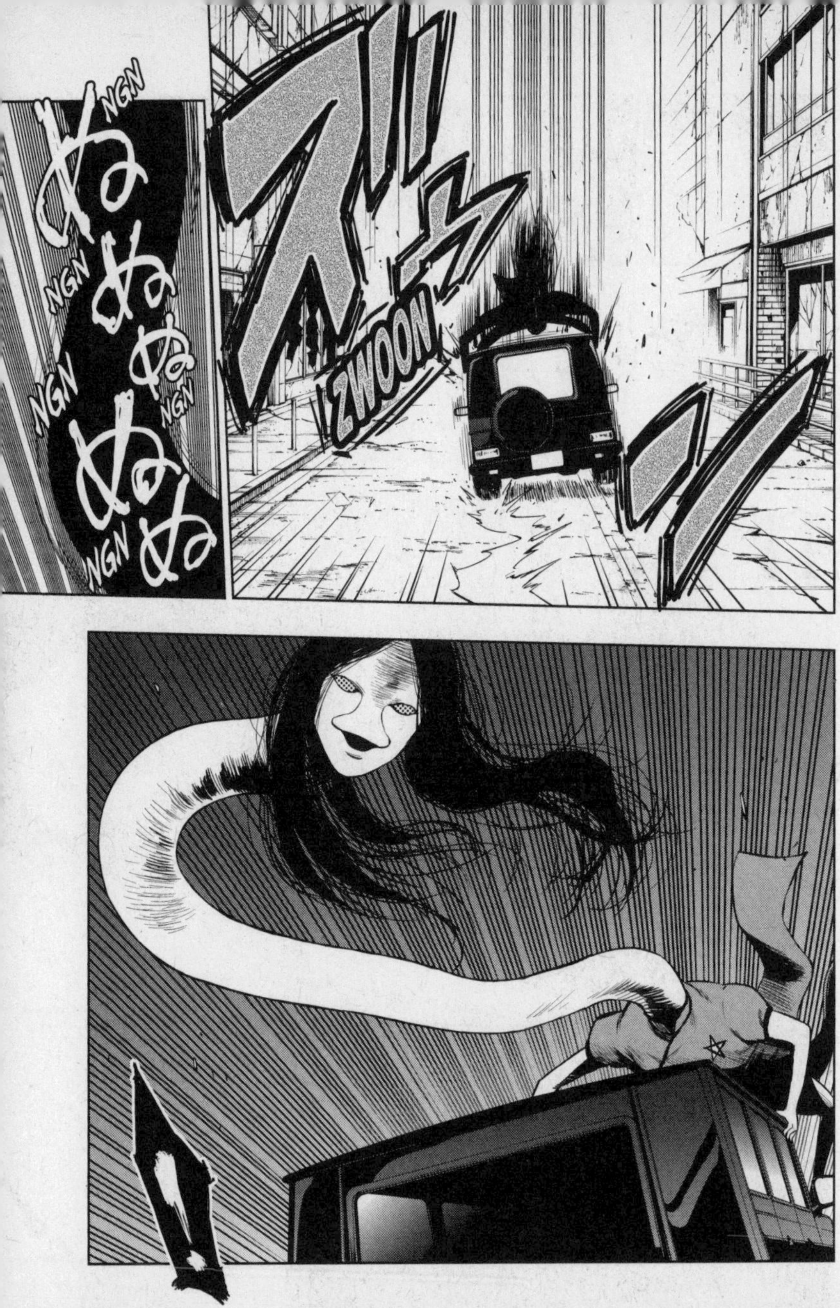
ZWOON
NGN NGN NGN NGN NGN NGN
!

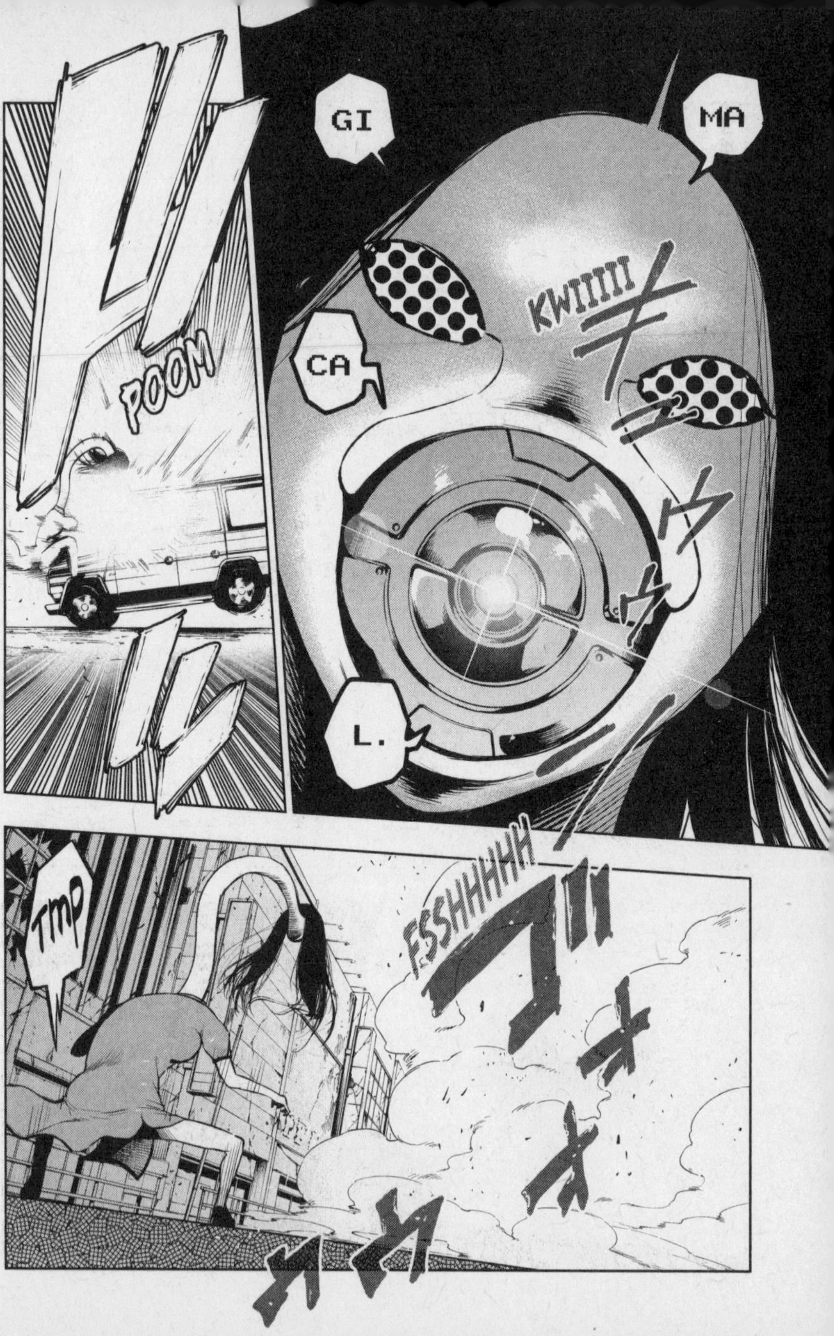
GI
MA
KWIIIII
CA
L.
POOM
FSSHHHHH
TMP

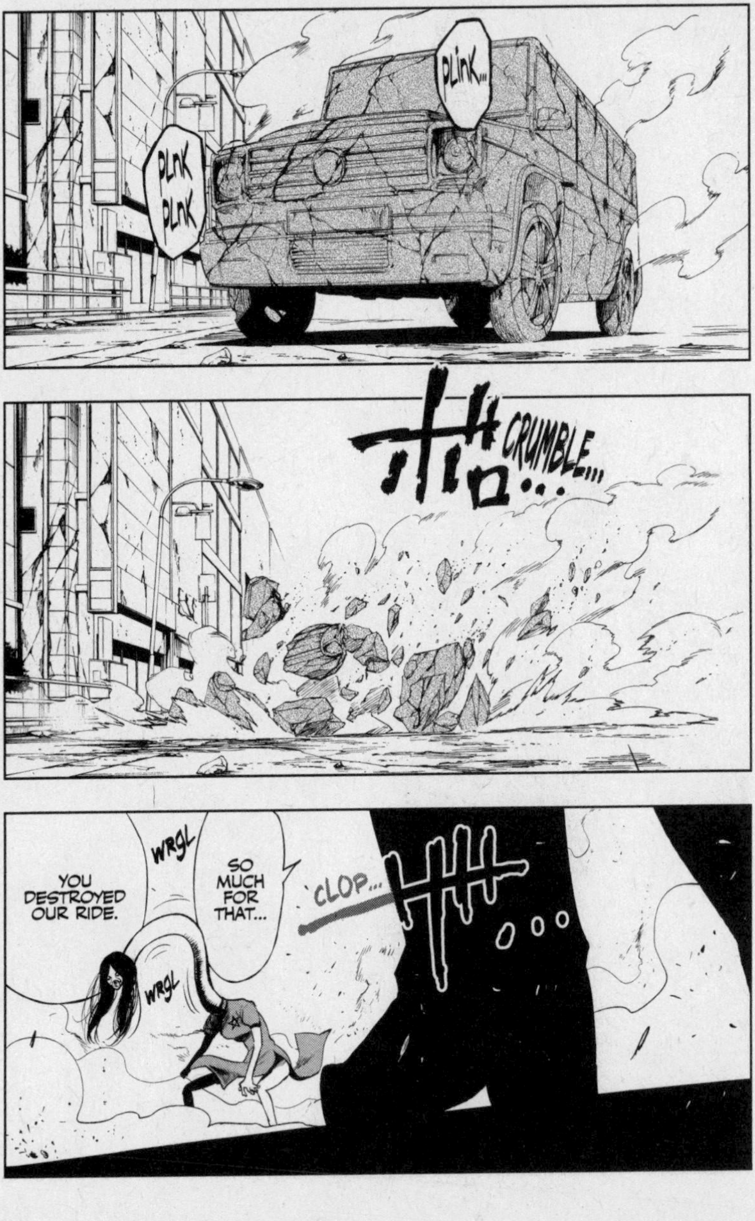
PLINK...
PLNK PLNK
CRUMBLE...
CLOP...
SO MUCH FOR THAT...
WRGL
YOU DESTROYED OUR RIDE.
WRGL

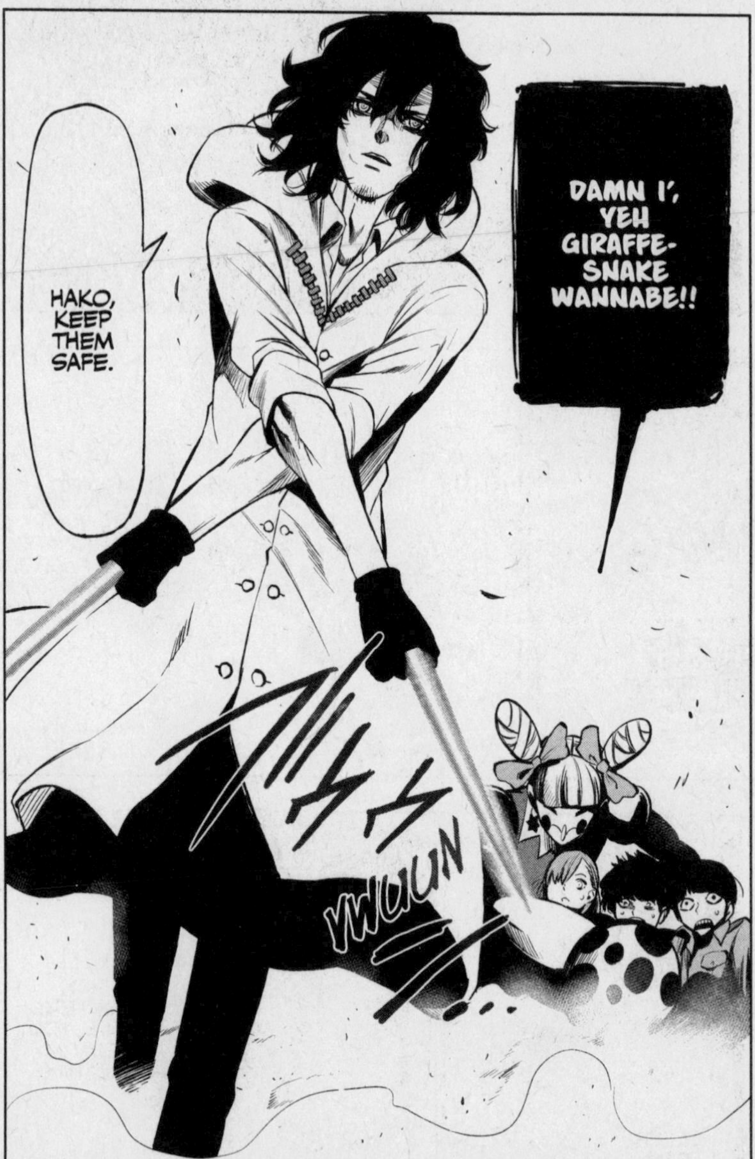
DAMN I', YEH GIRAFFE-SNAKE WANNABE!!
HAKO, KEEP THEM SAFE.
VWUUN

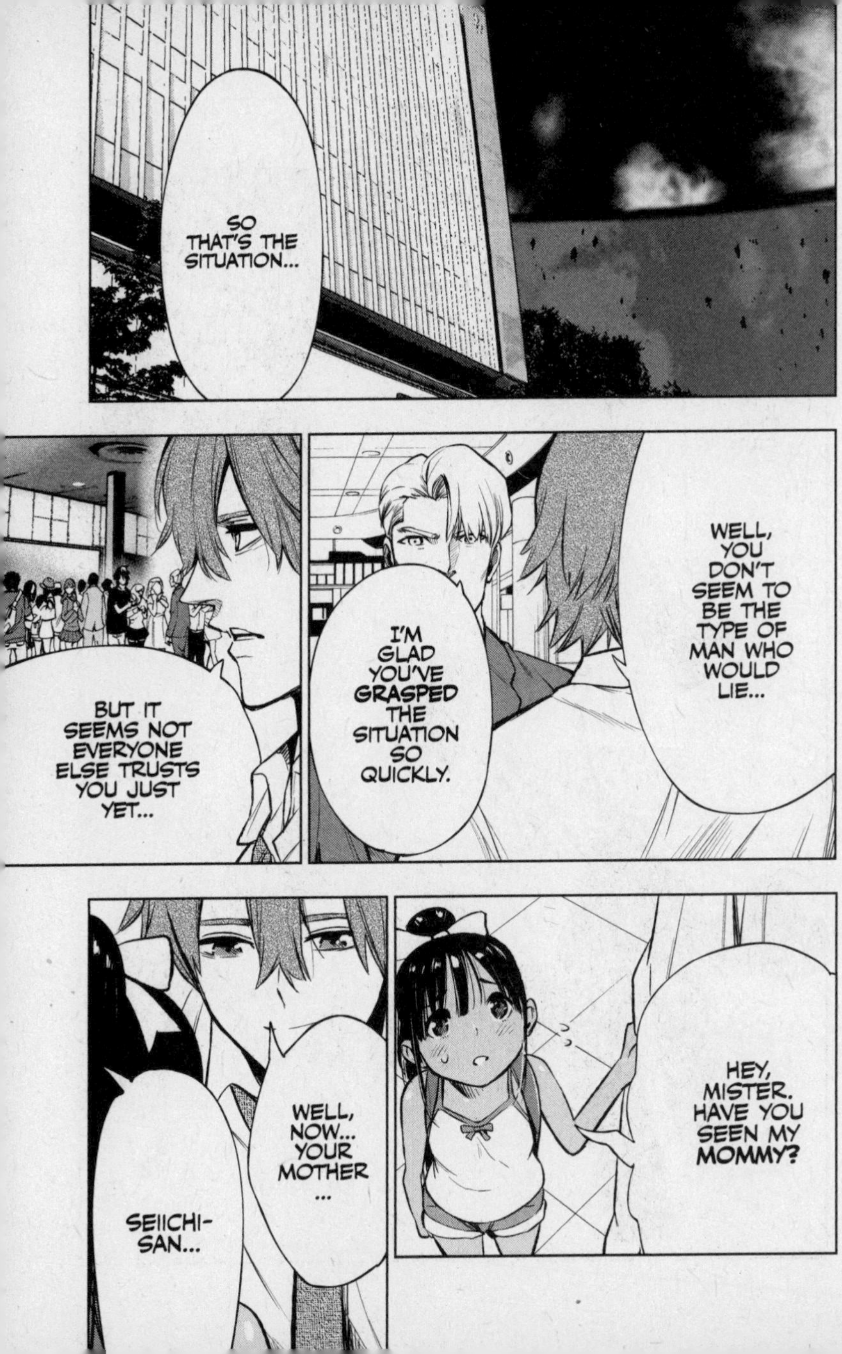
SO THAT'S THE SITUATION...
WELL, YOU DON'T SEEM TO BE THE TYPE OF MAN WHO WOULD LIE...
I'M GLAD YOU'VE GRASPED THE SITUATION SO QUICKLY.
BUT IT SEEMS NOT EVERYONE ELSE TRUSTS YOU JUST YET...
HEY, MISTER. HAVE YOU SEEN MY MOMMY?
WELL, NOW... YOUR MOTHER ...
SEIICHI-SAN...

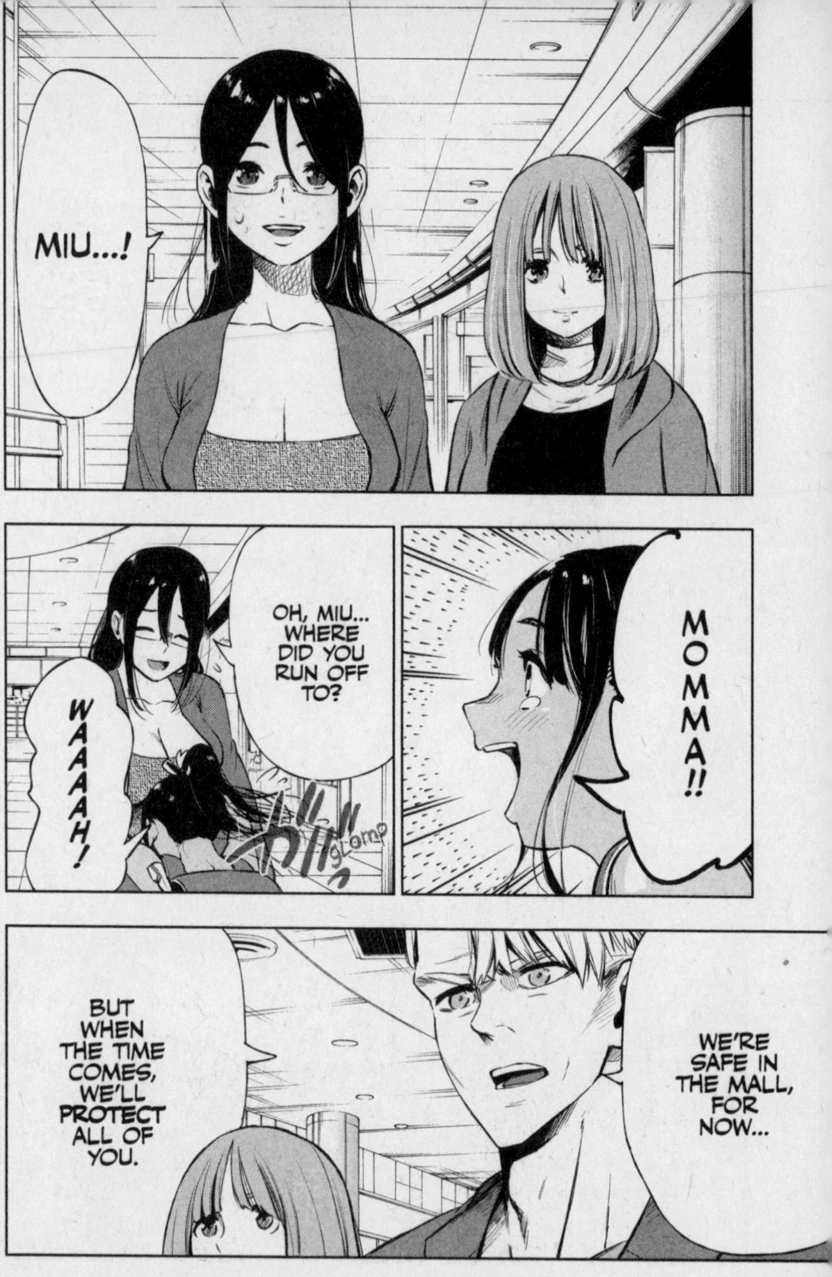
MIU...!
MOMMA!!
OH, MIU... WHERE DID YOU RUN OFF TO?
WAAAAH!
glomp
WE'RE SAFE IN THE MALL, FOR NOW...
BUT WHEN THE TIME COMES, WE'LL PROTECT ALL OF YOU.

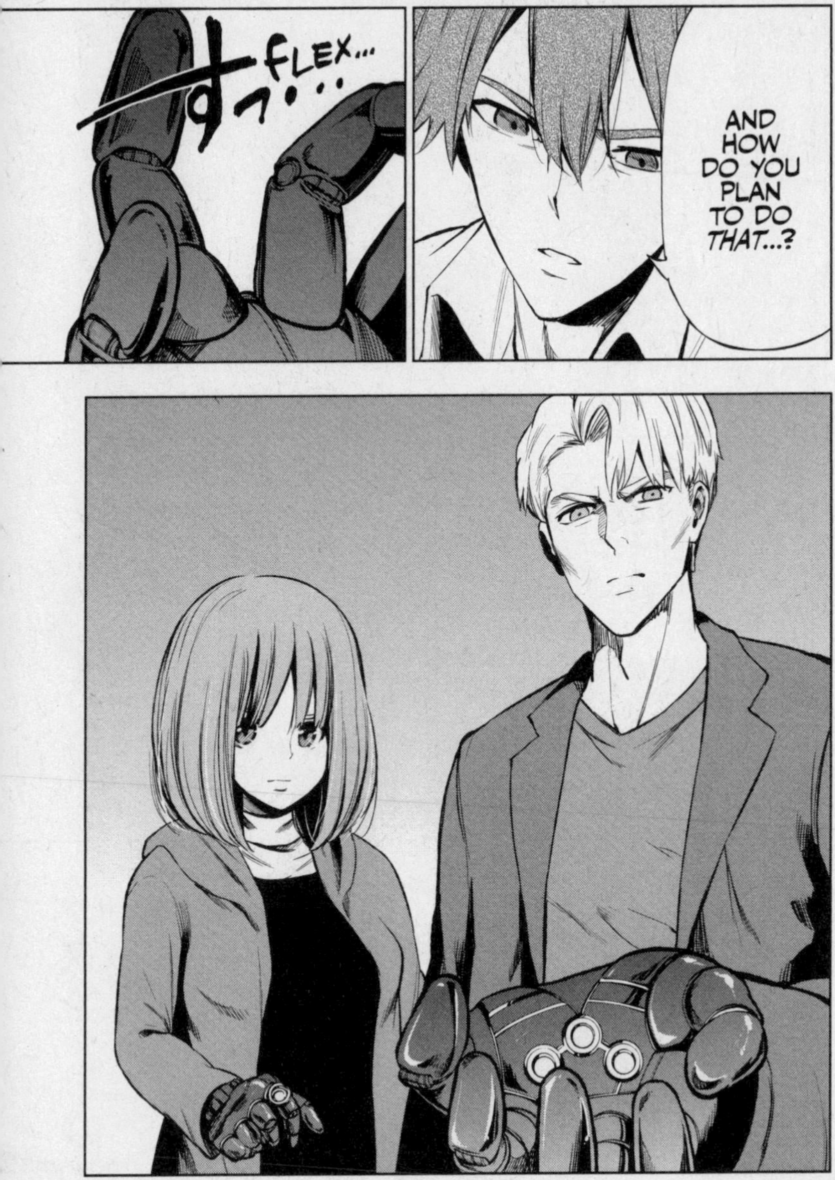
AND HOW DO YOU PLAN TO DO *THAT*...?
すっ...
FLEX...

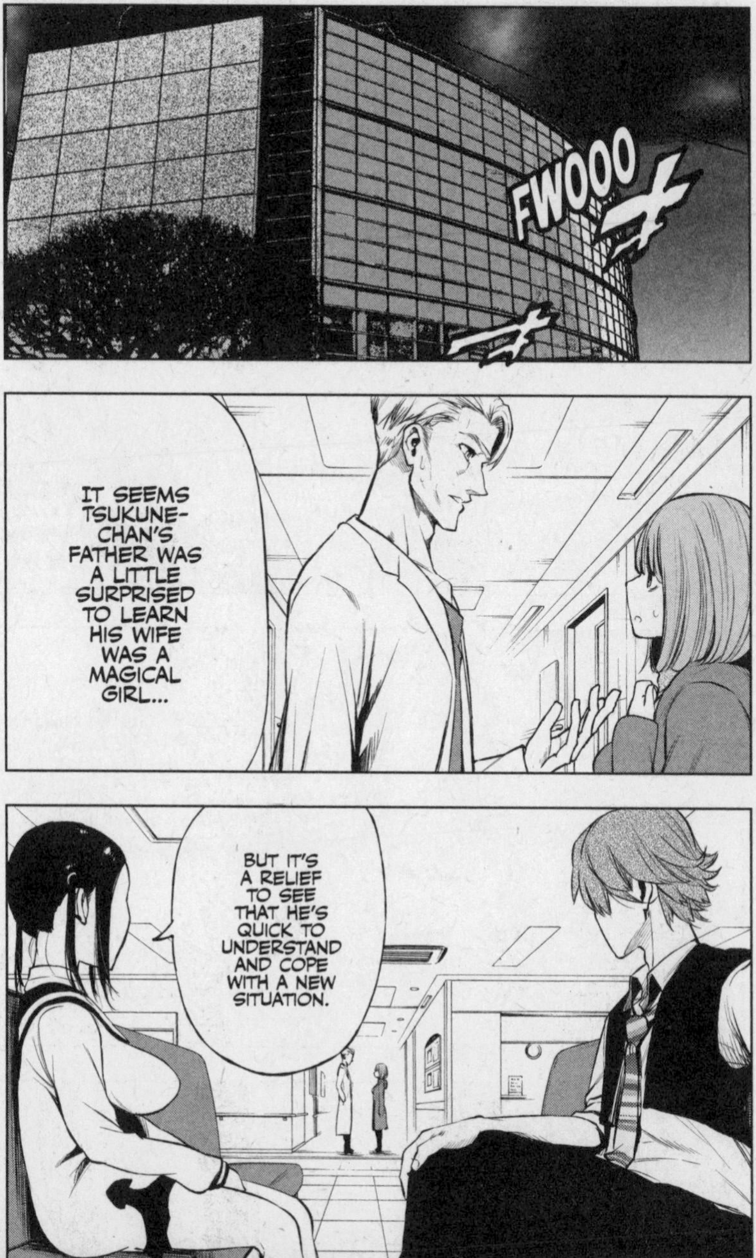
FWOOO
IT SEEMS TSUKUNE-CHAN'S FATHER WAS A LITTLE SURPRISED TO LEARN HIS WIFE WAS A MAGICAL GIRL...
BUT IT'S A RELIEF TO SEE THAT HE'S QUICK TO UNDERSTAND AND COPE WITH A NEW SITUATION.

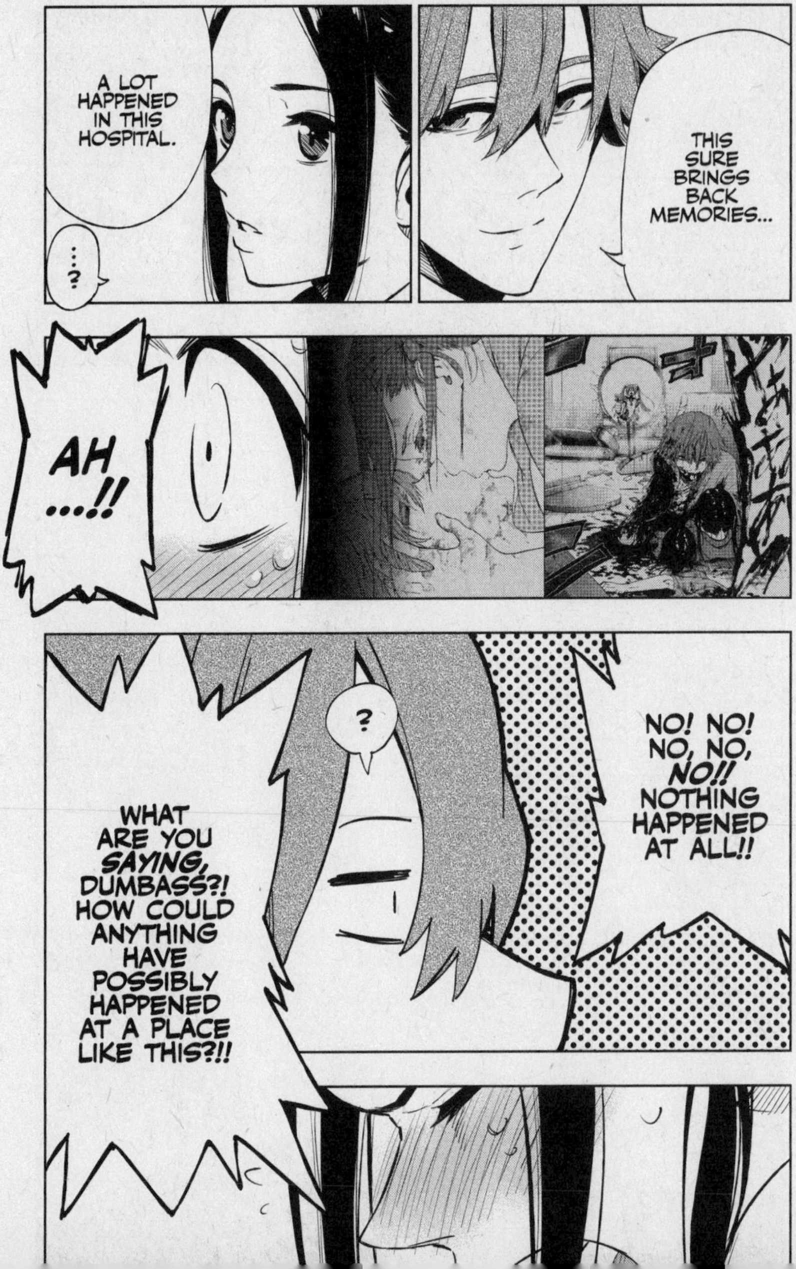
THIS SURE BRINGS BACK MEMORIES...
A LOT HAPPENED IN THIS HOSPITAL.
...?
AH ...!!
NO! NO! NO, NO, NO!! NOTHING HAPPENED AT ALL!!
?
WHAT ARE YOU SAYING, DUMBASS?! HOW COULD ANYTHING HAVE POSSIBLY HAPPENED AT A PLACE LIKE THIS?!!

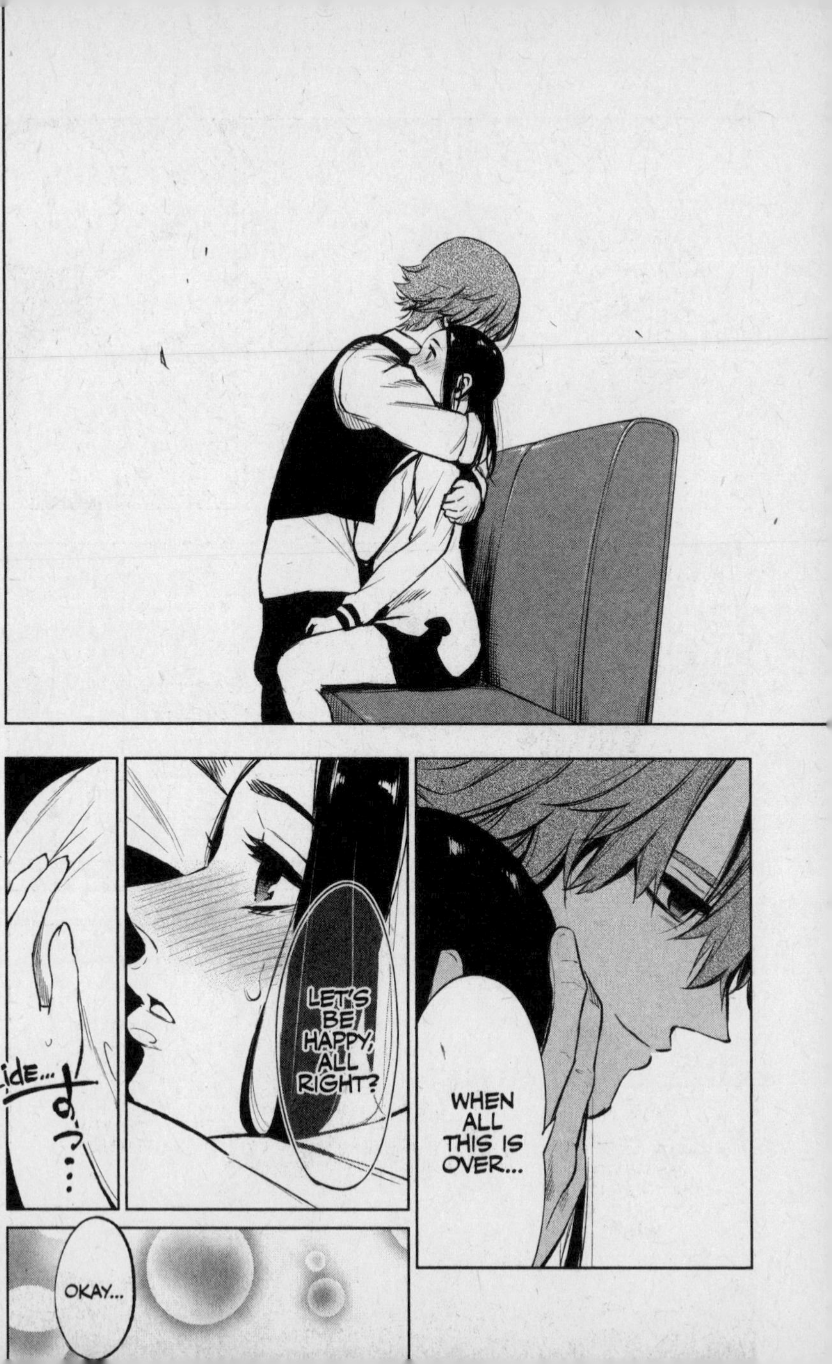
WHEN ALL THIS IS OVER...
LET'S BE HAPPY, ALL RIGHT?
SLIDE...
すっ…
OKAY...

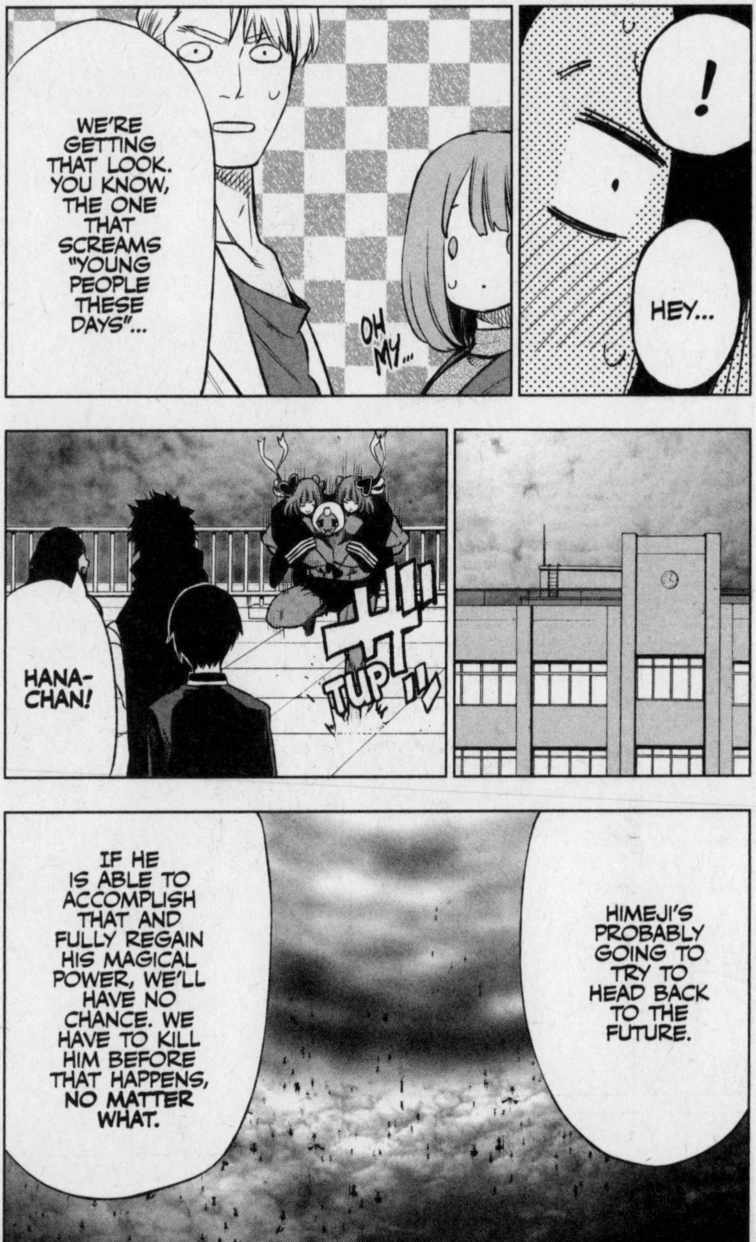
!
HEY...
WE'RE GETTING THAT LOOK. YOU KNOW, THE ONE THAT SCREAMS "YOUNG PEOPLE THESE DAYS"...
OH MY...
TUP
HANA-CHAN!
HIMEJI'S PROBABLY GOING TO TRY TO HEAD BACK TO THE FUTURE.
IF HE IS ABLE TO ACCOMPLISH THAT AND FULLY REGAIN HIS MAGICAL POWER, WE'LL HAVE NO CHANCE. WE HAVE TO KILL HIM BEFORE THAT HAPPENS, NO MATTER WHAT.

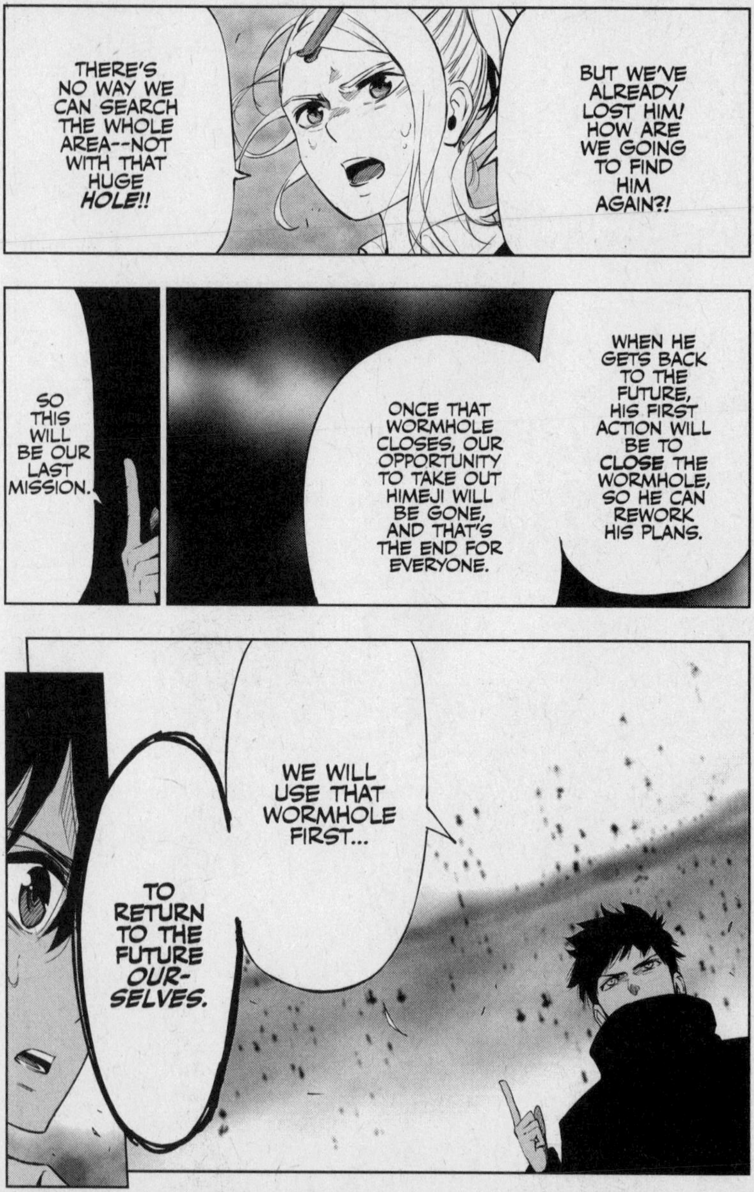
BUT WE'VE ALREADY LOST HIM! HOW ARE WE GOING TO FIND HIM AGAIN?!
THERE'S NO WAY WE CAN SEARCH THE WHOLE AREA--NOT WITH THAT HUGE *HOLE*!!
WHEN HE GETS BACK TO THE FUTURE, HIS FIRST ACTION WILL BE TO **CLOSE** THE WORMHOLE, SO HE CAN REWORK HIS PLANS.
ONCE THAT WORMHOLE CLOSES, OUR OPPORTUNITY TO TAKE OUT HIMEJI WILL BE GONE, AND THAT'S THE END FOR EVERYONE.
SO THIS WILL BE OUR LAST MISSION.
WE WILL USE THAT WORMHOLE FIRST...
TO RETURN TO THE FUTURE *OUR-SELVES*.

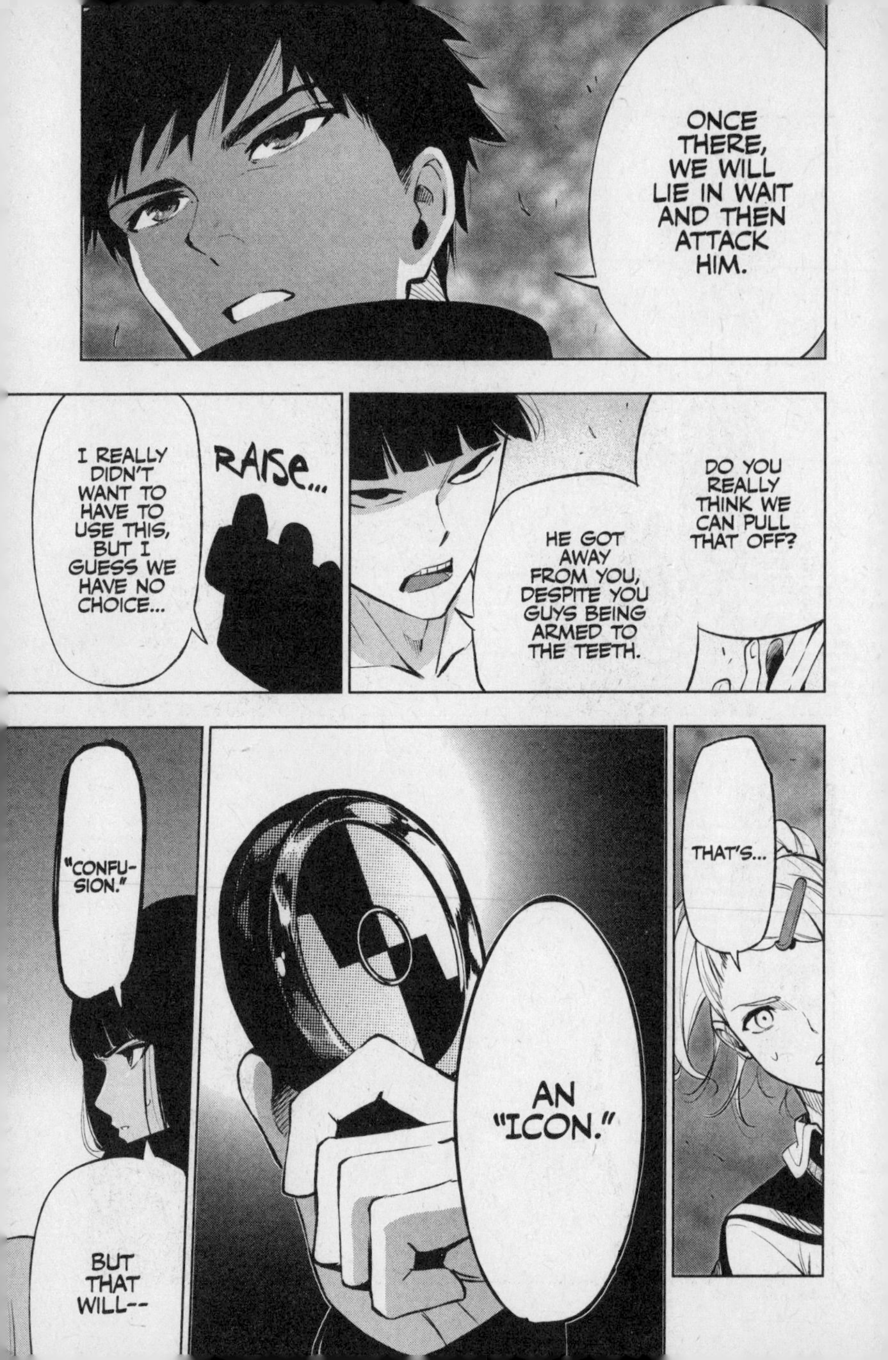
ONCE THERE, WE WILL LIE IN WAIT AND THEN ATTACK HIM.
DO YOU REALLY THINK WE CAN PULL THAT OFF?
HE GOT AWAY FROM YOU, DESPITE YOU GUYS BEING ARMED TO THE TEETH.
RAISE...
I REALLY DIDN'T WANT TO HAVE TO USE THIS, BUT I GUESS WE HAVE NO CHOICE...
THAT'S...
AN "ICON."
"CONFUSION."
BUT THAT WILL--

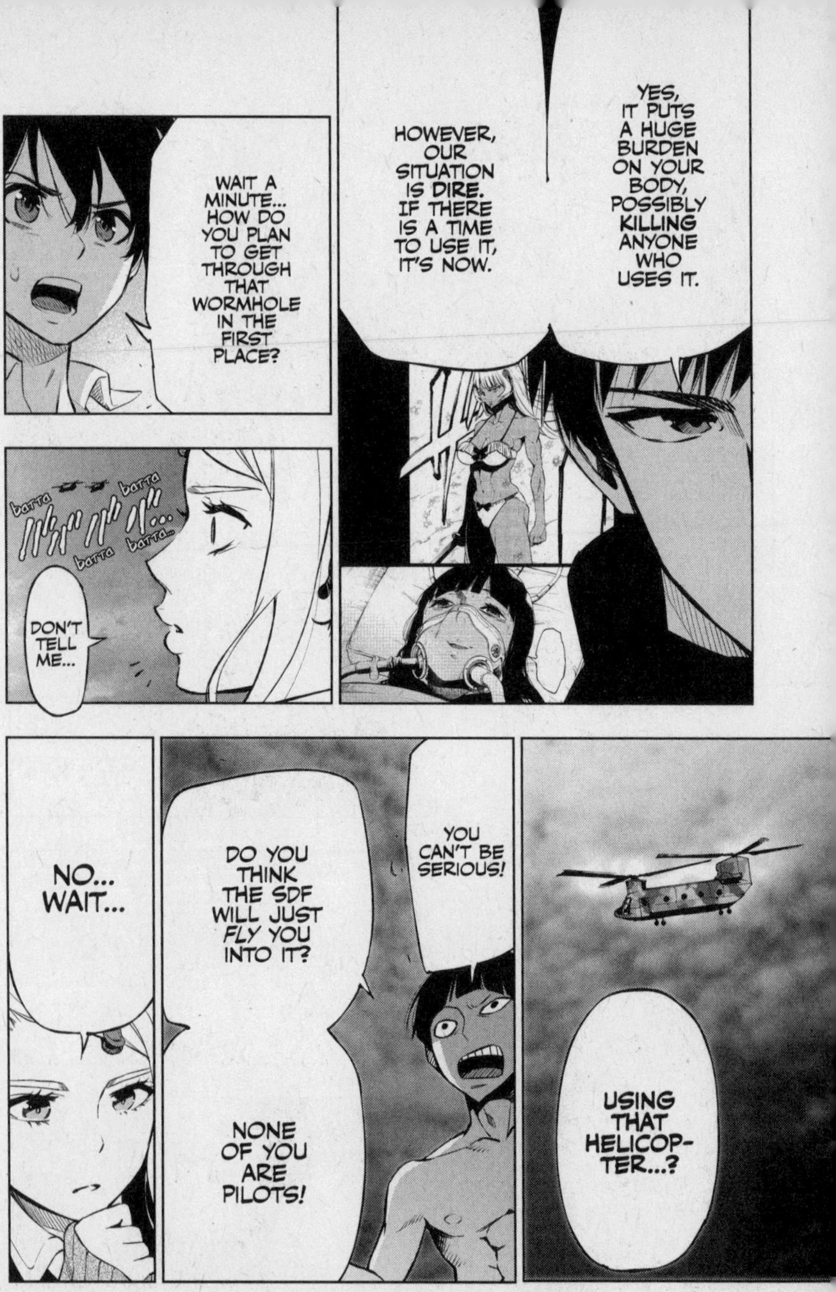
YES, IT PUTS A HUGE BURDEN ON YOUR BODY, POSSIBLY KILLING ANYONE WHO USES IT.
HOWEVER, OUR SITUATION IS DIRE. IF THERE IS A TIME TO USE IT, IT'S NOW.
WAIT A MINUTE... HOW DO YOU PLAN TO GET THROUGH THAT WORMHOLE IN THE FIRST PLACE?
batta batta
batta batta...
DON'T TELL ME...
USING THAT HELICOPTER...?
YOU CAN'T BE SERIOUS!
DO YOU THINK THE SDF WILL JUST *FLY* YOU INTO IT?
NONE OF YOU ARE PILOTS!
NO... WAIT...

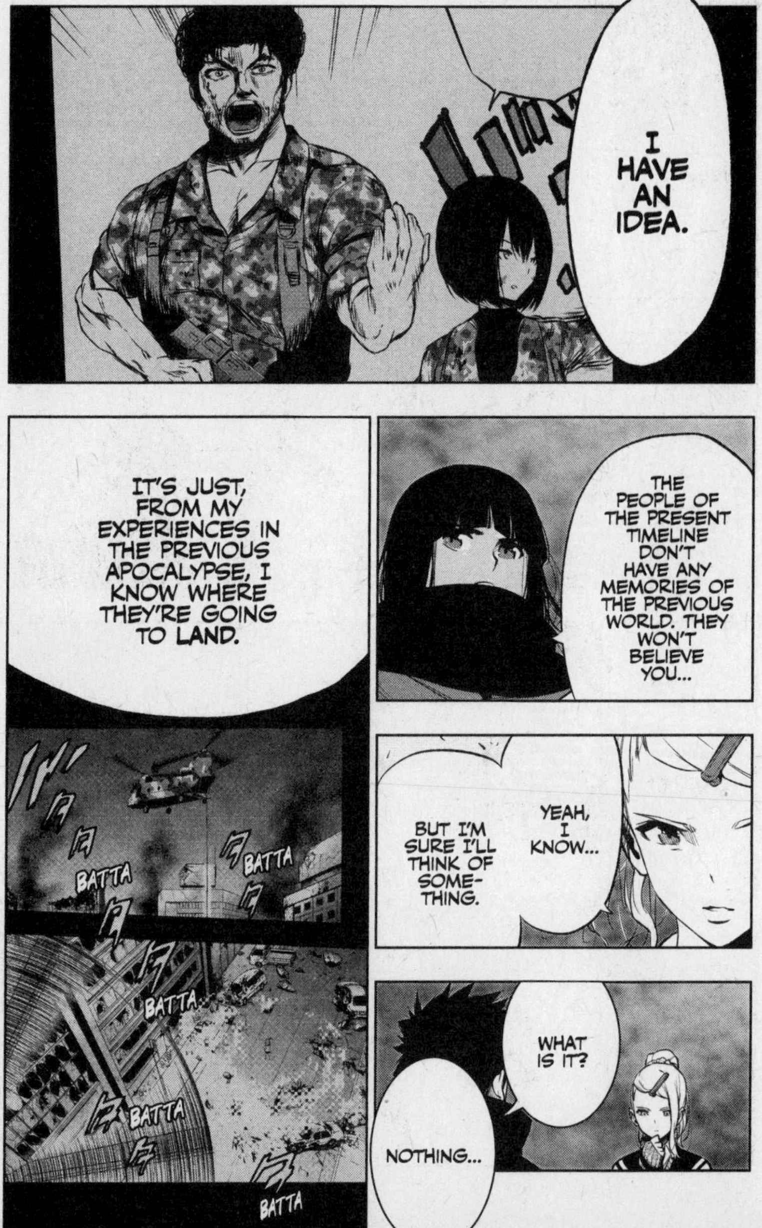
I HAVE AN IDEA.
THE PEOPLE OF THE PRESENT TIMELINE DON'T HAVE ANY MEMORIES OF THE PREVIOUS WORLD. THEY WON'T BELIEVE YOU...
IT'S JUST, FROM MY EXPERIENCES IN THE PREVIOUS APOCALYPSE, I KNOW WHERE THEY'RE GOING TO LAND.
YEAH, I KNOW...
BUT I'M SURE I'LL THINK OF SOME-THING.
BATTA
BATTA
WHAT IS IT?
NOTHING...
BATTA
BATTA
BATTA

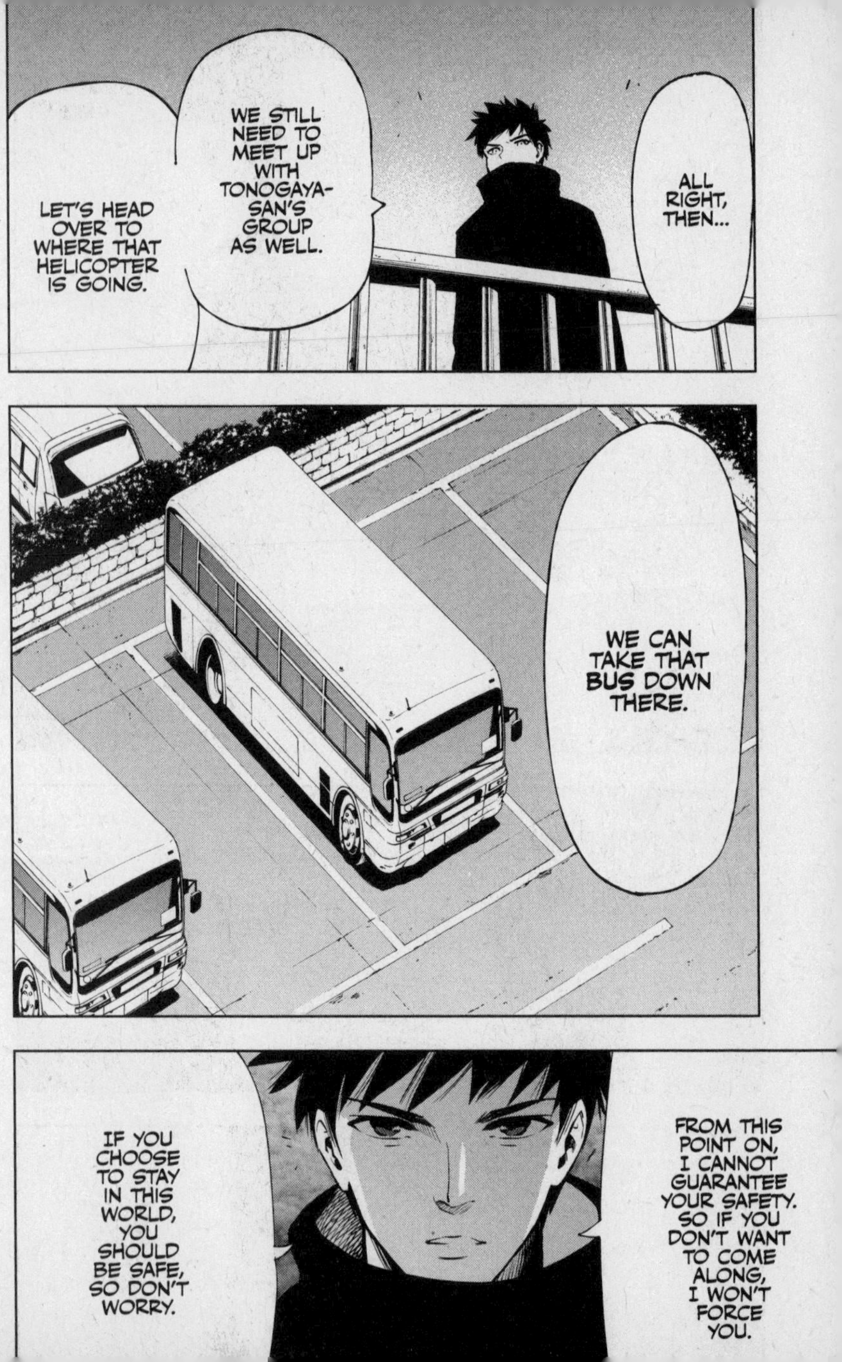
ALL RIGHT, THEN...
WE STILL NEED TO MEET UP WITH TONOGAYA-SAN'S GROUP AS WELL.
LET'S HEAD OVER TO WHERE THAT HELICOPTER IS GOING.
WE CAN TAKE THAT BUS DOWN THERE.
FROM THIS POINT ON, I CANNOT GUARANTEE YOUR SAFETY. SO IF YOU DON'T WANT TO COME ALONG, I WON'T FORCE YOU.
IF YOU CHOOSE TO STAY IN THIS WORLD, YOU SHOULD BE SAFE, SO DON'T WORRY.

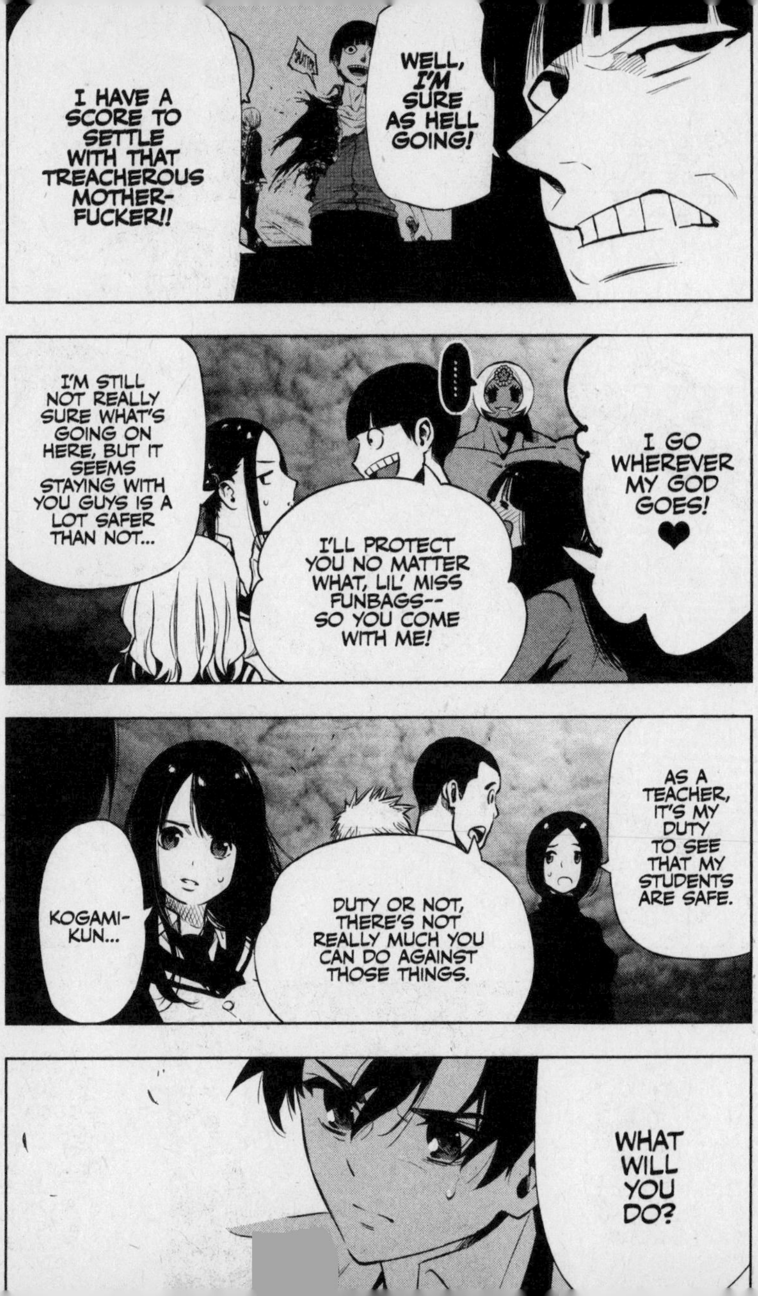
WELL, I'M SURE AS HELL GOING!
I HAVE A SCORE TO SETTLE WITH THAT TREACHEROUS MOTHER-FUCKER!!
I GO WHEREVER MY GOD GOES! ♥
......
I'LL PROTECT YOU NO MATTER WHAT, LIL' MISS FUNBAGS--SO YOU COME WITH ME!
I'M STILL NOT REALLY SURE WHAT'S GOING ON HERE, BUT IT SEEMS STAYING WITH YOU GUYS IS A LOT SAFER THAN NOT...
AS A TEACHER, IT'S MY DUTY TO SEE THAT MY STUDENTS ARE SAFE.
DUTY OR NOT, THERE'S NOT REALLY MUCH YOU CAN DO AGAINST THOSE THINGS.
KOGAMI-KUN...
WHAT WILL YOU DO?

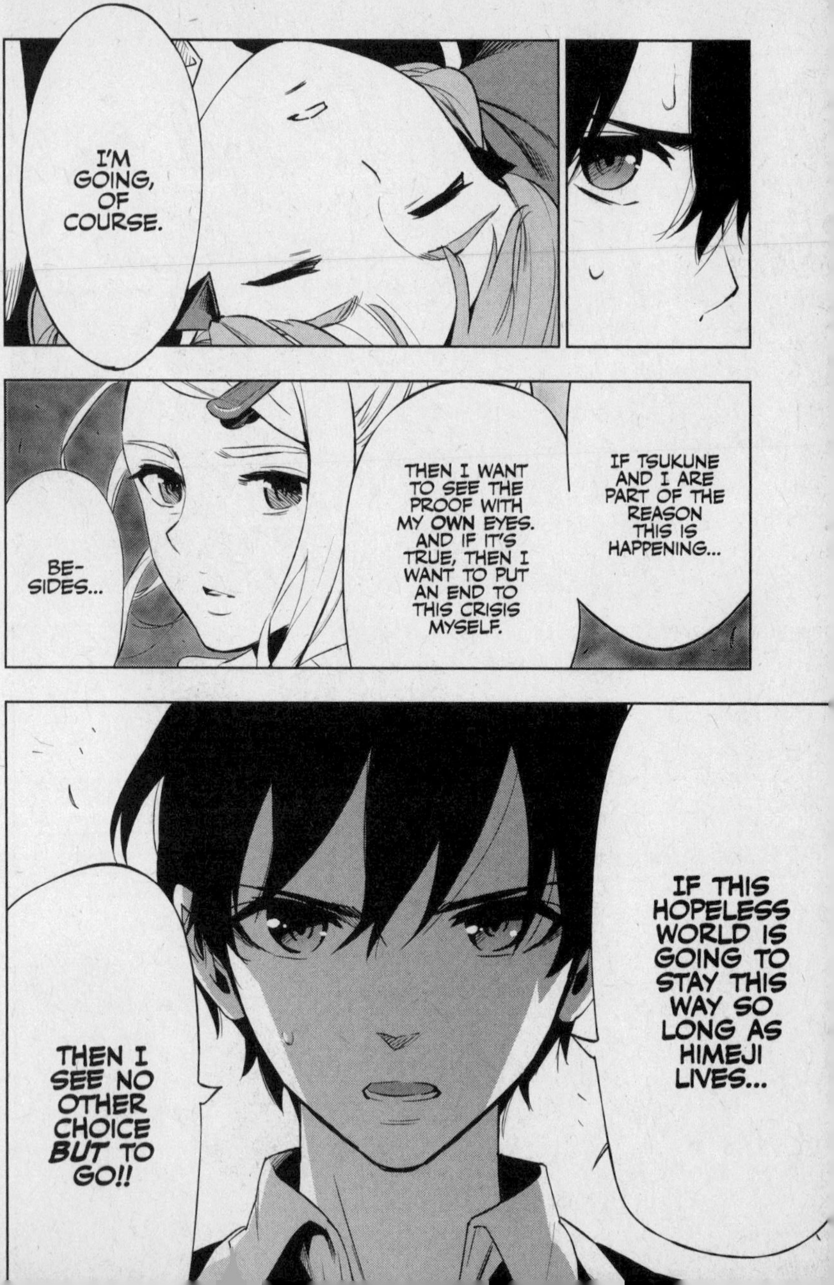
I'M GOING, OF COURSE.
IF TSUKUNE AND I ARE PART OF THE REASON THIS IS HAPPENING...
THEN I WANT TO SEE THE PROOF WITH MY OWN EYES. AND IF IT'S TRUE, THEN I WANT TO PUT AN END TO THIS CRISIS MYSELF.
BE-SIDES...
IF THIS HOPELESS WORLD IS GOING TO STAY THIS WAY SO LONG AS HIMEJI LIVES...
THEN I SEE NO OTHER CHOICE *BUT* TO GO!!

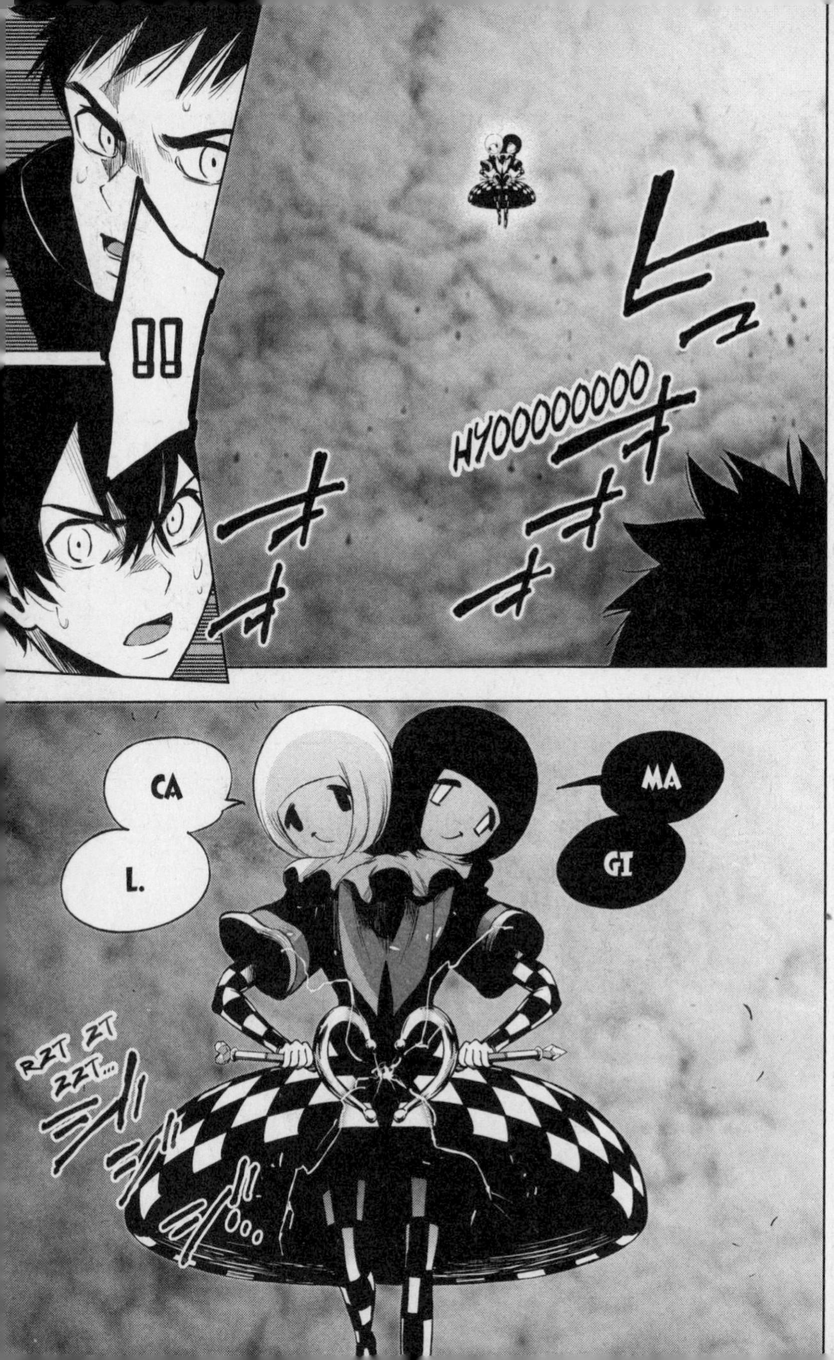

HYOOOOOOOO
!!
MA
GI
CA
L.
RZT ZT
ZZT...
Ooo

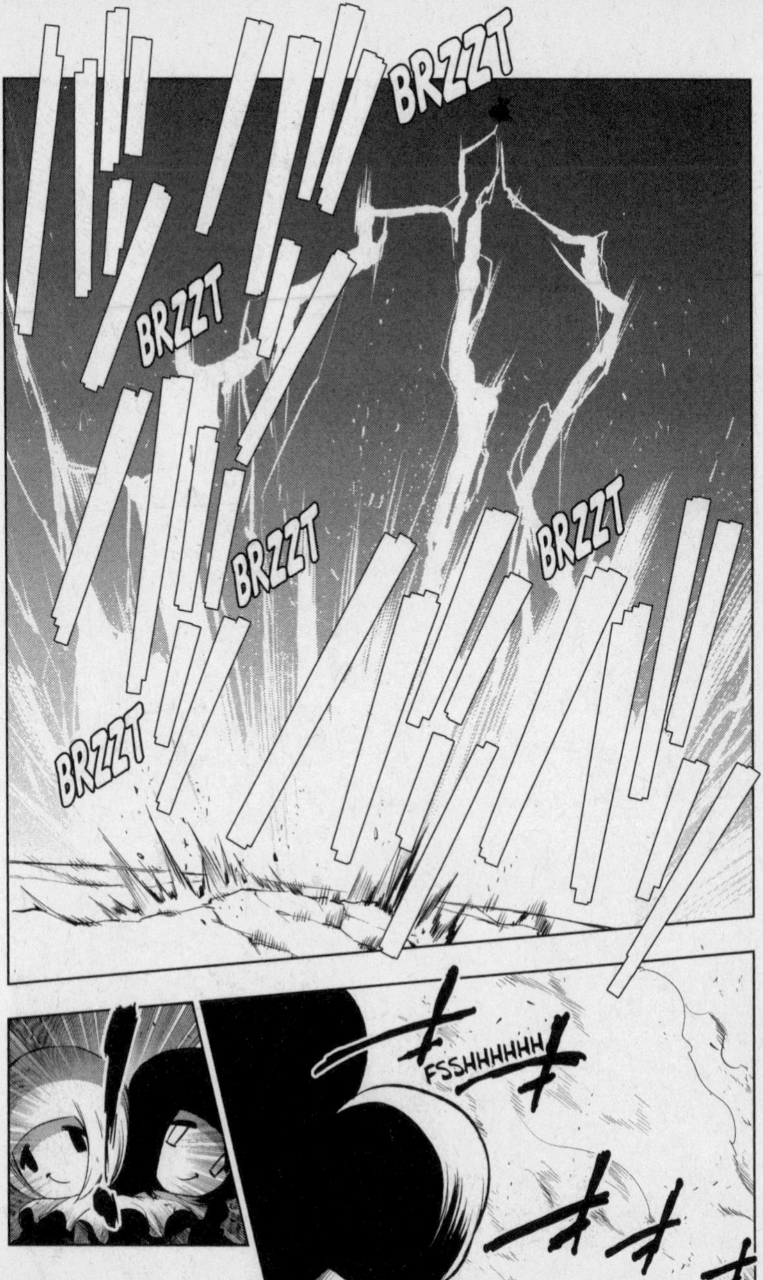
BRZZT
BRZZT
BRZZT
BRZZT
BRZZT
FSSHHHHHH

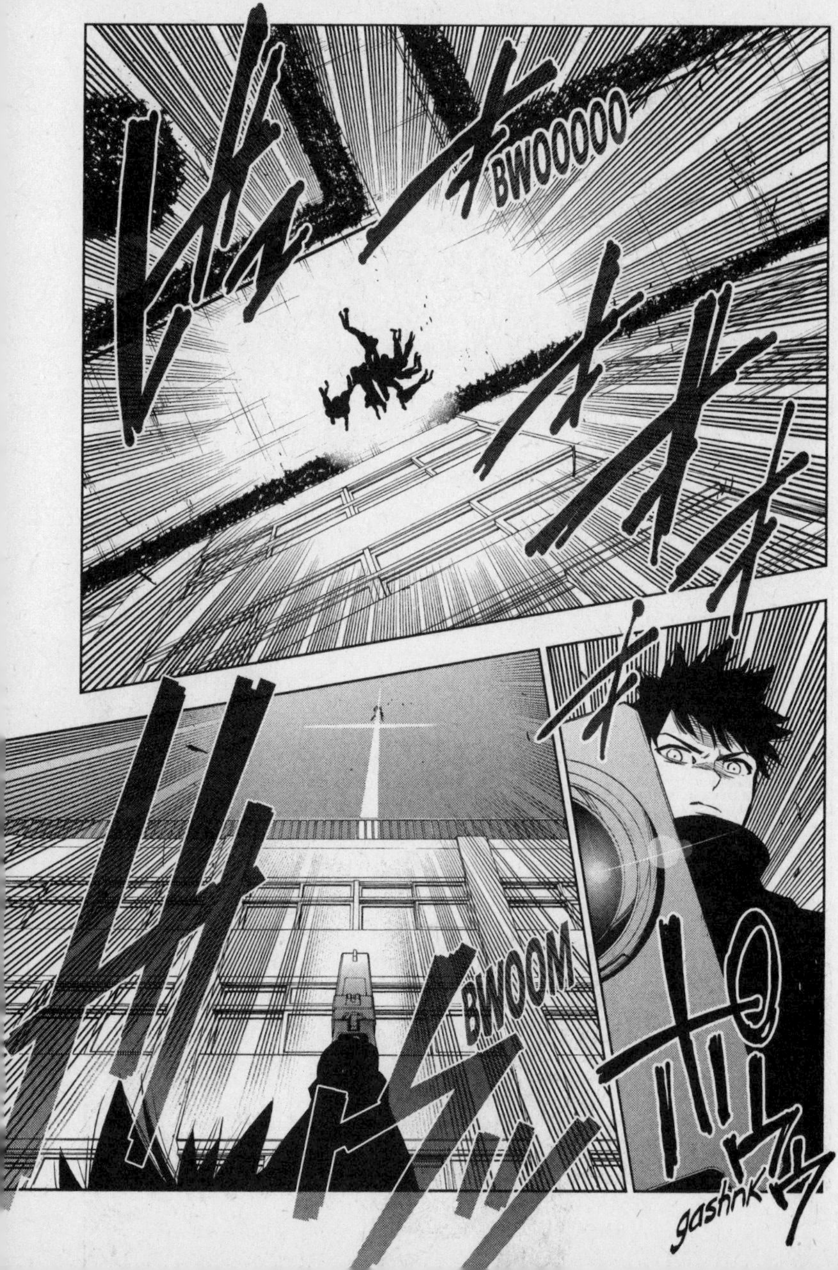
BWOOOOO
gashink
BWOOM

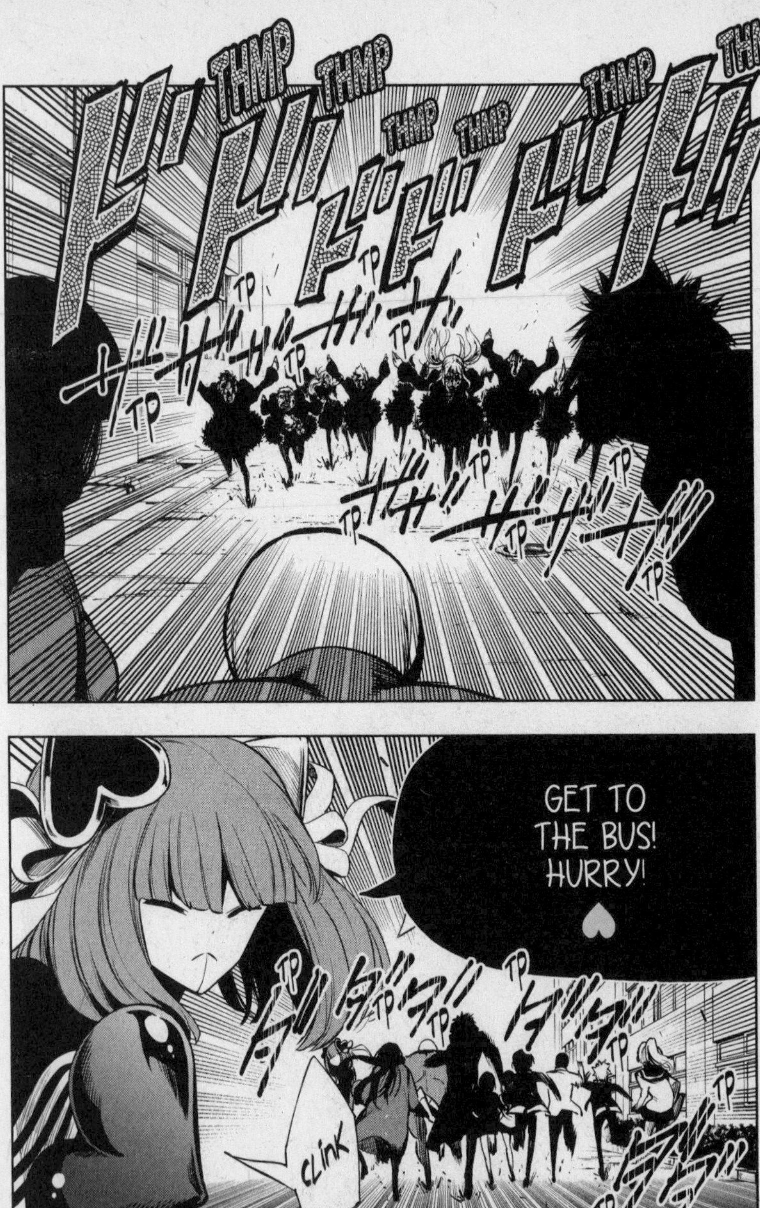
THMP THMP THMP THMP THMP THMP
TP TP TP TP TP TP TP TP TP TP
GET TO THE BUS! HURRY! ♥
TP TP TP TP TP TP
CLINK

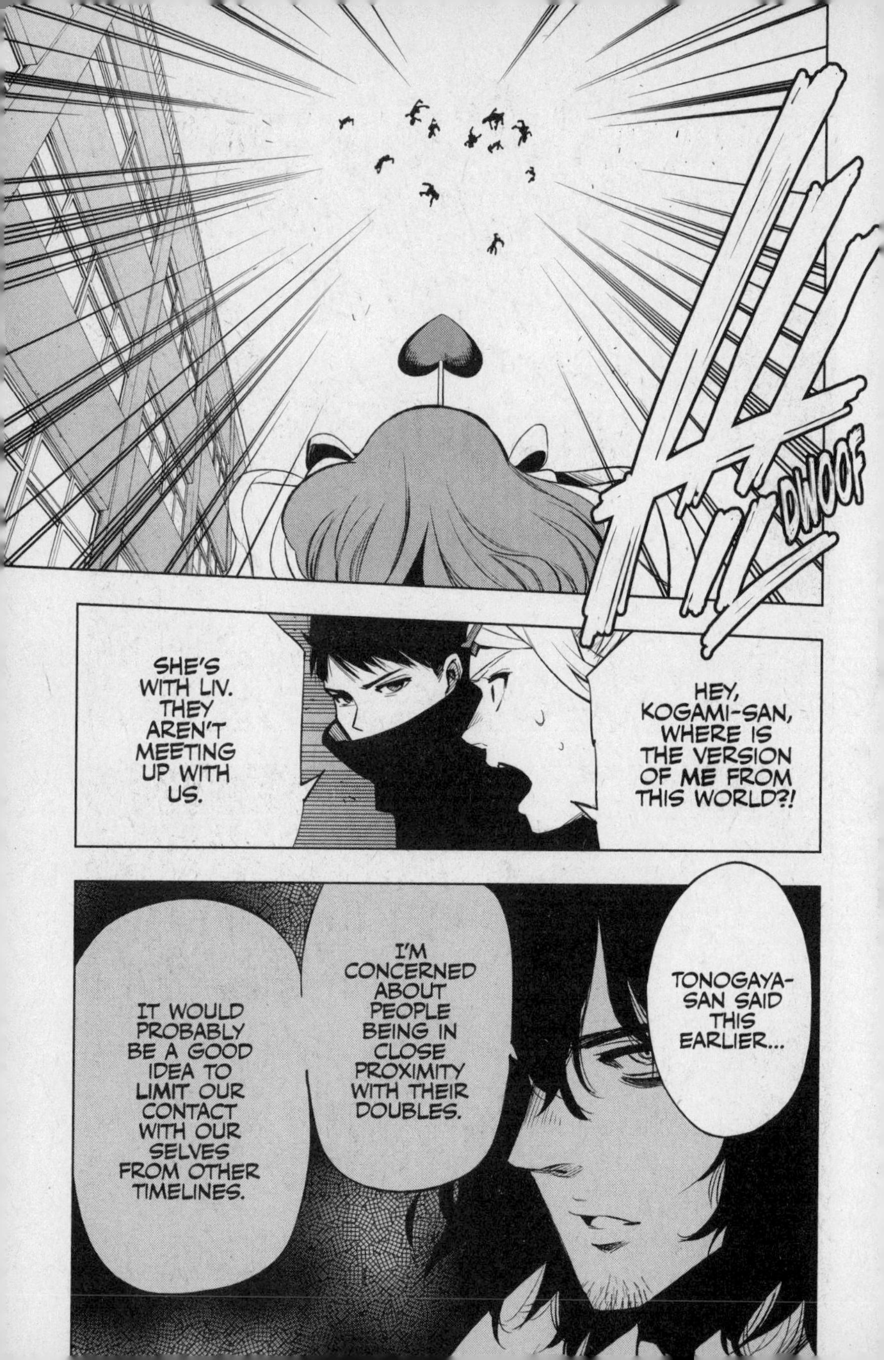
DWOOF
HEY, KOGAMI-SAN, WHERE IS THE VERSION OF ME FROM THIS WORLD?!
SHE'S WITH LIV. THEY AREN'T MEETING UP WITH US.
TONOGAYA-SAN SAID THIS EARLIER...
I'M CONCERNED ABOUT PEOPLE BEING IN CLOSE PROXIMITY WITH THEIR DOUBLES.
IT WOULD PROBABLY BE A GOOD IDEA TO LIMIT OUR CONTACT WITH OUR SELVES FROM OTHER TIMELINES.

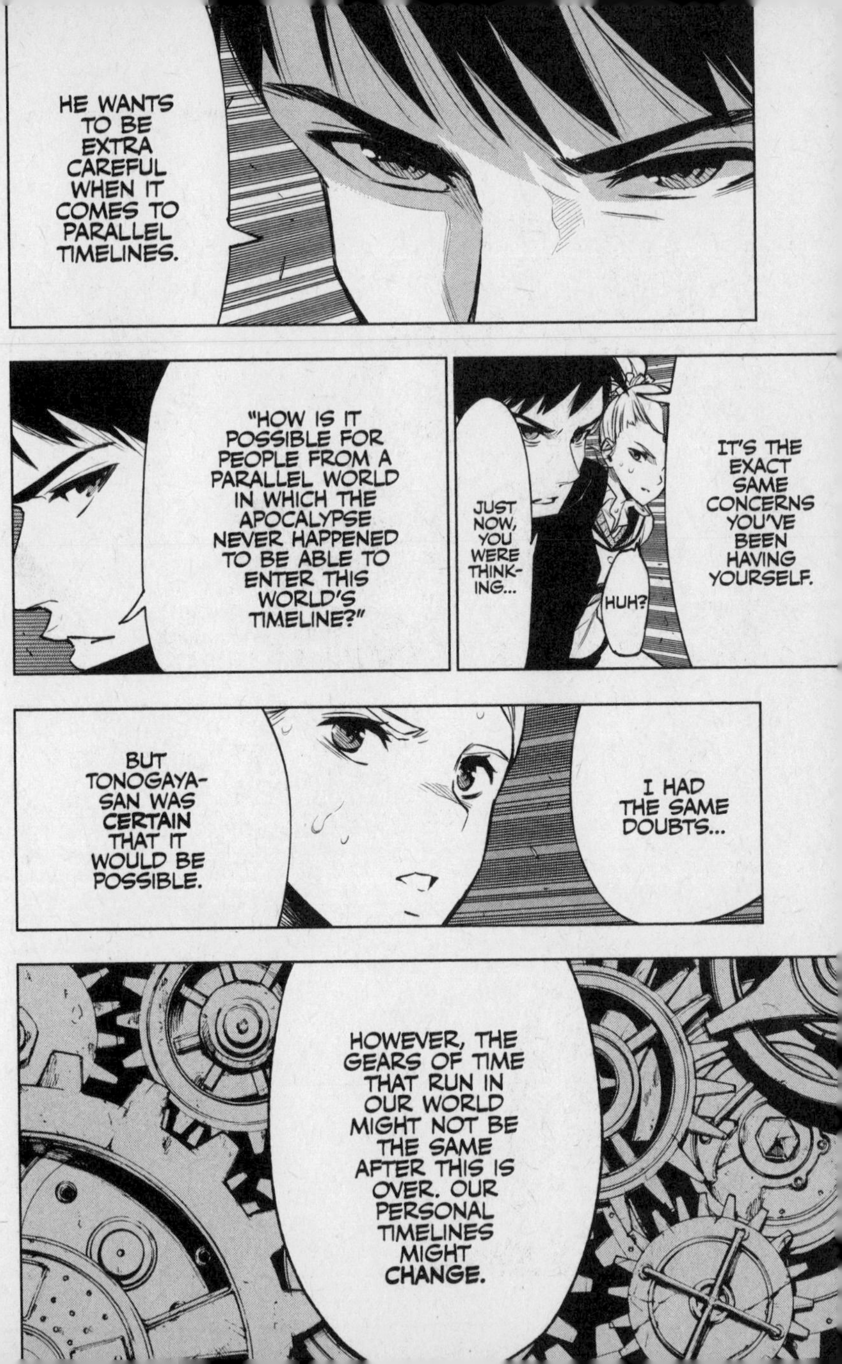
HE WANTS TO BE EXTRA CAREFUL WHEN IT COMES TO PARALLEL TIMELINES.
IT'S THE EXACT SAME CONCERNS YOU'VE BEEN HAVING YOURSELF.
HUH?
JUST NOW, YOU WERE THINK-ING...
"HOW IS IT POSSIBLE FOR PEOPLE FROM A PARALLEL WORLD IN WHICH THE APOCALYPSE NEVER HAPPENED TO BE ABLE TO ENTER THIS WORLD'S TIMELINE?"
I HAD THE SAME DOUBTS...
BUT TONOGAYA-SAN WAS CERTAIN THAT IT WOULD BE POSSIBLE.
HOWEVER, THE GEARS OF TIME THAT RUN IN OUR WORLD MIGHT NOT BE THE SAME AFTER THIS IS OVER. OUR PERSONAL TIMELINES MIGHT CHANGE.

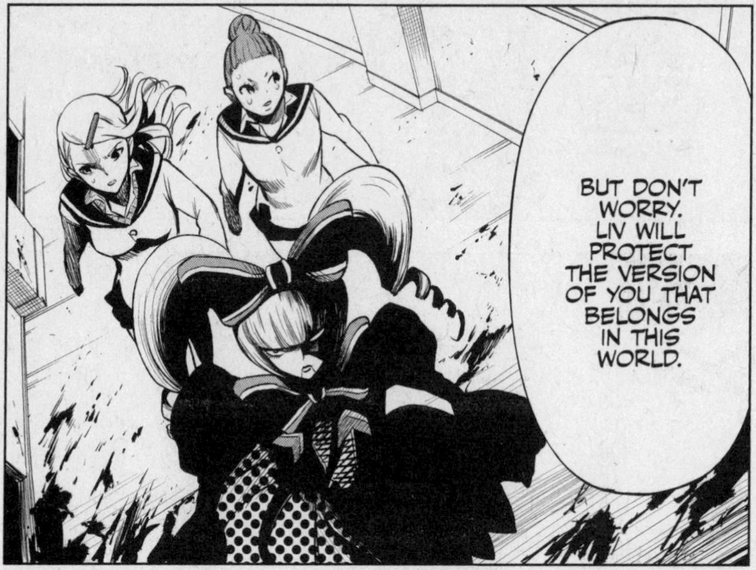
BUT DON'T WORRY. LIV WILL PROTECT THE VERSION OF YOU THAT BELONGS IN THIS WORLD.

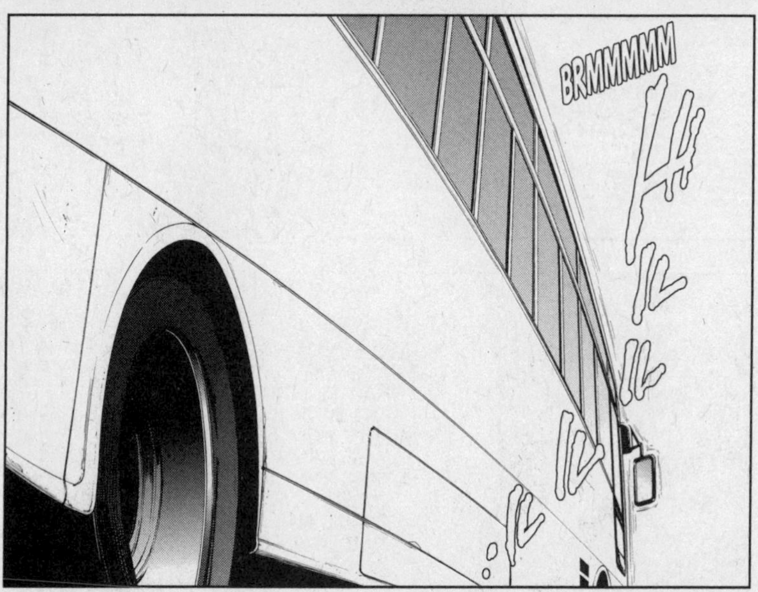
BRMMMMM

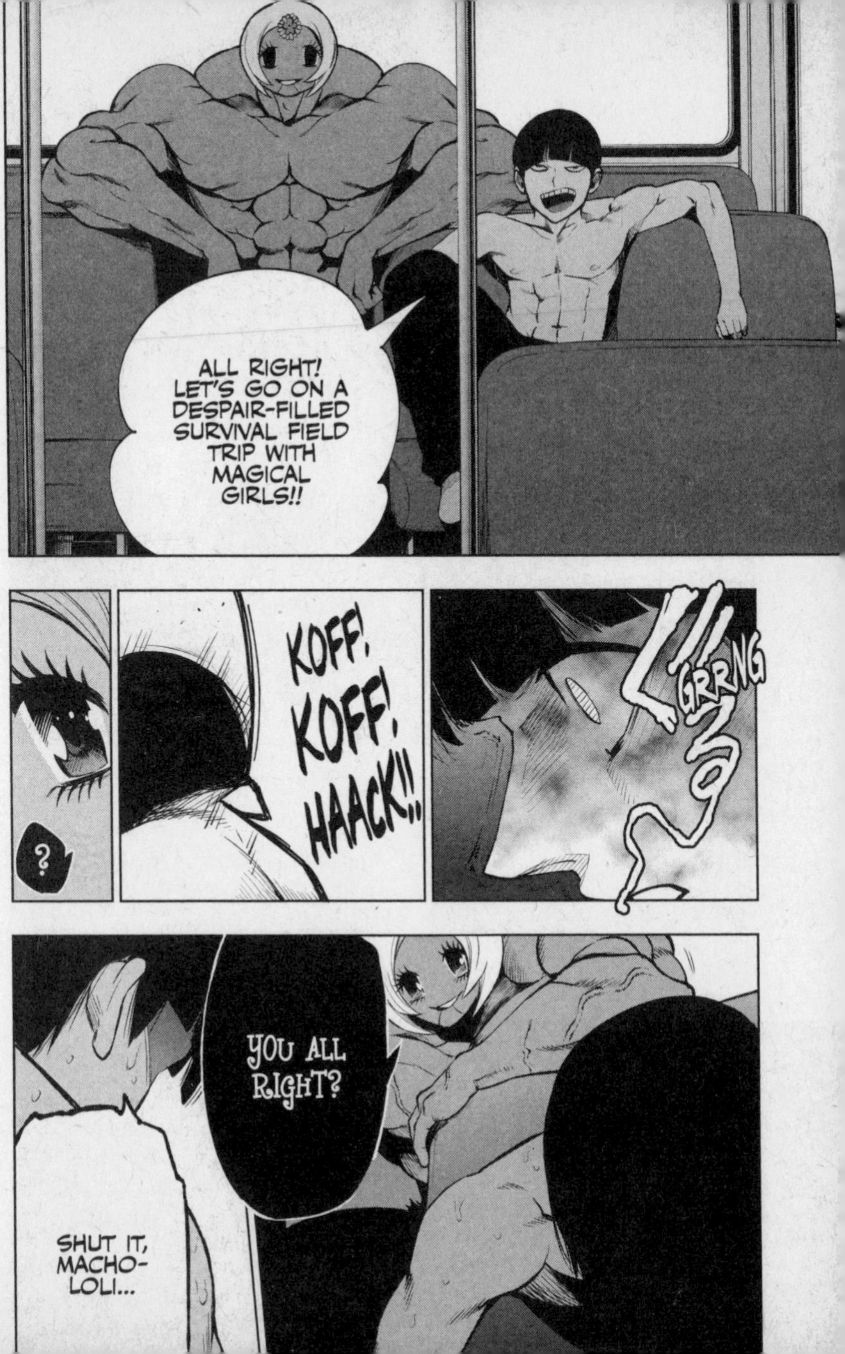
ALL RIGHT! LET'S GO ON A DESPAIR-FILLED SURVIVAL FIELD TRIP WITH MAGICAL GIRLS!!
GRRNG
KOFF! KOFF! HAACK!!
?
YOU ALL RIGHT?
SHUT IT, MACHO-LOLI...

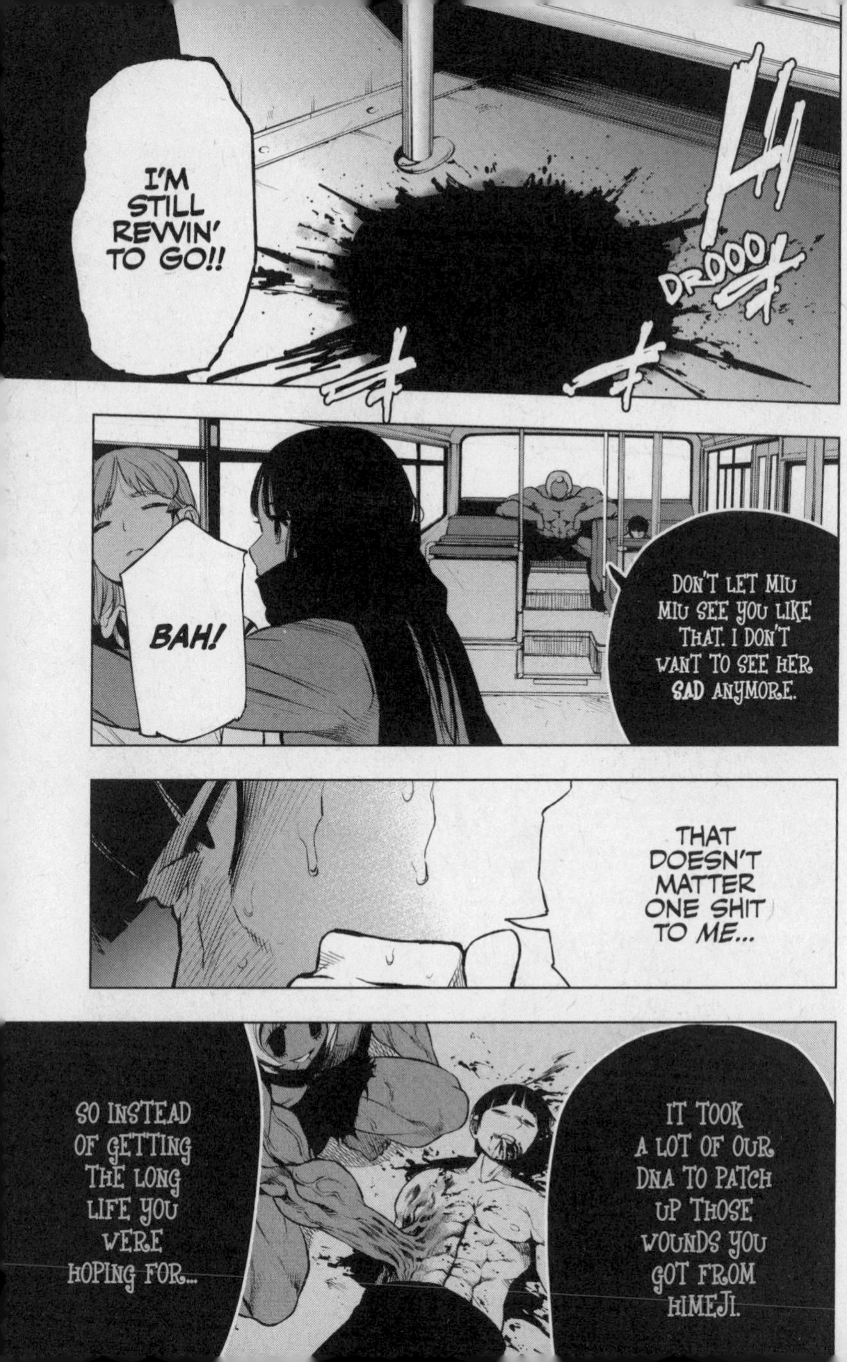
DROOO
I'M STILL REVVIN' TO GO!!
DON'T LET MIU MIU SEE YOU LIKE THAT. I DON'T WANT TO SEE HER SAD ANYMORE.
BAH!
THAT DOESN'T MATTER ONE SHIT TO ME...
IT TOOK A LOT OF OUR DNA TO PATCH UP THOSE WOUNDS YOU GOT FROM HIMEJI.
SO INSTEAD OF GETTING THE LONG LIFE YOU WERE HOPING FOR...

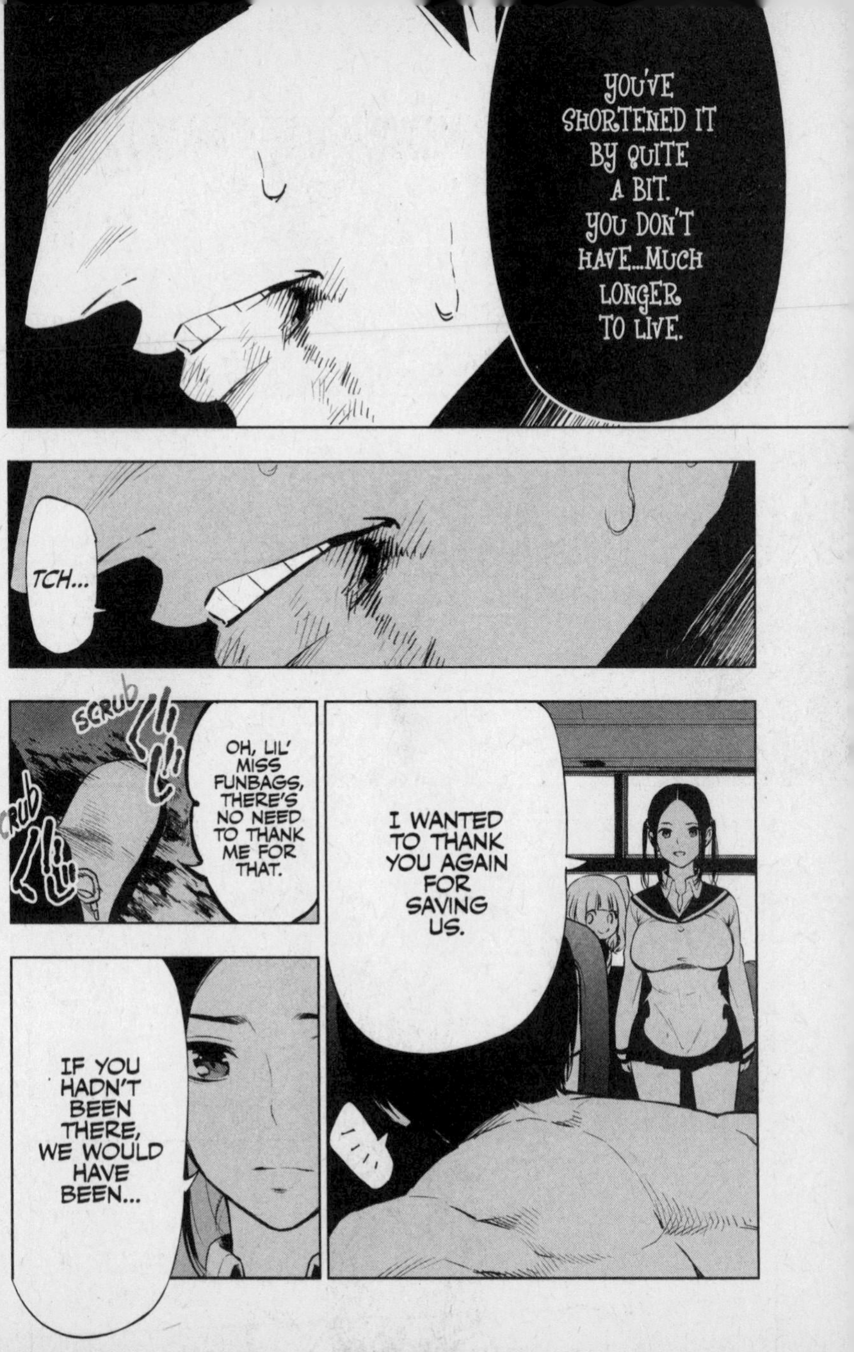
YOU'VE SHORTENED IT BY QUITE A BIT. YOU DON'T HAVE...MUCH LONGER TO LIVE.
TCH...
I WANTED TO THANK YOU AGAIN FOR SAVING US.
...
SCRUB
SCRUB
OH, LIL' MISS FUNBAGS, THERE'S NO NEED TO THANK ME FOR THAT.
IF YOU HADN'T BEEN THERE, WE WOULD HAVE BEEN...

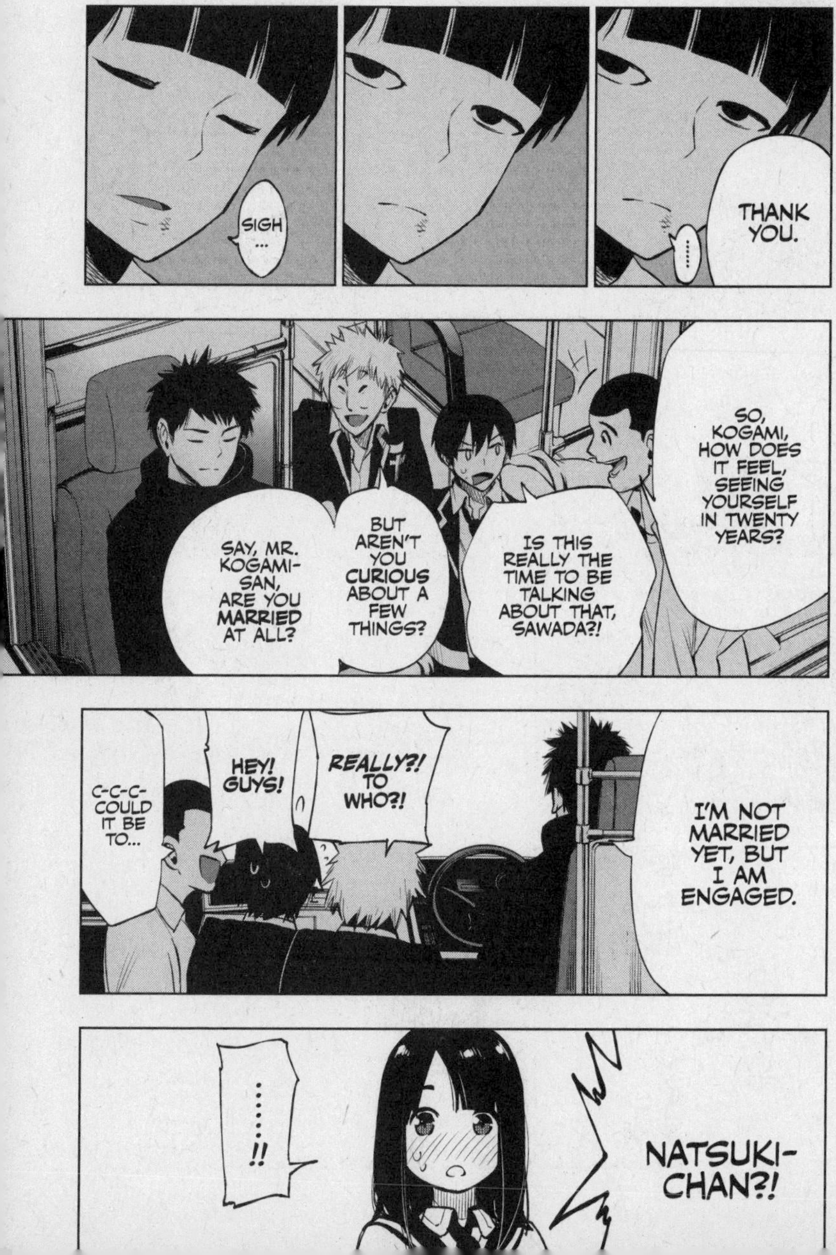
THANK YOU.
......
SIGH ...
SO, KOGAMI, HOW DOES IT FEEL, SEEING YOURSELF IN TWENTY YEARS?
IS THIS REALLY THE TIME TO BE TALKING ABOUT THAT, SAWADA?!
BUT AREN'T YOU CURIOUS ABOUT A FEW THINGS?
SAY, MR. KOGAMI-SAN, ARE YOU MARRIED AT ALL?
I'M NOT MARRIED YET, BUT I AM ENGAGED.
REALLY?! TO WHO?!
HEY! GUYS!
C-C-C-COULD IT BE TO...
NATSUKI-CHAN?!
......!!

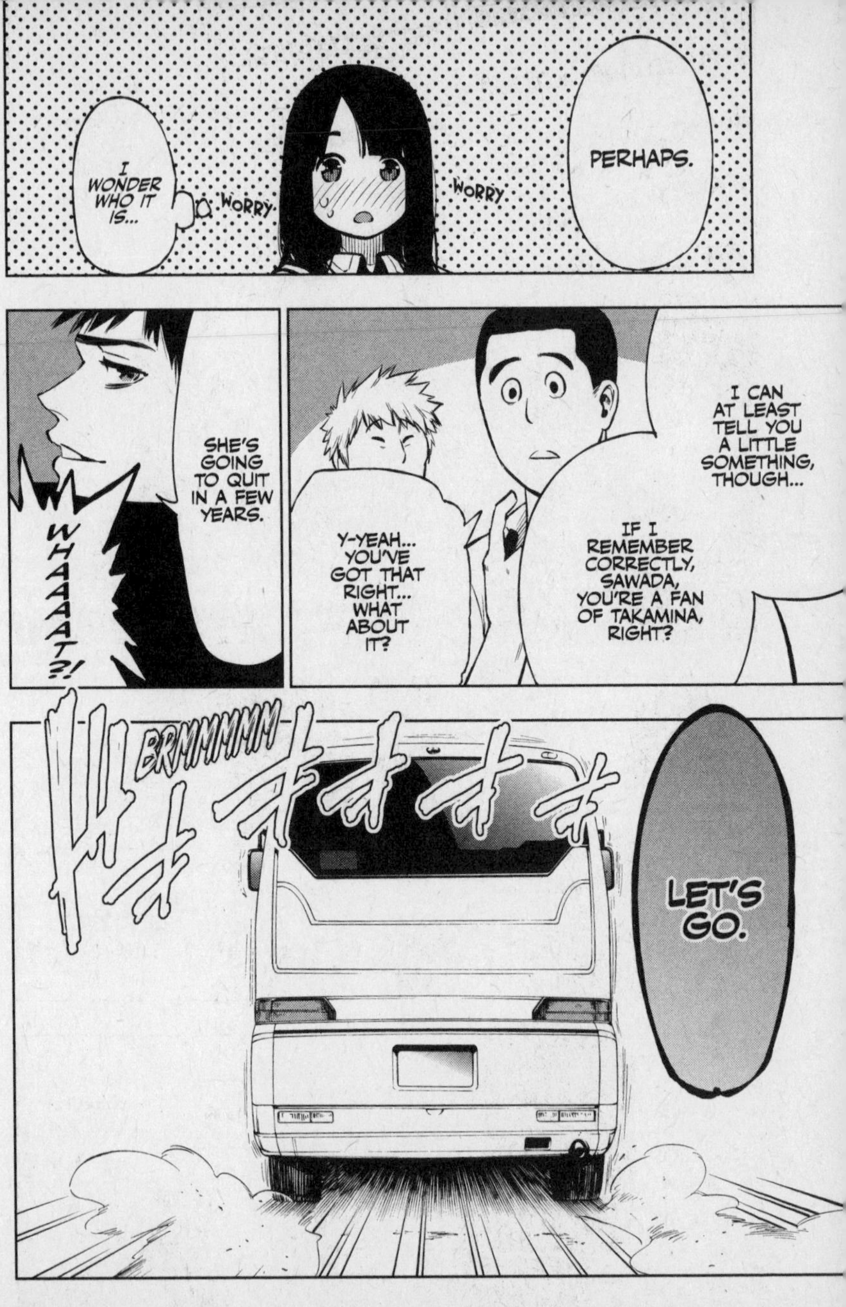
PERHAPS.
WORRY
WORRY
I WONDER WHO IT IS...
I CAN AT LEAST TELL YOU A LITTLE SOMETHING, THOUGH...
IF I REMEMBER CORRECTLY, SAWADA, YOU'RE A FAN OF TAKAMINA, RIGHT?
Y-YEAH... YOU'VE GOT THAT RIGHT... WHAT ABOUT IT?
SHE'S GOING TO QUIT IN A FEW YEARS.
WHAAAAAT?!
LET'S GO.
BRMMMMM

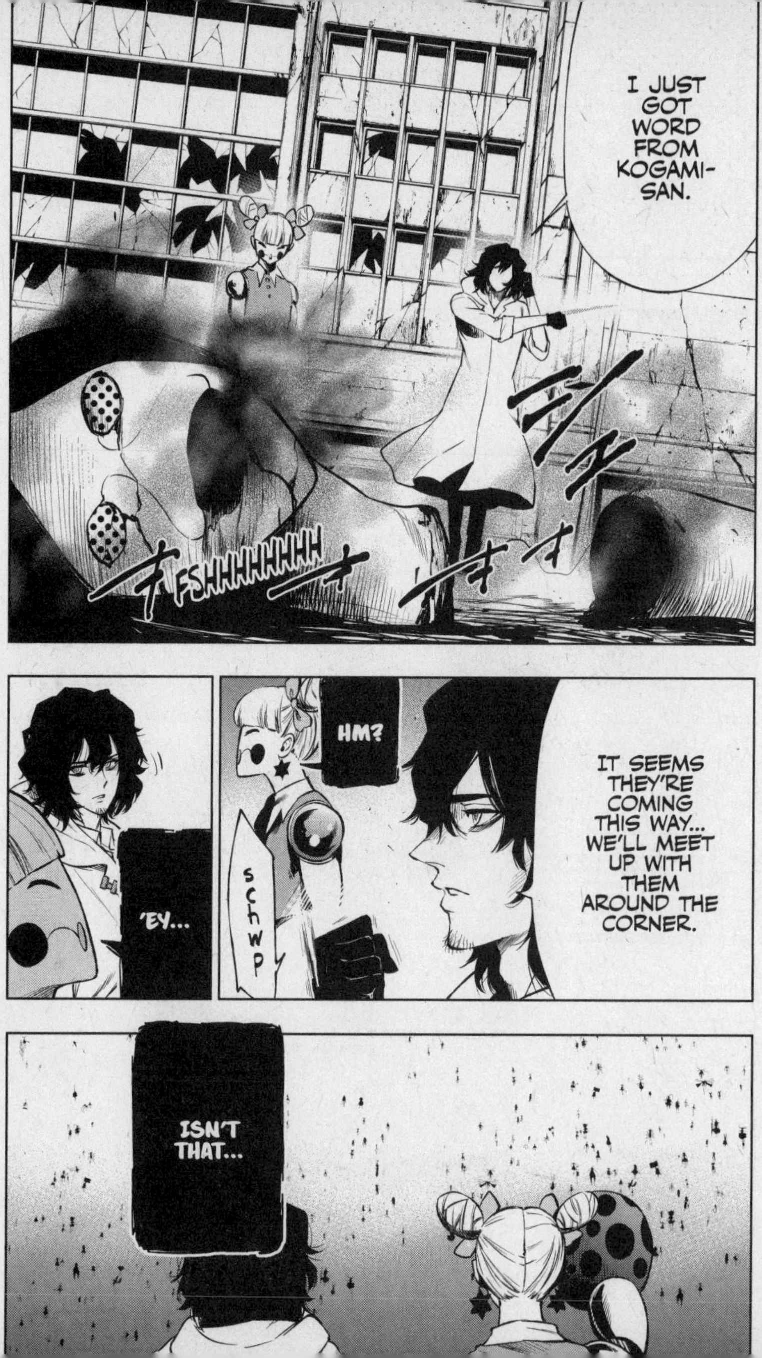
I JUST GOT WORD FROM KOGAMI-SAN.
FSHHHHHHHH
IT SEEMS THEY'RE COMING THIS WAY... WE'LL MEET UP WITH THEM AROUND THE CORNER.
HM?
schwp
'EY...
ISN'T THAT...

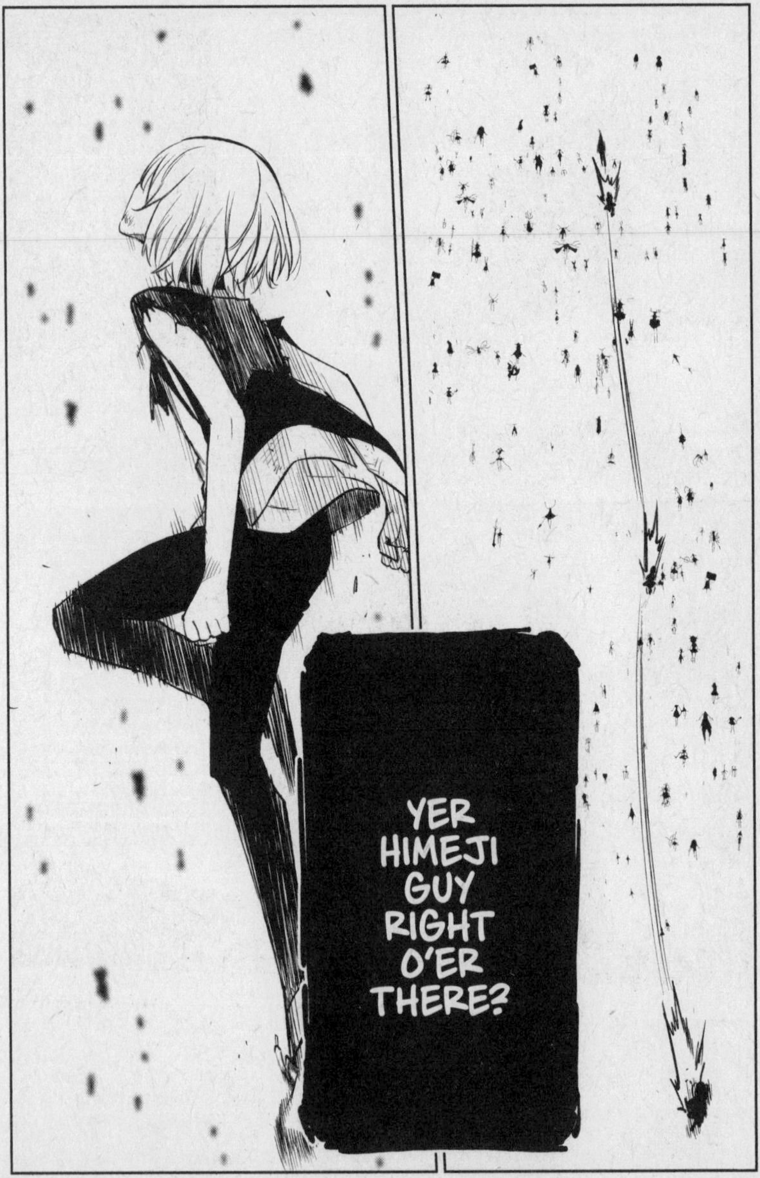
YER HIMEJI GUY RIGHT O'ER THERE?

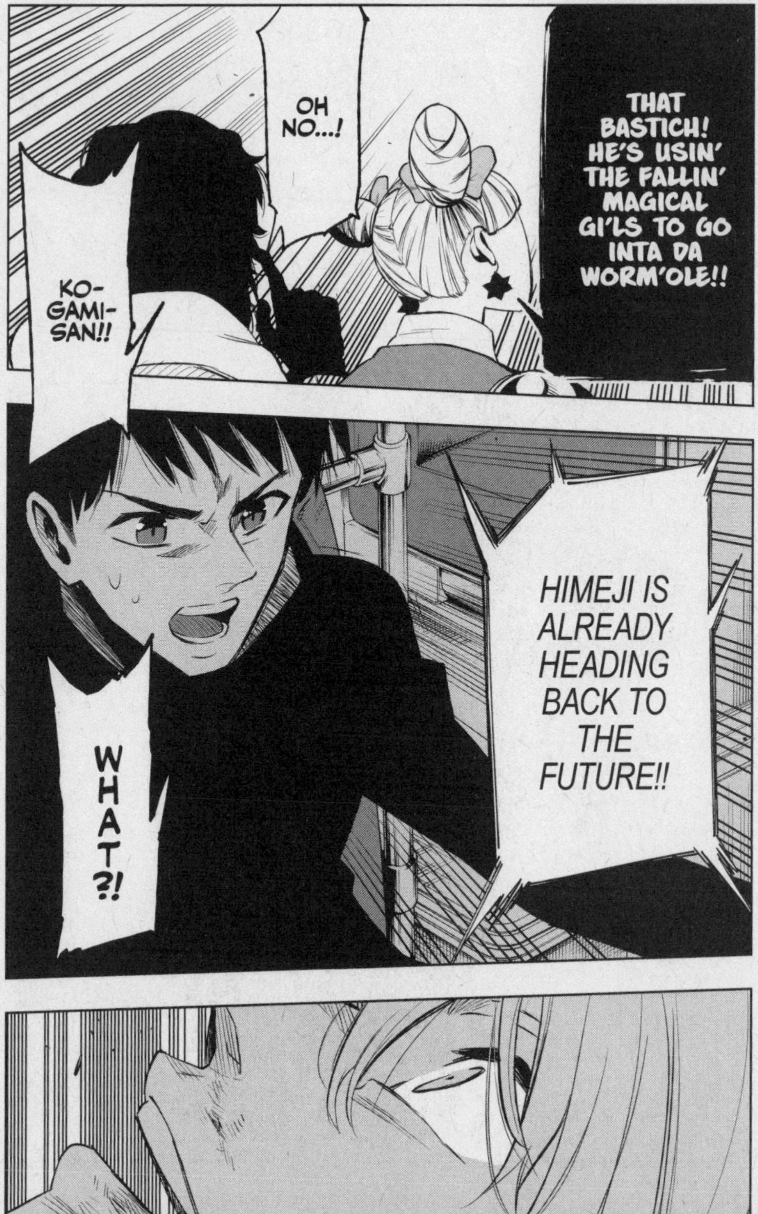
THAT BASTICH! HE'S USIN' THE FALLIN' MAGICAL GI'LS TO GO INTA DA WORM'OLE!!
OH NO...!
KO-GAMI-SAN!!
HIMEJI IS ALREADY HEADING BACK TO THE FUTURE!!
WHAT?!

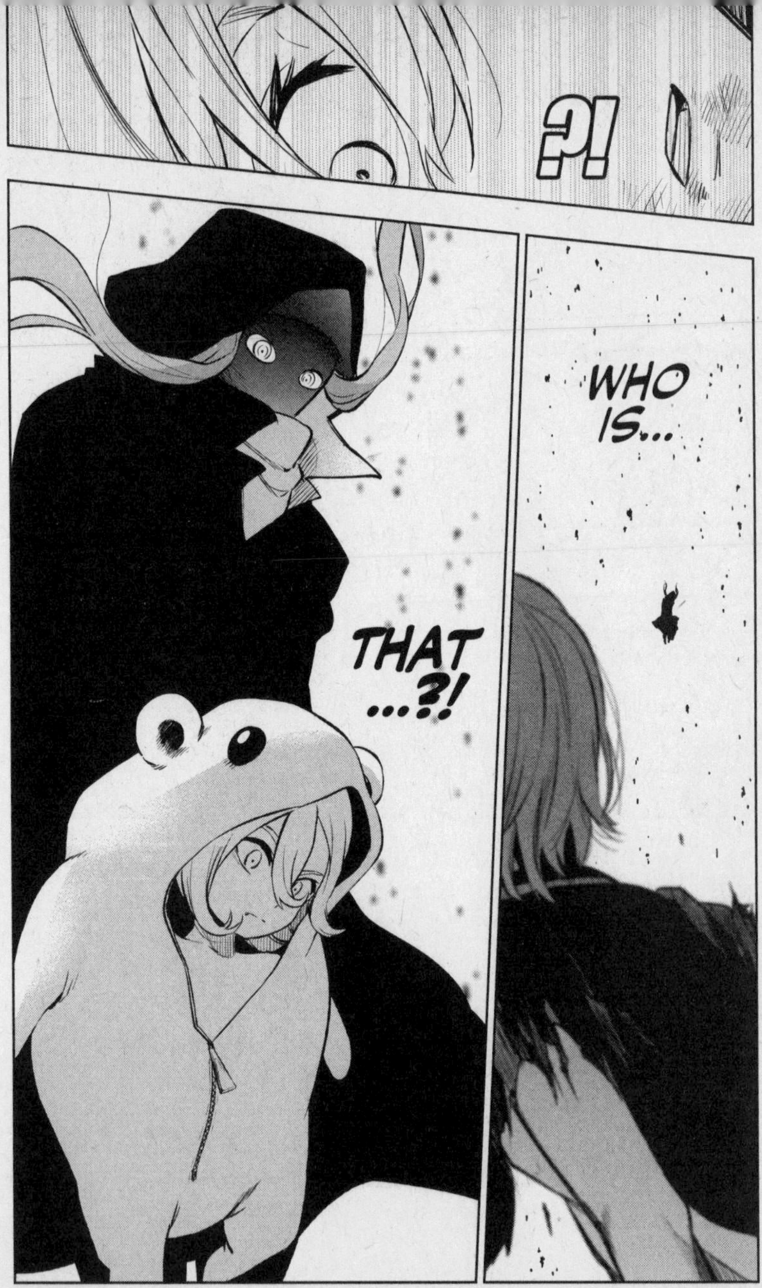
?!
WHO IS...
THAT ...?!

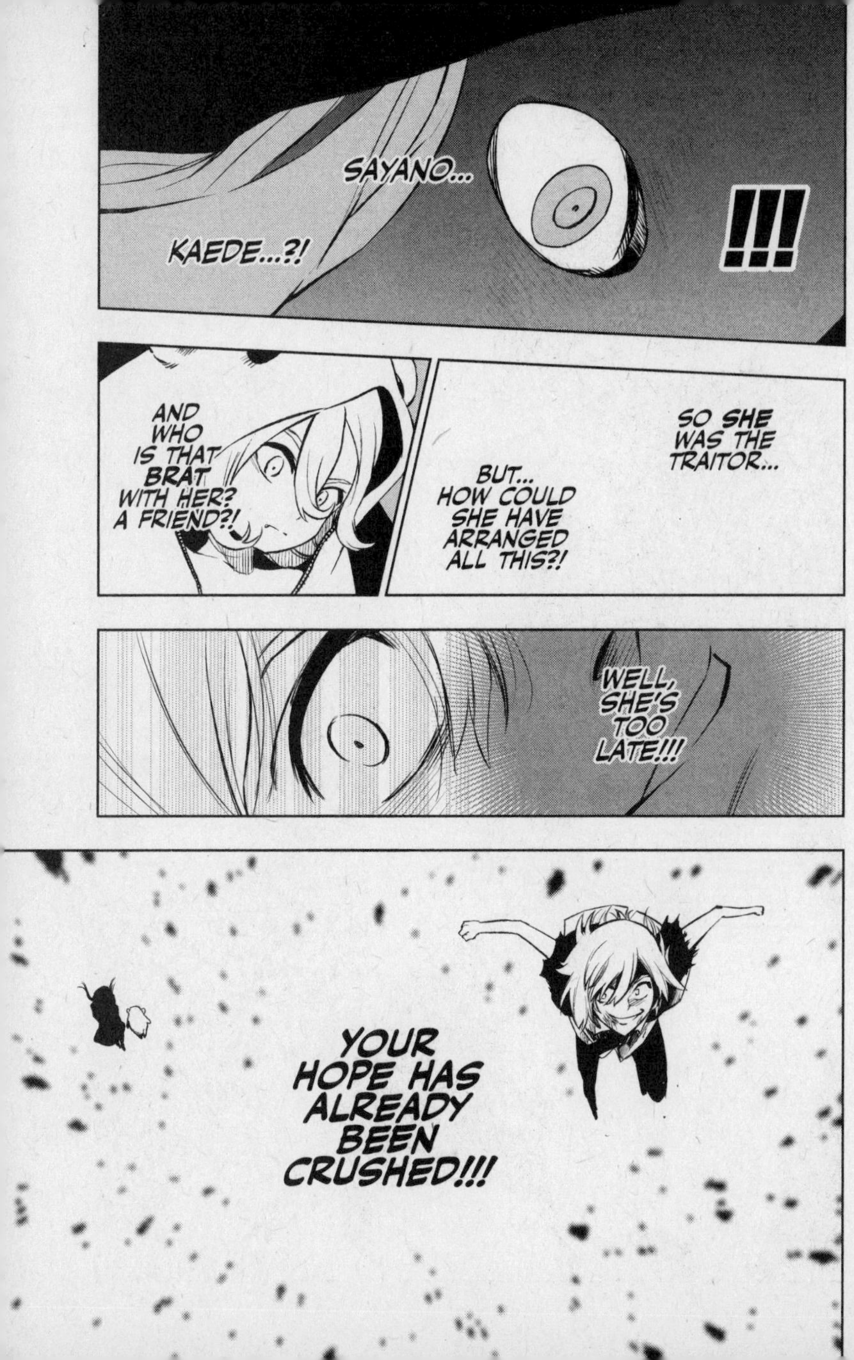
!!!
SAYANO...
KAEDE...?!
SO SHE WAS THE TRAITOR...
BUT... HOW COULD SHE HAVE ARRANGED ALL THIS?!
AND WHO IS THAT BRAT WITH HER? A FRIEND?!
WELL, SHE'S TOO LATE!!!
YOUR HOPE HAS ALREADY BEEN CRUSHED!!!

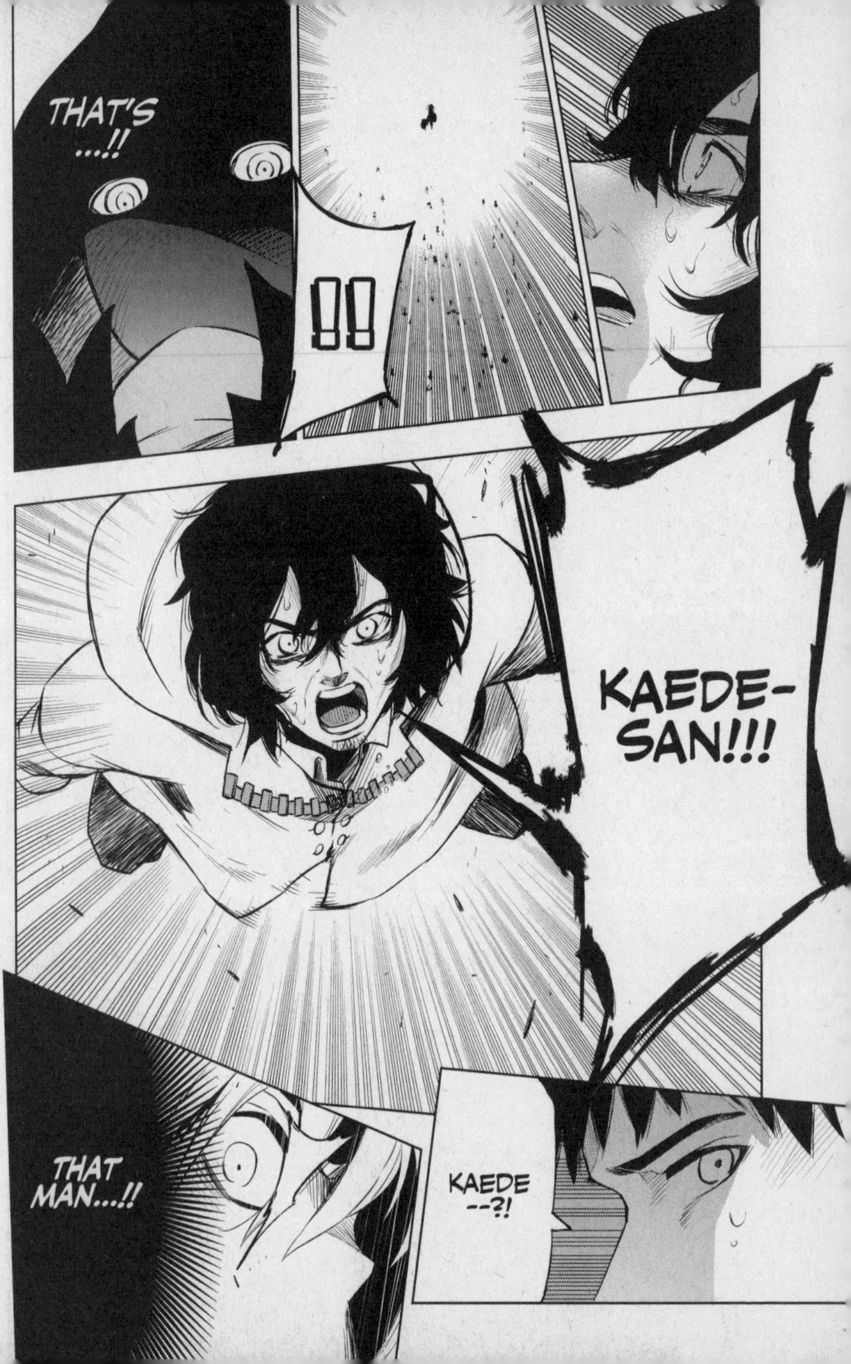
!!
THAT'S ...!!
KAEDE-SAN!!!
KAEDE --?!
THAT MAN...!!

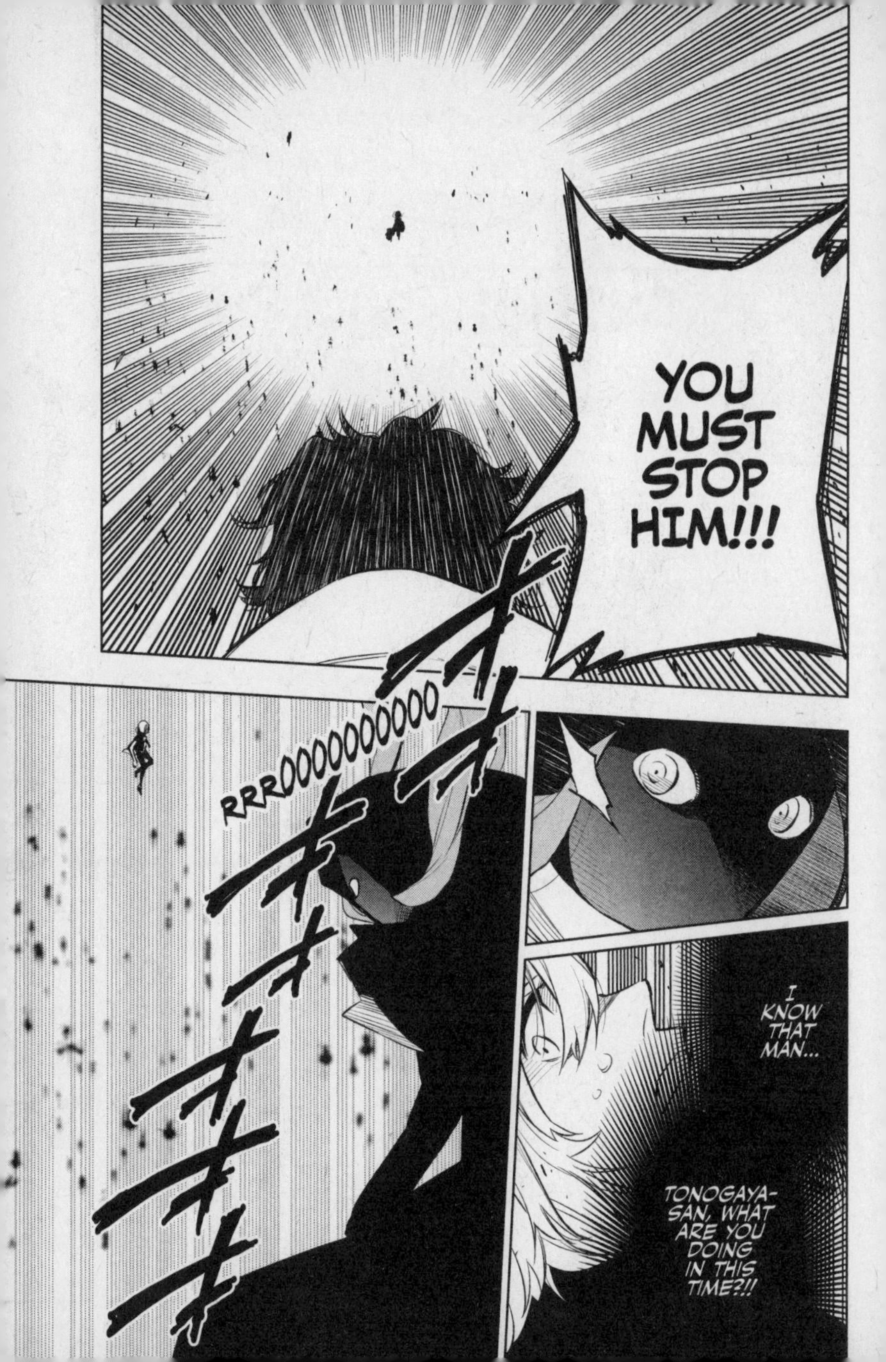
YOU MUST STOP HIM!!!
I KNOW THAT MAN...
TONOGAYA-SAN, WHAT ARE YOU DOING IN THIS TIME?!!
RRROOOOOOOOOOO

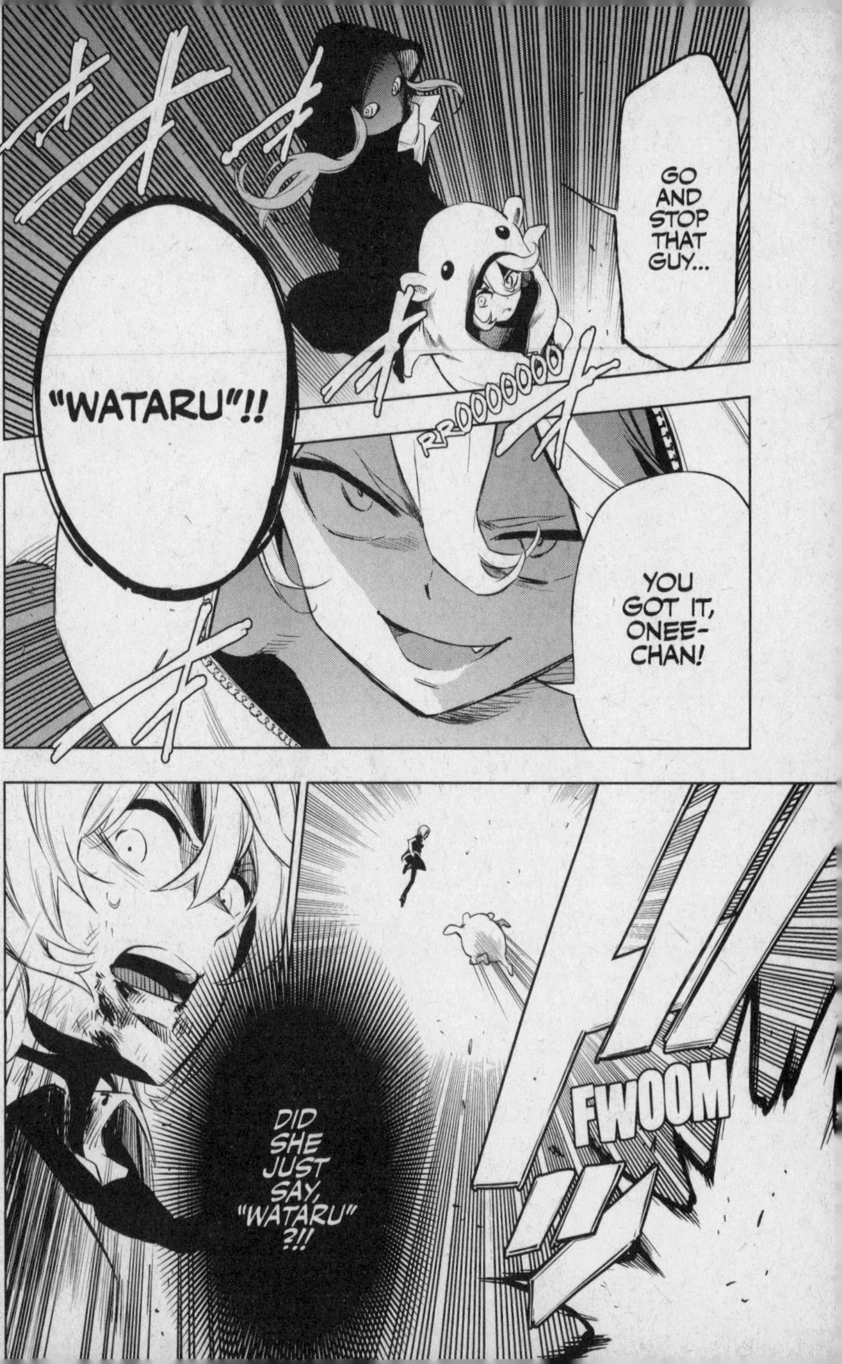
GO AND STOP THAT GUY...
"WATARU"!!
RROOOOOOO
YOU GOT IT, ONEE-CHAN!
FWOOM
DID SHE JUST SAY, "WATARU"?!!

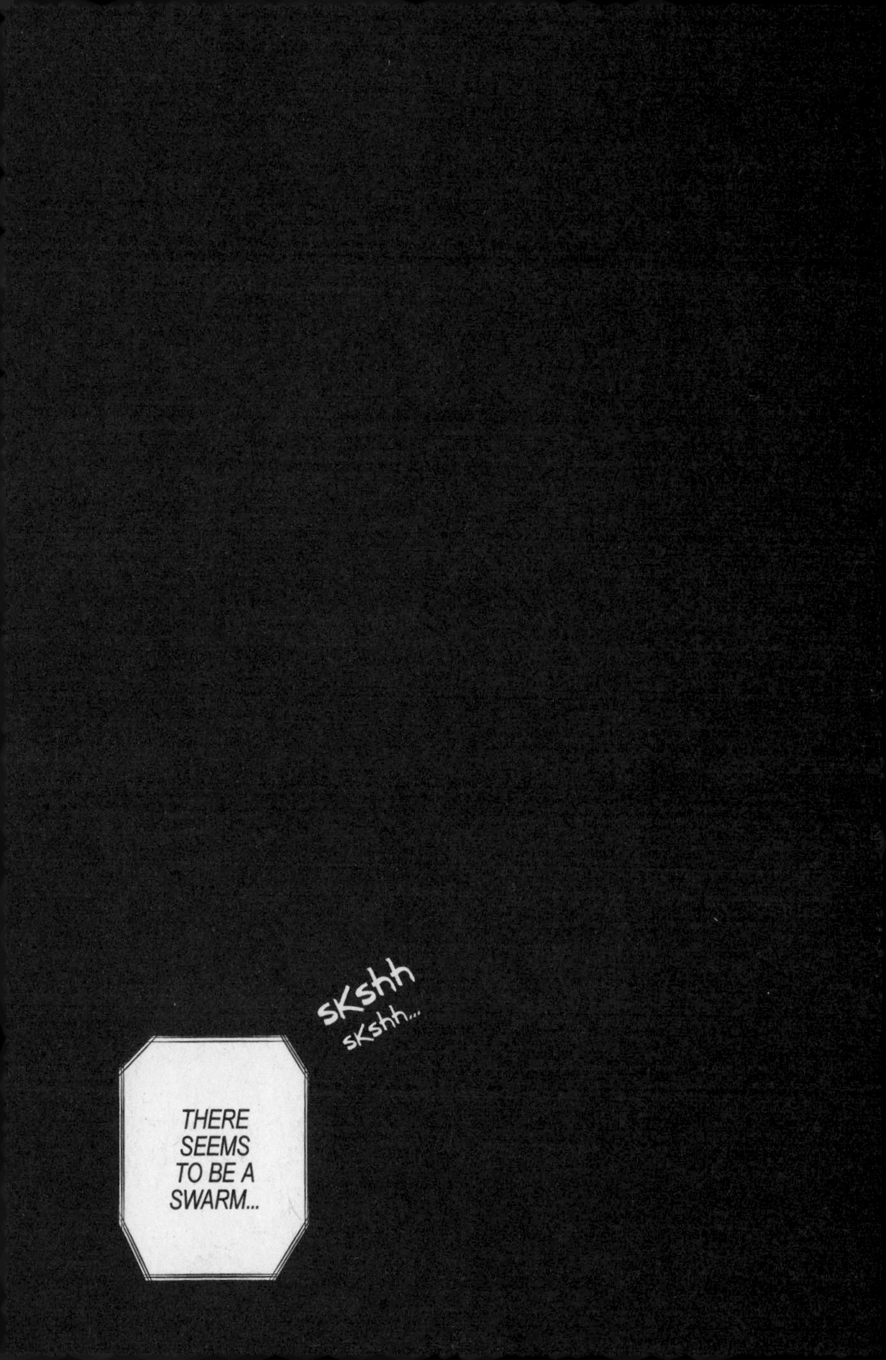
sKshh
sKshh...
THERE SEEMS TO BE A SWARM...

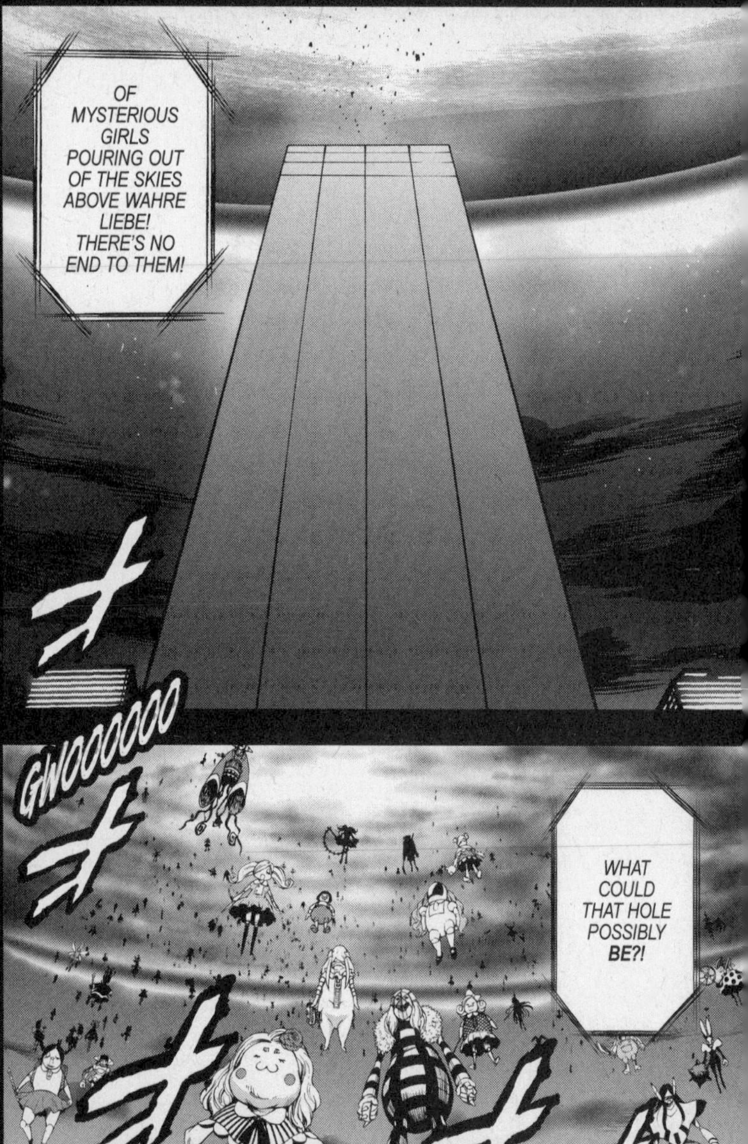
OF MYSTERIOUS GIRLS POURING OUT OF THE SKIES ABOVE WAHRE LIEBE! THERE'S NO END TO THEM!
GWOOOOOO
WHAT COULD THAT HOLE POSSIBLY BE?!

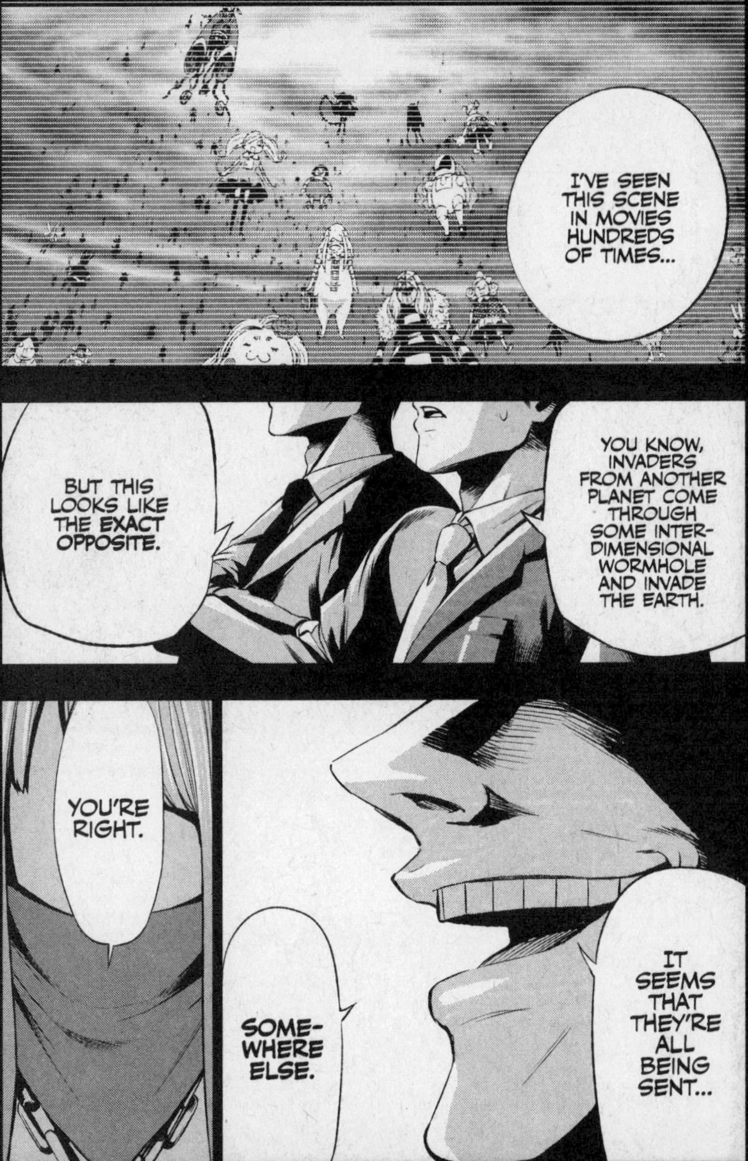
I'VE SEEN THIS SCENE IN MOVIES HUNDREDS OF TIMES...
YOU KNOW, INVADERS FROM ANOTHER PLANET COME THROUGH SOME INTER-DIMENSIONAL WORMHOLE AND INVADE THE EARTH.
BUT THIS LOOKS LIKE THE EXACT OPPOSITE.
IT SEEMS THAT THEY'RE ALL BEING SENT...
SOME-WHERE ELSE.
YOU'RE RIGHT.

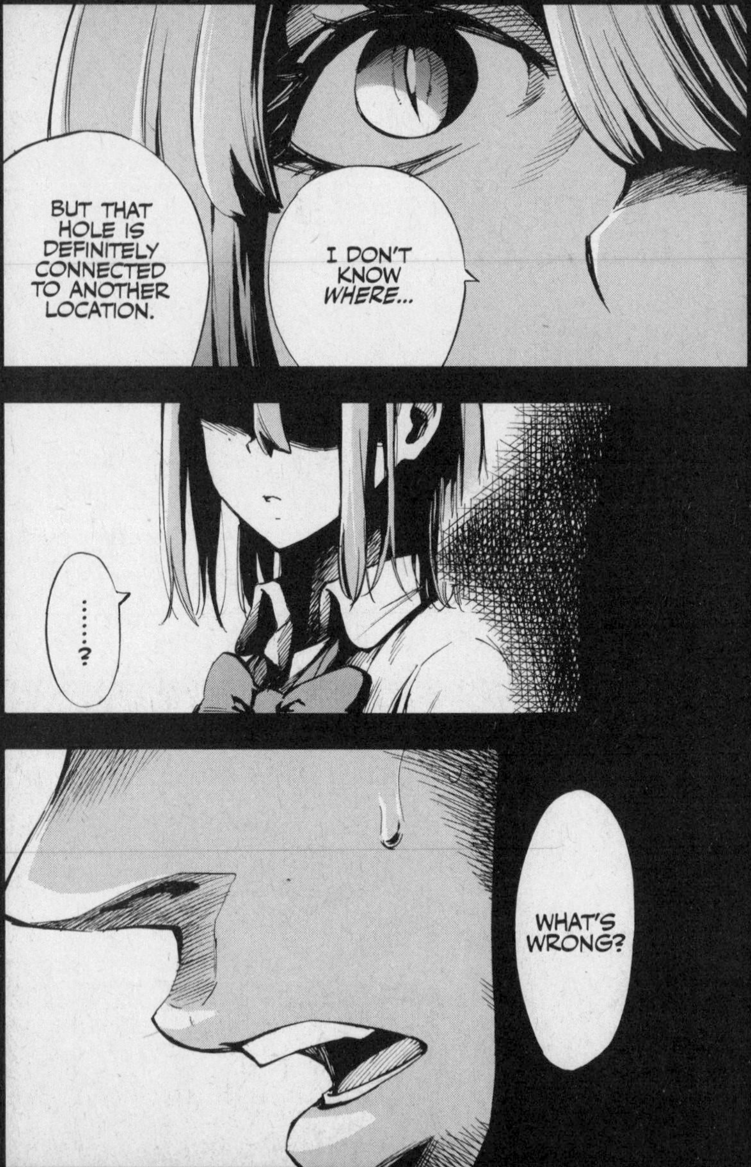
I DON'T KNOW *WHERE*...
BUT THAT HOLE IS DEFINITELY CONNECTED TO ANOTHER LOCATION.
......?
WHAT'S WRONG?

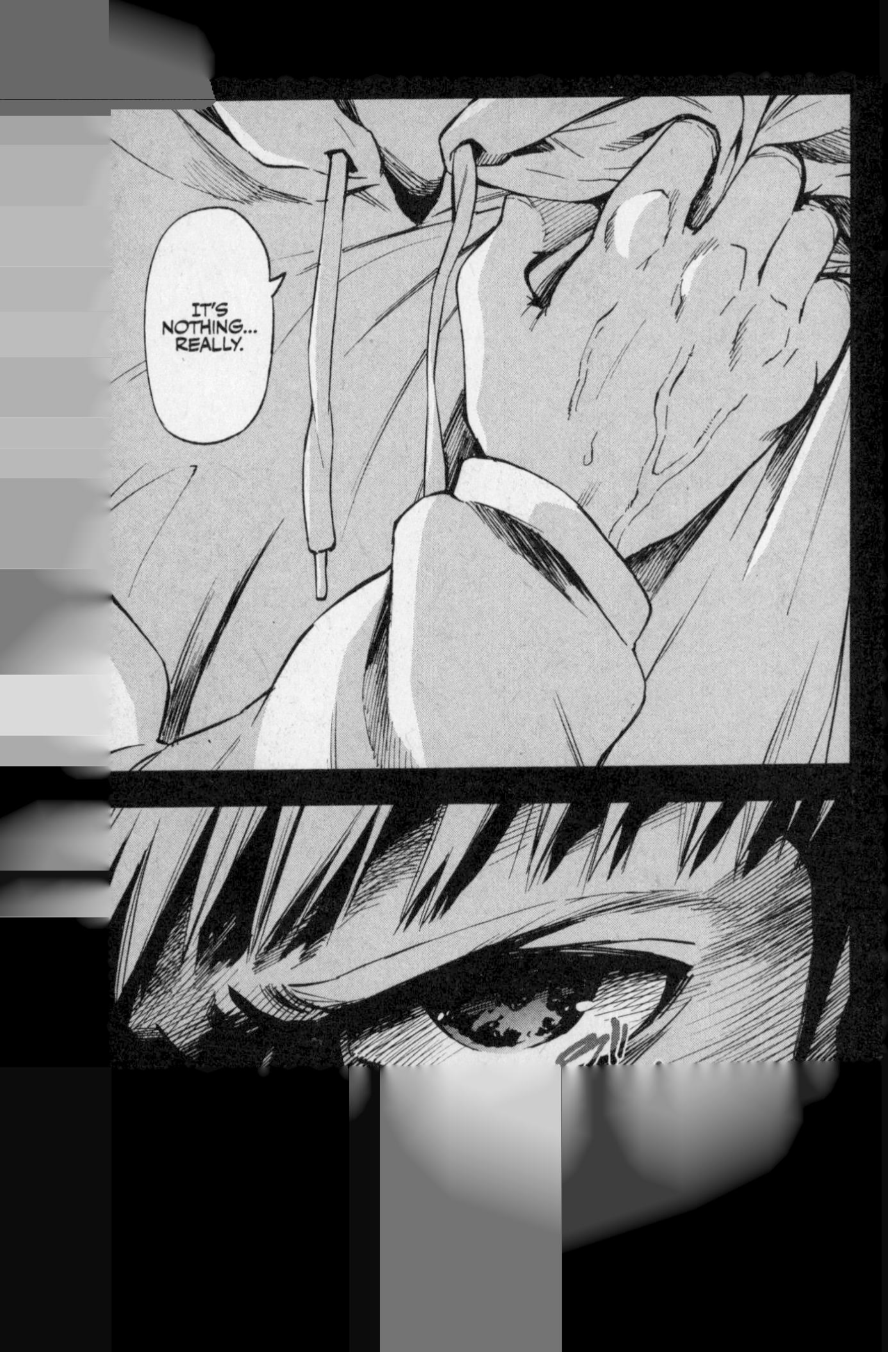
IT'S NOTHING... REALLY.

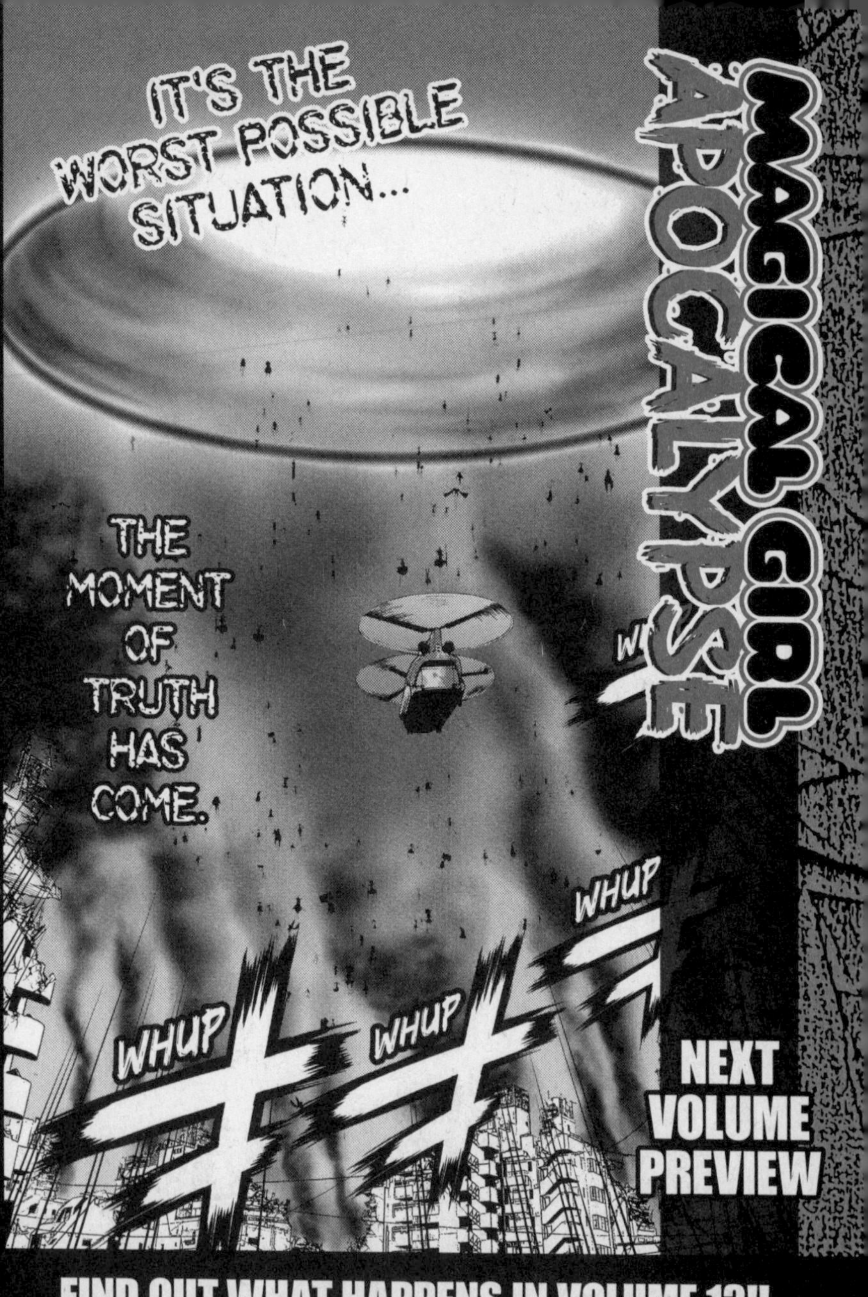
MAGICAL GIRL APOCALYPSE
NEXT VOLUME PREVIEW
IT'S THE WORST POSSIBLE SITUATION...
THE MOMENT OF TRUTH HAS COME.
WHUP
WHUP
WHUP

FIND OUT WHAT HAPPENS IN VOLUME 13!!

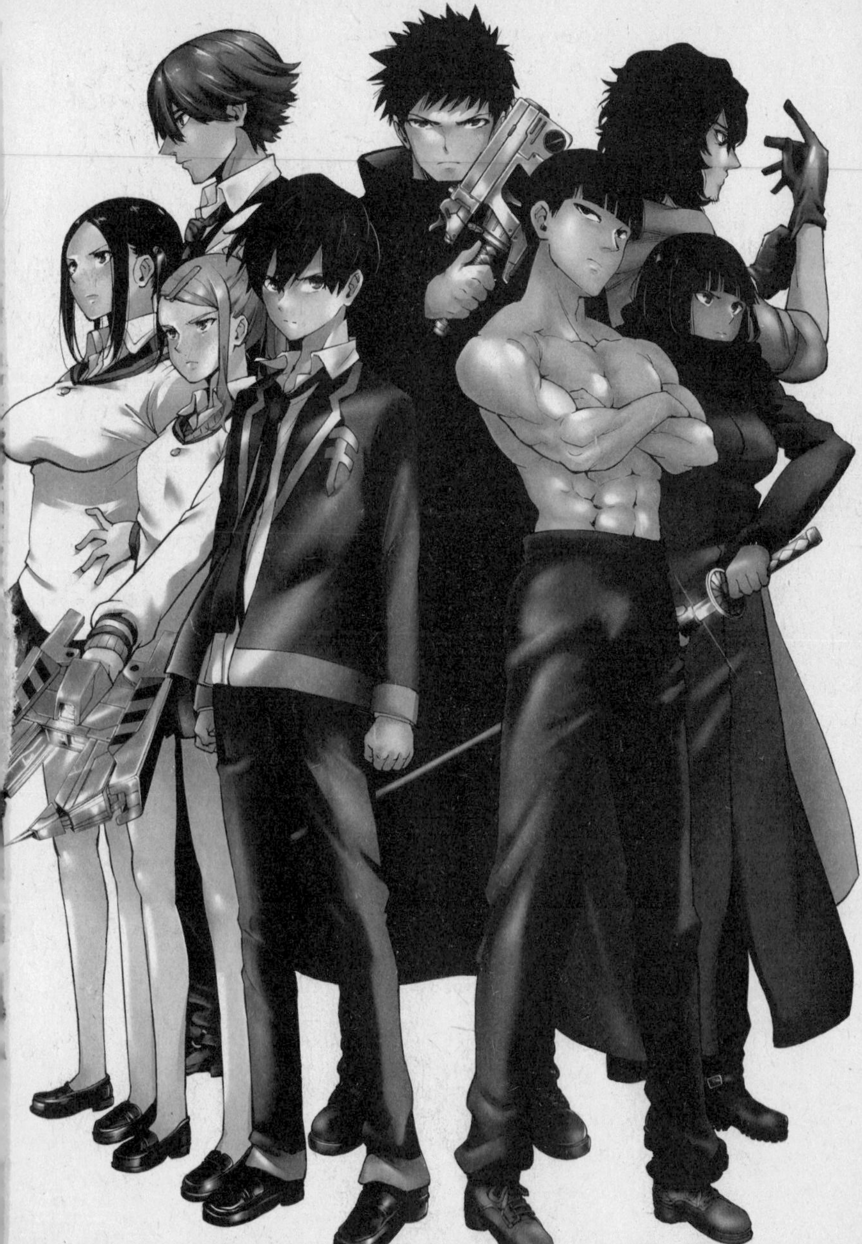